FANTASIES OF THE MASTER RACE

Other books by Ward Churchill

Authored: *Struggle for the Land:*
Indigenous Resistance to Genocide, Ecocide and Expropriation
in Contemporary North America (1993)

Indians Are Us?
Culture and Genocide in Native North America (1994)

Que sont les Indiens devenus? (1995)

Since Predator Came:
Notes from the Struggle for American Indian Liberation (1995)

From A Native Son:
Selected Essays in Indigenism, 1985-1995 (1996)

A Little Matter of Genocide:
Holocaust and Denial in the Americas, 1492 to the Present (1997)

Coauthored: *Culture versus Economism:*
Essays on Marxism in the Multicultural Arena
with Elisabeth R. Lloyd (1984)

Agents of Repression:
The FBI's Secret Wars Against the Black Panther Party
and the American Indian Movement
with Jim Vander Wall (1988)

The COINTELPRO Papers:
Documents from the FBI's Secret Wars
Against Dissent in the United States
with Jim Vander Wall (1990)

Pacifism as Pathology:
Reflections on the Role of Armed Struggle in the United States
with Mike Ryan (1998)

Edited: *Marxism and Native Americans* (1983)

Critical Issues in Native North America (1989)

Critical Issues in Native North America, Vol. II (1990)

Das indigene Amerika und die marxistische Tradition:
Eine kontroverse Debatte über Kultur, Industrialismus und Eurocentrismus
(1993)

Coedited: *Cages of Steel:*
The Politics of Imprisonment in the United States
with J.J. Vander Wall (1992)

FANTASIES OF THE MASTER RACE

Literature, Cinema and the
Colonization of American Indians

BY WARD CHURCHILL

CITY LIGHTS BOOKS
SAN FRANCISCO

Cover design by Rex Ray
Book design by Elaine Katzenberger
Typography by Harvest Graphics

Library of Congress Cataloging-in-Publication Data

Churchill, Ward.
    Fantasies of the master race : literature, cinema, and the colonization of American
Indians / Ward Churchill.
       p.   cm.
    Includes bibliographical references and index.
    Rev. and expanded from the 1992 ed.
    ISBN 0-87286-348-4
    1. Indians in literature. 2. Indians of North America—Public opinion. 3. Public
opinion—United States. 4. Racism—United States. 5 Indians in motion pictures.
I. Title.
PN56.3.I6C49   1998
810.9'3520397--dc21
                                                 98-36247
                                                  CIP

City Lights Books are available to bookstores through our primary distributor: Subterranean
Company, P. O. Box 160, 265 S. 5th St., Monroe, OR 97456. Tel: 541-847-5274. Toll-free
orders 800-274-7826. Fax: 541-847-6018. Our books are also available through library
jobbers and regional distributors. For personal orders and catalogs, please write to City
Lights Books, 261 Columbus Avenue, San Francisco, CA 94133. Visit our Web site:
www.citylights.com

CITY LIGHTS BOOKS are edited by Lawrence Ferlinghetti and Nancy J. Peters and
published at the City Lights Bookstore, 261 Columbus Avenue, San Francisco, CA 94133.

ACKNOWLEDGMENTS

Those familiar with the original version of *Fantasies of the Master Race* will undoubtedly note not only that the line-up of material in the second edition is stronger, but that there has been a marked improvement in quality control. Both matters are largely the result of the exemplary work performed by my editor at City Lights, Elaine Katzenberger. I would also like to thank Rex Ray for his superb execution of the cover and the Saxifrage Group for its assistance in preparing the index. Leah Kelly provided the photo of me used in the back of the book.

Appreciation is due to the original publishers of several of the essays for their generous permission to reprint. "Literature and the Colonization of American Indians" was first published in *Journal of Ethnic Studies*. "Lawrence of South Dakota" and "Hi Ho, Hillerman" both appeared initially in *Z Magazine*. "Interpreting the Indian" and "The New Racism" first came out in *Wicazo Sa Review*. "Fantasies of the Master Race" first appeared in *Book Forum*, while "A Little Matter of Genocide" saw the light of day in *Bloomsbury Review*. "Beyond Ethnicity" made its debut in *New Scholar* and "In the Service of Empire" first came out in *Great Plains Quarterly*.

for my maternal grandparents,
Minnie Idalee and Philip H. Allen, Sr.

CONTENTS

INTRODUCTION

Unraveling the Codes of Oppression
American Indians in Literature and Film

> It has been said that I dare to speak truth to power. Maybe so, but that's never
> been my objective. My job, as I see it, is to speak the truth to the great mass
> of people without political or economic power. . . . I take this as my task out
> of a firm conviction that knowledge of the truth is itself empowering.
> It follows that my goal is really to change current power relations in a
> constructive manner.
>
> —Noam Chomsky
> 1998

It is with considerable gratification that I write this introduction to the revised and expanded City Lights edition of my *Fantasies of the Master Race*. First released in early 1992, the book in its initial form captured a national award for writing on the topic of human rights in the United States, sold out through four consecutive printings, stimulated considerable discussion in activist/academic circles, has been widely referenced by other analysts and saw broad adoption as a course text before a dispute with the original publisher led to its withdrawal from circulation in mid-1996. All told, the record accrued by *Fantasies* has thus been quite remarkable, given the limited distribution channels available to it and the fact that its content is so frankly hostile to certain of the mythologies contrived to sustain the comfortability of North America's dominant settler society.[1]

The City Lights edition, born of the success enjoyed by its predecessor, promises to be a far stronger and more useful book. Shorn of items which now seem dated or otherwise extraneous, it nonetheless retains the best of what appeared in the 1992 compilation, much of it further developed and/or substantially reworked. It also incorporates material previously published elsewhere and an essay which was written specifically for inclusion in this edition.

Thematically, *Fantasies* remains very much the same, concentrating as it does upon exploring the ways in which literature and its celluloid stepchild, the cinema, have been employed in combination with supposedly nonfictional venues to falsify the realities of Euroamerica's interaction with the continent's indigenous peoples, both historically and in the contemporary setting. Its purpose is, as it has always been, to strip away at least some of the elaborate veil of misimpression and disinformation behind which the ugly countenance of Euroamerican conquest, colonization and genocide have been so carefully hidden.[2]

The Open Veins of Native North America

It is perhaps helpful to provide a backdrop to the analysis of films and written works which follow by providing a factual overview of the modern colonial context in North America. Although ideologues ranging in outlook from reactionary Republicanism to revolutionary marxism are wont to decry as "misleading and rhetorical" any application of such terms to the structure of relations prevailing on this continent, the fact is that the very core of U.S. imperialism lies not abroad in the Third World, but right here "at home."

As these words are written, more than 400 native peoples continue to exist within the boundaries of the 48 contiguous states of the United States alone, another 200 or so in Canada.[3] About half these peoples retain nominal possession of some reserved portion of their aboriginal territory (or "replacement lands"), a pastiche of areas comprising about 3 percent of the continental U.S. and a lesser portion of Canada. Moreover, these peoples, having never ceded it by treaty or other instrument of consent, still retain unassailable legal title to something more than ten times the territory now left to us. Put another way, the United States lacks even a pretense of legitimate ownership of about one-third of its claimed land mass, while in Canada the situation is rather worse.[4]

While pushing Indians off 90 percent of the land we'd retained by treaty — instruments through which both the U.S. and Canadian governments formally and repeatedly recognized indigenous peoples as comprising fully sovereign nations in our own right — the U.S. in particular consigned native populations to what were thought to be the least useful and productive portions of the continent, mostly arid and semi-arid tracts deemed unfit for ranching or agriculture, and typically lacking in timber and other renewable resources.[5] In effect, the reservations represent nothing so much as dumping grounds, out of sight and mind of polite society, where it was assumed that Native North Americans would die off altogether.[6]

It is one of history's supreme ironies that this same "worthless" acreage turned out to be extraordinarily rich in minerals, endowed with an estimated two-thirds of what the U.S. now claims as its own uranium assets, as much as a quarter of the readily accessible low-sulfur coal, 15-20 percent of the oil and natural gas, and appreciable deposits of copper, bauxite, zeolite and other strategically/commerically crucial ores.[7] These minerals, plainly belonging to the indigenous nations within whose reservation boundaries they lie, constitute what federal economic planners now like to call "U.S. domestic reserves." Without these resources, America's contemporary business as usual could never have been created, and would presently come to a halt in a hot minute.[8]

Using the term "colonization" to describe such circumstances stands to instill a certain unsettling, and perhaps "destabilizing," sense of cognitive dissonence among the Euroamerican citizenry. After all, they themselves, or rather their ancestors, once engaged in a decolonization struggle against England, a process inaccurately referred to at this juncture as having been a "revolution." Their success in that endeavor has with equal inaccuracy anchored their collective boast of having emerged as "the land of the free." To be confronted with the proposition that their ostensible heritage of staunch anticolonialism embodies instead as virulent a strain of colonialism as has ever been perfected is more than the average Joe can be expected to reconcile with any degree of psychological grace.

Hence, propagandists in service to elite interests have long been bent to the task of inventing a whole vernacular behind which to mask the true nature of U.S.-Indian relations. Rather than occupying and colonizing Native North America, for instance, it is asserted that the United States has merely assumed a permanent "trust" responsibility for indigenous land and lives, thereby accruing "plenary (full) power" over the disposition of native property.[9] Or, to take another prominent example, a bill designed to afford Indians a hiring preference in implementing federal Indian policy is titled—grotesquely, to anyone in the least familar with the meaning of the term—the "Indian *Self-Determination* Act" (emphasis added).[10] Illustrations of this sort could, of course, be easily continued at length and extended northwards across Canada.[11]

The systematic deployment of such euphemisms has allowed projection of the illusion that federal interaction with Indians, while displaying a variety of "errors" and "excesses" during the eighteenth- and nineteenth-century settlers' wars, has long been and remains well-intended, benevolent and "for the Indians' own good."[12] Thus, the average Joe, should he bother himself to think of Indians at all, has no reason to feel especially uncomfortable, much less outraged at what has been and continues to be done to us. Indeed, the opposite is often true. So relentlessly have official fables of federal largesse been put forth that many Euroamericans have come to feel resentment at what they see as the "free ride" bestowed upon Indians at their expense.[13]

The reality hidden behind this deceptive "spin" is, to be sure, very different. The true cost to native people bound up in the relationship providing the Euroamerican status quo its foundation is revealed in the federal government's own rather less publicized statistics. By any reasonable computation, a simple division of the fifty million-odd acres of land still in reserved status by the approximately 1.8 million Indians reflected in the last U.S. census should make us the largest per capita landholders of any group on the continent. Based upon its known mineral resources alone, our .6 percent of the total U.S. population should comprise its wealthiest segment, both as an aggregate and individually.[14]

Instead, we are as a whole the most impoverished by far, suffering the lowest annual and lifetime incomes, the worst housing and sanitation conditions, the lowest level of educational attainment and highest rate of unemployment.[15] The single poorest county in the United States over the past seventy-five years has been Shannon, on the Pine Ridge Sioux Reservation in South Dakota.[16] Counties on half-a-dozen other Indian reservations distributed across a wide geographic area make regular appearances among the ten poorest recorded by the U.S. Departments of Labor and Commerce.[17] That more do not appear in such listings is due mainly to the fact that non-Indians have long since infiltrated most reservation areas to monopolize such business, ranching and agriculture as exists there, thus skewing the data to a considerable extent.[18]

Correspondingly, Native Americans are currently afflicted with the most pronounced symptoms of destitution evidenced by any overall population group.

The Indian health level is the lowest and the disease rate the highest of all major population groups in the United States. The incidence of tuberculosis is over 400 percent higher than the national average. Similar statistics show that the incidence of strep infections is 1,000 percent higher, meningitis is 2,000 percent higher, and dysentery is 10,000 percent higher. Death rates from disease are shocking when Indian and non-Indian populations are compared. Influenza and pneumonia are 300 percent greater killers among Indians. Diseases such as hepatitis are at epidemic proportions. Diabetes is almost a plague. And the suicide rate for Indian youths ranges from 1,000 to 10,000 times higher than for non-Indian youths; Indian suicide has become epidemic.[19]

In addition, "between fifty thousand and fifty-seven thousand Indian homes are [officially] considered uninhabitable. Many of these are beyond repair. For example, over 88 percent of the homes of the Sioux in Pine Ridge have been classified as substandard dwellings."[20] One consequence is that Indians die from exposure at five times the national rate, twelve times the rate from malnutrition. The bottom line is that modern life expectancy among reservation-based men is 44.6 years; reservation-based women can expect to live only a little more than three years longer.[21]

Indicative of the depths of despair induced among native people by such conditions are the extreme rates of alcoholism, drug addiction, familial violence and teen suicide prevailing in most indigenous communities. The governmental response has been to imprison one in every four native men and to impose involuntary sterilization upon about 40 percent of all native women of childbearing age.[22] In sum, the sociophysical environment of contemporary Native North America far more closely resembles the sort of Third World colonial settings described by Frantz Fanon than anything one expects to encounter in the midst of a country enjoying one of the world's best standards of living.[23] The situation of Canada's indigenous peoples is a veritable carbon copy of that experienced by those in the United States.[24]

The vast gulf separating the potential wealth of Native North America on the one hand, and its practical impoverishment on the other, rests squarely upon what writer Eduardo Galeano has in another context aptly termed the "open veins" of the colonized.[25] In effect, the governments of both the United States and Canada have utilized their unilaterally asserted positions of control over native property to pour the assets of indigenous nations directly into the U.S./Canadian economies rather than those of native peoples.

A single illustration may suffice to tell the tale: Very near the disease-ridden and malnourished residents of Shannon County, on land permanently guaranteed to the Lakota Nation by the United States through the 1868 Fort

Laramie Treaty, the Homestake Mining Company has extracted billions of dollars in gold over the past fifty years.[26] Multiplying the Homestake example by the hundreds of United States corporations doing business on Indian land barely begins to convey the dimension of the process. Stripped to its essentials, the "American way of life" is woven from the strands of these relations. They comprise an order which must be maintained, first, foremost, and at all costs, because they more than any other definable factor constitute the absolute bedrock upon which the U.S. status quo has been erected and still maintains itself. Precisely the same can be said of Canada.

Semantic Subterfuge

As was suggested above, such things can never be admitted. On the contrary, it is most convenient from an elite perspective when they can be packaged to appear as exact opposites of themselves. A salient example, beginning with the 1934 Indian Reorganization Act (IRA), has been the supplanting of traditional indigenous forms of governance by a "tribal council" model. Devised in Washington, D.C., it was imposed over the vociferous objections of those now ruled by it. As with colonial/neocolonial régimes everywhere, the IRA councils owe their allegience not to their supposed constituents, but to the foreign power which created their positions and installed them, and which continues to fund and "advise" them.[27]

From the outset, these councils accepted a tacit quid pro quo attending their positions of petty power and imagined prestige. Theirs have been the signatures affixed to resolutions extending "Indian" approval to leases paying their people pennies on the dollar for the mineral wealth lying within their lands, waiving environmental protection clauses in mining contracts and all the rest. Theirs have also been the "Indian" voices adding illusions of "consensus" to the federal/corporate chorus proclaiming every agonizing step in the ongoing subjugation and expropriation of Native North America as "giant steps forward" while denouncing anyone insisting upon genuinely indigenous alternatives as a "barrier to progress."[28]

Altogether, this structure of "Indian self-governance" had become so entrenched and effective by the mid-1970s that it was cast under the rubric of "self-determination." This inherently anticolonialist concept, fully explained in black letter international law, was thus stood neatly on its head.[29] Advanced in its stead was a statutory formulation wherein all policy decisions affecting Indian Country would forever fall within the sphere of federal authority. Implementation of these policies would, to the maximum extent possible, be carried out by native people hired specifically for this purpose.[30] In many ways, since Canada shortly followed suit with its own version, this maneuver represented a consummation of the internal colonization of Native North America.[31]

As indigenous people were rendered increasingly self-colonizing during the 1980s and '90s, it became ever more possible to neutralize native opposition to internal colonization simply by juxtaposing it to the posturing of the growing gaggle of IRA "leaders" or preferred native employees within the federal bureaucracy. All of them were prepared at the drop of a hat to confuse critics through their own avid endorsement of the system. Additionally, such "professional Indians" have proven themselves quite willing to publicly dismiss bona fide native rights activists, usually in the face of overwhelming evidence to the contrary, as "self-styled and irresponsible renegades, terrorists and revolutionaries" who lack standing or credibility within their own communities.[32]

Within this painstakingly fabricated framework of duplicity and false appearances, all potential for coherent non-Indian understanding of the situation becomes increasingly difficult to realize. Consequently, the prospect of non-Indians developing any form of serious opposition to the internal colonization of Native North America has been diffused and dissipated, even among those committed to combatting U.S. neocolonial activities in Latin America, Southern Africa, the Mideast and elsewhere. In effect, the officially sponsored scenario fosters "mainstream" perceptions that, since we Indians ourselves cannot agree on the nature of our oppression, or even whether we are oppressed, then non-Indian intervention on our behalf is pointless at best. Worse, based on contentions put forth by the government and its "cooperating" cast of Indians that Native America is already self-governing and self-determining, non-Indian efforts to bring about U.S./Indian — or Canadian/Indian — relations can be interpreted as presumptious and counterproductive.

In the end, although each of the North American settler states has retained and perfected "sharp end" mechanisms of repression, the primary means by which they maintain their mutual internal colonial order has proven to be that of sheer sophistry.[33] Their joint deterrence of even the possibility that native rights will be defined in anticolonialist terms resides mainly in their successful peddling of the ridiculous notion that their structures of colonial oppression no longer "really" exist, if in fact they ever existed at all.[34]

Culmination of the process will rest on inculcation of the population at large with an "understanding" that the only "genuine," "authentic," "representative," and therefore "real" Indians are those who have elected to "fit in" most comfortably.[35] "Real" Indians, in other words, conform most closely to the needs and expectations of the "larger society." "Real" Indians provide "voluntary" and undeviating service to those "greater interests" associated with the Euroamerican status quo. All who resist will, to that extent and by the same definition, be relegated to the status of "fakes," "frauds" and "phoneys."[36]

Fantasies of the Master Race

Elsewhere, I have delved much more deeply into the form, substance and history of the official subterfuges and misrepresentations addressed above.[37] In the present volume, it is my objective to explore the modes, literary and cinematic, through which these officially sanctioned "interpretations" have been polished, popularized and foisted off upon the public at large.

To this end, several essays, most of them focusing on literature, have been retained from the first edition (two are substantially revised and expanded). These include "Literature and the Colonization of American Indians," "Carlos Castaneda," "Hi Ho, Hillerman...Away," "A Little Matter of Genocide," "It Did Happen Here," "The New Racism," "Interpreting the Indian" and "Beyond Ethnicity." Also retained from the first edition are two essays on cinema, "Fantasies of the Master Race" (which is also substantially revised and expanded) and "Lawrence of South Dakota." To these have been added a third essay on cinema, "And They Did It Like Dogs in the Dirt..." and a new essay on literary criticism entitled "In the Service of Empire."

Taken in combination, although they for the most part consist of a sequence of "case studies," the assembled essays are meant to provide an overview of how literature, whether fictional or ostensibly nonfictional, academic or poetic, has interacted with film to reinforce the hegemony by which the colonization of Native North America has been simultaneously denied, rationalized and, implicitly at least, legitimated. Taken as a whole, the book's objective, to borrow from the quotation of Noam Chomsky offered at the outset of this introduction, is to speak the truth and thus to facilitate a constructive alteration of the circumstances described herein.

Ward Churchill
Boulder, Colorado
May 1998

Notes

1. For explication of the idea of "settler societies" and "settler states," see J. Sakai, *Settlers: The Myth of the White Proletariat* (Chicago: Morningstar Press, 1983).

2. Terms like "conquest" and "genocide" are not used rhetorically. See, e.g., David E. Stannard's *American Holocaust: Columbus and the Conquest of the New World* (New York: Oxford University Press, 1992) and my own *A Little Matter of Genocide: Holocaust and Denial in the Americas, 1492 to the Present* (San Francisco: City Lights, 1997).

3. For particular data, see Francis Paul Prucha, *Atlas of American Indian Affairs* (Lincoln: University of Nebraska Press, 1990).

4. Russel Barsh, "Indian Land Claims Policy in the United States," *North Dakota Law Review*, No. 58, 1982; "Behind Land Claims: Rationalizing Dispossession in Anglo-American Law," *Law & Anthropology*, No. 1, 1986. Also see Bruce Clark, *Indian Title in Canada* (Toronto: Carswell, 1987).

5. For the texts of 371 ratified treaties between the United States and various indigenous peoples, see Charles J. Kappler, ed., *Indian Treaties, 1778-1883* (New York: Interland, 1973). For Canada, see *Canada: Indian Treaties and Surrenders from 1680 to 1890*, 3 vols. (Ottawa: Queen's Printer, 1891; reprinted by Coles [Toronto], 1971; reprinted by Fifth House [Saskatoon], 1992). On the process of expropriating treaty-secured territory in the United States, see Janet A. McDonnell, *The Dispossession of the American Indian, 1887-1934* (Bloomington: Indiana University Press, 1991). For explanations of the logical leaps employed by both settler states in trying to rationalize their abridgements of indigenous sovereignty, see Vine Deloria, Jr., and Clifford M. Lytle, *American Indians, American Justice* (Austin: University of Texas Press, 1983); Bruce Clark, *Native Liberty, Crown Sovereignty: The Existing Aboriginal Right of Self-Government in Canada* (Montréal: McGill-Queens University Press, 1990).

6. That this was the assumption, if not the intent, is well-remarked in early twentieth-century literature. See, as examples, James Mooney, "The Passing of the Indian," *Proceedings of the Second Pan American Scientific Congress, Sec. 1: Anthropology* (Washington, D.C.: Smithsonian Institution, 1909-1910); Joseph K. Dixon, *The Vanishing Race: The Last Great Indian Council* (Garden City, NY: Doubleday, 1913); Stanton Elliot, "The End of the Trail," *Overland Monthly*, July 1915; Ella Higginson, "The Vanishing Race," *Red Man*, Feb. 1916; Ales Hrdlicka, "The Vanishing Indian," *Science*, No. 46, 1917; J.L. Hill, *The Passing of the Indian and the Buffalo* (Long Beach, CA: n.p., 1917); John Collier, "The Vanishing American," *Nation*, Jan. 11, 1928.

7. Ronald L. Trosper, "Appendix I: Indian Minerals," in American Indian Policy Review Commission, *Task Force 7 Final Report: Reservation and Resource Development and Protection* (Washington, D.C.: U.S. Government Printing Office, 1977); U.S. Department of Interior, Bureau of Indian Affairs, *Indian Lands Map: Oil, Gas and Minerals on Indian Reservations* (Washington, D.C.: U.S. Government Printing Office, 1978).

8. See generally, Michael Garrity, "The U.S. Colonial Empire is as Close as the Nearest Reservation," in Holly Sklar, ed., *Trilateralism: The Trilateral Commission and Elite Planning for World Government* (Boston: South End Press, 1980) pp. 238-60.

9. For analysis of the U.S. plenary power doctrine, see Ann Laque Estin, "*Lonewolf v. Hitchcock*: The Long Shadow," in Sandra L. Cadwalader and Vine Deloria, Jr., eds., *The Aggressions of Civilization: Federal Indian Policy Since the 1880s* (Philadelphia: Temple University Press, 1984). It should be noted that the extention of perpetual trust by one nation over another is the essential condition defining colonial relations in international law and is thus flatly prohibited under the Charter of the United Nations and the U.N.'s 1960 Declaration on the Granting of Independence to Colonial Countries and Peoples. For texts, see Burns H. Weston, Richard A. Falk and Anthony D'Amato, eds., *Basic Documents in International Law and World Order* (St. Paul, MN: West Publishing, 1990) pp. 50-61, 343-4.

10. On the Act in question, see Rebecca L. Robbins, "American Indian Self-Determination: Comparative Analysis and Rhetorical Criticism," *New Studies on the Left*, Vol. XIII, Nos. 3-4, 1988, pp. 48-59. For analysis of the legal context and definition involved, see Michla Pomerance, *Self-Determination in Law and Practice* (The Hague: Marinus Nijhoff, 1982).

11. See generally, Menno Boldt and J. Anthony Long, *The Quest for Justice: Aboriginal People and Aboriginal Rights* (Toronto: University of Toronto Press, 1985).

12. Advancing such interpretations has been the stock in trade of such preeminent

"ethnohistorians" as the late Wilcomb Washburn and his heir apparent, James Axtell. See, e.g., Wilcomb Washburn, *The Indian in America* (New York: Harper & Row, 1975); James Axtell, *Beyond 1492: Encounters in Colonial North America* (New York: Oxford University Press, 1992).

13. Witness, as but one example, the virulent anti-Indian "backlash" manifested in Wisconsin during the 1980s when native people sought to assert treaty-secured off-reservation fishing rights guaranteed them in exchange for their land; U.S. Department of Justice, Commission on Civil Rights, *Discrimination Against Chippewa Indians in Northern Wisconsin: A Summary Report* (Milwaukee: Wisconsin Regional Office, 1989).

14. U.S. Bureau of the Census, *U.S. Census of Population: General Population Characteristics, United States* (Washington, D.C.: U.S. Dept. of Commerce, Economics and Statistics Div., 1990) p. 3; *Census Bureau Releases: 1990 Census Counts on Specific Racial Groups* (Washington, D.C.: U.S. Dept. of Commerce, Economics and Statistics DE., 1992) Table I.

15. See, e.g., U.S. Department of Health, Education and Welfare, *A Study of Socio-Economic Characteristics of Ethnic Minorities Based on the 1970 Census, Vol. 3: American Indians* (Washington, D.C.: U.S. Government Printing Office, 1974); U.S. Department of Education, Office of Research and Improvement, National Institute of Education, *Conference on the Educational and Occupational Needs of American Indian Women, October 1976* (Washington, D.C.: U.S. Government Printing Office, 1980); U.S. Senate, Committee on Labor and Human Resources, Subcommittee on Employment and Productivity, *Guaranteed Job Opportunity Act: Hearing on S.777* (Wasington, D.C.: 100th Cong., 1st Sess., U.S. Government Printing Office, 1980); U.S. Bureau of the Census, *1990 Census of the Population and Housing: Public Use Microdata A* (Washington, D.C.: U.S. Dept. of Commerce, Economics and Statistics Div., 1991).

16. In 1931, the average annual income for a family of five Lakotas in Shannon County was $152.80. By 1940, it had dropped to $120, one-third of the per capita income in Mississippi, the poorest state in the U.S.; Edward Lazarus, *Black Hills, White Justice: The Sioux Nation versus the United States, 1775 to the Present* (New York: HarperCollins, 1991) p. 163. By 1970, the figure had risen to just over $1,200; Cheryl McCall, "Life at Pine Ridge Bleak," *Colorado Daily*, May 16, 1975. At present, unemployment in the county still hovers in the upper-eightieth to lower-ninetieth percentile range, while real dollar income has remained almost constant.

17. See generally, Teresa L. Amott and Julie A. Mattaei, *Race, Gender and Work: A Multicultural History of Women in the United States* (Boston: South End Press, 1991) pp. 31-62.

18. For interesting assessments of how this happened, see Wilcomb E. Washburn, *Assault on Tribalism: The General Allotment Law (Dawes Act) of 1887* (Philadelphia: J.B. Lippencott, 1975); *Red Man's Land, White Man's Law* (Norman: University of Oklahoma Press, [2nd ed.] 1994) pp. 150-1.

19. Rennard Strickland, *Tonto's Revenge* (Albuquerque: University of New Mexico Press, 1997) p. 53.

20. Ibid.

21. U.S. Congress, Office of Technology Assessment, *Indian Health Care* (Washington, D.C.: 1986); U.S. Department of Health and Human Services, Public Health Service, *Chart Series Book* (Washington, D.C.: U.S. Government Printing Office, 1988).

22. On imprisonment rates, see Marc Mauer, "Americans Behind Bars: A Comparison of International Rates of Incarceration," in Ward Churchill and J.J. Vander Wall, eds., *Cages of Steel: The Politics of Imprisonment in the United States* (Washington, D.C.: Maisonneuve Press, 1992) pp. 22-37. On sterilization, see Janet Larson, "And Then There Were None," *Christian Century*, Jan. 26, 1977; Brint Dillingham, "Indian Women and IHS Sterilization Practices," *American Indian Journal*, Vol. 3, No. 1, 1977. Another very good study is Wellesley College student Robin Jerrill's unpublished 1988 undergraduate thesis entitled "Women and Children First: The Forced Sterilization of American Indian Women." It should be noted that compulsory sterilization of persons based upon their membership in a specific racial or ethnic group is a violation of the 1948 Convention on Prevention and Punishment of the Crime of Genocide; Weston, Falk and D'Amato, *Basic Documents, op. cit.*, p. 297.

23. Frantz Fanon, *Wretched of the Earth* (New York: Grove Press, 1966).

24. See, e.g., Terrance Nelson, ed., *Genocide in Canada* (Ginew, Manitoba: Roseau River First Nation, 1997).

25. Eduardo Galeano, *The Open Veins of Latin America: Five Centuries of the Pillage of a Continent*

(New York: Monthly Review Press, 1975).

26. Homestake, owned by the Hearst family and located outside the Black Hills town of Lead, is the richest gold mine in the western hemisphere, perhaps the world. Estimates of the gross value of the ore extracted from the still-operating mine run as high as $16 billion. In 1982, Pine Ridge (Oglala Lakota) tribal attorney Mario Gonzales filed a suit in federal court seeking to recover $1 billion for ore and $6 billion in damages for the company's illegal operations within the 1868 treaty territory. It was dismissed as being "frivolous"; Lazarus, *Black Hills, White Justice, op. cit.*, pp. 106, 412-3.

27. See generally, Vine Deloria, Jr., and Clifford M. Lytle, *The Nations Within: The Past and Future of American Indian Sovereignty* (New York: Pantheon, 1984).

28. For a survey of such activities, see "American Indian Self-Governance: Fact, Fantasy and Prospects for the Future," in my *Struggle for the Land: Indigenous Resistance to Genocide, Ecocide and Expropriation in Contemporary North America* (Monroe, ME: Common Courage Press, 1993) pp. 375-400.

29. For analysis, see Pomerance, *Self-Determination, op. cit.*; W. Ofuatey-Kodjoe, *The Principle of Self-Determination in International Law* (Hamden, CT: Archon Books, 1972); A. Rigo Sureda, *The Evolution of the Right to Self-Determination: A Study of United Nations Practice* (Leyden, Netherlands: A.W. Sijhoff, 1973); Lee C. Buchheit, *Secession: The Legitimacy of Self-Determination* (New Haven: Yale University Press, 1978); John Howard Clinebell and Jim Thompson, "Sovereignty and Self-Determination: The Rights of Native Americans Under International Law," *Buffalo Law Review*, No. 27, 1978.

30. Robbins, "American Indian Self-Determination," *op. cit.*; Michael D. Gross, "Indian Self-Determination and Tribal Sovereignty: An Analysis of Recent Federal Policy," *Texas Law Review*, No. 56, 1978.

31. Thomas Berger, "Native Rights and Self-Determination," *The Canadian Journal of Native Studies*, Vol. 3, No. 2, 1983; Leroy Little Bear, Menno Boldt and Jonathan Long, eds., *Pathways to Self-Determination: Canadian Indians and the Canadian State* (Toronto: University of Toronto Press, 1984). On the concept of internal colonization itself, see Robert K. Thomas, "Colonization: Classic and Internal," *New University Thought*, Vol. 4, No. 4, Winter 1966-67.

32. For further elaboration, see my "Renegades, Terrorists and Revolutionaries: The Government's Propaganda War Against the American Indian Movement," *Propaganda Review*, No. 4, 1989.

33. With respect to the "sharp end," see my and Jim Vander Wall's *Agents of Repression: The FBI's Secret Wars Against the Black Panther Party and the American Indian Movement* (Boston: South End Press, 1988); Peter Matthiessen, *In the Spirit of Crazy Horse* (New York: Viking, [2nd ed.] 1991); Rex Wyler, *Blood of the Land: The U.S. Government and Corporate War Against the American Indian Movement* (Philadelphia: New Society, [2nd ed.] 1992).

34. This is the tack taken by apologists such as Lazarus (*Black Hills, White Justice, op. cit.*) and Patricia Nelson Limerick in her much acclaimed book, *The Legacy of Conquest: The Unbroken Past of the American West* (New York: W.W. Norton, 1987). Also see Wilcomb E. Washburn's "Land Claims in the Mainstream of Indian/White History," in Imre Sutton, ed., *Irredeemable America: The Indians' Estate and Land Claims* (Albuquerque: University of New Mexico Press, 1985) pp. 21-34.

35. A classic example of this dynamic at play is to be found in self-styled "Indian rights activist" John LaVelle's lengthy review of my *Indians Are Us? Genocide and Colonization in Native North America* (Monroe, ME: Common Courage Press, 1994). Published in the *American Indian Quarterly* (Vol. 20, No. 1, 1997), the review denies, among other things, that genocide is an appropriate descriptor of the fate of indigenous peoples or that a race code was applied by federal authorities in compiling "tribal rolls" pursuant to the 1887 General Allotment Act. LaVelle, a Euroamerican, concludes his piece by insinuating that I am somehow anti-Indian because I object to use of the term "tribe"—as opposed to "nation" or "people"— to describe native groups. To top it off the journal's editor, Morris Foster, also a white man, never got around to publishing my reply (despite both verbal and written commitments to do so in Vol. 20, No. 4). Such is the devotion to "scholarly integrity" which supposedly protects us from the sort of outcome I depict in the text.

36. As illustration of precisely this thesis developed to booklength proportions, see Fergus M. Bordewich's *Killing the White Man's Indian: Reinventing Native Americans at the End of the Twentieth Century* (New York: Doubleday, 1996).

37. E.g., my *Struggle for the Land, op. cit.*

Literature and the Colonization of American Indians

> To retrench the traditional concept of Western history at this point would
> mean to invalidate the justifications for conquering the Western Hemisphere.
>
> —Vine Deloria, Jr.
> *God Is Red*

D URING the late 1960s American writers made inroads into advanced
literary theory by announcing their intent to offer "the journal as
novel/the novel as journal." Norman Mailer embarked overtly upon such a
course of action with his *Armies of the Night* in 1967; Tom Wolfe published
his *The Electric Cool Aid Acid Test* the same year. Such early efforts were soon
followed by a proliferation of journalist/novelist works including Kurt
Vonnegut's *The Slaughterhouse Five* and the great synthetic "gonzo"
excursions of Hunter S. Thompson. According to popular wisdom of the
day, a "new" literary genre had been born, a writing process defining the
emergent contours of American letters.

One might be inclined to agree with the assessment that this intentionally eclectic stew of fact and fiction constitutes a representative image of what
is characteristically American in American literature. One might also, with
equal certainty, dispute the notion that such a posture is new to the scene, particularly since the deliberate presentation of fictionalized material as fact has
marked the nature of American writing almost since the first English-speaking
colonist touched pen to paper. A symbiotic relationship has been established in
America between truly fictional writing on the one hand and ostensibly factual material on the other. Perhaps it is true that this principle prevails in any
literate culture. America, however, seems demonstrably to have gone beyond
any discernible critical differentiation between fiction and nonfiction, a condition which has led to an acute blurring of the line between "truth" and "art."

1

In locating the roots of such a situation, it becomes necessary to examine the content of early archetypal works originating in the Atlantic coastal colonies. By doing so, it is possible to distinguish a common denominator in terms of subject matter between the various modes of writing then extant (formal journals, reports, histories and narrative accounts, for the most part). This subject matter is the indigenous population of the region.

It next becomes necessary to determine concretely whether this early colonial preoccupation with "factually" fixing the realities of things Indian through fictive modes was a topical phenomenon or whether it has exhibited a longevity beyond its immediate context. An examination of 19th century American writing, including the emergence of the novel and epic poetry in North America, serves this purpose, albeit in cursory fashion. Interestingly, as fictional literature evolves in America, it is relatively easy to point both to its concern with the pronouncements of earlier "nonfictive" material as well as to the beginning of an active withdrawal of information from the "factual" treatments of the day. As American fiction developed during the 19th century, it provided a return of information (if only "themes") to be pursued in nonfiction forums. Again, the American Indian emerges as the common denominator blending these two types of writing.

Whether such literary trends are merely aspects of historical Americana or whether they retain a contemporary force and vitality is a question. Examination of several recent works in American letters tends to reveal that not only is the "Indian in American literature" genre alive and well but also that it has undergone something of an arithmetic progression, assuming a position occupying simultaneously both fictional and nonfictional frames of reference. Works that are secretly composed of pure imagination and conjecture are presented as serious factual writing; works of acknowledged fictive content are presented as "authentic." The journalist is and has always been novelist, the novelist has always pretended to journalistic "truth" in relation to the Native American, a condition which—in this sense at least—has served to define American literature itself.

We are not thus confronted with customary understandings of the status and function of literature. When fact and fiction fuse into an intentionally homogeneous whole, mythology becomes the norm. However, those who read, write and publish American literature are unused to and quite unwilling to acknowledge their "truth" as myth; it is insisted upon in most

2

quarters that that which is presented as fact *is* fact. Why this might be so constitutes a final question.

Viewed from the perspective of colonial analysis, I believe the enigmatic aspects of the handling of the American Indian in literature disappear. With literature perceived as a component part of a colonial system, within which Native America constituted and constitutes expropriated and subjugated peoples, the reworking of fact into convenient or expedient fantasies by the colonizer is a logical process rather than an inexplicable aberration. The merger of fact and fiction which was treated as such a rarified accomplishment by Mailer, Wolfe, Thompson, *et al.* was already a time-honored practice in a colonial nation which has always insisted upon viewing itself as free of the colonial aspirations marking its European antecedents.

The Colonial Period

> In May of 1607, three small ships sailed up the James River from Chesapeake Bay in search of a site for the first permanent English colony in North America. The prospective settlers chose a peninsula that had the clear disadvantage of being low and swampy. But it did provide a good anchorage, and the fact that it was a virtual island made it defensible against possible attacks by hostile Indians. By giving a high priority to physical security, the colonizers showed an awareness that this was not an empty land but one that was already occupied by another people who might well resist their incursion. Unlike earlier attempted settlements, Jamestown was not so much an outpost as a beachhead for the English invasion and conquest of what was to become the United States of America.
>
> —George M. Frederickson
> *White Supremacy*

American Indians seem to have provided the defining aspect of that portion of written expression which has come to be generically considered as "American literature." As early as 1612, Captain John Smith was offering observations on native peoples to an eager audience in the "Mother Country":

> They (the Indians) are inconstant in everything, but what fear constraineth them to keep. Crafty, timorous, quick of apprehension and very ingenious, some are of disposition fearful, some bold, most cautious, all savage . . . they soon move to anger, and are so malicious that they seldom forget an injury: they seldom steal from one another, lest their conjurers reveal it, and so they be pursued and punished.[1]

Smith's commentary was followed in short order by that of Alexander Whitaker:

3

Let the miserable condition of these naked slaves of the devil move you to compassion toward them. They acknowledge that there is a great God, but they know him not, wherefore they serve the devil for fear, after a most base manner. . . . They live naked of body, as if the shame of their sin deserved no covering. . . . They esteem it a virtue to lie, deceive, steal . . . if this be their life, what think you shall become of them after death, but to be partakers with the devil and his angels in hell for evermore? [2]

In 1632, Thomas Morton added to the growing list of English language publications originating in the Atlantic Seaboard colonies concerned with the indigenous population:

Now since it is but foode and rayment that men that live needeth (though not all alike), why should not the Natives of New England be sayd to live richly, having no want of either: Cloakes are the badge of sinne, and the more variety of fashions is but the greater abuse of the Creature, the beasts of the forest there deserve to furnish them at any time when they please: fish and flesh they have in great abundance which they roast and boyle. . . . The rarity of the air begot by the medicinal quality of the sweet herbes of the Country, always procures good stomaches to the inhabitants. . . According to humane reason guided only by the light of nature, these people leade the more happy and freer life, being void of care, which torments the minds of so many Christians: they are not delighted in baubles, but in useful things.[3]

And, in 1654, Edward Johnson penned the following concerning the English colonists' 1637 extermination of the Pequots:

The Lord in his mercy toward his poor churches having thus destroyed these bloody barbarous Indians, he returns his people safely to their vessels, where they take account of their prisoners. The squaws and some young youths they brought home with them, and finding the men guilty of the crimes they undertook the war for, they brought away only their heads.[4]

Each of the remarks quoted here serve at least a two-fold purpose: first, each contributed decisively to establishing Native Americans as a topic for English language writing originating in the Americas (in fact, it becomes difficult to conceive a colonial writing not preoccupied with things Indian); second, each established the groundwork for a stereotype which assumed increasing prominence in American literature.

Smith's writing played upon the persistent image of the Indian as a sort of subhuman, animal-like creature who was a danger to hardy Anglo settlers. Whitaker reinforced an already pervasive European notion of the Indian as godless heathen subject to redemption through the "civilizing" ministrations of Christian missionaries. Morton's often confused prattle went far in developing "noble savage" mythology in the Americas. Johnson mined the vein of a militaristic insistence that the native was an incorrigible (even criminal) hindrance to European "progress" in North America, a miscreant barrier to be overcome only through the most liberal applications of fire and cold steel.

With primary stereotyping trends isolated in letters, however, one must also be aware of another important genre of the same period, one which tends to cut across stereotypic lines and which might be perceived as generating a most heatedly emotional and decidedly anti-Indian popular response among readers: the so-called "narratives" of Indian captives. Perhaps the first manuscript of this school was published in 1682 by Mrs. Mary Rowlandson. Samples of her prose clearly meet the standards established above:

> Now away we must go with those barbarous creatures, with our bodies wounded and bleeding, and our hearts no less than our bodies. . . . This was the dolefullest night that ever my eyes saw. Oh, the roaring and singing and dancing and yelling of those black creatures in the night, which made the place a lively resemblance of hell. [5]

Such narratives were copiously cited as "evidence" by such unabashed white supremacists as Increase Mather in his 1684 epic, "Essay for the Recording of Illustrious Providences." Not to be outdone, brother Cotton joined in with his *Magnalia Christi Americana* of 1702:

> In fine, when the Children of the English Captives cried at any time, so that they were not presently quieted, the manner of the Indians was to dash out their brains against a tree . . . they took the small children, and held 'em under Water till they had near Drowned them. . . . And the Indians in their frolics would Whip and Beat the small children, until they set 'em into grievous Outcries, and then throw 'em to their amazed Mothers for them to quiet 'em as well as they could.[6]

This "accounting" was followed by others such as *William Fleming's Narrative of the sufferings and surprizing Deliverances of William and Elizabeth Fleming* in 1750 and the even more venomous (and very popular) *French and Indian Cruelty Exemplified, in the Life and Various Vicissitudes of Fortune, of Peter Williamson* in 1757:

> From these few instances of savage cruelty, the deplorable situation of these defenceless inhabitants, and what they hourly suffered in that part of the globe, must strike the utmost horror to a human soul, and cause in every breast the utmost detestation, not only against the authors of such tragic scenes, but against those who through inattentions, or pusillanimous and erroneous principles, suffered these savages at first, unrepelled, or even unmolested, to commit such outrages and incredible depredations and murders.[7]

In themselves, each of the works produced by the writers covered in this section ostensibly has more to do with the nonfictional strains which have developed over the years in America than with the generic or popular term "literature." Still, the allegedly nonfiction writing of the early English colonists noted above has had a large impact by creating the very conditions of stereotype and emotionalism from which later literary efforts sprang:

> From the initial poorly-informed reports on the Red Man emerged the bigoted and ethnocentric literary attitudes of pious but land-hungry Puritans. Soon were to follow the commercial and greatly fictional captivity narratives, and then the turn of the century "histories" of the Indian wars (never the "White," or "Settlers" or "Colonists" wars).... Perhaps the most tragic thing is that this was only the beginning.[8]

The Early United States

Perhaps the first American work which might appropriately be termed a novel concerning American Indians was Charles Brockden Brown's 1799 release, *Edgar Huntley*. It was followed, in reasonably short order for the time, by two chapters—"Traits of the Indian Character" and "Philip of Pokanoket"—devoted to the extermination of the Narragansets during what the colonists called "King Philip's War" in Washington Irving's *Sketch Book*, dating from 1819. The latter absorbs the "noble savage" stereotype associated with Thomas Morton's earlier work:

> Even in his last refuge of desperation and dispair a sullen grandure gathers round his (Philip's) memory. We picture him to ourselves seated among his careworn followers, brooding in silence over his blasted fortunes and acquiring a savage sublimity from the wilderness of his lurking place. Defeated but not dismayed, crushed to earth but not humiliated, he seemed to grow more haughty beneath disaster and experience a fierce satisfaction in draining the last dregs of bitterness.[9]

By 1823, James Fenimore Cooper was on the scene and between then and 1841 his cumulative novels—including *The Pioneers, The Last of the Mohicans, The Deerslayer, The Prairie* and *The Pathfinder*—had firmly established all four of the stereotypes denoted above within the popular consciousness. Of course, Cooper had considerable help. During the same period, Chateaubriand's *Atala* appeared, as well as novels by William Gilmore Simms including *The Yemasee* and *Guy Rovers*. Then, there were poems such as John Greenleaf Whittier's 1835 epic, *Mogg Megone* and, by 1855, Henry W. Longfellow's *The Song of Hiawatha, To the Driving Cloud* and *The Burial of Minnisink*. In a less pretentious vein, there was also during this general period the so-called "juvenile fiction" exemplified by Mayne Reid in *The Scalp Hunters* and *Desert Home*. The list is considerable.

The elements of this rapidly proliferating mass of creative output shared several features in common. For instance, none possessed the slightest concrete relationship to the actualities of native culture(s) they portrayed. Hence, each amounted to the imaginative invention of the authors, who by virtue of their medium were alien to the context of which they presumed to write. It can be argued, and has,[10] that such prerogatives rest squarely within the realm of the fiction writer. While this may be true in an aesthetic sense, the practical application of the principle breaks down for each of these works on at least two levels:

- The justifying aesthetic rationale is itself an aspect of the European cultural context which generated the literate format at issue. Hence, utilizing aesthetic "freedom" as a justifying basis for the distortive literary manipulation of non-European cultural realities is merely a logically circular continuum. It may perhaps be reasonable that Europe is entitled in the name of literature to fabricate whole aspects of its own sociocultural existence. However, the unilaterally extended proposition that such entitlement reaches into crosscultural areas seems arrogant in the extreme, little more than a literary "Manifest Destiny."

- Regardless of the contradictions implied through application of purely European aesthetic values within a crosscultural context, it must be held in mind that none of the authors in question operated in this abstract sense (such turf being generally reserved for their defenders). In each case, a more or less fictionally intended novel or poetic development was derived from the equally European (Anglo) but ostensibly nonfictive works referenced in the previous section. Consequently, each later literary figure could lay claim to the "authenticity" of a firm grounding in the "historical record." That such history utterly ignored the indigenous oral accountings of the people/events thus portrayed, and did so in favor of the thoroughly alien literary record, serves to illustrate the self-contained dynamic through which literature dismisses anything beyond its pale (including what is being written about). Again, the logic describes a perfect circle: product and proof are one and the same.

The advent of the treatment of American Indians within a formalized American literature does not imply a cessation or even necessarily a diminishing of the "nonfictional" writing from which the fictional material grew. Perhaps its most telling example rests within the introduction of "Indian Religions" to the readership(s) of popular magazines during the 19th century. For example, in an 1884 essay published in *Atlantic Monthly*, writer Charles Leland asserted that ". . .there is no proof of the existence among our [*sic*] Indians of a belief in a Great Spirit or in an infinite God before the coming of the whites." [11] William Wassell, in an article in *Harper's Monthly* felt a factual sort of hope in the freeing of "pagan savages" from "the sorcery and jugglery of weasoned medicine-men" by Christian missionaries who convinced them of "simple teachings of the Bible." [12] In the same vein, Amanda Miller celebrated the documentation of such "civilizing" successes in an 1869 issue of *Overland Monthly*:

> The contrast between the assemblage of hideously painted savages, whose countenances were rendered still the more revolting by their efforts to intensify their passions of hatred and revenge in their incantations of demonaltry, and the placid and devoted (Christian Indian) congregation at Simcoe, was wonderful and delightful. [13]

By 1891, a serious scholar such as Alfred Riggs could only conclude, on the basis of such a "factual" record, that the Christian influence was leading the American Indian to "a quickened conscience, a strengthened will, the power of self-restraint . . . power to labor patiently, economy, thrift . . . a new spiritual impulse, and a new revelation . . . and the customs of . . . a social order." [14] There were many similar pieces in journals with titles such as *Popular Science Monthly, North American Review, Nation, American Quarterly, Century, Scribner's Magazine, New Englander and Yale Review, Forum,* and others. [15] The conclusions of Alexander Whitaker were not only continued, but expanded upon.

It is relatively easy to perceive how, during the nineteenth century, any valid concept ever possessed by the English speaking population of North America as to Native Americans being peoples in their own right, peoples with entirely legitimate belief systems, values, knowledge and lifeways, had been lost in the distortion popularly presented through literature and pseudoscience. The stereotypes had assumed a documented "authenticity" in the public consciousness. Such a process cannot be viewed as meaningless distortion. For stereotyped and stereotyper alike, it becomes dehumanization. [16] As Russell Means put it in 1980:

> [W]ho seems most expert at dehumanizing other people? And why? Soldiers who have seen a lot of combat learn to do this to the enemy before going back into combat. Murderers do it before going out to murder. Nazi SS guards did it to concentration

camp inmates. Cops do it. Corporation leaders do it to the workers they send into uranium mines and steel mills. Politicians do it to everyone in sight. And what the process has in common for each group doing the dehumanizing is that it makes it alright to kill and otherwise destroy other people. One of the Christian commandments says, "Thou shalt not kill," at least not humans, so the trick is to mentally convert the victims into non-humans. Then you can claim a violation of your own commandment as a virtue.[17]

Viewed in this way, treatment of the American Indian in the arena of American literature must be seen as part and parcel of the Angloamerican conquest of the North American continent. How else could attitudes among the general public have been so massively conditioned to accept a system or policy of non-stop expropriation and genocide of the native population throughout U.S. history? The dehumanizing aspects of the stereotyping of American Indians in American literature may be seen as an historical requirement of an imperial process. No other description of the conquest of America seems adequate.

Conceptual Negation

The claim to a national culture in the past does not only rehabilitate that nation and serve as a justification for the hope of a future national culture. In the sphere of socioaffective equilibrium it is responsible for an important change in the native. Perhaps we have not sufficiently demonstrated that colonialism is not simply content to impose its rule upon the present and future of a dominated country. Colonialism is not merely satisfied with holding a people in its grip and emptying the native's brain of all form and content. By a kind of perverse logic, it turns to the past of an oppressed people, and distorts, disfigures and destroys it.

—Frantz Fanon
The Wretched of the Earth

The representation—indeed *mis*representation is a more accurate word—of indigenous people began with the advent of English colonization of the Western Hemisphere. Within a relatively short period, styles of exposition emerged which identified primary modes of stereotype, modes which are continued in evolved formations today and which must rightfully be viewed as having their roots within the literary culture of England itself. This latter seems true both on the basis of the sheer falsity of colonial pronouncements concerning the indigenous American population, which implies that the notions involved were imported rather than located upon arrival by the colonists, as well as on the identifiable prior existence of similar tendencies in "Mother England." Concerning this last:

> Whatever their practical intentions or purposes, the invaders did not confront the native peoples without certain preconceptions about their nature which help shape the way they pursued their goals. Conceptions of "savagery" that developed in the sixteenth and seventeenth centuries and became the common property of Western European culture constituted a distorting lens through which the early colonists assessed the potential and predicted the fate of the non-European peoples they encountered.[18]

The specific stereotypes of American Indians finally deployed in the New England colonies amount to elaboration and continuation of a stream of literary effort already sanctioned by the Crown and its subjects. In practical terms, the established contours of this writing may be assessed as following a roughly "them vs. us" pathway:

> There were two crucial distinctions which allowed Europeans of the Renaissance and Reformation period to divide the human race into superior and inferior categories. One was between Christian and heathen and the other between "civil" and "savage."[19]

As we have seen, the primary stereotypes developed in the Americas did not vary from the established categories. Rather, they represent merely the application of the prescribed generalities within a given context, that is, application to the indigenous populations within the territory of the New England colonies.

It is hardly an overstatement that the initial wave of any colonial invasion has been comprised of both the "cutting edge" and "hard core" of empire. These are the shock troops, arrogant, indoctrinated with the ideology of conquest, prepared to undergo hardship and sacrifice in order to actualize the ideal of their own inherent superiority to all they encounter. Small wonder that such "pioneers" would be prepared to bear false witness against those inhabitants of alien lands who might presume to stand in the way. A twofold purpose is served thereby: first, in an immediate tactical sense, the overtly physical elimination and expropriation of indigenous peoples, which is the abrupt necessity of any preliminary colonization, is provided self-justification and even (in the hands of able propagandists) righteousness; second, a longer-term, strategic consideration applies in that a less brutally doctrinaire segment of the Mother Country population must ultimately be attracted to the task of settling that which the invaders have conquered.

The latter cannot be emphasized too strongly. Mere conquest is never the course of empire. Colonial warriors tend to realize their limitations, their own mortality. The achievement of mission can only be attained through productive utilization of the captured ground, and this is the inevitable role of farmers, miners and merchants rather than soldiers. Hence, the literature of colonialism follows a course from the immediate self-glorifying accounts of first-wave assault troops such as John Smith and Alexander Whitaker, to the salesmanship of Thomas Morton, and on to the longer-term restructuring of the past to serve present and future needs at which Edward Johnson proved so adept. Things are never quite so clear cut in practice as they might be posed in theory. Smith blended his efforts at self-justification into sales pitches concerning colonial real estate. Morton's advertisements of terrain contain similar residues of self-justification. Johnson reveals both aspects of concern within his historiography. But the emphases hold, in the main.

It is at the point that historical recounting rather than more immediate polemics become feasible as an operant norm of literature that literary effort begins to proliferate within the colonial context. Understandably, this seems due to relaxation of initial tensions. The combat associated with the establishment of bridgeheads must end before significant writing can occur. In the Americas, this is evidenced through the work of the Mathers and others of the Puritan persuasion. Such material marks a shift from the need to establish that settlement was in fact both possible and justifiable, that the colonies were viable entities for occupation by farmers as well as assault troops, to emphasis upon the historical inevitability and moral correctness of colonial growth and perpetuation.

In inhabited areas, growth by one population segment is generally accommodated at the expense of another. And so it was in the Americas. The Puritan ideologues set the tone for a more or less continuous expansion of the English-speaking colonies, precipitating perpetual warfare with and expropriation of the various native peoples encountered in the process. John Smith had long since passed, and with him, the cutting edge. The Puritans' task was to deploy the means to provoke and sanctify systematic warfare on the part of the settler population itself. In this, the so-called captive narratives of Mary Rowlandson, William Fleming and others may be seen as having accrued a certain tactical utility.

At the onset of the nineteenth century, a new process had begun. Rebellion had stripped England of its external colonies in the Americas and consolidation of the American nation-state had begun. The emphasis in arts and letters became that of creating the "national heritage" of the emerging state, a source of patriotism and pride within which history (whether real or wholly fabricated) played no part. Hence, the preoccupation with "histories of the Americas" during this period and the historical "groundings" provided to incipient American fiction. But—and there was never a way to avoid this—the course of the European presence in the hemisphere had always been intertwined with that of the original inhabitants to the most intimate degree. The construction of the U.S. national heritage in terms of history therefore necessarily entailed the reconstruction of American Indian history and reality to conform to the desired image.

An obvious route along which to achieve this end was to incorporate preceding literature by English speakers (who constituted the preponderant population of the new American state) into the national heritage as the factual/perceptual basis for both current and future literature. The rupture of English colonization in North America really marked no change in the literary treatment accorded the American Indian. To the contrary, it marked both the continuation and intensification of practices initiated at the height of the colonial process. In both figurative and literal effect, the United States merely supplanted England as the new preeminent colonial power relative to Indians, with the alteration that where the colonies had been maintained as entities external to the British nation proper, they were ultimately to become internal to the territorial integrity of the United States.

In Fanon's terms, what was happening was that the colonist who had metaphorically stripped the native of his/her present through creation of a surrogate literary reality defined to the convenience of the colonizer, was now turning the metaphoric/mythic siege guns fully onto the past. In this way, the present for the native could be perpetually precluded through the maintenance of this seamlessly constituted surrogate reality. Clearly too, any perpetual "present" must encompass the future as well as the moment. The indigenous reality, the "national culture" of Fanon's thesis, is thereby hopelessly trapped within the definitional power of the oppressor, drifting endlessly in lazy hermeneutic circles, stranded in a pastless/presentless/futureless vacuum. The national identity of the colonizer is created and maintained through the usurpation of the national identity of the colonized, a causal relationship.

The final conquest of its continental landmass by the United States absorbed the whole of the nineteenth century, a period which coincided with the formal creation of American literature. Region by region, people by people, indigenous cultures were overwhelmed and consigned to the reservation status marking the physical characteristics of U.S. internal colonialism. Throughout this era an overarching theme in American writing, from the embryonic work of Charles Brockden Brown and Washington Irving to the late-century tracts of Charles Leland and Alfred Riggs, was the Indian. Or, rather, a certain image of the Indian which complemented the need of the nation's Euroamerican population to supplant the original inhabitants of the land.

Here, another shift occurs. Where initial English colonial writings seem primarily to be seriously concerned with the christian/heathen dichotomy, nineteenth-century American literature gravitates more and more toward themes involving the civil versus savage juxtaposition. The trappings of quasimissionary rhetoric are maintained in treatments such as that written by Amanda Miller, to be sure, but this is a blurring of distinctions of the same order as the overlapping of content evident between Smith, Whitaker and Morton in an earlier period. By the late 1800s, the original imperatives of missionarism, obvious enough in Puritan literature, had given way to a posture whereby christianization simply signalled the transition of the savage to "civilized" (nonobstructionist) status.

Another signification of the civilizing process was literacy itself. Therein, a primary tool of the formulation and justification of European colonialism was offered up as a focus for attainment to the colonized. As the articulation of its Manifest Destiny underscored Euroamerica's presumed right to concrete territorial ambitions, so too did articulation of aesthetic doctrine reserve unto the literate the right to interpret history and reality at will. In America, both theses were developed during the same period and progressed virtually in tandem. Both were designed to serve the population which invented them at the direct expense of others. But, while the most overt expressions of manifest destiny have become politically outmoded and have fallen into disrepute, the logic of literate aesthetic primacy has, if anything, become a dominant social norm.

The final absorption of the western United States into the national domain was accompanied by a constantly increasing public zeal to civilize the savage, or at least the popular conception of the savage. This latter is of considerable importance insofar as therein lies the primary function of literature within colonialism. The overwhelming preponderance of writing concerning the American Indian during the U.S. expansion was designed to create an image allowing conquest "for the Indians' own good," to effect "betterment" and "progress." The potential for a mass psychology of national guilt at its policy of genocide and theft could be offset in no other conceivable fashion at that time. Further, the imposition of literacy and "education" can be perceived as the most effective means to inculcate in the Indians themselves a "correct" understanding (in future generations, at least) of the appropriateness of their physical and cultural demise.

> Since schooling was brought to non-Europeans as a part of empire . . . it was integrated into an effort to bring indigenous peoples into imperial/colonial structures. . . . After all, did not the European teacher and the school built on the European capitalist model transmit European values and norms and begin to transform traditional societies into "modern" ones. . .(?)[20]

At this juncture, a truly seamless model of colonialism makes its appearance: The training of the colonized to colonize themselves. In this sense, hegemony over truth and knowledge replaces troops and guns as the relevant tool of colonization. Literature, always an important property of the European colonial process, assumes an increasingly important centrality to maintenance of the system. As Albert Memmi has observed:

> In order for the colonizer to be a complete master, it is not enough for him to be so in actual fact, but he must also believe in its (the colonial system's) legitimacy. In order for that legitimacy to be complete, it is not enough for the colonized to be a slave, he must also accept his role. The bond between the colonizer and the colonized is thus destructive and creative. It destroys and recreates the two partners in colonization into the colonizer and the colonized. One is disfigured into the oppressor, a partial, unpatriotic and treacherous being, worrying about his privileges and their defense; the other into an oppressed creature, whose development is broken and who compromises by his defeat.[21]

Such a view goes far towards answering the obvious questions concerning why, nearly a century after the conclusion of the primary U.S. territorial expansion, American literature still treats the Indian within its own desired framework. In the same sense, it explains the nature of the support for the situation from publishers, a massive reading audience, and the academic community as a whole.

Conclusion

That which is cannot be admitted. That which will be must be logically converted into that which cannot be. To this end, the publishers publish, the writers invent, the readers consume in as great a portion as may be provided, and the academics sanctify (over and over) the "last word" in "true" explanation as to where we've been, come and are going. None, or at least few, seem to act from outright malice; most are moved compulsively by internalized forces of fear (of retribution?), guilt and greed.

How then to best deploy the sophistry of literature within such a context? Certainly not in the crude polemical fashion of the Mathers and the Smiths. Those days passed with the need for blatant military suppression of tribal autonomy. No, direct attack is obsolete. In the post-Holocaust era there is no viable ability to justify Sand Creek, the Washita and Wounded Knee. Rather, these are to be purged through a reconstitution of history as a series of tragic aberrations beginning and ending nowhere in time. The literal meaning of such events must at all costs be voided by sentiment and false nostalgia rather than treated as parts of an ongoing process. The literal is rendered tenuously figurative, and then dismissed altogether.

From there, reality can be reconstructed at will. Witness the contemporary obsession with establishing "authenticity." Ruth Beebe Hill requires the services of an aging Indian to verify her every word. Cash Asher requires another aging Indian to step forward and attest to his version of "truth." Carlos Castaneda relies upon a truly massive and sustained support from both the publishing and professional academic communities to validate his efforts. Schneebaum, Waldo, Lamb, Storm, all within the recent years, receive considerable support from "reputable" publishers and from some of the most prestigious scholarly establishments in the country.[22]

It is not that they are "ordered" to say specific things about Indians, although the ancient stereotypes are maintained (albeit, in mutated form). Rather, it seems that the current goal of literature concerning Indians is to create them, if not out of whole cloth then from only the bare minimum of fact needed to give the resulting fiction a "ring of truth," to those Indians bound to colonialism as readily as to people of European heritage.

At the dawn of English colonization of the New World, Sir Walter Raleigh was able to write that the natives of Guiana, "have their eyes in their shoulders, and their mouths in the middle of their breasts." He was believed then by the English reading public, although his words assume proportions of absurdity today (as, one assumes, they must have to those in a position to know better at the time).

Things have come full circle on the literary front. Where, in the beginning, it was necessary to alter indigenous realities in order to assuage the invading colonial conscience, so it seems necessary today to alter these realities to assure the maintenance of empire. It seems to matter little what American Indians are converted into, as long as it is into other than what they are, have been and might become. Consigned to a mythical realm, we constitute no threat to the established order either figuratively (as matters of guilt and conscience) or literally (in terms of concrete opposition). That which is mythic in nature cannot be or has already been murdered, expropriated and colonized in the "real world." The potential problem is solved through intellectual sleight of hand, aesthetic gimmickry and polemical discourse with specters. The objective is not art but absolution. As Vine Deloria, Jr. has observed:

> [T]herein lies the meaning of the white's fantasy about Indians—the problem of the Indian image. Underneath all the conflicting images of the Indian one fundamental truth emerges—the white man knows that he is alien and he knows that North America is Indian—and he will never let go of the Indian image because he thinks that by some clever manipulation he can achieve an authenticity which can never be his.[23]

In this sense at least, literature in America is and always has been part and parcel of the colonial process. In this sense, too, it has always been that American literature constituted a confused netherworld wherein fictionalized journals met journalized fiction in a jumble of verbiage requisite only to the masking of a disavowed and painful reality.

Notes

1. John Smith, *A Map of Virginia, with a description of the Country, the Commodities, People, Government and Religion* (1621) as quoted in Reuben Post Halleck, *History in American Literature* (New York, 1911), p. 18.

2. Alexander Whitaker, *Good News from Virginia* as quoted in Moses Goit Tyler, *A History of American Literature, 1607–1765* (Ithaca, 1949), pp. 41–43.

3. Thomas Morton, *New English Canaan* (1632) as quoted in Wilcomb E. Washburn, ed., *The Indian and the White Man* (New York, 1965), pp. 35–38.

4. Edward Johnson, *Wonder-Working Providence of Zion's Savior in New England* (1654) as quoted in Tyler, *op cit.*, pp. 122–215.

5. Mary Rowlandson, *The Sovereignty and Goodness of God Together With the Faithfulness of His Promise Displayed: Being a Narrative of the Captivity and Restoration of Mrs. Mary Rowlandson* (1682) as quoted in R.H. Pearce, "Significance of the Captivity Narrative," *American Literature XIX* (Mar, 1947), 1–20.

6. Cotton Mather, *Magnalia Christi Americana* (1702), Ibid., pp. 3–4. *The Readers' Encyclopedia of American Literature*, Max J. Herzog, ed. (New York, 1962); also cites another work closely related to the Mather opus, but bearing the even more unlikely title of *The Redeemed Captive Returning to Zion or a faithful history of Remarkable Occurrences in the Captivity and Deliverance of Mr. John Williams (Minister of the Gospel in Deerfield) who in the Desolation which befell the Plantation by the incursion of the French and Indians, was by them carried away, with his family and his neighborhood into Canada* [!!!] (1707).

7. Peter Williamson, *French and Indian Cruelty Exemplified, in the Life and Various Vicissitudes of Fortune, of Peter Williamson* (1757) as quoted in Pearce, pp. 7–8.

8. David F. Beer, "Anti-Indian Sentiment in Early Colonial Literature," *The Indian Historian*, Vol. 2, No. 1, Spring, 1969, p. 48.

9. Washington Irving, *Sketch Book* (1819), as cited in C.F. Ten Kate, "The Indian in American Literature" (1919), *Smithsonian Annual Reports, 1921*, reprinted in *The American Indian Reader* (San Francisco: American Indian Historical Society, 1973). Citation is from p. 189 of the latter volume.

10. See, as but one example, the subtle justification(s) advanced in Ten Kate.

11. Charles G. Leland, "The Edda Among the Algonquin Indians," *Atlantic Monthly*, LIV (Aug, 1884), 223.

12. William Wassell, "The Religion of the Sioux," *Harper's New Monthly Magazine*, LXXXIX (Nov, 1894), 945.

13. Amanda Miller, "To Simcoe," *Overland Monthly*, III (Aug, 1869), 176.

14. Alfred Riggs, "Some Difficulties of the Indian Problem," *New Englander and Yale Review*, LIV (Apr, 1891), 329.

15. A sampling of the essays and articles intended here is: John Westley Powell, "Mythologic Philosophy I," *Popular Science Monthly*, XV (October 1879); Eugene J. Tripple, "Primitive Indian Tribes," *North American Review*, CI (July 1865); Frederick Schwatka, "The Sun-Dance of the Sioux," *Century*, XVII (Mar, 1890); Herbert Walsh, "The Meaning of the Dakota Outbreak," *Scribner's Magazine*, IX (April 1891); John G. Bourke, "The Indian Messiah," *Nation* (Dec 4, 1890); Hiram Price, "The Government and the Indians," *Forum*, X (Feb, 1891); Francis Parkman, "Indian Superstitions," *North American Review*, CIII (July, 1866). As noted in the text, the listing could be continued *ad nauseum*.

16. The sense of the definition of "dehumanization" intended here is as simple as that offered by *The Merriam-Webster Dictionary* (1974): ". . . the divestiture of human qualities or personality . . ." Surely this is an apt summation of the fate experienced by the native in the literature covered so far.

17. Russell Means, "Fighting Words on the Future of Mother Earth," *Mother Jones* (Nov, 1980), 26–27.

18. George M. Frederickson, *White Supremacy: A Comparative Study in American and South African History* (New York: Oxford University Press, 1981), p. 7.

19. Ibid., pp. 7–8.

20. Martin Carnoy, *Education as Cultural Imperialism* (New York: David McKay & Co., 1974), p. 16.

21. Albert Memmi, *Colonizer and Colonized* (Boston: Beacon Press, 1965), p. 89.

22. Some of the specific material intended within this observation includes Asher, Cash and Chief Red Fox, *The Memoirs of Chief Red Fox* (New York: Fawcett Books, 1972); Ruth Beebe Hill, with

Chunksa Yuha (Alonzo Blacksmith), *Hanta Yo: An American Saga* (Garden City, NY: Doubleday, 1979); Hyemeyohsts Storm, *Seven Arrows* (New York: Ballantine, 1972); Anna Lee Waldo, *Sacajawea* (New York: Avon, 1978); Tobias Schneebaum, *Keep the River on Your Right* (New York: Grove Press, 1970); as well as at least the first three books by Carlos Castaneda, the so-called "Castaneda Trilogy."

23. Vine Deloria, Jr., "Foreword: American Fantasy," in *The Pretend Indians: Images of Native Americans in the Movies*, Gretchen M. Bataille and Charles L. P. Silet, eds. (Ames: Iowa State University Press, 1980), p. xvi.

It Did Happen Here

Sand Creek, Scholarship and the American Character

> Nits make lice. . . . Kill all, big and little. . . . [And] damn any man who takes the side of the Indians.
>
> —Colonel John M. Chivington
> Commander, Colorado Volunteer Cavalry
> 1864

At a number of levels, the 1864 Sand Creek Massacre of Cheyenne and Arapaho Indians in what was then called Colorado Territory has come to symbolize the manner in which Euroamerica "settled" the entirety of the western United States. More than the comparable slaughters which ensued along the Washita River, Sappa Creek, Bear River, Wounded Knee and hundreds of other sites throughout the Plains and Great Basin regions, Sand Creek had everything necessary to commend it as an archetypal event: a white population, moved by gold fever, knowingly tramples upon legally binding treaty provisions with a massive invasion of Indian country; the federal government, rather than attempting to honor its own existing treaty obligations to protect the Indians' solemnly guaranteed national borders, engineers a second—utterly fraudulent—instrument purporting to legitimate its citizens' illegal occupation of the Cheyenne-Arapaho homeland; a conspiratorial circle of merchants and politicians among the invaders glimpses the potential for vast personal wealth and power in liquidation of the "savages" and the resultant Colorado statehood this might make possible. A propaganda campaign to whip up a public blood lust against the Indians is therefore initiated, a mostly phoney "war" is conjured up, and special dispensation is secured from Washington, D.C. to create bodies of soldiers devoted exclusively to Indian killing.

The Indians, pushed to the wall, are divided as to whether they should fight back or simply surrender to the onrushing wave of national and cultural oblivion which threatens to engulf them. Either way, they are tremendously outgunned and beset by the murderous frenzy of an alien population bent upon their eradication as "a species." A large number of the Cheyennes and a few Arapahoes attempt to remain at peace with their opponents, allowing themselves to be mostly disarmed and immobilized in exchange for official assurances that they will be safe from attack so long as they remain at a location selected for them at Sand Creek, in southeastern Colorado. They live there quietly, under protection of a white flag flown above the lodge of their leader, Black Kettle, until the very moment of the preplanned attack which decimates them. No sparkling hero arrives to save the day at the last moment, and the matter is never "set right." A large though undetermined number of Indians, mostly women, children and old people, are killed and grotesquely mutilated. Those who survive are driven permanently from the territory, and the plotters' plans are largely consummated. Colorado duly becomes a state. Many of the conspirators prosper. Evil wins out, pure and simple.

Literature concerning the wanton butchery occurring at Sand Creek on November 29, 1864 began to emerge almost immediately. This was first the case in the pages of jingoist local tabloids like the *Rocky Mountain News*, where the massacre was heralded as a glorious event, and then in lengthy reports issued by three separate governmental commissions charged with investigating what exactly had happened. Each of these—*Massacre of Cheyennes* (U.S. Congress, 1865), *The Chivington Massacre* (U.S. Congress, 1865) and *Sand Creek Massacre* (Secretary of War, 1867)—concluded unequivocally that there was no merit to the rationalizations advanced by those responsible concerning why they'd acted as they had, and that mass murder had indeed been perpetrated against the Cheyennes and Arapahoes. That said, however, each report stopped well short of recommending any sort of criminal punishment for any of the perpetrators, never mind abortion of the process of state formation their collective misdeeds had set in motion. To the contrary, the only tangible consequence visited upon anyone who had played a major role accrued to Colonel John Milton Chivington, a former Methodist minister *cum* overall commander of the troops (the 3rd and portions of the 1st Colorado Volunteer Cavalry Regiments) who'd done the actual killing. "Disgraced" by the official findings, Chivington was forced to abandon his previously promising political career in favor of other lines of work.

Over the years since then, Sand Creek has found a ready place in recountings of Euroamerica's takeover of the Great Plains ranging in tone, tenor and intent from Frank Hall's four volume *History of the State of Colorado* (Blakely, 1899), through Frederick Jackson Turner's *The Significance of the Frontier in American History* (Holt, 1947), to S.L.A. Marshall's *The Crimsoned Prairie* (Scribner, 1972) and E.S. Connell's *Son of the Morning Star* (North Point, 1984). Similarly, it has been integral to those works—such as George Bird Grinnell's *The Fighting Cheyennes* (Scribner, 1915) and *The Cheyenne Indians* (Yale University, 1923), or J.H. Moore's *The Cheyenne Nation* (University of Nebraska, 1987)—seeking to chronicle the effects of U.S. westward expansion upon the indigenous people at issue.

The massacre and its implications have also been central to biographies of certain of the non-Indian principles involved—Edgar Carlisle MacMechen's *Life of Governor John Evans, Second Territorial Governor of Colorado* (Wahlgreen, 1924) and Reginald S. Craig's sympathetic study of Chivington, *The Fighting Parson* (Westernlore, 1959), spring immediately to mind—as do the autobiographical accounts of lesser players like Morse Coffin in his *The Battle of Sand Creek* (W.M. Morrison, 1965).

The authors of the biographies in particular have taken considerable liberties with the record, both factually and philosophically, in their quest to, if not completely vindicate and rehabilitate their subjects, then at least neutralize the genocidal negativity of their central figures' words and conduct. In this, they are joined by the writers of several books focusing directly upon the massacre itself, notably Eugene F. Ware's *The Indian War of 1864* (Crane & Co., 1911) and William R. Dunn's *"I Stand by Sand Creek": A Defense of Colonel John M. Chivington and the Third Colorado Cavalry* (Old Army Press, 1985).

Such lies, distortions and unabashed polemics in behalf of Sand Creek's perpetrators have, in combination, provided a convenient umbrella under which "more responsible" scholars have persistently sheltered, avoiding the unpleasantness inherent not only to the specifics of Sand Creek itself, but of the far broader sweep of policy to which it was inextricably linked. The conventional academic wisdom has thus landed squarely on the comfortable proposition that, while the massacre was undoubtedly a "tragedy," its real meaning and place in American history remains somehow "unknowable" or "stubbornly mysterious" (see Raymond G. Carey's "The Puzzle of Sand Creek" [*Colorado Magazine*, 41:4, 1964] and Michael A. Sievers' "Shifting Sands of Sand Creek Historiography" [*Colorado Magazine*, 49:2, 1972]).

There have, to be sure, been efforts which have gone in decidedly different directions. Noteworthy in this regard, albeit to varying degrees, have been

William H. Leckie's *The Military Conquest of the Southern Plains* (University of Oklahoma, 1963), Ralph K. Andrist's *The Long Death* (Collier, 1964), Dee Brown's *Bury My Heart at Wounded Knee* (Holt, Rinehart and Winston, 1970), and John Selby's *The Conquest of the American West* (Rowman and Littlefield, 1976), each of which treats the massacre for what it was and attempts to situate it within an accurate contextual rendering of overall policy and public sentiment. Paramount among this genre is Stan Hoig's *The Sand Creek Massacre* (University of Oklahoma, 1961), an honest and meticulously researched volume which has stood for nearly thirty years as the definitive study for those pursuing a genuine understanding of the whole affair.

Aside from the obligatory inclusion of Sand Creek in Father Peter Powell's works on the Cheyenne, however, there has since the mid-'70s been something of a hiatus on the generation of worthwhile material. It is thus a circumstance of some interest and importance that a single six-month period, spanning the years 1989 and '90, saw the release of two new book-length examinations of the topic.

Of the two — David Svaldi's *Sand Creek and the Rhetoric of Extermination: A Case Study in Indian-White Relations* (University Press of America, 1989) and *Month of the Freezing Moon: The Sand Creek Massacre, November 1864* by Duane Schultz — Schultz's book follows by far the more shopworn and predictable pattern. It is a standard history of the "who did what to whom" variety, tracing the by now familiar progression of events leading up to, comprising and immediately stemming from the massacre itself. In this, it is accurate enough on the main points, although essentially duplicative of Hoig's earlier and much better written volume.

Were this all that was involved, *Month of the Freezing Moon* would be nothing so much as a vaguely plagiaristic redundancy, more or less harmless despite its tendency to include easily avoidable errors of detail which serve to muddy rather than further clarify the record. A good example of this comes at page 135, where Schultz places Left Hand, a primary Arapaho leader, among those slain at Sand Creek. This myth, created by the glory-seekers of the Colorado Volunteers, has been debunked long since by Hoig (p. 154) and Margaret Coel in her exhaustive biography of the supposed victim, *Chief Left Hand: Southern Arapaho* (University of Oklahoma, 1981), among others.

Schultz, however, goes much further, and this is where his work is transformed from being merely irrelevant into something truly malicious and objectionable. This comes with his adoption of the Euroamerican standard of "academic objectivity" decreeing that whenever one addresses the atrocities committed by the status quo, one is duty-bound to "balance one's view" by depicting some negativity as being embodied in its victims. This holds as an iron law of "responsible scholarship" even when counterbalancing information must be quite literally invented. Hence, while Schultz follows Hoig's lead in dissecting and refuting assorted untruths about specific Cheyenne actions manufactured and disseminated by the perpetrators in the process of entering their own justification of the massacre, he simultaneously embraces those same sources—or those like them (e.g., Richens Lacy "Uncle Dick" Wooten)—as credible and valid when it comes to describing the broader dimensions of Indian character and behavior:

> [B]efore there were whites to rob and plunder and steal from, the [Indians] robbed and stole from each other. Before there were white men in the country to kill, they killed each other. Before there were white women and children to scalp and mutilate and torture, the Indians scalped and mutilated and tortured the women and children of the enemies of their own race. They made slaves of each other when there were no palefaces to be captured and sold or held for ransom, and before they commenced lying in ambush along the trails of the white man to murder unwary travelers, the Indians of one tribe would set the same sort of death traps for the Indians of another tribe (p. 16).

None of this is substantiated, or even substantiable. It instead flies directly in the face of most well-researched and -grounded contemporary understandings regarding how the Cheyennes did business in precontact times as well as the early contact period. Deployed in the otherwise "critical" (of the whites) and "sympathetic" (to the Indians) setting so carefully developed by the author, such disinformation serves a peculiarly effective propaganda function. The general reader is led to conclude that, while it's "a shame" the good citizens of Colorado were forced to comport themselves as they did, the intrinsic bestiality of their enemies led inevitably to this result. The inherently horrible nature of the victims themselves—*not* the fundamental nature of the process by which they were victimized—accounts for the nature of the fate imposed upon them. The process itself thereby becomes "necessary" and consequently beyond need of justification.

In this construction, Evans, Chivington and the others are indeed guilty, but only of what are conventionally described as "excesses." This is to say, by definition, that they undertook a good thing (the conquest of native nations) and "pushed it too far" (using methods which were overly crude). The reader is the left to ponder whether even this might not be excusable—

or at least "understandable" (which is to say, "forgivable")—"under the circumstances" or "in the heat of the fray."

Such techniques of presentation are hardly novel or unique to Schultz, having been well-refined since 1950 by various apologists for nazism seeking to vindicate the "core impulse" guiding the Waffen SS to its gruesome performance in eastern Europe during World War II. That the author of *Month of the Freezing Moon* might actually desire that his revision of Hoig join the ranks of North American corollaries to such Germanic endeavors would not seem especially out of character in view of his earlier record of cranking out uniformly hyper-patriotic accounts of U.S. military prowess: *Hero of Bataan: The Story of General Jonathan M. Wainwright* (St. Martins, 1981), *Wake Island: The Heroic Gallant Fight* (Jove, 1985), *The Last Battle Station: The Story of the USS Houston* (St. Martins, 1986), and *The Doolittle Raid* (St. Martins, 1988). To observe from this perspective that Schultz makes no worthwhile or commendable contribution to the literature on Sand Creek is to extend a very substantial bit of understatement.

David Svaldi's first book commands an altogether different assessment. Anchoring his analysis in the whole range of public pronouncements emerging in Colorado contemporaneously with the massacre, the author drives home the point that the will to exterminate Indians (*any* Indians, of *whatever* character) was an hegemonic force among the territory's settler population throughout the crucial period. There simply was no generalized dissent from the prevailing view—isolated figures like Edward Wynkoop and Silas Soule are rightly treated as such exceptions as to prove the rule—to be found in this quarter until well after the fact. Meaning is assigned to this phenomenon through reliance upon already established theoretical structures elaborated in William Stanton's *The Leopard's Spots: Attitudes Towards Race in America, 1815–1859* (University of Chicago, 1960), Murray Edelman's *Politics as Symbolic Action: Mass Arousal and Quiescence* (Markham, 1971), Reginald Horsman's *Race and Manifest Destiny* (Harvard University, 1981), and elsewhere.

The broader insights gained from these latter connections entail extension of Svaldi's rhetorical examination comparatively and longitudinally from the moment of Sand Creek to a number of other instances occurring both earlier and later in U.S. history. Following the same sort of trajectory plotted by Richard Drinnon in his superb *Facing West: The Metaphysics of Indian Hating and Empire Building* (University of Minnesota, 1980), the analysis offered in *Sand Creek and the Rhetoric of Extermination* therefore picks up the thread of Euroamerica's genocidal mentality in colonial New England during the mid-eighteenth century, and carries it through to the Mylai Massacre in Vietnam more than 200 years later. Under such scrutiny, any notion that Sand Creek was an "aberration" is rapidly dispelled. Although U.S. citizens residing east of the Mississippi River widely condemned the massacre at the time, such condemnation fell uniformly short of demanding either criminal prosecution for the perpetrators or redress for surviving victims. Why? Because the inhabitants of each state of the union were uncomfortably aware that their own antecedents had, in the not-so-distant past, done precisely the same thing to the indigenous people of their region.

No area within what are now the forty-eight contiguous states of the United States is exempt from having produced its own historical variant of the Sand Creek phenomenon. The very existence of the U.S. in its modern territorial and demographic configuration is contingent upon this fact. Racially oriented invasion, conquest, genocide and subsequent denial are all integral, constantly recurring and thus defining features of the Euroamerican makeup from the instant the first boat load of self-ordained colonists set foot in the "New World." At base, nothing has changed for the better in this regard up through the present moment. Nor will things be likely to improve until such time as denial is supplanted by a willingness to face such things squarely, without evasion or equivocation. Towards this positive objective, David Svaldi has performed sterling service, joining the still tiny group of Hoigs and Drinnons who strive to inject a measure of accuracy into the popular consciousness of what has transpired in North America since 1600.

This is by no means to say that *Sand Creek and the Rhetoric of Extermination* is a perfect book. It suffers from being written in a dry, overly academic, almost dissertationish, manner. It passes over numerous examples—from Lord Jeffrey Amherst's use of bacteriological warfare against Indians in 1763, to the slaughter of a million "Moros" by U.S. forces in the Philippines at the end of the nineteenth century—which were deserving of mention and would have provided further support to the author's thesis. Similarly, it would have been useful and instructive had Svaldi devoted time and attention, even transiently, to exploration of the rhetorical similarities (and dissimilarities) between exterminationists in the U.S. and those of the third reich. A sharper comprehension of that ugly relationship might well have emerged from such handling, strengthening our grasp of Svaldi's overall premises.

It is nonetheless apparent that the book accomplishes much in improving our posture of understanding about Sand Creek and its implications. It also lays a sound foundation for investigating the conceptual crosscurrents between nazism and Euroamerican ideologies of exterminationism called for above. Perhaps this will be David Svaldi's next project. Be that as it may, *Sand Creek and the Rhetoric of Extermination* must be assessed as tangible proof that the whole truth of "the American experience" will eventually come out despite the best efforts of those who would seek to block or confuse it. There is reason enough in this for us to enter a certain hopeful applause.

Carlos Castaneda
The Greatest Hoax Since Piltdown Man

> Since the American public has already become accustomed to seeing Jerome Rothenberg "translations," the poetry of "white shamans" such as Gary Snyder, Gene Fowler, Norman Moser, Barry Gifford, and David Cloutier, to name a few, and other neo-romantic writers posing as Indians and/or Indian experts/spokes[persons], such as Carlos Castaneda, Hyemeyohsts Storm, Tony Shearer, Doug Boyd, the Baha'i influenced "Indian" works of Naturegraph Publications, contemporary Indian writers are often discounted or ignored since they are not following or conforming to the molds created by these "experts."
>
> —Geary Hobson
> *The Remembered Earth*

In 1968, a book appeared on the American literary scene bearing the rather unlikely title, *The Teachings of Don Juan: A Yaqui Way of Knowledge*. Even less probable, on the surface at least, was that the publisher of this overnight bestseller was not a commercial publishing house, but the academically prestigious UCLA Press. In 1971, the successful author followed up with a sequel volume, *A Separate Reality: Further Conversations with Don Juan*, and in 1972, *Journey to Ixtlan: The Lessons of Don Juan*.

In contrast to the initial book, the second pair were published by a popular press, Simon & Schuster, perhaps because the author was simultaneously preparing to submit his third manuscript under the title *Sorcery: A Description of the World* to his UCLA doctoral committee.[1] On the other hand, his motivation was perhaps more oriented toward Simon & Schuster's lucrative bid to package all three efforts as a "Don Juan Trilogy" available to all those seeking initiation into the "innermost secrets" of American Indian spirituality. In any event, the transition from a scholarly press, with its inherent limitations on readership and sales, to the mass market of Madison Avenue publishing seems to have presented the author with no discernible difficulty. Indeed, the product peddled was the same in each case.

As a certified Ph.D. in anthropology, the writer went on to crank out *Tales of Power* in 1974, following up with *The Second Ring of Power* in 1977 and *The Eagle's Gift* in 1981, all of them published by Simon & Schuster. Along the way, he also found time to undergird his academic stature by publishing a ponderous short essay entitled "The didactic uses of hallucinogenic plants: An examination of a system of teaching" in *Abstracts of the 67th Annual Meeting of the American Anthropological Association* (1968), and to add luster to his place in the cash-rich cosmos of pop psychology with articles like "The Art of Dreaming" in *Psychology Today* (Dec. 1977). By 1979, as Simon & Schuster was preparing to go to press with *The Art of Stalking*, which, had it been published (mysteriously, it was not), would have been the author's sixth book, he had by various estimates grossed from $1 million to $3 million as a result of his literary output.[2]

Such cashflow undoubtedly accrued not simply from the books' reputed merits, but from the sort of publicity attending their release. As early as 1969, *New York Times* reviewer Charles Simmons, for example, was informing its millions of readers that Carlos Castaneda, at the time an obscure graduate student writing on what was ostensibly an equally obscure subject matter, was plainly "destined for fame."[3] The "newspaper of record" followed up, in May 1971, with a review by Roger Jellinik in which it was proclaimed that Castaneda's books represented an authentic accounting of "a pre-logical form that is no-one-knows how old," and that it was thus "impossible to exaggerate the importance" of his work.[4] By February 1972, it was running pieces such as that by William Irving Thompson to the effect that Castaneda was the first scholar to effectively integrate science with the occult in an anthropologically valid sense.[5]

At about the same time, *Saturday Review* published a review by Joseph Canon saluting Castaneda as one of the few "serious" current anthropological experimenters in "reality perception and psychic phenomenon."[6] Both books were described as being "consistent, luminous [and] profoundly exciting" in *Publishers Weekly* the same year.[7] An avalanche of other highly favorable reviews also appeared in such widely circulated periodicals as *Natural History* (1971), *Esquire* (1971 and 1975), *Harper's* (1973 and 1974), *New Statesman* (1975), *Sunday Times* (1975), *Cultural Information Service* (1976), and *CoEvolution Quarterly*, *Booklist* and *New Age* (all in 1977), the tenor of which may best be exemplified by lengthy interviews published in *Penthouse* (1972) and *Playboy* (1975).[8]

Popular reviewers and interviewers were by no means alone in bolstering Castaneda's burgeoning reputation, a matter readily evidenced by humanities professor Albert William Levi's 1971 tribute to both *The Teachings of Don Juan* and *A Separate Reality*, published in *Saturday Review*.[9] In October 1972, respected Africanist Paul Reisman used the *New York Times* as a podium from which to endorse all of the first three Don Juan books as "milestones in [the] science of anthropology."[10] Noted anthropologist Stan Wilk chimed in the same year—in the *American Anthropologist*, no less—to assert that *A Separate Reality* might "be beneficially viewed as a sacred text," and to personally thank Castaneda for writing it and thereby "saving the discipline" from the doldrums which had afflicted it for some time.[11] Of all the material recently published in its vein, Carl Rogers informed readers of *American Psychologist*, only Castaneda's "rings true," a conclusion endorsed not only by a range of less eminent psychoanalysts and psychiatrists like Marie Coleman Nelson, Bruce Scotton and William Stillwell, but such heavies as Robert E. Ornstein.[12]

In 1973, anthropologist Mary Douglas, another prominent academic voice by any estimation, held forth in the *Times Higher Educational Supplement*, pronouncing Castaneda's work to be a "substantial pedagogical breakthrough."[13] Two years later, she included a revised and expanded version of the same essay in one of her books, intended as a text for broad consumption by undergraduates.[14] In the interim, educational theorist Ronald Cohen proclaimed the Don Juan/Castaneda interaction to be an extraordinarily promising model for revamping prevailing notions of pedagogy across-the-board.[15] There were literally scores of such "reputable" intellectual voices filling in the published chorus of applause.

And, to be sure, "countercultural" theoreticians were quick to join the queue. From the outset, Theodore Roszak, to name one significant example, consistently championed Castaneda, opining that he had brought out as no one else "the ritualistic precision and pedagogical discipline surrounding Don Juan's teachings [which] resound with generations of meditation and philosophical experiment."[16] Lucius Outlaw, Beatrice Bruteau and others added amplification, asserting that, through Castaneda, Don Juan's Yaqui teachings "radically challenge our present modes of understanding" by opening our minds to "the totality of the infinite intercommunicating universe."[17] Even into the 1990s, writers like Jerry Mander have persisted in offering Castaneda's material as an example of "the indigenous alternative" to Western thought.[18]

In view of such hype, it is small wonder that as of the spring of 1977 Simon & Schuster was reporting aggregate sales of more than four million

Castaneda books, UCLA Press an additional several hundred thousand.[19] Today, after twenty years of shelf-life (unlike many extremely important offerings, no Castaneda book has ever been taken out of print), myriad course adoptions, translation into two dozen languages and publication of a further three volumes—*The Fire from Within* (1984), *The Power of Silence: Further Teachings of Don Juan* (1991) and *The Art of Dreaming* (1993)—the total likely falls in the range of fifteen-to-twenty million.[20] In sum, it is more than probable that Carlos Castaneda ranks as the most widely read—or, in any event, best selling—author in the history of American anthropology.

The Sanctity of "Academic Standards"

All of this devolves upon the notion that Castaneda, at the time a beginning grad student in anthropology, set off at some point in 1960 into the wilds of the Sonora Desert for purposes of conducting "field research." Once there, so the story goes, he encountered and was allowed to understudy an aging "Yaqui sorcerer," Don Juan Matus.[21] For the next eight years, according to Castaneda, Don Juan unraveled the deepest intricacies of a genuine indigenous belief system while his erstwhile protégé scribbled notes in Spanish at what must have been a truly furious rate. At the end of this period, although still apprenticed to his master, the latter began to publish the fabulous results, albeit in edited and translated form. And the rest, as they say, is history.

The tale is at least superficially plausible, of course, if just barely. Given even minimal critical scrutiny, however, it can be seen that major problems beset the entire proposition, starting with legitimate questions as to the very identity of the researcher/author involved. Carlos César Salvadore Araña Castaneda has claimed to have been born in São Paulo, Brazil, in both 1931 and 1935. In actuality, he was born in Cajamarca, Peru, in 1925. He's claimed that his father was a professor of literature while, according to a 1973 *Time* magazine article, the man was actually a goldsmith. He's claimed to have served as a U.S. Army paratrooper during the Korean War and that he was badly wounded (both testicles shot away). During that period, however, he was actually in Brazil. There is no record of his ever serving in any unit or branch of the U.S. military—before, during or after Korea—much less that he was wounded.[22]

While spinning out this multiplicity of personal fables, Castaneda has also claimed, falsely, that the spelling of his father's family name is the

Portuguese "Aranha" rather than the Spanish "Araña" (Castaneda is actually his mother's family name). This is interesting in terms of his literary/academic career in that, unlike its Spanish variant, the Portuguese word means "trickster" or "deceiver," an altogether appropriate self-characterization, as we shall see.[23]

One would think that such a startling willingness on the part of any candidate to twist facts—or to lie outright—about things this fundamental might have prompted Castaneda's doctoral committee to question their student's veracity in other respects as well. At the very least, it seems reasonable to expect that they might have scrutinized his data more closely than usual. This should have been especially true after anthropologist Ralph Beals, the sole member of the panel in any way conversant with Yaqui culture, resigned not only because he was suspicious of Castaneda's "preliminary findings" but also because of the student's refusal to verify them.[24] There is no indication that the balance of the committee—a rather luminous group chaired by Philip Newman and including Clement Meighan, Harold Garfinkle (of ethnomethodology fame), Kees Bolle and Theodore Graves (later replaced by Robert Edgerton)—ever seriously interrogated the supposedly factual content of Castaneda's material.

On the contrary, in 1967 four of them—Garfinkle, Bolle, Meighan and Graves—teamed up to recommend *The Teachings of Don Juan* for publication as a reputable anthropological text. In this, they were joined by Walter R. Goldschmidt, chair of the anthropology department as well as the editorial committee presiding over manuscript review for UCLA Press. Not only did Goldschmidt shepherd the material through the process at a very rapid rate—it seems he was the sole in-house reader prior to its acceptance as a "brilliant piece of ethnography"—he provided a glowing forward to the published version.[25] It also appears that he collaborated with sponsoring editor Robert Zachary—who lent the final copy an appropriately "scholarly" flavor—to arrange the book's promotional campaign, kicked-off with a full-page ad on the back cover of *American Anthropologist* in which it was asserted that *Teachings* was "nothing less than a revelation, [an] unprecedented . . . living document to the spirit."[26]

Given the strength of the support letters it received, and the direct involvement of Goldschmidt throughout the review and production processes, it may seem that UCLA Press was on firm ground in publishing and promoting Castaneda's first book as it did. Such an impression holds up only until the press's own rules are considered, however. A basic requirement is that the merit of all submissions be assessed, not only by in-house personnel but by several outside individuals qualified as experts in the field addressed by the potential publication.[27] *None* of those involved in recommending or otherwise supporting Castaneda's manuscript were remotely qualified to serve as peer reviewers. In fact, while it was common knowledge around campus that the only person in the mix with a competence concerning Yaquis, Ralph Beals, had openly expressed suspicions that the whole thing might well be a fabrication, his opinion was (emphatically) never solicited.[28]

Meanwhile, the doctoral committee was also quietly engaging in waivers of protocol and relaxations of conventional academic standards, first by failing to require any sort of tangible proof that Castaneda had actually done what he said he'd done—or even that "Don Juan" existed—and then by allowing the earlier-mentioned retitled version of *Journey to Ixtlan* to be submitted and defended as a dissertation without so much as a major revision (Newman, Meighan and Graves administered the student's written exams; Garfinkle and Bolle joined in for the orals). Being a bona fide doctoral candidate, of course—and ultimately receiving his degree—anchored Castaneda's pretensions to scholarly legitimacy and integrity as nothing else could. Hence, as late as 1975, sociologist Lewis Yablonski was still insisting in the *Los Angeles Times Book Review* that, "There is no question that Carlos Castaneda is an able anthropologist who has performed at a unique level of excellence in his field."[29]

Projecting Fantasy as Fact

The question really at issue here, aside from the sanctimony and duplicity involved in the mechanics of careermaking in U.S. citadels of higher learning, is this: What sort of content were the preceding academic and commercial heavies opting to sell? What are they still selling, for that matter? What have a "Yaqui way of knowledge," "Don Juan" and Carlos Castaneda to do with Yaquis, either in reality or as one might anticipate seeing them reflected through the filters of genuine anthropological lensing? Or, to put it still another way, what has any of the above to do with factual circumstances of any sort?

While the final answer(s) to such queries must go to the accuracy and validity of the manner in which Yaqui culture has been portrayed by Castaneda, there have always been a raft of clues imbedded in the Don Juan writings, none of them requiring any particular expertise in things Yaqui to understand, which plainly prefigure the outcome of any honest investigation. Each of them is approximately as transparent as were the assorted falsehoods and prevarications with which Castaneda adorned his personal history. All of them should—indeed, *would*—have been detected by his committee and various publishers, had any of them displayed the least interest in assuring that what they were vouching for as being "true" bore even the slightest relationship to truth.[30]

Take, for example, the physicalities Castaneda recounts in descriptions of his "research activities and resulting experiences." Bear in mind that these supposedly occur in the vast outback of the southern Sonora, a region in which summer daytime temperatures all but invariably exceed 100° Fahrenheit, commonly go above 110°, and tend to prevail with little abatement around the clock. Castaneda nonetheless rather flippantly referred his UCLA professors and colleagues to dates like "June 29," "July 24" and "August 19" as days when, allegedly under the tutelage of a veteran desert dweller who would have known better even if the urbanized Carlos had not, he "roamed for hours across the desert" hunting quail,[31] becoming so absorbed in this activity that "a whole day went by and [he] had not noticed the passage of time. [He] even forgot to eat lunch."[32] He was also known to "stop around noon . . . to rest in an unshaded area."[33]

As has been pointed out elsewhere, any such behavior would be virtually guaranteed to induce delirium, coma and death among mere mortals, yet Castaneda's doctoral committee allowed him to pretend that he and Don Juan performed such superhuman feats on a more-or-less incessant basis.[34] Moreover, such never-never land descriptions of the summers are well-matched by his inaccurate descriptions of Sonoran winters. Castaneda describes the generally frigid rains as "lukewarm" and refers to spending at least one night sleeping in them, in the open and unprotected.[35] Again, such activity would have proven all but suicidal for even the heartiest native of the desert, never mind a campus type like the author.

Nor are climactic conditions the end of such physical nonsense. At one point, Castaneda refers to the desert as "crawling with mountain lions,"[36] a circumstance which would contradict not only the big cats' decided preference for living as territorial loners but the fact that they'd been all but exterminated in Sonora long before Castaneda set foot there. At another point, he recounts being charged by an uncornered puma,[37] another distinctly mythical mountain cat characteristic, but a trait he might easily have confused with readings about jaguars (which, although they've long since become extinct in Sonora, did inhabit the region a few centuries back). In still another instance, he tells of being forced to take refuge in a tree in order to escape one particularly bloodthirsty beast (in reality, mountain lions are considerably more adept at tree-climbing than are humans).[38]

And then there is the matter of Don Juan himself. At no point has Castaneda ever offered a photograph, a tape recording or any other form of concrete evidence that the fabled "Yaqui sorcerer" exists, or ever existed, in a dimension other than the author's own imagination. While this does not in itself establish that the man is a fiction—Castaneda insists that Don Juan categorically rejected use of either cameras or tape recorders (another superficially plausible scenario)[39]—the fact is that an equal lack of corroboration accrues from indirect forms of evidence. More to the point, such indirect evidence as has ever been produced points unerringly to the idea that Don Juan was invented.

Consider the question of Castaneda's field notes, which he always claimed were voluminous, and which might have gone far towards confirming—or refuting—the author's contention that the sorcerer was/is a real person. It might be expected, for instance, that the primary language of an individual so steeped in Yaqui traditionalism as Don Juan would be Yaqui. This presents a certain problem in that Yaqui language is an area in which Castaneda is—and he's always been smart enough to never pretend otherwise—abysmally ignorant. The matter was finessed to some extent when Castaneda claimed that Don Juan was essentially as fluent in Spanish as in Yaqui, and he therefore addressed his apprentice all but exclusively in their common tongue. Ipso facto, the vaunted field notes were rendered both verbatim and in Spanish.[40]

Certain concepts, however—especially those associated with highly specialized practices like sorcery—are simply not translatable from one language to the next. In such instances, it is standard practice to retain the term in its native form, with a sometimes lengthy explanation accompanying its first usage. Castaneda occasionally relies upon this convention in his books.[41] In every instance, however, the attending definition fails to conform to any known Yaqui usage.[42] Hence, either the Spanish-speaking Don Juan didn't really understand his own language, or the muddle-headed Carlos managed to get it wrong every single time (a possibility which lessens confidence in the accuracy/validity of the rest of what he says), or Carlos simply made up the whole thing.

The latter prospect receives substantial reinforcement from Castaneda's Spanish-language notes, or, rather, the handful of them he made available to mycologist Gordon R. Wasson in 1968. Not only did the content of these fail to match that appearing on corresponding pages of text, but they were noticeably tainted by Castaneda's own Peruvian dialect rather than reflecting the Mexican idiom which might have been expected from a lifelong Sonora resident like Don Juan.[43] So, either the aging Yaqui sorcerer spent a very large portion of his life in South America, far from his people and the traditions he supposedly exemplified, or Castaneda spent a lot of time interviewing himself.[44] On balance, it seems fair to observe at this point that the last is far and away the most likely. With all due credulity, no other possibility may be reasonably said to exist, a matter which means Don Juan doesn't. Or, conversely, the truth is and always was that Carlos Castaneda *is* Don Juan.[45]

Snapshot of a Culture Fraud

Although it is plain that much contained in the Don Juan books is fraudulent, it remains possible that Castaneda's interpretation of Yaqui culture is valid (this would be true whether his data base was obtained through field research, via lengthy stints in the basement of the UCLA library, or some combination). If so, there might be something salvageable in his work, at least in terms of its potential—once the wheat is separated from the chaff, so to speak—to provide a popularized understanding of a given indigenous society. Once again, however, even the most cursory examination of his material leads to an exactly opposite conclusion.

Take the above-mentioned misuse of actual Yaqui terminology as an example. Castaneda's deployment of the word "*tonal*," encompassing as it does a specifically Yaqui spiritual concept, serves as a perfect illustration. According to Yaqui specialists Richard Adams and Arthur Ruble, "The *tonal* is a companion animal or destiny . . . subject to stealing and specifically of concern in becoming ill."[46] While Castaneda demonstrates an awareness of this actual meaning of the term in Yaqui life, he then proceeds to utilize the "authenticating and interpretive medium" of Don Juan (i.e., himself), to offer a completely opposing—or negating—definition of his own.[47]

> The tonal is *not* an animal which guards a person. . . . [It] is the social person . . . the organizer of the world . . . everything we know . . . everything that meets the eye. . . . [It] begins at birth and ends at death. . . . [It] is a creator which doesn't create a thing. . . . [It] is but a reflection of that indescribable unknown filled with order.[48]

The process is repeated with "*nagual*," another key term. According to Adams and Rubel, as well as George Foster, another recognized expert on the Yaqui language and spiritual concepts, "The *nagual* is a special transformation of a man into an animal, and the term helps to define a witch."[49] Castaneda agrees that this is the accepted usage, only to use Don Juan as a vehicle upon which to dub the notion "pure nonsense."[50] The *nagual* is then redefined as being "the part of us which we do not deal with at all . . . for which there is no description. . . . [It] never ends . . . has no limit . . . is the only part of us we can create. . . . [It] is but a reflection of the indescribable void that contains everything."[51]

If the connotations with which Castaneda imbues Yaqui terms seems decidedly un-Yaqui, there is good reason. Consider the following juxtaposition of quotations.

> My eyes were closed, and a large pool started to open up in front of them. I was able to see a red spot. I was aware of an unusual odor, and different parts of my body getting extremely warm, which felt extremely good.

> What was very outstanding was the pungent odor of the water. . . . I got very warm, and blood rushed to my ears. I saw a red spot in front of my eyes. "What would happen if I did not see red?" "You would see black." "What happens when you see red?" "An effect of pleasure."

The first quotation is a condensation of material published in *Psychedelic Review*. The second is from *The Teachings of Don Juan*.[52] The first quotation predates the second, and the journal in which it appeared was readily available in the UCLA library during the late 1960s. This could, of course, be purely coincidental, two authors describing similar drug-induced experiences. The possibility of coincidence begins to evaporate, however, when we consider a second juxtaposition.

> The Human Aura is seen by the psychic observer as a luminous clouds, egg-shaped, streaked by fine lines like stiff bristles standing out in all directions.

> A man looks like an egg of circulating fibers. And his arms and legs are like luminous bristles bursting out in all directions.

This time, the first quotation originates with an obscure early twentieth century text by a hack mystic called Yogi Ramacharaka while the second is attributed by Castaneda to Don Juan.[53] Similar echoes of Sufism, Tantric Buddhism and the Hindu chakras permeate the wisdom of Castaneda's supposed Yaqui sorcerer, who appears equally prepared to offer discourses drawn straight from Wittgenstein, Sapir and Husserl, all the while paraphrasing the occultism of Govinda, Artaud, Ouspensky, Gurdjieff and Madame Blavatsky. Such things could be charted in great depth, and have been elsewhere.[54]

Castaneda's wholesale and often absurd infusion of non-Yaqui characteristics into what he was telling readers was a literal portrayal of a specific people's thought and lifeways hardly ended there, nor did his plagiarism. Ultimately, he incorporated "yards of tangled Amerindian folklore" into his tale, none of it discernibly Yaqui, "borrowing" a story here, a ceremony there, a concept somewhere else.[55] None of these are offered with attribution to the print source from which they were paraphrased, of course, or to the indigenous societies in which they originated. Invariably, the form in which these thefts were foisted off upon the unknowing Yaquis was distorted almost — but never quite — beyond recognition, rewritten in a manner carefully calculated to appeal to the tastes and desires of the mostly white counterculturalists comprising the lion's share of Castaneda's mass market.[56]

One of the more egregious examples concerns Barbara Myerhoff, a graduate student in anthropology at UCLA during the late 1960s, who conducted research among the Huichol people near Guadalajara, Mexico. Given their mutual interest in "shamanism," and the supposedly more advanced state of his own field work, she shared her draft dissertation material with Castaneda.[57] In the final version, she includes the following sentence while describing a peyote gathering among the Huichols: "We were puzzled but fell into our places at the end of the line and found ourselves barely able to keep up, for the group was nearly running."[58] In *Journey to Ixtlan*, and also in his dissertation, Castaneda virtually duplicates the passage while claiming to be describing a hunt by his Yaqui sorcerer for psylocibin mushrooms: "I followed him, but . . . could not keep up . . . and he soon disappeared into the darkness."[59]

Myerhoff also recounts a 1966 incident in which Ramón Medina, the Huichol spiritual leader she worked with most closely, performed a trick to demonstrate the principle of balance to the anthropologist and several associates who accompanied her.[60] As Richard de Mille has summarized,

> Ramón led the party to a spectacular waterfall, from whose edge the water dropped hundreds of feet to the valley below. As his Huichol companions sat in a semicircle to watch, Ramón took his sandals off, gestured to the world directions, then leapt. . .from one rock to another with arms stretched wide, often landing but a few inches from the slippery edge. Now he vanished behind a boulder, now he stood motionless on the

brink of destruction, but never did he or his Huichol observers show the slightest concern that he might fall, though the visitors from California were terrified.[61]

Enter Castaneda, describing an event he dates as occurring two years after Ramón performed his feat.

On narrative 17 October 1968, don Genaro [a Mazatec sorcerer friend of Don Juan's] led his party to the bottom of a roaring waterfall, where Don Juan, Carlos, Nestor, and Pablito sat down in a straight line to watch. Genaro took his sandals off, then climbed the hazardous 150 feet, several times seeming to lose his footing and hang in the air by his fingertips. Reaching the top, he leapt out upon the edge of the fall, where he seemed to be standing on the water. There he perched for a long time, occasionally leaning out into space with no visible support, but mostly standing unaccountably still, resisting the rushing current. Though his performance struck terror to Carlos's heart, the watching Indians evinced no concern for his safety. At the end, Genaro turned a lateral somersault to vanish behind a boulder.[62]

De Mille has catalogued some 200 comparable examples and admits that his list is probably far from complete.[63] Misimpressions that this incredible hash of sheer invention and jazzed up but plainly pilfered prose constituted an accurate reflection of Yaqui realities were boosted continuously, not only through the earlier-mentioned onslaught of favorable reviews and articles in the popular and academic press, but the incorporation of Castaneda's material into standard undergraduate texts. Walter Goldschmidt's broadly required introductory anthropology reader, *Exploring Ways of Mankind*, for example, contained an excerpt from *The Teachings of Don Juan*, complete with a chapter heading reading "A Yaqui Man of Knowledge." Following the "standard" he'd set for himself in writing the foreword to *The Teachings*, Goldschmidt introduced this chapter as a bona fide account of how a Yaqui "shaman" led his apprentice "down the road . . . of knowledge of the Yaqui Indians."[64]

The major competitor to Goldschmidt's book, L.L. Langness' *Other Fields, Other Grasshoppers*, also included a substantial excerpt from *The Teachings*. Captioned "Listen to the Lizards," the segment was introduced to students as providing insight into "how the Yaqui themselves understand knowledge."[65] By conservative estimate, and leaving aside course assignments of his own books, Castaneda's ersatz version of "Yaquiness" was incorporated into more than 130 anthologies—required not just for anthropology majors but those pursuing disciplines as diverse as philosophy, education, psychology, literature and sociology—between 1970 and 1985.[66] The *English Journal* even went so far as to prescribe *Journey to Ixtlan* as an "antidote to fake Indian books,"[67] while *American Anthropologist* continued to run Simon & Schuster's ads describing the Don Juan Trilogy as serious studies on "the religious practices of Yaqui Indians" as late as 1977.[68]

Such systematic misrepresentation has been actively aided and abetted in official quarters. Whatever might be a proper classification for Castaneda's books—and, here, one is hard-pressed to come up with a useful suggestion—it is certain that it bears no connection at all to Yaquis. Yet, all three volumes in the Don Juan Trilogy remain classified within the Library of Congress cataloging system as 399.Y3 material. The 399 code number indicates "Indians of North America," while Y3 indicates "Tribes: Yaqui." Moreover, although they have precious little relationship to American Indians of any denomination, every Castaneda title with the exception of *Journey to Ixtlan* has been coded under the Dewey Decimal system as 299.7; that is, as books concerning "Religions of North American Indian Origin." This has led to subject heading assignments such as "YAQUI INDIANS— RELIGION AND MYTHOLOGY." Attribution is also made, straight-facedly, to one "JUAN, DON, 1891-_____."[69]

Small wonder, under the circumstances, that by the mid-'70s Castaneda's had become the most popular readings in beginning anthropology and many other courses, or that graduate students were beginning to grind out theses and dissertations on *him*.[70] To quote anthropologist Eugene Anderson's masterly passing of the buck, "students raised on television spectaculars and science fiction novels expect anthropological studies to read the same way."[71] Castaneda's writings did, of course, with ample dashes of Timothy Leary, Baba Ram Dass and R. Crumb thrown in for good measure. And so, as Anderson put it, he and his colleagues habitually assigned the Don Juan material, "which [students] were reading anyway," rather than "more serious tomes" for which they failed to display "equal enthusiasm."[72]

Such practices, to be sure, did nothing to "help a myriad of trusting undergraduates who learn[ed] from Castaneda's books about a supposed community of mystical magicians quaintly miscalling themselves sorcerers and wandering about an air-conditioned desert positing koans and twanging their lutes."[72] To the contrary, the "pedagogy" at issue served only to foster illusions that even the bizarrest forms of falsehood had been "objectively" confirmed as fact.[73] Thus were an entire generation of American university students conned—indoctrinated might be a better word—into viewing

Yaquis in particular, and Native Americans more generally, in terms of self-serving fantasy projections.[74]

Of Mescalito and Magic Smoking Mushrooms

Nothing provides a better proof than his treatment of psychotropic substances that Castaneda was all along tailoring his material to fit pop sensibilities rather than factual circumstance.[75] In the initial pair of Don Juan books—the first published at the very peak of the U.S. "psychedelic" drug craze, the second written during more-or-less the same period—there are accounts of not less than 22 hallucinatory "trips" supposedly taken by the author and his mentor under the influence of everything from peyote to jimson weed to hallucinogenic mushrooms.[76] By 1972, with evaporation of public enthusiasm for hallucinogens, Castaneda has a suddenly transfigured Don Juan holding forth in *Journey to Ixtlan* on the principle that *real* power cannot be attained through resort to chemical crutches, and revealing a wealth of drugless techniques for "mind expansion."[77] As this shift is explained still later, in *Tales of Power*:

> The extraordinary effect that psychotropic drugs had had on me was what gave me the bias that their use was the key feature of the teachings. I held on to that conviction and it was only in the later years of my apprenticeship that I realized that meaningful transformations and findings of sorcerers were always done in sober states of consciousness.[78]

Along the way, however, he had saddled the unsuspecting Yaquis—and the world—with "Mescalito," a "berry-headed, green-warted, cricket-bodied, choral-voiced, cinema-handed supernatural personage" or "ally" whom the Indians allegedly believe materializes whenever they've swallowed peyote buttons, which Castaneda claims they refer to as "mescal."[79] Predictably, Yaqui culture yields no counterpart, direct or indirect, to the mystical Mescalito, and only the Spaniards, never the Indians, have been in the habit of confusing peyote with mescal.[80] Such realities notwithstanding, this particular Castanedan concoction was sufficiently appealing in 1968 to afflict the traditionally reclusive residents of southern Arizona's Nueva Pascua Yaqui community for several years with an apparently endless stream of oddly painted Volkswagen buses, each filled with its own gaggle of wide-eyed white hippies, all of them devoutly hopeful of meeting Don Juan and, thence, obtaining an introduction to their favorite cactus demon.[81]

More concrete was Castaneda's claim, offered for the first time on page 63 of *The Teachings*, that under Don Juan's tutelage he had used an hallucinogenic mushroom, referred to as both "*homitos*" and "*honguitos*," which was smoked rather than ingested. Since his only technical description of the organism in question comes by way of calling it *Psilocybe mexicana* on page 7 of the same book, and since neither that mushroom nor any other is known to render the least effect when smoked, the story immediately piqued the interest of ethnobotonists.[82] This was especially true of eminent mycologist Gordon R. Wasson, who wrote a letter to Castaneda on August 26, 1968—very shortly after *The Teachings* hit the market—containing a series of questions about the younger scholar's apparent discovery of a species "previously unknown to science."[83]

Uncharacteristically, Castaneda—who was then preparing his paper on the didactic use of hallucinogens for presentation to/publication by the American Anthropological Association, and could hardly afford at that moment to invite open challenge by a senior scholar—replied.[84] In his September 6, 1968, missive, he hedges his bets by stating that while his own identification of the fabulous mushroom was "terribly unsophisticated," he and an unidentified member of the UCLA Department of Pharmacology had determined it was "probably" *Psilocybe mexicana*.[85] Replying to Wasson's questions on whether and where he himself had participated in gathering the mushrooms—*Psilocybe mexicana* are not known to grow in the desert localities of Sonora or adjoining Chihuahua—Castaneda stated that he'd personally gathered "perhaps hundreds," finessing the geographic issue by revealing for the first time that he and Don Juan made an annual pilgrimage to Oaxaca for that purpose.[86] He also notes that the mushrooms grew on the trunks of dead trees and rotting shrubbery.

In response to Wasson's query as to whether he had obtained specimens, Castaneda said that he had—not in Oaxaca, but in the Santa Monica Mountains, near Los Angeles—but that he'd conscientiously turned it over to "the laboratory at UCLA" for analysis.[87] There, it went the way of his field notes, which he would later claim were destroyed in a flood of his basement, having been "carelessly lost" by an unidentified lab technician.[88] Nonetheless, he promised, it was certain that he could bring back "perhaps a dab" from his next trip to see Don Juan, and would send it along for Wasson's inspection before the end of 1968.

On October 4, Wasson sent another letter, thanking Castaneda for his expeditious reply to the first missive and encouraging him produce a whole specimen of the magic mushroom as rapidly as possible. His interest was even more highly aroused than before, Wasson noted, since *Psilosybe mexicana* never grows on trees. Perhaps, he suggested, Castaneda had encountered *Psilocybe yungenis*, a rarer but related type of fungus, or, reiterating his earlier suggestion, a "previously undiscovered species."[89] Having thus bought himself sufficient time to make his presentation to the anthropological society unhampered, and garnering a reasonably favorable review by Wasson of *The Teachings* in the process, Castaneda never bothered to answer the second letter. And, although he would claim in subsequent writings to have smoked mushrooms on at least eight separate occasions after promising to do so, he never provided a sample of his mythic psychedelic.[90]

Once burned, twice wary, Wasson was one of a growing number of academics, many of whom had experienced comparable examples of such manipulative behavior firsthand, who by 1974 had begun to publicly question the factuality of Castaneda's increasingly implausible and self-contradictory material.[91] Over the next few years, their ranks continued to swell, and their database to grow, until, by 1978, the Don Juan books and their author were being openly characterized as fraudulent even in the formerly laudatory popular press.[92] Here, the reaction of an appreciable segment of the "responsible" academic community is illuminating.

"I think Castaneda's work is 110 percent valid," wrote anthropologist Michael Harner in 1978, without remarking on its authenticity and in the face of overwhelming evidence to the contrary.[93] "I have no reason whatsoever to suspect a hoax," added anthropologist C. Scott Littleton, "I have known [Castaneda] too long and too well to doubt his professional integrity."[94] The point should be to "praise Carlos, not to bury Don Juan," anthropologist Philip Stanford asserted.[95] Jungean scholar Daniel Noel chimed in with the observation that Castaneda provides a valid "lesson in 'lived hermeneutics,' the actual *experience* of interpretation's role in interpreting experience so as to constitute what we know as the 'world,' 'reality,' 'meaning.' [His is] a practical, existential exercise in hermeneutics, one which he himself *lived*."[96] "It makes no difference whether the books [derive from] an actual encounter or whether Castaneda is the author of a clever fiction," philosophy professor Joseph Margolis summed up, "If the system is valid, its source is rather irrelevant."[97]

Such "scholarly" prattlings were indistinguishable, in substance if not always in rhetorical style, from the kind of mindless apologetics oozing from the huge and spreading pool of Castaneda groupies which had coagulated outside the halls of ivy by the late 1970s. A letter to *Time*, written by a reader greatly offended that the magazine's "hired leeches" had exposed Castaneda's assorted lies about his own identity, insisted that the "facts" encompassed in the Don Juan books were "no less true or honest" if they were entirely invented.[98] Castaneda "may be lying," the editors of *New Age* followed up, "but what he says is true."[99] Celebrated novelist *cum* independent naturalist Peter Matthiessen also got in his two cents' worth, using the pages of his award-winning book, *The Snow Leopard*, to explain to his readers not only that American Indians — or at least their ways of thinking and knowing — come from Tibet, but that it was "no matter" if Don Juan were imaginary: "whether borrowed or not, the teaching rings true."[100]

Others were more militant. Erin Matson, for example, opined in a letter to *High Times* that while Don Juan was certainly real enough, it was equally certain that Castaneda critics like Richard de Mille and Gordon Wasson were not.[101] Robert Holbrook, a resident of Warren, Ohio, upset that the editors of *Fate* had begun referring to Castaneda as a fraud, went Matson one better by observing that it didn't matter whether Don Juan was real because "we are all [merely] hallucinatory projections of each other" anyway.[102] He was, however, already contradicted by Ralph Ullman, who claimed in the pages of *New Age* not only to have met the fabled sorcerer a year earlier, but published photos of three different old men to prove his point.[103]

Confronted with a crisis in credibility unprecedented in its history, the American Anthropological Association decided to conduct a special session at its 1978 annual meeting to "clear the air" (actually, there had long been a desire in some quarters of the association for such an event but Walter Goldschmidt, who had risen from his station prefacing *The Teachings* to preside over the AAA in 1975 and '76, had been "rather less than interested" in the organization's sponsoring it).[104] When it finally occurred, during the late afternoon of November 15, it turned out to be little more than an exercise in attempting to keep the lid on things.

Although several critics were allowed to speak, briefly, the main attraction was Goldschmidt, who arrived bearing a delegation of authority to speak for his colleagues on Castaneda's doctoral committee at UCLA and launched into a truly grotesque display of stonewalling and half-truth.[105] Castaneda's missing field notes, photographs, tape recordings, plant specimens and all other forms of supporting evidence of his "research" didn't matter one whit, Goldschmidt informed the assembled scholars, because he had once shown committee member Clement Meighan several Yaqui baskets "of a type that had to be obtained directly from the Indians as they could not be collected from commercial sources."[106]

"We know of no evidence whatever that would support charges of [fraud, or even deceit] that have been made," Goldschmidt went on, ignoring a recent itemization published by Jacques Maquet, a faculty member in good standing of the UCLA Department of Anthropology, in *American Anthropologist*, the AAA's own leading journal.[107] "We cannot confirm or deny fraud," he concluded, and "do not consider it appropriate here to evaluate the work of Carlos Castaneda" (where, precisely, he/the committee felt it *would* be appropriate, if not in session of the AAA devoted to the matter, was left unstated). As for himself, he said, "I am not going to say *mea culpa!*"[108]

In the aftermath, nothing much really happened, other than a quiet retreat by most anthropologists from the "controversy" attending Castaneda's work. Meanwhile, damage control specialists like Steven O. Murray began the delicate process of recasting the record in such a manner as to deflect all onus of responsibility away from the discipline of anthropology itself.[109] So pathetic was this response that a frustrated sociologist, Marcello Truzzi, was provoked into publicly observing why he was "concerned about what all this says not about Castaneda but about anthropology."[110]

> What I've been hearing suggests an incredible scientific disarray. Anthropologists are quick to criticize exoheretics like von Däniken, but when it comes to endoheretics [deviant insiders] there's a great reluctance to talk. Most criticism has not come from anthropologists, and when anthropologists do speak, they say something oblique. . . . Students find Castaneda in [their] introductory readers and think they are getting ethnography about a typical shaman. Do [we] really need a "smoking gun" before [we] can do something about this? Normally the burden of proof is on the claimant. If you [abandon this standard], what will we do with all the subjective and fraudulent dissertations we will get — say they resonate beautifully, say they're symbolically true? What's happened to the canons of science? Where are organized skepticism, empirical falsibility, and logical consistency in anthropology today? Or don't [we] know what anthropology is anymore?[111]

The answers to these queries was probably provided, however unintentionally, by Barbara Myerhoff, a close confidant of Castaneda during his student days, who admitted in a 1977 interview that she'd been fully aware from the outset that her friend's sorcerer was a fiction and that his "ethnography" had nothing at all to do with Yaquis or any other identifiable human group. Indeed, she professed to have been "offended" by his gross distortions of the "beautiful indigenous concepts" of *tonal* and *nagual*, and claimed that she'd attempted before the fact to both persuade him to jettison the Don Juan moniker with which he proposed to anoint the central character of his stories and to delete all reference to Yaquis, both in his titles and in the text.[112] Yet, when he declined to follow her advice, when he instead published as fact increasingly preposterous material which she knew beyond question was plagiarized, bastardized and invented, she remained silent.

Although Barbara Myerhoff can hardly be accused of publicly endorsing Castaneda's material, neither can it be said that she met her fundamental professional—and social—obligation to expose it for what it was. She maintained this posture, not of a perpetrator but of one who was nonetheless by virtue of her moral and ethical defaults directly complicit in the Castanedan scam, for nearly a decade, long after her own degree was awarded, her own books published, and she had come to chair a department of her own.[113] Much more than that of the Don Juan enthusiasts, such behavior, representative in its way of that displayed by the discipline of anthropology as a whole, is what made Castaneda's fraud possible.

The Greatest Hoax Since Piltdown Man

It is not that there was no warning. "Don Juan is quite a find," read a letter from a skeptic named Paul Zakaras published by *Esquire* in May 1971, "He is probably as much a reflection of our time as Piltdown was of his." Another six years were to pass, however, before even the harshest of Castaneda's academic critics, Marcello Truzzi and J. Gordon Melton among them, had begun to publicly make the same connection.[114] By then, it should have long been clear to anyone willing to look that such comparisons were by no means a matter of petty mudslinging by those caught up in defense of "older" or more "conservative" methods of research against displacement by some newer, sleeker variety. Nor were they merely the chatter of assorted intellectual mediocraties jealous of, and thus wishing to smear a "native genius."[115]

Piltdown Man (*Eoanthropus dawsoni*), it will be recalled, was a set of skeletal remains supposedly discovered by an amateur geologist named Charles Dawson in 1912 in a gravel pit at the Piltdown historic site, near Sussex, England. Turned over to the British Museum, where the fragmentary skull—five pieces of humanoid braincase and part of a simian-appearing lower jaw—was reassembled by Dawson's friend, the eminent paleontologist

Arthur Smith Woodward, and the "find" was shortly being celebrated as the "missing link" between man and monkey (a distinction now held by *Austalopithecus africana*).[116] Smith Woodward was knighted for his work while Dawson was quickly catapulted to the station of scientific celebrity.[117]

Over the next 41 years, an entire school of evolutionary/social theory, much of it devoted to "proving" the basic tenets of eugenics and white supremacist ideology, was developed on the basis of the Piltdown skull.[118] Courses were taught, degrees bestowed, books and literally hundreds of scientific articles were published (more than on all other "missing links" combined), while the bones were safely tucked away in a museum vault, unavailable for direct examination, and skeptics were banished from the scientific mainstream. The "essential truth" of Piltdown, convenient as it was in many circles, continued to be treated as self-evident even as the allegedly factual context in which it had been advanced eroded.

It was not until 1953 that the cumulative weight of other anthropological discoveries was sufficient to force a reexamination of the Piltdown remains. At that point, it turned out that the cranial fragments were of modern origin, chemically aged, and that the jawbone was actually that of an orangutan, cleverly broken off at just the point at which its real identity would have become unmistakable, its teeth carefully filed to further the misimpression.[119] Discovery of the forgery had the effect of instantly rearranging the posthumous image of Charles Dawson. For the next nineteen years, as the scientific community closed ranks to protect the reputations of their own, he was projected as having been the "Wizard of Sussex," a brilliant if misguided outsider who had singlehandedly deceived the scholarly community, violating their collective trust to perpetrate "the greatest hoax of all time."[120]

Finally, in 1973, researcher Ronald Millar was able to demonstrate that, whatever his personal abilities, Dawson simply could *not* have pulled it off alone. Millar offered a convincing case that Dawson's collaborator had been Grafton Eliot Smith, a capable though less respected paleontologist.[121] Others, taking Millar's cue, nominated Oxford University professor William J. Sollas, dissident priest Teilhard de Chardin, and Smith Woodward as accomplices.[122] More important than the identities of the actual conspirators, as Harvard evolutionist Steven Jay Gould would later reflect, is that Piltdown was so quickly and so avidly embraced, even without substantive offers of proof, by a fairly lopsided majority of anthropologists and other scientists. This made the hoax relatively easy to accomplish, Gould observes, a matter plainly facilitated by the fact that the hoaxers were saying more-or-less precisely what the bulk of the scholarly community wanted to hear anyway.[123]

Following the Piltdown example, Richard de Mille has classified Don Juan as "*Uclanthropus Piltdunides Castanedae*" ("UCLA-Man, Son of Piltdown, Belonging to Castaneda").[124] More seriously, he has schematized the Zakaras/Truzzi/Melton comparison of Castaneda and the earlier hoax in a fashion which is well worth repeating here.

- Each was hailed as a giant step in science but was doubted from the beginning by [some].

- Each was the product of a clever deceiver who was very knowledgeable about the relevant scientific theory.

- Each combined disparate elements—Piltdown bones of man and ape, Don Juan pre-literate and modern conceptual systems.

- Each provided superficially plausible support for a particular theoretical tendency—Piltdown for brain primacy, Don Juan for ethnomethodology.

- Each could have been exposed at once by a competent, skeptical inquiry—into the shape of Piltdown's teeth, into the existence of Carlos's voluminous Spanish field-notes, never offered for examination and now said to be destroyed by flooding of Castaneda's basement.

- Each wasted the time or made fools of trusting colleagues.

- Each implicated possible but uncertain accomplices—Piltdown Teilhard de Chardin, William Sollas, and Arthur Smith Woodward; Don Juan the professors who should have known they were dealing with an illusionist but [claim] they did not.

- Neither hoaxer confessed. Castaneda's flagrant fourth and outlandish fifth books [not to mention the even more ridiculous sixth and seventh] constitute a sort of implicit confession.

- Each was supported by a faction—Piltdown by British paleoanthropologists, Don Juan by anyone who thought publishing *The Teachings* or granting a doctorate to Castaneda would make merit for ethnomethodology or UCLA anthropology.

- Each was rendered more congenial by cultural bias—Piltdown for favoring intelligence and white superiority, Don Juan for demonstrating that an antirationalist noble savage could reflect 1960s idealism back to dissident but regular consumers of electricity and Kool-Aid as though from an ancient culture.

- Each enjoyed the benefits of fallible recognition—as when [one early observer] thought he saw an orang's forehead on Piltdown's skull; as when academic readers consistently failed to notice how seriously the Don Juan books contradicted one another.

- Each was protected by taboo and tact—Piltdown must not be challenged by mere suspicions; Carlos's Spanish fieldnotes could not be demanded by scholars who deferred to colleagues on his committee, or by committee members [unwilling for whatever reason to require Castaneda] to bear the normal burden of proof.[125]

This last bears amplification. As Kenneth Oakley has pointed out in a fine study of scientific attitudes attending the Piltdown hoax, while most researchers were precluded by museum policy from examining *Eoanthropus* directly—Louis Leakey, to name a prominent example, was consigned to working only with plaster replicas of the skull parts in 1933 because curators were unwilling to risk their "priceless" artifacts under the ravages of his scrutiny[126]—there were at least three exceptions. One of them, paleontologist Carleton Coon, believed as early as 1930 that he had detected certain markings, indicative of doctored evidence, on the Piltdown molars. Instead of disclosing his discovery and demanding further investigation, however, he, as Barbara Myerhoff would do with respect to Castaneda, maintained a "tactful" silence, telling no one but his wife of his suspicions.[127]

At about the same time, zoologist Gerritt Miller also concluded—although he, like Leakey, had been restricted to working with plaster replicas—that Piltdown's dentures had been fabricated. Colleagues convinced him not to publish his findings, arguing that his was "too serious an accusation to make without absolute proof" of the very sort denied by museum policy. Adopting a "prudent" stance, Miller too held his tongue.[128] How many more scientists may have pursued a similar course is unknown, but there were certainly others. Be that as it may, the defaults of Coon and Miller in themselves allowed the Piltdown hoax to be sustained for an additional quarter-century.

Cost and Consequences

As de Mille observes, the period in which Castaneda's hoax reigned unchecked lasted nowhere near as long as Piltdown's 41-year lifespan. One is disinclined, however, to share his opinion that "the scientific cost of Piltdown was [therefore] high, of Don Juan low."[129] For one thing, the latter can hardly be said to have run its course. While exposure of the physical forgeries underpinning Piltdown instantly destroyed both its scientific credibility and popular influence, Castaneda's inherently more subjective fraud continues to thrive some twenty years after it was conclusively unmasked in de Mille's *Castaneda's Journey* and elsewhere.[130] Unlike those of the Piltdown proponents—or de Mille's own—the books of Carlos Castaneda remain in print,

48

sell very well, and are favorably cited in a wide range of scholarly and pseudoscholarly literature.[131] Moreover, they are still assigned as readings in university courses as of 1997.[132] Hence, the true costs of Don Juan, scientific and otherwise, can as yet scarcely be calculated.

There are nonetheless several sorts of indicators, all of which should give pause to anyone prepared to accept the notion that the continuing cost of Castaneda has been low. One of them, voiced by anthropologist Marvin Harris at the time, is that the perverted pathways to "power" presented as revealed truth in the Trilogy, centering as they did/do in the purely personal, had done much to dissipate the potential for accomplishing constructive sociopolitical and economic change manifested by the "youth movement" of the 1960s.[133] With dissidents increasingly inclined not just to "drop out" of mainstream structures in the manner recommended by LSD guru Timothy Leary, but to follow Don Juan's lead in copping out on social obligation altogether, any possibility that the '60s radical impulse might gather sufficient mass and momentum in the 1970s to transform the status quo quickly disappeared.[134]

Moreover, as Harris observed, the philosophical terms in which Castaneda's work was so consistently couched—the idea that, to quote critic/novelist Ron Sukenick, "All versions of 'reality' are of the nature of fiction. There's your story and my story, there's the historian's story and the journalist's story, there's the philosopher's story and the scientist's story. . . . Our common world is really a description . . . only imagined"—were *bound* to yield lingering effects of the sort precluding formation of coherent oppositional movements, once they'd been popularized to the point of fad proportions via the Don Juan books.[135] Indeed, we are still suffering fallout in the guise of that theoretically sterile and politically neutralizing phenomenon known as "postmodernism" which has come to predominate in left intellectual circles during the '90s.[136]

Harris aptly describes the "invitation to intellectual suicide" presented by Castaneda's "ethnomethodological phenomenology" as a form of "obscurantism" remarkable for its "moral opacity."[137]

> The doctrine that all fact is fiction and all fiction is fact is a morally depraved doctrine. It is a doctrine that conflates the attacked with the attacker; the tortured with the torturer; and the killed with the killer. It is true that at Dachau there was the SS's story; and the prisoners' story; and that at Mylai, there was Calley's story and the kneeling mother's story; and that at Kent State there was the guardsmen's story and the story of the students shot in the back, five hundred feet away. Only a moral cretin would wish to maintain that all these stories could be equally true.[138]

Left out of this discussion is the functioning of power. In any system where absurdity and objective falsehood are privileged at the outset to equal standing with logic, common sense and verifiable fact—"it all depends on your point of view," "he's entitled to his opinion" (no matter how ridiculous or repugnant)—all humanly achievable approximations of "truth" are likely to be displaced in favor of whatever complex of *un*truths best serves the needs and interests of the status quo at any given moment.[139] The proverbial "playing field" is *never* "level," all stories are *never* treated equally, and pretenses to the contrary serve only to guarantee the ease with which fresh elements of disinformation can be injected into the ever-evolving mythic structure which constitutes the hegemony we intellectually inhabit.[140]

To put it most simply, when the attackers' power prevails in a systemic sense, their story will *always* be privileged over that of the attacked; the torturers' over that of the tortured; the killers over that of the killed. American Indians—and, notwithstanding his own and his apologists' assorted *post hoc* disclaimers, this *is* who Castaneda has used as a prop in his extended shadow play—have of course already suffered, and continue to suffer, the true consequences of such mainstream mythmaking in a fashion which is perhaps unparalleled in its sheer horror.[141]

From 1492 onward, literary apparitions taking the form of savages both "bestial" and "noble" have been used as devices with which to mask the intrinsic humanity of entire nations exterminated, degraded and dispossessed, the survivors consigned to live in perpetual destitution, during the course of Europe's invasion, conquest and colonization of America.[142] All the while, historians, anthropologists and other scholars—indeed, the academic edifice as a whole—has bent itself all but unerringly to the task of rendering such fiction into "fact."[143] Unsurprisingly, given this backdrop, the newer medium of cinema has both reflected and amplified these inverted interpretations of reality, unleashing some 2,000 consecutive iterations of the theme that indigenous people whose homelands were being overrun were, whenever they sought to avert their fate, guilty of gratuitously attacking, torturing and killing the "peaceful settlers" or "pioneers" who were in fact invading and often annihilating them.[144]

If, as Norman Cohn has observed, certain myths can serve as outright "warrants for genocide," so too can others serve as veils behind which genocidal realities, past and present, are conveniently hidden.[145] It changes nothing to argue, as Castaneda's admirers often do, that his "Yaqui" mythos merely exotifies Indians rather than denigrating or demonizing us. Exotification is, after all, every bit as much an aspect dehumanization as demonization, and, as analysts as diverse as Russell Means, Robert Jay Lifton, Eric Markusen and Tzvetan Todorov have long observed, it is precisely the psychology of dehumanizing "others" which makes possible the malignant processes of genocide, colonization and group oppression.[146]

In this connection, the Castanedan legacy has been, first and foremost, to facilitate a peculiarly virulent pathology of "plausible deniability" within the supposedly most "progressive" sectors of the dominant society. In 1980, de Mille, following Harris to some extent, wondered in print whether the rush to embrace Castaneda exhibited by an uncomfortably large share of dissident white intellectuals wasn't born simply of a wish to shirk the arduous responsibilities—and risks—which attend any serious real world confrontation with state power. Was the deification of Don Juan, he asked, "an insidious manifestation of our middle-class desire to maintain a privileged position in the world by claiming that realities like racial oppression, colonialism, or militarism will somehow go away if we stop thinking they are there?"[147]

Today, a quarter-century after the Don Juan Trilogy replaced Che Guevara's *Bolivian Diary* as the reading matter of choice on campus, he has his answer. It comes neatly packaged in the form of a postmodernist subgenre known as "postcolonialism," an increasingly vapid and detached preoccupation with the textual analysis of "master narratives" offered up as "cutting edge oppositional theory" at a time when not only neocolonialism but colonialism of the direct variety continues to be a normative condition for non-whites the world over.[148] In thus relegating the victims of contemporary systems of colonial domination to the status of historical anachronism, postcolonialism not only precludes the very possibility of forging a viable anti-imperialist praxis, it demotes the plight of the colonized to that of "just another story among many" (and hardly the "most interesting," at that).[149]

In effect, had Carlos Castaneda not come along when he did, it might well haven proven necessary for America's elites to have invented him. Far from occupying the niche of one who opened the door to a liberatory reordering of consciousness once assigned him by radical anthropologists like Kurt Wolff, Castaneda has ultimately proven to have been a crucially important cog in the machinery with which the status quo has sustained itself, its stability not only restored but substantially reinforced in the aftermath of the "almost revolution" of the 1960s.[150] His service in repairing what Paul Joseph termed the "cracks in the empire," creating the space which allowed

51

a relatively unhampered "reconstruction of imperial ideology," have been immense.[151]

We are all paying and will continue to pay the price for this, whether we know it or not, Third Worlders and people of color most of all.[152] The costs and consequences of Don Juan and the "Shaman of Academe" who manufactured him thus exceed, by any reasonable estimation and by an already incalculable margin, those which may be associated with the Piltdown hoax.[153] If there is any bright side at all to Castaneda—and it is difficult to imagine that there is—it must reside in his having so abundantly punctuated certain lessons we should all have understood well before his arrival on the scene:

1) There are no shortcuts to accomplishing constructive social change, nor are there easy ways out of the requirements to achieving it. There are no pills or herbs we can swallow (or smoke) which will make things better. Struggle is called "struggle" for a reason.

2) Unpleasant realities remain real, even though we wish they weren't, and they will remain so until we collectively do whatever is necessary—in the real world, not in our minds—to change them for the better. Wishful thinking is just that: wishful thinking. It changes nothing unless it is harnessed to concrete and concerted lines of action.

3) If something seems "too good to be true"—say, for example, by offering flashy, feel-good "alternatives" to either of the above—it *is* untrue. Those actually committed to attaining genuine social transformation need to discard it as just another pleasant fantasy designed and intended to get in the way of our *changing* the unpleasant realities we must otherwise escape through resort to drugs, occultism, fake mysticism and other fantasies.

Lessons learned (again)? Alright then, perhaps now we can at last set aside our silly, self-serving subjectivities and get on with it. Much time has been wasted, much damage done, by pretending we have the option to do otherwise.

Notes

1. *Dissertation Abstracts*, 1973, 33 (12 Part 1, Jun) 5625.B. UCLA library call number LD 791.9 A6 C275.

2. The $1 million estimate accrues from Richard de Mille in his *Castaneda's Journey: The Power and the Allegory* (Santa Barbara, CA: Capra Press, 1976). The higher figure is from Simon & Schuster by way of Castaneda's agent, Neil Brown.

3. Charles Simmons, "The Sorcerer's Apprentice," *New York Times*, Aug. 14, 1968. It should be noted that it was during this very period that the *Times* was employing its vaunted "editorial objectivity" to freeze from print individuals of the philosophical stature of Bertrand Russell and Jean-Paul Sartre, and declining to review books by high caliber intellectuals like Noam Chomsky. The distinction to be drawn is perhaps that people like Russell, Sartre and Chomsky were explicitly engaged in organizing a coherent resistance to the politicoeconomic status quo (of which the *Times* is an integrally important part) while Castaneda's bizarre "get into your own head" message went in precisely the opposite direction. Be that as it may, the *Times'* early and enthusiastic embrace of Castaneda was certainly no more "revolutionary"— to borrow from the vernacular of "New Agers" like Theodore Roszak—than were the Don Juan epics themselves. On Russell's experience with the *Times*, which may be extended to Sartre, see the chapter entitled "The Press and Vietnam," in his *War Crimes in Vietnam* (New York: Monthly Review, 1967). Concerning Chomsky, one will look in vain for a mention, whether positive or negative, of his crucially important *American Power and the New Mandarins* (New York: Pantheon, 1968). The same principle holds true with respect to antiwar and dissident literature in general; Todd Gitlin, *The Whole World Is Watching: mass media in the making & unmaking of the new left* (Berkeley: University of California Press, 1980).

4. *New York Times*, May 14, Oct. 14, 1971.

5. *New York Times*, Feb. 13, 1972. Perhaps most nauseating was Elsa First's "Don Juan is to Carlos Castaneda as Carlos Castaneda is to us," *New York Times Book Review*, Oct. 27, 1974.

6. *Saturday Review*, Nov. 11, 1972.

7. Favorable reviews appeared in *Publishers Weekly* in 1968, 1969, 1971, 1972, 1974, 1976 and 1977. The remarks quoted are taken from the latter.

8. These "mainstream" reviews—and there are many others—are aside from the vast gush of ink devoted to praising Castaneda in the myriad "alternative" or "underground" publications extant in this period. For the interviews, see John Wallace, "The Sorcerer's Apprentice: Conversations with Carlos Castaneda," *Penthouse*, Dec. 1972; Craig Karpel, "Conversations without Don Juan," *Playboy*, Aug. 1975.

9. *Saturday Review*, Aug. 21, 1971.

10. Paul Riesman, "The Collaboration of Two Men and a Plant," *New York Times Book Review*, Oct. 22, 1972. True to form, when anthropologist Weston La Barre, author of *The Peyote Cult* (New York: Schocken Books, [2nd ed.] 1969) and infinitely more qualified to assess Castaneda' work than Reisman, submitted a review describing it as "pseudo-profound, deeply vulgar pseudo-ethnography," the *Times* flatly rejected it; see La Barre's account in *Journal of Psychological Anthropology*, Vol. 2, No. 3, 1979.

11. Stan Wilk, untitled review in *American Anthropologist*, Vol. 74, No. 4, 1972.

12. C.R. Rogers, "Some New Challenges," *American Psychologist*, No. 28, 1973; Marie Coleman Nelson, "Paths of Power: Psychoanalysis and Sorcery," *Psychoanalytic Review*, Vol. 63, No. 3, 1976; Bruce W. Scotton, "Relating the Work of Carlos Castaneda to Psychiatry," *Bulletin of the Menninger Clinic*, Vol. 42, No. 3, 1978; William Stillwell, "The Process of Mysticism: Carlos Castaneda," *Humanistic Psychology*, Vol. 19, No. 4, 1979); Robert E. Ornstein, "A Lesson of Carlos Castaneda," in his *The Mine Field* (New York: Grossman, 1976).

13. Mary Douglas, "Torn Between Two Realities," *The Times Higher Education Supplement*, June 15, 1973.

14. Mary Douglas, "The Authenticity of Castaneda," in her *Implicit Meanings* (London: Routledge and Kegan Paul, 1975).

15. Ronald D. Cohen, "Educational Implications of the Teachings of Don Juan," *Phi Delta Kappan*, Vol 55, No. 7, Mar. 1974.

16. Theodore Roszak, "A Sorcerer's Apprentice," *The Nation*, Feb. 1969.

17. Lucius Outlaw, "Beyond the Everyday Life-World: A Phenomenological Encounter with Sorcery," *Man & World*, Vol. 8, No. 4, 1975; ; Beatrice Bruteau, "The Grid-Maker," *Fields Within Fields*, No. 14, 1975.

18. Jerry Mander, *In the Absence of the Sacred: The Failure of Technology and the Survival of Indigenous Nations* (San Francisco: Sierra Club, 1991) pp. 207–8.

19. Michael Korda, "A Conversation About Carlos Castaneda," *Simon & Schuster News*, Dec. 1979. It should be noted that Korda himself cashed in on the Castaneda craze, authoring a silly little psychic instruction manual entitled *Power! How to Get It, How to Use It* (New York: Random House, 1975) which garnered him more than $100,000 in royalties and a momentary celebrity of the minor sort.

20. *The Fire Within* and *The Power of Silence* were published by Simon & Schuster, *The Art of Dreaming* by HarperCollins.

21. One is never quite certain the term "sorcerer"—although it is the author's—even applies to the Don Juan Castaneda depicts. The Spanish language equivalent would be *brujo*, "one who makes one's enemies sick with the help of the devil, an evil person." Nowhere in Castaneda's books is the old Yaqui—supposedly 71 years of age in 1960—characterized in this fashion. A more accurate term might in some ways have been "healer" (*curandero*, in Spanish), but Castaneda's Don Juan, who is more-or-less a hermit, hardly spends enough time in the company of people to function as a *curandero* in any real sense. Essentially, he is a magician (*mago*), but to have employed the term—smacking as it does of carnival-style hocus pocus—would have been to semantically forfeit many of the mystical connotations surrounding Don Juan, thus undercutting the seriousness with which Castaneda's writing was received, and thus its sales potential.

22. Robert Hughes, et al., "Don Juan and the sorcerer's apprentice," *Time*, Mar. 5, 1973. Also see Richard de Mille's "A Portrait of the Allegoricist" and "Sergeant Castaneda and the Photos of Don Juan: Transforming the Special Consensus," in his edited volume, *The Don Juan Papers: Further Castaneda Controversies* (Santa Barbara, CA: Ross-Erikson, 1980). Another interesting read is that provided by Castaneda's former wife, Margaret Runyon (as told to Wanda Sue Parrot), "My Husband Carlos Castaneda," *Fate*, Feb. 1975.

23. Bruce-Nova, "Chicanos in the Web of Spider Trickster," ibid., p. 274.

24. As Beals later recounted, when, skeptical of Castaneda's claims, he began to press for verbatim copies of the student's field notes, Carlos "simply disappeared" for several months. When other committee members suggested, in order "to get things back on track," that Beals should relent, he withdrew from the process altogether; Ralph Beals, "Sonoran Fantasy or Coming of Age?" *American Anthropologist*, June 1978.

25. The process was later described by UCLA Press Director James H. Clark, who did not hold that position in 1967, and Associate Director Philip Lilienthal, who did.

26. *American Anthropologist*, June 1968. Among the other devices employed for purposes of making *The Teachings* appear to be a "factual" book was the appending of a ponderous section in which Castaneda explains in some detail the actual "scientific methods" by which he'd arrived at his marvelous results.

27. Both Clark and Lilienthal have confirmed that such procedures were as much required in 1967 as they are thirty years later. In other words—although this is hardly how they put it—the press quite blatantly scuttled its own rules in order to rush Castaneda's tome into print. Under the circumstances, one may perhaps be forgiven for detecting the vulgar scent of profit motive wafting through the story. In the emergent "New Age" environment of the late 1960s, Castaneda's peculiar blend of pseudomysticism and psychedelia was all but guaranteed to sell quite well—albeit, it's likely nobody foresaw *how* well—especially if it were packaged as academically-ordained "Truth." The motive of the professors who participated in the charade? To produce a "star" in one's department is to bask in reflected glory, thereby attracting bigger budget allocations, hefty raises, grant monies and better book contracts of their own. A further incentive has been suggested by University of Colorado anthropologist Deward E. Walker, Jr., a longtime Castaneda critic: "He made the discipline seem sexy for a while," Walker says, "and that's no small thing in a profession reputedly filled with pencil-headed little geeks. Anthros like to get laid just like everybody else, so a lot of my colleagues seem to have endorsed Castaneda without ever looking at what he had to say, and for quite a while after it had become clear the man was a fraud." No better commentary on the "permeability" of academic standards can be envisioned.

28. Beals, *op. cit.*; the same can be said with respect to Edward Spicer, widely considered to be *the* preeminent anthropological authority on Yaquis in the U.S. at that time, and a regular consultant to the press.

29. *Los Angeles Times Book Review*, Nov. 30, 1975. It is noteworthy that Yablonski was bothered by "rumors"—surfaced most prominently by that point in Daniel C. Noel's *Seeing Castaneda: Reactions to the*

"*Don Juan*" *Writings of Carlos Castaneda* (New York: Putnam's, 1976)—that *Journey to Ixtlan* and *Sorcery* were one and the same. Rather than securing a copy of the dissertation to find out for himself, however, he "researched the matter" (as he put it in his review) by simply phoning a member of Castaneda's committee to inquire. For his trouble, Yablonski was informed by his "reliable source" that "contrary to the opinions of several critics in *Seeing Castaneda*, [*Sorcery*] was not the same as *Journey to Ixtlan.*" On this basis, he proceeded to write his whitewash.

30. This is so at least within the generally-accepted definition of "truth." A major insight into the Castaneda saga, however, may be gained through appreciation of the implications of the involvement of sociologist Harold Garfinkle, a leading advocate of an "alternative" anthropological practice called "ethnomethodology." Stripped of its more verbose intellectual trappings, this bizarre "method of research and analysis" not only stands scientific method squarely on its head but reduces to the most virulent sort of etic imposition on understandings of whatever culture it encounters. The ethnomethodologist first decides what it is he or she would like to be true about a given society. S/he then proceeds by way of "allegory"—that is, by making up stories—to explain *why* it is true. If one decides the Yanomamis are cannibals, for instance, one "proves" this is so by simply writing believable accounts of Yanomami cannibalism. Mere facts don't enter in. This is because, according to proponents of the approach, "validity is more important than authenticity" where "truth" is concerned. Hence, the ethnomethodologically revealed truth of Yanomami culture is that it is cannibalistic even though, in actuality, cannibalism may be utterly unknown to, or at least unpracticed in, Yanomami society. The ultimate beauty of this "analytical breakthrough" for its adherents is that no tedious and time-consuming research is required. One need never have gone to Yanomami territory, laid eyes on a Yanomami, nor even have read a book about them, in order to "understand them better than they understand themselves." From there, one may rely upon the credulity of the public concerning the pronouncements of academically-pedigreed "experts"—all the more so if you're telling them something they wanted for whatever reason to believe anyway—to consumate one's undertaking through publishing one's "findings." On the face of it, Castaneda may be guilty of nothing so much as applying his mentor's method in a most spectacular fashion. For Garfinkle, and perhaps his committee associates as well, the whole thing may simply have been a grand experiment to determine just how well such an approach might work on the stage of big time publishing. If so, there is a certain irony attending their endeavor: While the project certainly bore fruit, it did so essentially by replicating the very models of falsehood and distortion concerning American Indians unstatedly employed by more conventional anthropologists and historians all along. Thus, in their elaboration of a thoroughly dishonest method, ethnomethodologists end up being far more honest than their mainstream counterparts, who do precisely the same thing but deny it. For a good taste of Garfinkle's theory, see his *Studies in Ethnomethodology* (New York: Prentice-Hall, 1967). On his role in the development of ethnomethodological theory and technique, see John Heritage, *Garfinkle and Ethnomethodology* (New York: Polity Press, 1984); Wes Sharrock and Bob Anderson, *The Ethnomethodologists* (New York: Tavistock, 1986); Richard L. Hilbert, *The Classical Roots of Ethnomethodology: Durkheim, Weber, and Garfinkle* (Chapel Hill: University of North Carolina Press, 1992). On the ethnomethodological handling of facts, see Hugh Mehan, *The Reality of Ethnomethodology* (New York: Wiley, 1975); Pierce J. Flynn, *The Ethnomethodological Movement: Sociosemiotic Interpretations* (Berlin, NY: Mouton de Gruyter, 1991); Graham Button, ed., *Ethnomethodology and Human Sciences* (Cambridge: Cambridge University Press, 1991).

31. *Journey to Ixtlan*, p. 83.

32. Ibid., p. 124.

33. Ibid., p. 105.

34. Hans Sebald, "Roasting Rabbits in the Tulameria, or the Lion, the Witch and the Horned Toad," in *The Don Juan Papers, op. cit.*, p. 35.

35. *Journey to Ixtlan, op. cit.*, p. 161.

36. Ibid., pp. 144–51.

37. *A Separate Reality, op. cit.*, p. 186.

38. Ibid., p. 296.

39. As Castaneda was undoubtedly aware, it is not uncommon for traditional elders to refuse to have their pictures taken or voices recorded. While the expression of such sentiments hardly corresponds with much of the rest of the behavioral portrait painted of Don Juan, the rejection of cameras and tape

recorders therefore remains entirely possible. The problem is that, while Castaneda makes the "no photos, no recorders" claim in his dissertation elsewhere, he states on two occasions in *A Separate Reality* that he *did* in fact use a tape recorder to collect the wit and wisdom of Don Juan Matus. Obviously, the matter can't be had both ways.

40. This was explained, among other places, in a 1968 interview—"Don Juan: The Sorcerer" (Tape Cassette #25021)—conducted by Theodore Roszak at radio station KPFA, Berkeley. Interestingly, during the course of the interview Castaneda also describes a process in which he typically took copious "mental notes" while under the influence of hallucinogenics. These, he claimed, were later transcribed. So much for the pretense that what he published was a verbatim reiteration of what Don Juan or anyone else had to say. It should be noted also that, as R. Gordon Wasson observed in a review of *The Teachings of Don Juan* published the April 1969 issue of *Economic Botany*, Don Juan's alleged command of Spanish seemed extraordinary, since "most genuine shamans in Mexico are locked behind...linguistic barriers."

41. *Very* occasionally. As Bruce-Nova observes (*op. cit.*, p. 273): "Miguel Méndez is a Yaqui Indian, whose first short story was published in 1969. Méndez used more Yaqui words in those 14 pages than Castaneda used in 1400." He is referring to Miguel Méndez, "Tata Casehua," in Octavio I. Romano and Herminio Ríos, eds., *El Espejo: An Anthology of Chicano Literature* (Los Angeles: Quinto Sol, 1969).

42. Beals, *op. cit.*, p. 357. The matter is blurred somewhat by Castaneda's claims, advanced at various points in his books, that, in addition to Yaqui and Spanish, Don Juan is also fluent in Yuma, Mazatec, Toltec and, perhaps, other native languages. One can never be quite certain, therefore, exactly which conceptual vernacular he is supposedly drawing upon.

43. About half the twelve pages of hand scrawled notes supposedly provided the basis for pages 56–60 of *The Teachings*. Strikingly, while the descriptions of physical events survive the transition more-or-less intact, Castaneda has elected to change not only how "Don Juan" says things, but *what* he says. While this is certainly a legitimate option to be exercised by a novelist reworking the first draft of a manuscript prior to publication, it is by no means an acceptable approach for an anthropologist—or anyone else—laying claim to standing as a scholarly writer. This undoubtedly explains why Castaneda never provided copies of his notational material to his doctoral committee—why the committee never bothered itself to demand at least samples is another matter—at least to substantiate a few of the more obviously outlandish claims made in his dissertation, why he never tried to find a home for his field notes at the UCLA library or some other safe archive (fairly standard practice with such "important" work), and why he never offered copies of such material to those engaged in the laborious task of translating his English language books into Spanish (a gesture which would, under normal circumstances, have facilitated both the ease and the accuracy of their work). It also explains why, once he'd begun to come under serious pressure to produce his notes after publication of his third book (and the granting of his degree), Castaneda suddenly announced that they'd been destroyed in their entirety during a "catastrophe" in which his basement flooded. Even if one is inclined to accept this feeble excuse on its face, it remains appropriate to ask, since they tend to overlap heavily with the first three, what, exactly, it was upon which he based his *next* six "nonfiction" books.

44. Paul Preuss, "Does Don Juan Live on Campus?" *Human Behavior*, Vol. 7, No. 11, 1978, pp. 53–7. Preuss does not state this categorically. I infer it.

45. To Joyce Carol Oates goes credit for being first to publicly suggest—in a letter to the *New York Times* published on Nov. 26, 1972—that Don Juan was invented and that the Castaneda books should be viewed as works of fiction rather than anthropology. She followed up with a superb little essay, "Don Juan's Last Laugh," in the September 1974 issue of *Psychology Today*. Aside from Oates, Richard de Mille and myself, a sampling of others who have drawn more-or-less the same conclusion include Eric J. Dingwall, "The end of a legend: notes on the magical flight," in Allan Angoff and Ciana Barth, eds., *Parapsychology and Anthropology* (New York: Parapsychology Foundation, 1974); Gordon G. Globus, "Will the real 'Don Juan' please stand up?" *The Academy*, Vol. 19, No. 4, 1975; Michael W. Whan, " 'Don Juan,' Trickster, and Hermeneutic Understanding," *Spring*, 1978; Tom Bourne, "Carlos Castaneda: Genius or Hoax?" *Bookviews*, Nov. 1978; Don Strachan, "In Search of Don Juan," *New West*, Jan. 29, 1979; Gerald Sussman, "Don Juan Revisited," *National Lampoon*, Jan. 1980.

46. Richard N. Adams and Arthur J. Rubel, "Sickness and Social Relations," *Handbook on Middle American Indians* (Washington, D.C.: Smithsonian Institution, 1973) p. 336.

47. "The 'tonal'. . .was thought to be a kind of guardian spirit, usually an animal, that a child obtained at birth and with which he had intimate ties for the rest of his life"; *Tales of Power*, p. 121.

48. Ibid., pp. 122–5, 270–1.

49. Adams and Rubel, *op. cit.*, p. 336; George M. Foster, "Nagualism in Mexico and Guatemala," *Acta Americana*, Vol. 2, Nos. 1–2, 1944.

50. "Nagual. . .was the name given to the animal into which sorcerers could allegedly change themselves, or to the sorcerer who elicited such transformation"; *Tales of Power*, p. 121.

51. Ibid., pp. 126, 141, 271. In *The Second Ring of Power*, Castaneda goes on to define nagual as "a person" (p. 69), "a substance" (p. 219), "a perception" (p. 220) and "a place" (p. 261).

52. The juxtaposition is borrowed, in slightly modified form, from Richard de Mille's "The Shaman of Academe," in *The Don Juan Papers*, *op. cit.*, p. 20.

53. Yogi Ramacharaka (William Walker Atkinson), *Fourteen Lessons in Yogi Philosophy and Oriental Occultism* (New York: Yogi Publication Society, 1903); *The Second Ring of Power*, p. 87.

54. See especially, Richard de Mille's "Epistemallegory: I fly, therefore. . ." in *The Don Juan Papers*, *op. cit.*, at p. 283.

55. Agehananda Bharati, "Castaneda and His Apologists: A Dual Mystical Fantasy," ibid., p. 148.

56. A good early assessment of Castaneda's market will be found in James Collins, "Carlos Castaneda. . .or the making of a guru," *Fate*, Apr. 1974. Also see Herbert Mitgang, "Behind the best sellers: Carlos Castaneda," *New York Times Book Review*, Mar. 5, 1978; Korda, *op. cit.*

57. The word "shaman" originates with the Tungus people of Siberia and thus—the wishes of anthropologists and New Agers notwithstanding—has no more real applicability to American Indian spiritual practices than do European terms like "minister" and "deacon."

58. Barbara Myerhoff, *The Deer-Maize-Peyote Complex among the Huichol Indians of Mexico* (*Dissertations Abstract Index* 30/02–B475; XUM 69–11899 (1968)).

59. Quoted in Richard de Mille's "Validity is not Authenticity: Distinguishing Two Components of Truth," in *The Don Juan Papers*, *op. cit.*, pp. 40–1.

60. Myerhoff, *op. cit.*, p. 94.

61. De Mille, *Castaneda's Journey*, *op. cit.*, p. 112.

62. Ibid.

63. See his 46-page "Alleglossary" at the back of *The Don Juan Papers*, *op. cit.*

64. Walter R. Goldschmidt, *Exploring Ways of Mankind* (New York: Holt, Rinehart & Winston, [3rd ed.] 1977) pp. 187–90.

65. L.L. Langness, *Other Fields, Other Grasshoppers: Readings in Cultural Anthropology* (Philadelphia: Lippencott, 1977) p. 59. It should be noted that the selection used by Langness contains Don Juan's instruction on how to sew lizards' eyelids, a practice not only unknown among Yaquis, but—using the tools indicated—later found to be "utterly impractical" by Hans Sebald in his *Witchcraft: The Heritage of a Heresy* (New York: Elsevier, 1978).

66. Tentative count made via universal database search at Norlin Library, University of Colorado at Boulder, 1997.

67. G. Robert Carlson, Tony Manna and Betty Lou Tucker, "Books for Young Adults 1974 Honor Roll Listing," *English Journal*, Vol. 64, No. 1, 1975.

68. This was in the usual full-page format, guaranteeing attention from incipient scholars.

69. Stanford Berman, "Cataloging Castaneda," *HLC Cataloging Bulletin*, Sept./Oct. 1978, pp. 38–9.

70. See, e.g., Steven Jeffrey Hendlin, *Toward a Converging Philosophy: Don Juan Matus and the Gestalt Therapy of Frederick Perls* (Master's Thesis, United States International University, 1973); Carl Ray Vernon Brown, *A Phenomenological Study of Carlos Castaneda: Educational Implications and Applications* (Doctoral Dissertation, Stanford University, 1977). A database search reveals more than three-dozen other works by graduate students featuring Castaneda and/or Don Juan in the title (none of them appear to be efforts at debunking). It is impossible to determine how many more rely on the factual integrity of Castaneda's work without making such titular reference.

71. See the exchange of letters between Eugene Anderson, Marcello Truzzi and Richard de Mille in *Zetetic*, Vol. 2, No. 1, 1977. A broader framing of their debate will be found in Lawana Trout's "Paperbacks in the Classroom," *English Journal*, Vol. 63, No. 9, 1974.

72. De Mille, *The Don Juan Papers, op. cit.*, p. 67.

73. Truzzi, a professor apparently less concerned with popularity than Anderson (and perhaps more concerned with little things like honesty and accuracy), responded that the fact that students were reading them anyway "should be...a major reason for *not* assigning Castaneda's books in the classroom." He insisted instead that the very "tomes" for which students displayed "less enthusiasm" were exactly what they *should* be required to read in the name of "higher" education. In the alternative, Anderson and others of the "give 'em what they like school" might as well—and as justifiably—have assigned the collected works of Eric von Däniken and a complete set of *Zap Comics* as readings.

74. The idea that Castaneda's specific misrepresentation of Yaquis might translate into misrepresentation of Native Americans in general comes from the second sentence of his dissertation abstract, which states that "sorcery does not have a cultural focus, but is, rather, a series of skills practiced, in one form or another, by all American Indian societies of the New World." It also comes from the nature of his polemical defense, undertaken after critics had begun quite literally to shred his linkage of "Don Juan" and Yaqui culture, that—despite his having subtitled *The Teachings* a "Yaqui Way of Knowledge," despite his explicit and profusely repeated characterizations of Don Juan as a Yaqui in all of his first three books, and despite numerous advertisements labeling his work an exploration of "Yaqui religion"—he had never intended the trilogy as an ethnographic depiction of any "specific cultural milieu." Rather, he claimed at that point, Don Juan was "culturally ambiguous," a sort of generic representative of American Indians as a whole.

75. There are, of course, other examples which might be used. While the early, drug-drenched work, as well as the transcendental alternatives presented in *Journey to Ixtlan*, all follow then wildly popular trajectories of employing altered states of consciousness to explore reality, *Tales of Power* shifts—in keeping with the changing public mood, manifested through the success accorded Uri Geller and movies like *The Exorcist*—to an emphasis of revealing the ways in which sorcery dominates it. A bit later, with "the women's rights agenda" grabbing center stage in the national political discourse, *The Second Ring of Power* explains how Castaneda had actually, contrary to his earlier preoccupation with the decidedly masculine realm of Dons Juan and Genaro, been all along hobnobbing with a bevy of indigenous protofeminist occultists who possess an underlying matrix of knowledge which allows the more ostentatious cast of male characters to thrive.

76. It should be noted that Yaquis do *not* use jimson weed (*Datura*) as an hallucinogen. The question of where Castaneda came up with the idea that they might has always been perplexing, since it is mentioned in none of the standard literature. It appears he lifted it from José Pérez de Paradas' *Plantas Mágicas Americanas* (Madrid: Instituto Sahaguin, 1957), an obscure and often unreliable tract available in the Spanish language section of the UCLA library. Pérez, in turn, seems to have borrowed it from a still earlier pamphlet, *La Flora Diabólica de México*, put out by occultist Victor A. Reko. Meanwhile, on the U.S. "drug culture" of the 1960s, see generally Charles Perry, *The Haight-Ashbury: A History* (New York: Random House/Rolling Stone Press, 1984). For political applications, see Abbie Hoffman, *Revolution for the Hell of It* (New York: Dial, 1968).

77. The transfiguration of Don Juan was not merely technical and philosophical. In keeping with the "revolutionary" sensibilities of a broad segment of the American "youth culture" at the time, *The Teachings*, depicts him as a somber figure, even intimidating at times, driving his apprentice rather hard and seldom relying on humor while imparting his lessons. In *A Separate Reality*, as the New Left went into sharp decline, the old sorcerer is drawn in much more relaxed terms. By the time *Journey to Ixtlan* made its appearance in 1973, the period of serious sociopolitical activism had spent itself altogether, replaced by a mood of individual self-indulgence. Don Juan joins in, adopting what might best be described as a "Conan O'Brien mode of teaching." It should be borne in mind that all three mutually contradictory depictions supposedly accrue from the same set of field notes, often covering the same time frames or events.

78. *Tales of Power*, p. 238.

79. De Mille, *The Don Juan Papers, op. cit.*, pp. 418–9.

80. Weston La Barre, for one, has catalogued all two-dozen terms for peyote employed by the indigenous peoples of the region in which Don Juan and Castaneda supposedly gathered and consumed it. The word "mescal" does not appear; *Peyote Cult, op. cit.*, pp. 14–5. It follows that neither the Yaquis nor

any other group would call a spirit entity associated with peyote use "Mescalito." Indeed, the Yaquis are not known to express belief in such an entity by *any* name; see, e.g., the review of *Teachings* written by the eminent authority on Yaquis, Edward H. Spicer, and published in *American Anthropologist*, Vol. 71, No. 2, 1969. The closest approximation may be the Tarahumara *hikuri*, a matter suggesting that the drug passages of Castaneda's first two books may be influenced by his reading the poet Antonin Artaud's "artistic" descriptions of that people's peyote use in his *Peyote Dance* (at least Castaneda has he and Don Juan journeying to Tarahumara territory in order to gather peyote buttons). It should be noted that, in 1976, Farrar, Strauss & Giroux released a new edition of *Peyote Dance*, following the lead established in UCLA's and Simon & Schuster's handling of Castaneda by listing Artaud's obvious fantasy as "anthropology" rather than as "literature" or "fiction."

81. On the onslaught and the defensive measures eventually developed by the Pascua Yaquis, see, e.g., Jane Holden Kelley, "A Yaqui Way of Kidding," in *The Don Juan Papers*, *op. cit.*, p. 33. For an account of the travails of one of the legions of gullible young whites duped into setting out on a quest to find Don Juan and Mescalito, see Neil Ericson, "Seven Years with Don Juan," ibid., at p. 227. According to Lakota scholar Vine Deloria, Jr., who worked in those days at the University of Arizona, the waiting room of the Tucson bus station was for years frequently haunted by "young white kids hoping to encounter Don Juan" in the same manner Castaneda claimed to have in nearby Nogales during the summer of 1960.

82. It should be noted that the in the Popayan area of the Columbian Andes—not far from Castaneda's native Peru—there *are* people known to smoke mushroom in powdered form. Consumed in this way, however, the mushroom, believed to be *Stropharia cubensis*, produces no appreciable hallucinogenic effect. Moreover, it has been suggested that the practice evident at Popayan actually derives from Castaneda's claims vis-à-vis "*humito*," a term unknown to ethnobotanists, mycologists and others who have studied mushroom usage by the indigenous peoples of central Mexico; Steven Hayden Pollack, "The Psilocybin Mushroom Pandemic," *Journal of Psychiatric Drugs*, Vol. 7, No. 1, 1975.

83. The second volume of Wasson's major work, *Mushrooms, Russia and History* (New York: Pantheon, 1957), coauthored with Valentia Pavlovna Wasson, contains a lengthy description of mushroom usage by the native peoples of Oaxaca. Wasson also authored a pair of articles on the topic, "The Divine Mushroom: Primitive Religion and Hallucinatory Agents (*Proceedings of the American Philosophical Association*, Vol. 102, No. 3, 1958) and "The Hallucinogenic Fungi of Mexico: An Inquiry into the Origins of the Religious Ideal Among Primitive Peoples (*Harvard Botanical Museum Leaflets*, Vol. 17, No. 1, 1961), as well as coauthoring a book with George Cowan, Florence Cowan and Willard Roads, *María Sabina and Her Mazatec Mushroom Valeda* (New York: Harcourt, Brace, Jovanovich, 1974). All but the latter were available at the UCLA library during the period the Don Juan books were being researched. Since Castaneda informed Wasson in his letter of September 6, 1968, that he was already "very familiar" with the mycologist's ethnobotanical work, it can be presumed that what Wasson was actually querying were regurgitations of his own material, albeit in a form so grossly distorted by Castaneda as to be unrecognized by the real author. The text of Wasson's letter to Castaneda appears in *The Don Juan Papers*, *op. cit.*, pp. 319–21.

84. Castaneda's response is aptly summarized by Richard de Mille in a piece entitled "Allegory is not Ethnobotany"; ibid., pp. 321–8.

85. Predictably, no one on staff at the laboratory recalled such an interaction.

86. This marks a pronounced shift in Castaneda's storyline since he had nowhere before mentioned Oaxaca as an area frequented by either Don Juan or himself. Moreover, in *The Teachings*, he explicitly identifies the place in which he found his first mushroom as being near the city of Durango, in Chihuahua. Since Castaneda was by his own account already familiar with Wasson's research in Mexico, which had centered among the Huichol of Oaxaca, he was simply feeding the mycologist's own findings back to him in altered form (as an expedient to making his own fable seem more credible).

87. Once again, a major contradiction. The climate and topography of the Los Angeles area are much more similar to those of Chihuahua and Sonora than to those of Oaxaca.

88. There is no record of the UCLA lab having received a specimen of any sort from Carlos Castaneda. Nor did Castaneda himself ever provide a receipt or any other sort of documentation that this presumably precious specimen ever existed.

89. This second letter is summarized in The Don Juan Papers, *op. cit.*, p. 328.

90. Wasson's review appeared in *Economic Botany*, Vol. 23, No. 2, 1969. Subsequent reviews of the next two Don Juan books—published in *Economic Botany*, Vol. 26, No. 1 (1972) and Vol. 27, No. 1 (1973)—displayed increasing skepticism.

91. See, e.g., Wasson's review of *Tales of Power*, published in *Economic Botany*, Vol. 28, No. 3, 1974. On the kinds of contradictions at issue, as de Mille has pointed out, after comparing texts, "Carlos meets a certain witch for the first time in 1962 and *again* in 1965. Though he learns a lot about *seeing* in 1962, unaccountably he has never heard of it in 1968," and so on, ad infinitum; *The Don Juan Papers*, *op. cit.*, p. 18.

92. See, e.g., Douglass McFerran, "The Castaneda Plot," *America*, Feb. 26, 1977; Sam Keen, "Don Juan's Power Trip," *Psychology Today*, Dec. 1977; Robert Bly, "Carlos Castaneda Meets Madame Solitude," *New York Times Book Review*, Jan. 22, 1978; Richard de Mille, "Explaining Anomalistic Anthropology with Help from Castaneda," *Zetetic Scholar*, Vol. 1, Nos. 3–4, 1979. Earlier doubts had been raised not only by Joyce Carol Oates (*op. cit.*), but by Donald Barthelme, "The Teachings of Don B.: A Yankee Way of Knowledge," *New York Times Magazine*, Feb. 11, 1973, and Martin E. Marty, "The Castaneda Cult," *Christian Century*, Mar. 21, 1973.

93. Letter to the *New York Times*, May 7, 1978. Harner had done excellent work on the Jívaro people of the Amazon Basin (*The Jívaro: People of the Sacred Waterfalls* [New York: Doubleday/Anchor, 1973]) and the use of consciousness-altering substances among indigenous peoples (see his edited *Hallucinogens and Shamanism* [New York: Oxford University Press, 1973]), so his affirmation of Castaneda's credibility was not insignificant. Even demonstrations of the fact that Castaneda appeared to have lifted passages on "soul stealing" from his own "Jívaro Souls" (*American Anthropologist*, Vol. 64, No. 2, 1962) and applied them in garbled form to the Yaquis failed to deter him from pronouncing, again contrary to available evidence, that such practices are "universal" among natives, and that no plagiarism had thus occurred.

94. C. Scott Littleton, "An Emic Account of Sorcery: Carlos Castaneda and the Rise of a New Anthropology," *Journal of Latin American Lore*, Vol. 2, No. 2, 1976.

95. Philip Staniford, "I Come to Praise Carlos, Not to Bury Don Juan," in *The Don Juan Papers*, *op. cit.*, at p. 151.

96. Daniel C. Noel, "Makings of Meaning: Carlos Castaneda's 'Lived Hermeneutics' in the Cargo Culture," *Listening: Current Studies in Dialog*, Vol. 7, No. 1, 1972. This early quote is included because Noel never recanted his affirmation of Castaneda's validity *and* authenticity. Instead, he elected to pen a less effusive but nonetheless supportive biographical entry for the fifth volume of *Collier's Encyclopedia* (New York: Macmillan, 1980).

97. "Don Juan as Philosopher," in Noel's *Seeing Castaneda*, *op. cit.* Margolis' position obviously begs the question of why, if sources are so "irrelevant," Castaneda and his publishers went to such lengths in casting an aura of empirical authenticity around his project. Such rules may be appropriate to the subjective mishmash of metaphysics, but not to a purported human "science" like anthropology.

98. Ron Fisher, letter to the editors of *Time*, Mar. 26, 1973.

99. *New Age*, Feb. 1975.

100. Peter Matthiessen, *The Snow Leopard* (New York: Viking, 1978) p. 326; on diffusion, see pp. 55–6.

101. Erin Matson, "R. de Mille Doesn't Exist," reproduced in *The Don Juan Papers*, *op. cit.*, pp. 175–6.

102. Robert Holbrook, letter to the editors of *Fate*, Oct. 31, 1978. Holbrook also observes that the targets of his wrath were likely misled by Richard de Mille's *Castaneda's Journey*, "an asinine book which I will not read."

103. Ralph Ullman, "I Found Don Juan," *New Age*, June 1977. Ullman claims that, inspired by a photo of an elderly Indian, perhaps a Yaqui and reputedly Don Juan, taken in secret by Castaneda crony Al Egori and reproduced on p. 33 of *Castaneda's Journey*, he set out to find the legendary sorcerer himself. Traveling to Sonora and taking up the provincial telephone directory—Where else would one look for one of Don Juan's attributes? One suspects Ullman searched first in the yellow pages, under "Sorcery"—and finding no Matuses, he switched to "Matos." There, he hit paydirt. After 2,999 phone calls he finally reached the individual who confirmed that yes, indeed, he *was* the very person depicted in the Castaneda books and, contrary to what he'd always told his apprentice, didn't mind being photographed at all. How,

exactly, this translated into Ullman's coming back with pictures of three different people, all of them supposedly Don Juan, is a bit mysterious. Nonetheless, such a compelling gathering of proof by one qualified as an "art history major at the University of Michigan" was sufficient to cause the magazine's editors to engage their usual evidentiary standards by announcing unequivocally, in reference to Castaneda, that "this is no hoax."

104. In his chapter entitled "Sonoragate or Tales of Folly" in *The Don Juan Papers (op. cit.,* pp. 126–8), Richard de Mille recounts writing a letter to Goldschmidt in 1975, asking that he explain his version of events. Not only did Goldschmidt fail to reply, he contacted the Ethics Committee of the American Psychological Association, to which de Mille belonged, charging that the raising of questions about his own role in the career of Carlos Castaneda constituted "intellectual blackmail" and insinuating that de Mille should be "disciplined."

105. Among the critics who were allotted time were session organizer Joseph K. Long, Richard de Mille, Agehananda Bharati, Marcello Truzzi, and Ralph Beals, who publicly apologized for the "mistake" made by the UCLA anthropology department in the case of Carlos Castaneda. It should be noted that Long had himself been something of a Castaneda believer. See his "Shamanism, Trance, Hallucinogens, and Physical Events: Concepts, Methods and Techniques for Working Among Primitives," in Agehananda Bharati, ed., *The Realm of the Extra-Human* (New York: Mouton, 1976). Also see his introductory remarks in his edited volume, *Extrasensory Ecology: Parapsychology and Anthropology* (New York: Scarecrow Press, 1977).

106. How Goldschmidt knew the basketry was not commercially available in villages along the Yaqui River has never been made clear. In any event, how, exactly, showing a few rare baskets to an archaeologist in 1962 serves to establish the authenticity of a dissertation having nothing at all to do with either basketry or archaeology, and delivered a full decade later, is even more unfathomable. By that standard of evidence, I could as easily show the pair of aluminum cylinder heads I just bought for my car to a member of the coaching staff at the University of Colorado and then offer them as verification that I'd actually engaged in research proving that the universe orbits the Earth. At that point, my dissertation, carefully paraphrased from medieval manuscripts lodged in the rare books collection of the campus library, perhaps with a few tidbits gleaned from Velikovsky and *Hot Rod* magazine thrown in, should not only be accepted by the university's physics department, apparently without my having to defend it in any tangible way, but published by the University Press of Colorado, complete with a foreword by the physics chair in which it is proclaimed "a revolutionary breakthrough in our understanding of the inner functioning of the cosmos." Afterwards, everyone can all sit around and talk about how my work was "allegorically true, even if literally false." After all, there are those cylinder heads corroborating that, at some level, I "must have" actually done the math. This is "science"?

107. Jacques Maquet, "Castaneda: Warrior or Scholar?" *American Anthropologist,* Vol. 80, No. 2, 1978. For an apologist's refusal to accept the obvious, see Stan Wilk's "On the Experimental Approach to Anthropology: A Reply to Maquet" in the same issue.

108. Quoted in *The Don Juan Papers, op. cit.,* pp. 131–2.

109. Murray argues, counter to the great weight of facts, that Castaneda "deceived" both his committee and the UCLA Press, and that the "scientific community" paid scant heed to Castaneda all along. More than that, he claims, is "beyond the capacity" of the profession in terms of enforcing standards. Whatever stigma should be assigned in the Castaneda case, he suggests, belongs exclusively to Castaneda, and to a public gullible enough to believe him; Steven O. Murray, "The Invisibility of Scientific Scorn," ibid., at p. 198. The idea that the academic status quo lacks the ability to "defrock" those it *wishes* to brand as charlatans will undoubtedly come as a surprise to a great number of scholars who have set out to challenge orthodoxy. One need only consider the case of Immanuel Velikovsky, examined quite well by Vine Deloria, Jr., in his *Metaphysics of Modern Existence* (New York: Harper & Row, 1978), to get the point. As concerns the alleged "silent rejection" of Castaneda by the scholarly community, even a cursory review of the literature reveals the precise opposite. In addition to material already cited, see, e.g., David A. Aberle's review of *The Teachings* in *Man: Journal of the Royal Anthropological Institute,* Vol. 4, No. 2, 1969; Edward Spicer's review in *American Anthropologist,* Vol. 71, No. 2, 1969; Peter T. Furst, ed., *Flesh of the Gods: The Ritual Use of Hallucinogens* (New York: Praeger, 1972); Paul Heelas, "Expressing the Inexpressible: Don Juan and the Limits of Formal Analysis," *Journal of the Anthropological Society of London,* Vol. 3, No. 3, 1972;

Marlene Dobkin de Rios, "The Anthropology of Drug-Induced Altered States of Consciousness: Some Theoretical Considerations," *Sociologus*, Vol. 22, Nos. 1–2, 1972; Keith H. Basso, "Southwestern Ethnology," *Annual Review of Anthropology*, 1973; Janet Siskind, "Visions and Cures among the Sharanahua, in *Hallucinogens and Shamanism, op. cit.*; James W. Boyd, "The Teachings of Don Juan from a Buddhist perspective," *Christian Century*, Mar. 28, 1973; Michael S. Kimmel's review of the Don Juan Trilogy in *American Journal of Sociology*, Vol. 79, No. 4, 1974; Jerry H. Gill, "The World of Don Juan: Some Reflections," *Soundings*, Vol. 57, No. 4, 1974; David Silverman, ed., *Reading Castaneda: A Prologue to the Social Sciences* (London: Routledge & Keegan Paul, 1975); John Ryle's review of *Tales of Power* in *Journal of the Anthropological Society of Oxford*, Vol. 6, No. 2, 1975; Joseph L. Zentner, "Pathways to the Supernatural," *Journal of Interamerican Studies and World Affairs*, Vol. 18, No. 3, 1976; Joseph L. Zinker, "Castanedian Vision," in Brunner/Maztel, eds., *Creative Process in Gestalt Therapy* (???, 1977); Marlene Dobkin de Rios and David E. Smith, "Drug Use and Abuse in Cross-Cultural Perspective," *Human Organization*, Vol. 36, No. 1, 1977; Klaus-Peter Koeppling, "Castaneda and Methodology in the Social Sciences: Sorcery or Genuine Hermeneutics?" *Social Alternatives*, Vol. 1, No. 1, 1977; Stan Wilk, "Castaneda: Coming of Age in Sonora," *American Anthropologist* (Vol. 79, No. 1, 1977); "Therapeutic Anthropology and Culture Consciousness," *Anthropology and Humanist Quarterly* (Vol. 2, No. 3, 1977) and review of *Castaneda's Journey* in *American Anthropologist* (Vol. 79, No. 4, 1977); Ronald Palmer, "Carlos Castaneda and the Phenomenology of Sorcery," *Humbolt Journal of Social Relations*, Vol. 4, No. 2, 1977.

110. Quoted in *The Don Juan Papers, op. cit.*, p. 125.

111. Ibid., pp. 125–6.

112. Myerhoff's interview with Richard de Mille, entitled "Conversations with Yoawima," is included in ibid., at p. 336.

113. To be clear about this, Myerhoff had precisely the same obligation to blow the whistle on Castaneda as does a person who is aware that a friend who happens to be a building contractor is planning to cut corners on a construction project in such a way as to make likely a structural collapse which could kill hundreds of people. One may be obligated, out of a sense of loyalty or whatever, to try and dissuade the contractor friend from following through with his/her plan before doing anything else. If the effort fails, however, and s/he persists, one has an unequivocal moral/ethical obligation to warn the public. If this responsibility is defaulted upon, and a structural collapse does in fact occur, then the defaulter is properly viewed as an accomplice in the resulting deaths (murders). While the circumstances pertaining to our imaginary contractor are different than those associated with Castaneda—more urgent, let's say— the principle is precisely the same.

114. See Truzzi's review of *Castaneda's Journey* in *Zetetic*, Vol. 1, No. 2, 1977; Melton's review of the same book in *Fate*, June 1977.

115. The characterizations accrue from Michael Harner and others.

116. C. Dawson and A.S. Woodward, "On the Discovery of a Paleolithic Skull and Mandible at Piltdown with an Appendix by Elliot Smith," *Quarterly Journal of the Geological Society of London*, LXIX, 1913.

117. See generally, Ronald Millar, *The Piltdown Men* (New York: St. Martin's Press, 1972).

118. The premise here is that evolutionary advancement is reflected in the expansion of cranial capacity, that cranial capacity itself correlates to intellect and, thus, to "innate superiority." Since the Piltdown skull was clearly caucasoid in its configuration, and since it exhibited a far larger cranial capacity than other paleolithic skulls, it was advanced as "proof" that whites were biologically superior to other human groups; Ian Langham, "Talgai and Piltdown: The Common Context," *Artefact*, Vol. 3, No. 4, 1978, at p. 196. On "scientific racism" more broadly, see William Stanton, *The Leopard's Spots: Scientific Attitudes Towards Race in America, 1815–1859* (Chicago: University of Chicago Press, 1960); Steven Jay Gould, *The Mismeasure of Man* (New York: W.W. Norton, 1981). It should be noted that exactly the same kind of pseudoscientific sludge is still being published in the U.S., and is being received with an uncomfortable degree of acclaim. See, e.g., Richard J. Herrnstein and Charles Murray, *The Bell Curve: Intelligence and Class Structure in American Life* (New York: Free Press, 1994). For analysis, see Russell Jacoby and Naomi Glauberman, eds., *The Bell Curve Debate: History, Documents, Opinions* (New York: Times Books, 1995). A good related read is Troy Duster's *Back Door to Eugenics* (New York: Routledge, 1990).

119. For an interesting examination of how the same process has worked in other contexts, see

Steven O. Murray, *Group Formation in Social Science* (Edmonton: Linguistic Research, Inc., 1980).

120. J.S. Weiner, *The Piltdown Forgery* (London: Oxford University Press, 1955). Weiner was one of those who initially exposed the hoax; see J.S. Weiner, W.E. Le Gros Clark and K.P. Oakley, "The Solution of the Piltdown Problem, *Bulletin of the British Museum*, Vol. II, No. 3, 1953; "Further Contributions to the Solution of the Piltdown Problem," *Bulletin of the British Museum*, Vol. II, No. 6, 1953.

121. Millar, *op. cit.*

122. See, e.g., L.B. Halstead, "New Light on the Piltdown Hoax?" *Nature*, Nov. 2, 1978; J.S. Weiner, "Piltdown Hoax: New Light," *Nature*, Jan. 4, 1979; Ian Langham, "The Piltdown Hoax," *Nature*, Jan. 18, 1979; Frank Spencer, *Piltdown: A Scientific Forgery* (New York: Oxford University Press, 1990).

123. Steven Jay Gould, "Smith Woodward's Folly," *New Scientist*, Apr. 5, 1979. Also see Kenneth Oakley, "Suspicions About Piltdown Man," *New Scientist*, June 21, 1979.

124. *The Don Juan Papers, op. cit.*, pp. 112, 456.

125. Ibid., pp. 114–5.

126. L.S.B. Leakey, *By the Evidence: Memoirs, 1932–1951* (New York: Harcourt, Brace, Jovanovich, 1974) p. 22–5. It should be noted that Leakey, discoverer of *Australopithicus*, had already expressed skepticism about Piltdown's implications, a matter which rendered him "undependable" in the view of F.A. Bather, who had succeeded Smith Woodward as Curator of Paleontology at the British Museum. In attempting to reconcile the almost blanket rejection which greeted his own genuine 1932 discovery and the "strange acceptance by all but a few scientists of the Piltdown skull and jaw during 1912 and 1913," Leakey suggests that "the Piltdown specimens were accepted with such ease because they fitted readily into the generally agreed pattern of what an ancestral skull *ought* to look like." In other words, don't confuse us with facts, feed our preconceptions.

127. Oakley, *op. cit.* Oakley succeeded Bather as the British Museum's paleontological curator in 1953 and immediately made it possible for skeptics such as J.S. Weiner and Sir Wilfred Le Gros Clark to conduct the test of *Eoanthropus* which disclosed its fraudulent nature. Obviously, such tests could—and certainly should—have been performed decades earlier, thus doing much to preempt consolidation of an utterly spurious body of racist theory into academic dogma.

128. Oakley, *op. cit.*

129. *The Don Juan Papers, op. cit.*, p. 115.

130. *Castaneda's Journey, op. cit.*

131. E.g., Mander, *op. cit.*

132. This is true, not just at such officially accredited "institutions of higher learning" as Boulder's Naropa Institute and the California Institute for Integral Studies—where it might perhaps be expected (if not forgiven)—but at academically prestigious institutions like the University of Colorado, U Cal/Berkeley and—you guessed it—UCLA.

133. Marvin Harris, *Cultural Materialism: The Struggle for a Science of Culture* (New York: Random House, 1979) pp. 319–32. On the movement, see Milton Viorst, *Fire in the Streets: America in the 1960's* (New York: Touchstone, 1979); George Katsiaficas, *The Imagination of the New Left: A Global Analysis of 1968* (Boston: South End Press, 1987). For what is probably the best documentary history—if you can find it—see Mitchell Goodman, ed., *The Movement Toward a New America: The Beginnings of a Long Revolution* (Philadelphia/New York: Pilgrim Press/Alfred A. Knopf, 1970).

134. For Leary's eclectic view of things, complete with a quest for some personal connection to what he called "*curanderos*," see his *High Priest* (New York: World, 1968). De Mille makes an interesting case that Castaneda was heavily influenced by Leary's promotion of LSD as a chemical device for "unleashing revolutionary forms of human consciousness" during the early '60s, a point of view which itself derived from Aldous Huxley's experiments with psilocybin mushrooms a few years before. In fact, de Mille argues, "la Catalina," a female character deployed in the Don Juan books, may well have gotten her name from a hotel in the Mexican fishing village of Zihuatanejo (now a resort town), where Leary maintained a short-lived acid colony which Castaneda alludes to having visited during the summer of 1962; *The Don Juan Papers, op. cit.*, pp. 309–18. On Huxley, who, by his own account, was one of Castaneda's favorite authors, see *The Doors to Perception* (New York: Harper, 1954) and, esp., "Drugs that Shape Men's Minds," *Saturday Evening Post*, Oct. 18, 1958. Another text which Castaneda mentioned as

having "helped" him realize the psychedelic properties of fungus and its spiritual applications in some indigenous societies was Andreja Puharich's *The Sacred Mushroom* (New York: Doubleday, 1959). To be fair, it should be admitted that Castaneda synthesized a system of "self-actualization"—actually, self-negation—through drug consumption which was far more elaborate, and in many ways more convincing, than those offered by his predecessors.

135. Ronald Sukenick, "Upward and Juanward: The Possible Dream," in Noel, *Seeing Castaneda*, *op. cit.*, p. 113.

136. For what is in many ways an excellent analysis, but one offering few if any viable alternatives, see Alex Callinicos, *Against Postmodernism: A Marxist Critique* (New York: St. Martin's Press, 1989). To again be fair, neither Harris nor Callinicos nominates Castaneda to a position of sole responsibility for this intellectual/conceptual impasse (Callinicos, in fact, fails to even mention him). Rather, it is argued that Castaneda became the popularizer of the degenerate ideas of other, far more important, theorists such as Garfinkle and the phenomenologist, Paul Feyerabend; Harris, *op. cit.*, pp. 22–4, 319–22. For a good dose of Feyerabend, see his *Against Method* (Atlantic Highlands, NJ: Humanities Press, 1975).

137. The characterization of Castaneda's philosophical stance as "ethnomethodological phenomenology" is apparently his own, made during lectures delivered at U Cal/Irvine in 1972; Russ Rueger, "Tripping the Heavy Fantastic," *Human Behavior*, Vol. 2, No. 3, 1973, p. 74.

138. Harris, *op. cit.*, p. 324. The analogy to Dachau presumably bears no further explanation, but a good overview is provided in Marcus J. Smith's *Dachau: The Harrowing of Hell* (Albany: State University of New York Press, 1995). For those unfamiliar with what happened at Mylai 4 (Son My), and the role played by Lt. William Calley, see Joseph Goldstein, Burke Marshall and Jack Schwartz, *The Mylai Massacre and Its Cover-Up: Beyond the Reach of the Law?* (New York: Free Press, 1976). On the 1970 killing of four students at Kent State University—and the wounding of several others—by Ohio National Guardsmen, see Joseph Kelner and James Munves, *The Kent State Coverup* (New York: Harper & Row, 1980).

139. At the most immediate level, this devolves upon the official or quasiofficial propaganda (in the vulgar sense). For general theory, see Jacques Ellul, *Propaganda: The Formation of Men's Attitudes* (New York: Alfred A. Knopf, 1965). For concrete applications to U.S. society, see, e.g., Edward S. Herman and Noam Chomsky, *Manufacturing Consent: The Political Economy of the Mass Media* (New York: Pantheon, 1988); Michael Parenti, *Inventing Reality: The Politics of the News Media* (New York: St. Martin's Press, 1993).

140. Ask yourself how a patent ignoramus like Rush Limbaugh—or Howard Stern—ends up with a weekly slot to opinionate via the mass media while so lucid and informed an observer as Noam Chomsky—or Angela Davis—is consistently denied so much as a sound bite, and you'll start to get the drift. To pontificate on "all stories being equal" in such a context, even in the most abstract sense, is preposterous. The "stories" of Limbaugh and Stern, Chomsky and Davis, are by no defensible estimation "equal," whether one is using their veracity, their accuracy or their quantitative degree of exposure as a standard of measure. On the concept of hegemony, hammered out in the sense intended here during the 1920s and '30s by Italian theorist Antonio Gramsci, see Walter L. Adamson, *Hegemony and Revolution: Antonio Gramsci's Political and Cultural Theory* (Berkeley: University of California Press, 1980).

141. Some points are worth making more than once. At p. 8 of *Journey to Ixtlan*, Castaneda makes an initial effort to parry the thrusts of critics, and to shift blame for any "misunderstandings" which may have arisen from himself to his imaginary indigenous source: "So far I have made no attempt whatsoever to place Don Juan in a cultural milieu. The fact that he considers himself to be a Yaqui Indian does not mean that his knowledge of sorcery is known to or practiced by the Yaqui Indians in general." This is an interesting statement, to say the least, coming from a man who had insisted, apparently over the objections of at least one knowledgeable colleague, to make it clear in the subtitle to his first Don Juan book that what was at issue was a specifically "*Yaqui* way of knowledge."

142. See, e.g., Robert F. Berkhofer, Jr., *The White Man's Indian: Images of the American Indian from Columbus to the Present* (New York: Alfred A. Knopf, 1978). On the process masked by such misrepresentations, see David E. Stannard, *American Holocaust: Columbus and the Conquest of the New World* (New York: Oxford University Press, 1992), as well as my own *A Little Matter of Genocide: Holocaust and Denial in the Americas* (San Francisco: City Lights, 1997).

143. One would do well ask the difference in principle between Castaneda's brand of mythologizing on the one hand and the deliberate falsification of American Indian demographics by a

"reputable historian" like John Gorham Palfrey—or the Smithsonian Institution's anthropological enshrinement of his and his colleagues' spurious estimates—on the other. For solid documentation of this and a range of comparable offenses committed in the name of orthodox historiography, see Francis Jennings, *The Invasion of America: Indians, Colonialism and the Cant of Conquest* (Chapel Hill: University of North Carolina Press, 1975). For a broader view, see Robert Young's *White Mythologies: Writing History and the West* (New York: Routledge, 1990).

144. Although dated, the best treatment is still Ralph and Natasha Friar's *The Only Good Indian: The Hollywood Gospel* (New York: Drama Book Specialists, 1972). Also see Raymond William Stedman, *Shadows of the Indian: Stereotypes in American Culture* (Norman: University of Oklahoma Press, 1982).

145. Norman Cohn, *Warrant for Genocide: The Myth of the Jewish World Conspiracy and the Protocols of the Elders of Zion* (New York: Harper & Row, 1967).

146. There is an overall consensus on this point. The works referenced are Russell Means, "The Same Old Song," in my *Marxism and Native Americans* (Boston: South End Press, 1983) at p. 22; Robert Jay Lifton, *The Nazi Doctors: Medical Killing and the Psychology of Genocide* (New York: Basic Books, 1986); Robert Jay Lifton and Eric Markusen, *The Genocidal Mentality: Nazi Holocaust and Nuclear Threat* (New York: Basic Books, 1988); Tzvetan Todorov, *The Conquest of America: The Question of the Other* (New York: Harper Colophon, 1985).

147. *The Don Juan Papers, op. cit.*, pp. 209–10.

148. A pair of collections should prove sufficient to make my point. See Chris Tiffin and Alan Lawson, eds., *De-Scribing Empire: Post-colonialism and textuality* (New York: Routledge, 1994); Patricia Williams and Laura Chrisman, eds., *Colonial Discourse and Post-Colonial Theory: A Reader* (New York: Columbia University Press, 1994). Meanwhile, anyone wishing to question the ongoing existence of direct colonialism, even after dissolution of the classic European empires during the 1950s and '60s, need only consider with some degree of honesty the situation of Hawai'i, Puerto Rico, the "U.S." Virgin Islands, "American" Samoa, Guam, the Marshall Islands and every Indian reservation in North America to start to get the picture. See generally, my own *Struggle for the Land: Native North American Resistance to Genocide, Ecocide and Colonization* (Winnipeg: Arbiter Ring, [2nd Ed.], 1998).

149. Actually, a very good case can be made that postcolonialism assigns "most interesting" status—and, hence, top political priority—to itself, or at least the "found oppressions" of its adherents, especially among those who have come to view antiracism and anti-imperialism as "boring." Astonishingly, I have increasingly encountered Euroamerican "dissidents" who are prepared to explain how internally colonized African Americans, American Indians and Latinos are actually oppressive to *them*.

150. Kurt Wolff, "This is the Time for Radical Anthropology," in Dell Hymes, ed., *Reinventing Anthropology* (New York: Random House, 1972).

151. Paul Joseph, *Cracks in the Empire: State Politics in the Vietnam War* (Boston: South End Press, 1981); Noam Chomsky and Edward S. Herman, *After the Cataclysm: Postwar Indochina and the Reconstruction of Imperial Ideology* (Boston: South End Press, 1979).

152. On the Third World, see Noam Chomsky, *Year 501: The Conquest Continues* (Boston: South End Press, 1992) and *World Orders, Old and New* (New York: Columbia University Press, 1996). Domestically, see Leslie W. Dunbar, ed., *Minority Report: What Has Happened to Blacks, Hispanics, American Indians and Other Minorities in the Eighties* (New York: Pantheon, 1984) and Andrew Hacker, *Two Nations: Black and White, Separate, Hostile and Unequal* (New York: Scribner's, 1992).

153. The descriptor used is once again attributable to Richard de Mille; *The Don Juan Papers, op. cit.*, p. 17.

Hi-Ho, Hillerman . . . (Away)
The Role of Detective Fiction in Indian Country

> My theory is that people who don't like mystery stories are anarchists.
>
> —Rex Stout

Over the past thirty years, a string of novels—*The Blessing Way* (1970), *Dance Hall of the Dead* (1973), *Listening Woman* (1978), *People of Darkness* (1980), *The Dark Wind* (1982), *The Ghostway* (1984), *Skinwalkers* (1986), *A Thief of Time* (1988), *Talking God* (1989),*Coyote Waits* (1990) and *Sacred Clowns* (1993)—have in some ways changed the face of detective fiction in the United States.[1]

Each of them is set against the backdrop of the Navajo Reservation in the Four Corners region where the states of Arizona, New Mexico, Utah and Colorado meet, a remote and thinly populated desert locale about as different from the usual scene of an American detective yarn as it is possible to conceive. Each of them, moreover, features one or both of a pair of Navajo police officers, Joe Leaphorn and Jim Chee, as its central character(s); they too represent an abrupt departure from the sort of sleuth we have become accustomed to expect when consuming a who-done-it from either the literary menu or its cinematic counterpart. Finally, the non-Indian author of this body of work, Tony Hillerman, is himself far from fitting the image of the detective writer typically projected for public consumption.

Despite, or perhaps because of, the seemingly anomalous nature of the man and his material, Hillerman has been cast by the *Dallas Morning News* as standing among "any list of the best living mystery writers." The *New Yorker* describes his work as being "agile . . . reflective . . . absorbing," and the *San Diego Union* calls him a "gifted, skillful and . . . unique writer." The *Boston Globe* asserts that Hillerman "is surely one of the finest and most original craftsmen at work in the [detective] genre today," while the *Washington Post Book World* has claimed he "transcends the . . . genre" altogether. *People Magazine* holds that he is a "keen observer in a world not his own," critic Phyllis A. Whitney states categorically that he "evokes the Arizona desert and Navajo lore as no other writer can," and the *Denver Post Magazine* goes even further, proclaiming that, "The magic of his mysteries is in the world he creates: a sense of intimacy he builds within a structure that seems whole, unbreakable, unassailably true." Critic Ursula LeGuin sums up, announcing emphatically: "The only mysteries I read are Hillerman's."[2]

Unquestionably, superlatives such as this are reserved for writing which is not only acceptable in content to the establishmentarian voices uttering them, but yielding—or expected to yield—a maximal impact upon the national consciousness. Correspondingly, conservative newspapers like the Asheville, North Carolina *Citizen Times* have concurred with the East Coast liberal perspective, solemnly intoning that the essential purpose of Hillerman's thrillers is "to teach." The Oklahoma City *Oklahoman* has advised that "readers who have not discovered Hillerman should not waste one more minute."[3]

Such consensus among "responsible" critics is perplexing insofar as the work in question reputedly flies in the face of many rules of orthodox detective fiction and, for that matter, the mores usually associated with the North American status quo itself. There is a paradox involved in the idea that books as seemingly deviant from the norm as this should be so warmly—effusively might be a better word—embraced by those most committed to enforcing sociopolitical convention. This is all the more true when the very same material is generally endorsed by self-proclaimed (and sometimes genuine) opponents of the status quo as being socially and politically progressive. Overall, the Hillerman phenomenon bears close scrutiny on the part of serious analysts.

A Bit of Background on the Detective Genre

It seems most unlikely, on the face of it, that a paunchy, sedate, middle-aged family man *cum* reformed journalist/graduate student and all around "nice guy" like Tony Hillerman should become premier detective novelist of the moment. Little in the history of the genre would lead one to conclude the man would ever secure such a lofty place within it. Beginning perhaps in the 1840s with "The Murders in the Rue Morgue" and other short stories by Poe, who has typically been considered a bit mad by even his most devoted admirers, detective fiction has been for the most part forged and perfected by individuals as antithetical to Hillerman's seemingly staid temperament as is possible to imagine.[4]

During the late nineteenth and early twentieth centuries it was mainly the purview of social dilettantes, fallen British aristocrats like Wilkie Collins and Arthur Conan Doyle.[5] Theirs was the age — when England was still the reigning world power, before the Great War and at the very beginnings of real U.S. international muscle-flexing — of the "soft-boiled sleuth" and manor house murders, as G.K. Chesterton once noted, cast in the impossibly sentimental tones of snobbish rural ambiance derived from landed gentry and country estates.[6]

By the late 1920s, the detective venue had been largely taken over by commoners across the Atlantic, appropriated as *the* exemplary American literary enterprise, and redeployed in emblematic urban landscapes like San Francisco, Los Angeles and New York. It was honed and polished by a school of writers perfecting their craft in the pages of pulp magazines like *Black Mask*, creating a style of exposition stretched so taut and descriptive as to sometimes make the sparse sentences of Hemingway seem flabby by comparison.[7] It was riveting and exciting stuff, its pages literally crackling with tension, and it quickly attracted a mass audience. In short order, the idiom set the stage for a transcendence of itself, a translation into Humphrey Bogart's playing of Sam Spade in the Hollywood adaptation of Dashiell Hammett's *The Maltese Falcon* and Philip Marlowe in Raymond Chandler's *The Big Sleep*, movies which stamped notions of "heroically" bare-fisted, leadslinging, hard-drinking, chainsmoking, wisecracking, womanizing and (above all) "virile" and "hard-boiled" private-eyes indelibly upon the American consciousness.[8]

The authors of the stories, books and scripts making up the formative body of American detective fiction often, both as a matter of ego and as a calculated promotion of their work, associated themselves personally and directly with the characters they created. Chandler, Cornell Woolrich, Paul Cain, Jim Thompson, and many others were inveterate alcoholics and carousers who typically dressed in the manner attributed to their characters.[9] Hammett, anchored by his real-life status as a former Pinkerton detective, was — despite a severe lung disorder which eventually killed him — a three-pack-a-day smoker and near-legendary consumer of straight scotch.[10] In the end he was so possessed of the carefully nurtured image that he was actually the model upon which his *Thin Man* series was based and at least one contemporary writer has produced a novel (and resulting movie) in which

Hammett himself appears as the chief protagonist, a seedy but somewhat sexy synthesis of pulp writer and private eye which conforms quite well to the intricate web of misimpressions about the man so carefully spun by Hollywood publicists more than thirty years earlier.[11]

Mickey Spillane (Frank Morrison), to take another prominent if somewhat later example, tied his own persona so closely with that of Mike Hammer, the central figure in his dozens of novels, that he tended to speak only in a close approximation of the character's salty vernacular during radio and television interviews, and refused for years to appear in public without the trenchcoat and snap-brimmed fedora which were Hammer's trademarks. Rumors, untrue but well cultivated, that Spillane was himself a "hard case," packing a pistol in a shoulder holster and helping New York police detectives solve some of their really tough cases were far-flung during the 1950s and on into the '60s, during the period when the first *Mike Hammer* TV series was a weekly event. By the end of that decade, the author himself had been transformed into something of a cult personality.[12]

For its part, the *Hammer* show aired in the midst of what can only be fairly described as a saturation bombardment of programming devoted to comparable detective (and police) "realism." Fact and fantasy were deliberately blurred through such techniques, the posture and attitudes of fictional tough guys extrapolated into a sort of "reactionary hip" iconography absorbed by the population at large, particularly that segment composed of young white males (all detective characters of the period, like all the writers, being decisively Euroamerican and masculine).[13] Unquestionably, the sort of ideological and psychic conditioning which was occurring conformed quite nicely—despite the vaguely antiestablishmentarian aura with which tough guy detectives were conventionally imbued, a matter calculated to make such characters appealing to the masses of working class people their message was intended to reach—to the needs of the corporate elites who underwrote and produced them, week after week, year after year.[14]

Most illuminating in this proposition is the sort of value schemes and personal codes of conduct which the status quo considered it useful to inculcate among those considered to comprise the core of its military capacity. To illustrate, as the critic Julian Symons points out with regard to the sexual dimension imbedded in Spillane and other tough guy detective writing:

Women are seen as sexually desirable objects, and there are a good many descriptions of their bodies, but intercourse is often replaced by death or torture. In *I, the Jury*

70

(1947), Charlotte the beautiful psychiatrist makes several unsuccessful attempts to get Hammer into bed. At the end, when she turns out to be a multiple murderess, he shoots her in the stomach with pleasure. "How could you?" she asks incredulously, and he replies: "It was easy." At the end of *Kiss Me Deadly* (1952), the apparently lovely Lily reveals herself as "a horrible caricature of a human' whose body has been burned so that it is "a disgusting mass of twisted, puckered flesh from her knees to her neck." Hammer goes on to burn her to death, so that she becomes "a mass of flame tumbling on the floor with the blue flames of alcohol turning the white of her hair into black char and her body convulsing under the agony of it."[15]

There can be no doubt that the "ideal" represented in such admiring—one is tempted to say masturbatory—depictions of extreme psychosexual violence has had an incalculably negative effect in deforming gender relations in the United States, intensifying an already existing subjugation of women as a group and reinforcing the tacit social sanction which not only okayed rape as a male "sport," but fed into to all manner of other misogynist atrocities. And there is more, much more. In the metaphorical structure of the tough guy detective genre, strength and power (hence superiority, and therefore goodness) are invariably equated to masculinity, weakness and powerlessness (inferiority and badness) to feminity.[16]

The metaphors can plainly be extended beyond literal gender assignations, orchestrated to encompass virtually *any* set of power relations (race or international relations say, or matters devolving on class and ideology) in which *we* are to project *our* innate strength and the goodness. As the nazi leader Heinrich Himmler once formulated it in a speech to the officers of his Waffen SS—a select group within the German "master race" he was actively attempting to transform into psychological "supermen"—it is possible for a relatively small group of superior types to assert their "proper" role of domination over much larger bodies of inferiors only by realizing the "vision and, most of all, the *will*" to adopt a posture of "utmost hardness, even cruelty," to be "merciless" and overwhelmingly "virile."[17]

"Achieving the correct attitude of harshness" by which average people can be made to "do what must be done" to become dominant, Himmler concluded, "is by no means inevitable."[18] It requires concerted psychological conditioning, often by means which seem oblique, through constant bombardment with "parables," projection of "culture figures" (role models) appropriate to the purpose, and so forth. What is necessary is to create a requisite orientation and sensibility among the target population as a whole.[19] This sentiment can then be "sharpened" through more specific modes of ideological indoctrination, at least among selected subgroups such as police and military personnel, for purposes of practical application by the state. The nazis used tales of the Teutonic Knights and other Germanic legends to accomplish their mission.[20] In the post-war United States, detective fiction, and the deluge of films and television programs which attended it, served as a major component of the drive by socioeconomic and political elites to inculcate the desired sense of "toughness" of perspective within the public at large.[21]

In either case, the outlook insinuated into the collective consciousness was as logically perfect in its way as it was monstrous: Those who inflict torture and death are able to do so only because they possess and are willing to assert the power (and therefore the "goodness") to do so. Those who suffer such things do so only because they are weaker and therefore unable to avoid it. They are therefore bad ("evil"), and thus *deserve* their fate. The latter postulation affords not only the essential justification necessary for torture and murder to be properly systemic, but a basis for satisfaction, pride, even glee, on the part of the torturer-murderers. Reflections of Spillane's burning women may thus be glimpsed in the flaming peasant huts and napalmed children of Southeast Asia barely a decade after *Kiss Me Deadly* hit the stands, or, for that matter, in the charred corpses of a quarter-million fleeing Iraqis scattered along the "Highway of Death" in 1991.[22]

Similarly, echoes of Mike Hammer permeate such utterances as U.S. troops' laughing and habitual references to Vietnamese victims of the massive American use of incendiary weapons as "crispy critters," their cavalier dismissals of civilian dead under the contention that "if it's dead, it's a Vietcong" (known, "in country," as "the dead gook rule"), and the jovial, self-congratulatory descriptions of these same soldiers as "a damn fine bunch of killers" by officers like Brigadier General George S. Patton, III.[23] And again, much more recently, there are the haunting descriptions by U.S. pilots, quite literally leering at the recollections, of their roles in slaughtering already-defeated Iraqi opponents: "It was fun, kind of like a video arcade."[24] Needless to say, Himmler's SS troops—or the Marquis de Sade or Ted Bundy—would have felt perfectly at ease in such company.

The Ideological Function of Detective Fiction

All appearances to the contrary notwithstanding, the purpose of detective fiction has always been to reinforce the status quo. It was thus no accident that the genre arose when, where, and in the forms it did. In the context of late nineteenth century England, a mature but decaying empire, it was useful as a popular medium through which to transmit the message that the aristocracy, whatever its defects and idiosyncrasies, was inherently smarter and more able than those of lower station. The latter, it was explained, when left to their own devices, would inevitably engage in all manner of self-destructive mayhem. Hence, the function of the *private* detective in this venue, whether a semipro like Sherlock Holmes or a persistent amateur like Agatha Christie's Miss Marple, was and is to set an example of "social responsibility," providing an additional, usually unsolicited and entirely *voluntary* dimension of investigative acumen to an often less competent body of state officials. Institutional authority, often in spite of itself, might thus be preserved and strengthened through such well-directed "citizen participation." The underlying theme, of course, has always been that it is in everyone's best interests — and is therefore everyone's fundamental obligation — to do whatever he or she can to see the existing social order maintained.[25]

The United States of the early twentieth century, on the other hand, represented a very different setting, a burgeoning empire struggling to assume what its elites perceived as their "world historic role" of exercising first dominant, then hegemonic global power. It was a context in which a premium was placed, not upon the credentials and internal positioning requisite to management of a finished system of hierarchy, but upon savvy individual initiative and the ability to project the sheer physical force needed to expand an as yet incomplete imperialist structure.[26] The private eye in 1930s American fiction and film is meant not simply to reinforce or enhance the institutional order, but to assist directly in finalization of its symbolic terrain and contours. Always, they "walk point" on the fringes of official authority, serving as figurative expeditionary hunter-killer teams along its frontiers, intuitively serving that "higher law" from which the codified civic version derives, expanding the psychic territory of the state at every step along the way.[27]

Whatever the imagined tension between those "irregular" methods utilized by tough guy fiction's private-eyes and the supposedly tame, incompetent or corrupt orthodoxy of regular police investigators and public officials, both sides ultimately realize they are the *same* side, that each is necessary if an implicitly understood "greater good" is to be accomplished. Ends inevitably justify means, and only "bad guys" get killed along the way. By the time Spillane came along in the aftermath of World War II, with America standing supreme on the world stage, the pathology was thoroughly established. As Symons puts it:

> Power is the law of the world to Spillane's Mike Hammer, who says, "The cops can't break a guy's arm to make him talk, and they can't shove his teeth in with the muzzle of a .45 to remind him that they aren't fooling." Hammer, however, can and often does do these things, and they are described with relish. When he breaks a man's fingers and then smashes an elbow into his mouth, the "shattered teeth tore my arm and his mouth became a great hole of welling blood" while "his fingers were broken stubs sticking back at odd angles."[28]

At base, this is little different than the sort of characters and thematics developed much earlier by writers—from James Fenimore Cooper's Natty Bumppo to Ned Buntline's Wyatt Earp and Wild Bill Hickock—of "rugged individualists" motivated by the narrow tedium of "civilized life" to repeatedly denounce its constrictions, "escaping" into one or another "untamed wilderness" in which the are "free" to conduct themselves with utmost barbarity. Inevitably, such antisocial behavior is necessary and commendable, providing sometimes inadvertent but always sterling service to the very order against which it is ostensibly posed, its consequences being an ultimate "taming of the wilds" and ushering in of civilization.[29] The fictive literature elaborating this "adventurous" dialectic of conquest for mass consumption served the systemic needs of its day, providing the popular rationalizations and motivations necessary to energize Euroamerica's "Manifest Destiny" of inexorable expansion across the face of North America.[30] It is but a short step from conquest to consolidation:

> Actually, as critics have pointed out, the private detective [in the U.S.] is a direct carryover from the lone western gunfighter, that mythic folk hero who righted wrongs with a weapon at his hip and who preserved ideals of justice in the face of raw frontier violence. In later years, as *Black Mask* put its full emphasis on big city crime, the old and new West blended into the figure of the mythic private eye who rode into the sunset at the wheel of a Ford and who packed a .45 in his armpit in place of a Colt at his hip. But, basically, he was the same man.[31]

Where "savage" Indians, "dirty" Mexicans, "greasy" Latins (usually "spics" or Italian gangsters) and other such racially defined barriers to the orderly progression and functioning of American empire had been the typical targets of WASPish heroes in previous western and detective fiction, Spillane's work assumed an increasingly overt and reactionary political cant. "I killed more people tonight than I have fingers on my hands," Mike

Hammer recounts in *One Lonely Night* (1951). "I shot them in cold blood and enjoyed every minute of it. . . . They were commies . . . red sons-of-bitches who should have died long ago."[32] By such means as western and detective novels, and the movies made from them, "criminality" had by then become identified primarily with "un-American" deviation from the "values" underlying presumptions of natural class (as well as racial and gender) supremacy by North America's ruling elites, a matter amply reflected in the McCarthyite witch-hunting of the same period. Whatever "Senator Joe" and the boys dished out to those guilty of thinking impure thoughts, it was okay, because subversives were deserving of far worse in the mass fantasizing inspired but Spillane's "gritty" phrasing.[33] The books sold by the millions.

Whatever else might be said, such conditioning of public sensibilities could not help but play a significant role in shaping the mentality, and Middle America's tacit acceptance of it, that went into development of sophisticated, highly secretive and virulently reactionary political repression components within most big city police departments during the 1960s. The same principle might be applied to the FBI's COINTELPROs, operations devoted explicitly to the extralegal "neutralization" of "politically objectionable" citizens between 1955 and 1971.[34] It is further applicable with regard to the CIA's various programs during the same period to destabilize or destroy popular movements and governments abroad, often through the literal murder of selected organizers, leaders and heads of state.[35] On the contrary, the latter agency's activities in prosecuting what policymakers liked to call the Cold War were simply and neatly sanitized for public acceptance through the fashioning of a whole new subgenre of detective novels and films called "spy thrillers."[36]

Nor were such things restricted to a relatively abstract coaxing of the body politic to go along with or even applaud the systematic "excesses" of investigative, intelligence and police operatives. The average citizen was also expected, upon demand by "higher authority," to participate directly, putting such sentiments into practice. Domestically, this was manifested in such phenomena as the "Legion of Justice" in Chicago, an outright vigilante organization interlocked with police and intelligence agencies.[37] Another salient illustration was creation of the "Secret Army Organization," a private paramilitary formation, controlled to a considerable extent by the FBI and devoted to assisting in the curtailment of political "subversion" via a campaign of terrorism, including assassination of key activists.[38]

The sense of what was going on at home, and its relationship to U.S. activities elsewhere in the world, was perhaps captured most succinctly by an American colonel in Vietnam, early in 1968: "We had to destroy the village," he said, "in order to save it."[39] Yes, and Wyatt Earp, Philip Marlowe and Mike Hammer *must* habitually ignore the law if the order it supposedly represents is to be maintained, the government *must* destroy its political opposition if it is to guarantee "our political liberty," and everyone *must* "do what they're told," meekly taking their assigned places within the carefully crafted American socioeconomic hierarchy so that we may all "live free."[40] Obviously, if detective fiction had never come to exist on its own, it would have been vitally necessary for the status quo to invent it.

Why Hillerman?

The question remains as to how any of this might apply to Tony Hillerman. Far from wandering about in trenchcoat or slouch hat (or jack-boots), he usually appears casually attired in slacks or Levis and a sports shirt, sometimes a cardigan or crew-neck sweater. There is no indication at all that he suffers a speech impediment causing him to utter clipped phrases from the corner of his mouth, nor has he proven himself prone to inflammatory polit-ical statements of any sort; in conversation, his orientation seems blandly lib-eral, a bit preoccupied with matters like "social equality" and "environmental standards." Nor does he lay claim to the "authenticity" of a real-life back-ground in police or intelligence work, not even to having emphasized these areas during his stints as a reporter and newspaper editor; the one time he was asked to appear as an expert witness in a murder trial, he declined on the basis that he lacked anything which might be reasonably described as exper-tise on the subject at hand.[41] The overt celebrations of racism, misogyny and sadism infesting so much earlier detective fiction are not only missing from, but seem entirely antithetical to both his personality and his manner of exposition; he appears almost squeamish about discourses on blood and guts. So, how is it he has attained such standing and credibility as a writer of mod-ern American detective novels?

Let it be said, first of all, that the man can write. While clearly not the literary equal of either Hammett or Chandler, the last of whom he claims as a figurative mentor,[42] Hillerman can at least hold his own with the "second tier" standards of wordsmithing set by Spillane and, more recently, Ross Macdonald and Charles Willeford.[43] Needless to say, the quality of his material far surpasses that of assembly line hack writers like S.S. Van Dine, Leslie Chartiris, Earl Stanley Gardiner, Rex Stout, and Ellery Queen.[44] The spare style of structure and exposition he acquired in his years as a journalist has plainly stood Hillerman in good stead during his shift to penning novels. His books are, technically speaking, always an abundantly "good read." Yet, undeniably, there is no great shortage of equally talented writers out there. There is something much more, something of decisive utility to the status quo, involved in Hillerman's success than his ability to turn a crisp and tidy phrase.

To find this "something," we must look to certain critical factors which have come to alter the style with which power has been wielded in the U.S. since the 1960s. Salient in this regard is the U.S. defeat in Southeast Asia and the concomitant exposure of the sheer falsity bound up in the myth of white male invincibility this entailed. Certainly, the agony of losing in a major military adventure precipitated a crisis of confidence (and loss of consensus about how to proceed), even among U.S. elites.[45] This brought on a lengthy period during which America's imperial ideology was reconstructed in an effort to overcome what was called the "Vietnam Syndrome."[46] One means to this reconstruction was inculcation of a new sense of "participation and inclusiveness" centered on the imperial core of North America itself, a structure in which even the most oppressed would be increasingly solicited and employed to impose the order which formed the basis of their oppression. Popular literature and electronic media, of course, played primary roles in bringing about this necessary transition in public sensibilities.

As concerns the utilization of detective fiction as a medium by which to attain such results, the process was laid out rather clearly by Roger Simon, creator of the Moses Wine character portrayed by Richard Dreyfus in the movie version of *The Big Fix*, during the 1988 International Crime Writers Conference: After the U.S. military loss in Indochina, Watergate, the rise of feminism, the black liberation movement, the new left, and gay rights activism, those famous "mean streets" of Philip Marlowe and Mike Hammer have become at best passé. More often, they are downright embarrassing, the image of Euroamerican supermen they represent having been so thoroughly discredited over the preceding thirty years by everyone from Ho Chi Minh to Rita Mae Brown.[47]

In 1958, the public was glued to its collective television set watching *M-Squad*, an unabashed celebration of white male violence proudly proclaimed by its star, Lee Marvin, to portray "Chicago's SS."[48] By 1968, such fare had been replaced with programs like *The Mod Squad*, a much less graphically violent series featuring three young "countercultural" figures, including a woman and a black man, "doing the right thing" by working as snitches for the police.[49]

The writer who wishes to succeed in attaining the goals of contemporary detective writing can do so only by creating characters which eschew conventional formulas in favor of apparent opposites. The hero may be a heroine, as in the work of Sara Paretsky and Sue Grafton, but never (ever!) in the clichéd, frumpy manner of Miss Marple.[50] He or she may be gay or lesbian, as Joseph Hansen and others have lately demonstrated, but only when portrayed in a manner reflecting "credit" on his or her preference.[51] In the event a heterosexual male is selected as a lead character, he need be "sensitive," not particularly good looking, frequently fallible, and usually "not-quite-white" (e.g., Jewish). It has proven helpful to provide such characters with a slightly stale but still noticeable "rad-lib" political cant.[52]

Another helpful twist is to have him married, but to a wife who has left him because of his obvious shortcomings; a sizable portion of his usually meager earnings should go by court order to support of his several children, preferably daughters requiring expensive dental work.[53] Neat bourbon by the shot should whenever possible be replaced by Perrier water (or at least white wine), appreciable time and emotional energy should be spent trying to kick a persistent smoking habit, and firearms should be treated as something to be fumbled with in moments of extreme peril (proving that violence in behalf of order is, however much we might wish it otherwise, is still an "unfortunate necessity").[54]

The resulting stew is extremely and intentionally deceptive. While first appearances are carefully crafted to suggest a thoroughgoing deconstruction and disposal of everything Hammeresque in detective fiction, the reality is quite the reverse. In the manner of George Bush's speech writers, the new stable of "innovative" detective novelists have simply offered up a "kinder, gentler" impression of business-as-usual. The central values defended by today's private sleuths—regardless of their race or ethnicity, gender, sexual proclivities, degree of addiction to health food, or inability to place a bullet in the center of the target—are exactly those held by earlier tough guys like Spade and Marlowe. Although they might never agree on the menu for lunch, yesterday's private eyes and today's "more diverse" roster share an inherent consensus about who are the bad guys and who are the good.

Whatever their stylistic differences, *M-Squad* and *Mod Squad* remain equally committed to serving the same master, accepting precisely the same structure of order and hierarchy, and pursuing exactly the same goals and objectives.

The key to the success of any endeavor of this sort lies squarely in fostering the delusion among the population at large that the emergence of such tendencies within various oppressed groups represent a dimension of "good," while simultaneously reinforcing preexisting notions that tendencies which go in other directions—resisting or seeking dismantlement of the oppressing system—represent "bad."[55] In this way a broker or *comprador* class is drawn from among the oppressed themselves, participating in their own colonization through acceptance of managerial and/or enforcement positions within the colonial system, thereby lending an impression, carefully orchestrated for general consumption by propagandists for the status quo, that a consensus on the legitimacy of the system has been reached between colonizer and colonized.[56] The new detective fiction, and the characters who inhabit it, are an integral component in this process of U.S. imperial maturation, and it is here that Tony Hillerman may be said to have truly come to the fore.

Colonial Structure in Native North America

Unlike most empires, the heart of that manifested by the United States is its own "homeland." Approximately one-third of the continental U.S. was never, by any definition, legally acquired from its native owners and is therefore illegally occupied at the present moment.[57] Within this utterly usurped landbase lies a vast proliferation of mineral resources (see p. xi of this volume).[58] Maintenance of unrestricted internal colonial control over these assets belonging to the 400-odd indigenous nations resident to the "lower forty-eight" and Alaska is an absolute cornerstone to continuation of the U.S. as a world power.[59] The question, of course, is how best to accomplish this objective.

As has been remarked elsewhere, colonialism—whether internal or external—evidences several distinct stages. First there are processes of conquest, subordination and direct rule by the colonizing power. Direct rule is then usually replaced by sectors of the colonized population subverted into serving the colonizer, both in terms of administration and in terms of muscle. This is a lesson the British learned long ago, when they discovered that, "properly oriented," the Gurkha Rifles and Bengal Native Light Infantry might serve as better, more efficient keepers of England's imperial order than could English troops themselves.[60] The French, too, arrived at such a realization, developing as a result the concepts of the Foreign Legion and the use of Algerians rather than Frenchmen as colonial police.[61] The same thrust in thinking is readily apparent in the U.S. "Public Safety Program" of the 1960s, training Latin American police operatives to "autonomously" impose the order of North American interests on their own people.[62]

With regard to Native North America, the script needed for this purpose might be expected to follow a course lifted straight out of *The Legend of the Lone Ranger*, that time-honored medium for explaining the proper roles of Indians and whites to children of both groups. In the new "enlightened" and *adult* version, Tonto — having long-since aligned himself with the Ranger's (Euroamerica's) intrinsic goodness (superiority) by habitually ("faithfully") licking his better's boots — finally reaches the point of "realizing himself as a total human being." The route to this end will not be found in Tonto's original identity and autonomy as a nonwestern being. No ending of his degradation will come through, say, a richly deserved slitting of his master's throat.[63]

Instead, with the Hillerman mystery novel as his vehicle, Tonto demonstrates that his polished self-denigration and subservience has at last prepared him, the Indian, to assume the Ranger's mantle, proving once and for all that he too can be "just as good" ("civilized") as his master ever was. The latter can thus retire to enjoy the fruits of his labor, the long, lonely, and often brutal toil of imposing the hallowed virtues of rational order upon a world filled with the irrational evils of disorder.[64]

Readers can thus relax, secure in the cunningly implanted knowledge that even the most obviously colonized segment of the North American population, the Indians, now agree that "the system works" for one and all. It took a while to figure it out, but we really *do* share the same essential values and beliefs when we get right down to it. At a "gut level," we all want the same things, for the same reasons, and are prepared to do the same things to get them.[65] Exotic little differences in pigmentation aside, we are all — "black, white, yellow, red, brown, purple and polka dot" — distinguishable primarily on the basis of mere cultural particularities, diversity around a common theme, the spice of life in a "pluralistic society" which is moving (or has moved) "beyond substantial questions of race and ethnicity."[66] We can now all "feel good about ourselves." Why worry? Be happy. I'm okay, you're okay. Meanwhile, despite the pleasurable hallucinatory sensations produced by this narcotizing facade, the perpetual hemorrhaging of Native America goes on and on, unconstrained by public outcry, safely out of sight and mind.

Hillerman Stew

The conventional wisdom holds that Hillerman's singular achievement, aside from bringing the western and the detective novel together in a uniquely sustained fusion, has been "humanitarian," even "liberatory" with regard to Native America. His books, beginning with their main characters, are populated by American Indians who, in ways and to an extent previously absent in the tradition of Euroamerican letters, are provided the dimensionality, motivation and nuance necessary to establish them as bona fide people rather than mere props in the popular mind. Further, for one of the very few times in popular fiction, the Indians in his work—the lead characters at least—are projected unqualifiedly as good guys; they are honest and courageous, courteous and strong, beset by just enough doubt, confusion and frailty to make them wholly believable. By contrast, the white folk who inhabit these tales, from anthropologists to FBI agents to erstwhile girl-friends, come off rather the worse for wear, at least in terms of personal integrity and likability. Such "role reversal" takes on a handy appearance of "pro-Indianism."

Indeed, at one level, Hillerman has managed—almost singlehandedly, to hear his enthusiasts tell it—to reverse the stream of the kind of anti-Indian sentiment which has flowed virtually without interruption across the pages of American literature since British colonists first set foot in Virginia in 1607.[67] Through his efforts, an appreciable portion of the American reading public, few of whom are actually Indians, have for the first time found themselves identifying directly with native characters, thereby understanding the modern Indian circumstance in ways which have never before been possible for them. The question before us, however, is the matter of exactly *which* Indians—or tendencies within native communities—Hillerman has selected to treat sympathetically in his books and thus legitimate as being emblematic of Native America as a whole. Conversely, there is a question as to which persons and tendencies his formulations tend (and are intended) to discredit.

Here, there really is no mystery. Hillerman's two heroes, Joe Leaphorn and Jim Chee, are members of the Navajo "tribal" police force. The police units in question, at Navajo and everywhere else, were formed during the nineteenth century, not by the indigenous people they were designed to "regulate," but by the U.S. Army in collaboration with an assortment of agents sent by the Departments of War and Interior.[68] Plainly, the federal rationale in creating and maintaining these paramilitary entities among peoples the U.S. had recently conquered was never remotely concerned with seeing to it that they retained (or regained) a capacity to enforce their own laws among themselves. To the contrary, the express intent of the exercise was from the outset to usurp and destroy native concepts of legality and order, imposing in their stead a system of rules devised in Washington, D.C., all of them meant to subordinate indigenous nations to the will of the United States, undermining their sociocultural integrity and destroying their ability to resist domination by Euroamerica.[69]

The role of these Indian surrogates for U.S. power has never been especially abstract. In a number of instances, those who were to become the nucleus of the original police units had served as scouts for the army, fighting against their own people's struggles to remain free and independent. Subsequently, they were used, notably in the cases of the great Lakota patriots Crazy Horse and Sitting Bull, to assassinate key leaders of the ongoing indigenous resistance to U.S. rule.[70] During the late nineteenth and first half of the twentieth centuries, they also lent themselves consistently to putting teeth into programs meant to eradicate even deeper layers of internal cohesion within native cultures, targeting the traditional spiritual leadership by arresting and sometimes imprisoning those "guilty" of conducting such central religious ceremonies as the Sun Dance and Potlatch.[71] Once federal authorities had installed outright puppet governments on most reservations pursuant to their 1934 "Indian Reorganization Act" (IRA), the Indian police were included as subparts.[72] As early as the mid-'70s, they played a key role in repressing efforts by traditional Oglala Lakota people on the Pine Ridge Reservation to depose an exceptionally corrupt IRA regime; at least sixty-nine Indians were murdered during this counterinsurgency campaign, mostly at the hands of Leaphorn's and Chee's real-life counterparts.[73]

In the context of other nations—Norway, say, or France—the word normally used to describe such outlooks and behaviors is "treason." To clarify by analogy, if Hillerman were to write a novel set in occupied Norway during World War II, and remain consistent with the character formulations he has used throughout the Chee/Leaphorn novels, he would have no alternative but to script the notorious nazi collaborator and puppet leader, Vikdun Quisling, as the book's most heroic figure.[74] Perhaps a better analogy would be if the hypothetical novel were set in nazi-occupied France. Then the heroes would have to be the police of the Vichy puppet regime, working closely with the Gestapo while enforcing Hitler's New Order upon their people.[75] In context, these *are* the only counterparts to Chee and Leaphorn. One might find interesting precedents to such "unique" and "innovative" story lines in the material produced by Josef Goebbels' nazi propaganda ministry during the period in which Germany occupied both countries. Certainly, there are more than ample antecedents to Hillerman's characterizations of American Indians in "Gunga Din" and others of Rudyard Kipling's literary apologetics for British colonialism in East India.[76]

In a manner typical of imperial literature everywhere, the sympathetic portrait Hillerman draws of the most traitorous elements resident to North America's Indian Country carries in it undeniable implications regarding how he *must* depict the remainder of the native societies with which he deals. Put simply, if his heroes are to be those most sold out to the colonizing order, then it stands to reason that the less sold out, more traditionally oriented a character, the greater the degree of silliness and/or negativity which must be assigned to him or her.[77] Hence, a theme running like a river through the Leaphorn/Chee novels is that traditional Navajo and Hopi societies are predicated in an inexplicably irrational complex of beliefs infested by all manner of goblins and demons. These childlike outlooks give rise to a steady series of innately evil individuals, "witches" who adopt the personae of "skinwalkers," "bad kachinas" and the like.[78] Because of the inordinate power held by these witches within their own cultures — traditional folk are as a whole usually terrorized by them to the point of trauma in Hillerman's stories — they are often selected for manipulation by sinister non-Indians pursuing an assortment of nefarious ends.

Since the traditionals are automatically incapacitated by the evil ones among them, and thus subject to endless victimization by a seemingly infinite array of villains, it falls to a nice, college-educated, Euro-oriented boy like Jim Chee — or his older and crustier, but equally Euro-oriented police mentor, Joe Leaphorn — to save them, protecting them from their own naïve fallibilities over and over and over again (*Listening Woman* is a prime example of this emphasis developed to its full potential). Small wonder that Leaphorn professes a near-total disinterest in Navajo tradition. Chee, for his part, is cast as being curious but perpetually baffled by the sheer and often perverse stupidity imbedded in the culture of which he is supposedly a part. It is easy to understand why he might be given to endless deep contemplation of the meaning of it all, perched as he is upon the peak of superior knowledge provided him by the anthropology department at Arizona State University. He is bound up irretrievably in the world of Kipling's discourses on "wogs" and "white man's burdens."[79]

Hillerman, as even his staunchest admirers have been sometimes willing to admit, has had to engage in considerable distortion of Navajo ethnography in order make the good and evil dimensions of his heavily larded moral plays work out.[80] And there is much more to it than that. There are two absolutely unbreachable rules the author deploys when developing every one of his "Indian" novels (most emphatically in *Skinwalkers*, *Talking God* and *Dancehall of the Dead*):

- First, Euroamericans are *always* the smart guys, manipulating Indians in criminal endeavors, *never* the other way around. Although usually understated in Hillerman's work, this no is more than a conventional ploy to reinforce the smug sense of Eurosupremacism permeating the U.S. reading mainstream. The only reasonably intelligent Indians on the scene are invariably Leaphorn and Chee, adherents to the rules of the Euroamerican status quo. The message to be drawn is that if Indians wish to stop suffering, they should abandon all this "Other Cultural" claptrap, and buy into the system as rapidly as possible. As a whole, Hillerman's construction speaks sly volumes about the "inevitability" of native subordination to Eurocentric values and ideologies. Such themes play well these days, not only among Wall Street conservatives, hard-hat types and federal officials, but more especially liberal yuppie readers who have "grown tired" of hearing that their position and mobility are based in the oppression and exploitation of non-white peoples.[81]

- Second, Euroamerican bad guys are *always* individuals, "criminals" who have deviated from the rules of procedure laid down by the status quo while striking out on their own for unapproved purposes (in other words, their actions stand to interfere with more orderly and institutionalized forms of criminal conduct). They are *never* representatives of the governmental/corporate entities—the Bureau of Indian Affairs, Bureau of Reclamation, Bureau of Land Management, Army Corps of Engineers, U.S. Marshals Service, FBI, Peabody Coal, Anaconda, Kerr-McGee, Westinghouse, et al.—which have demonstrably victimized Indians far more extensively and systematically than any individual(s). This too is a standard device, consistently used by detective novelists and other propagandists to divert attention away from the real nature of the problems suffered by "common people," replacing it with the illusion that "real" issues are caused by the "deviant" actions—often on the part of the victims themselves—which are always systemically solvable. Resolution of fictional problems can thus be located in the very structures which generate the real-world problems of the oppressed.[82] Needless to say, both conservative and liberal Euroamericans are delighted to learn that the source of daily agony for oppressed people of color lies not in the structure of white supremacism, but in deviation from its order and values.

So conscientious has Hillerman been in the latter regard that he has managed to write ten consecutive novels providing ostensibly detailed descriptions of the habitat of Navajoland, and the people who reside in it, without ever once mentioning the vast proliferation of uranium tailings piles abandoned by U.S. corporations—with full governmental complicity—on the reservation since 1952. He makes no remark at all upon the cancers, congenital birth defects, and other health problems among the Navajo brought on by such government-corporate practices, matters which presently constitute a major crisis for the Navajo Nation.[83]

Nor does he refer in any way to the massive and ongoing stripmining for coal which is destroying the Navajo and Hopi landbases, or the forced relocation of more than 13,000 traditional Navajo sheepherders which is accompanying this mining in the Big Mountain area. Missing too is mention of the catastrophic depletion of ground water, chemical and radioactive contamination of surface water, rapidly deteriorating air quality due to the location of massive coal-fired electrical generating facilities on Navajo land, destruction of sacred sites, and all the rest of the damage done by the Euroamerican status quo to the land and peoples depicted so "sympathetically" in the Chee/Leaphorn novels.[84] The list of omissions might be continued at length, but suffice to say simply that such "politically sensitive" issues are strictly off-limits within the framework of Hillerman's literary project.

The Political Message of Tony Hillerman

With such sincerely posed dexterity does he pull this off that one might almost be willing to accept, despite the highly politicized nature of his cross-cultural characterizations, Hillerman's own and oft-repeated assertion that his is an apolitical intent. Depiction of the colonial police as honorable and value-neutral figures might, after all, be merely a regrettable, even reprehensible, but nonetheless unwitting regurgitation of Indian-white stereotypes subconsciously absorbed during a lifetime's furtherance of "objective journalism."[85] It might also be plausible, just barely, that his decision to avoid completely the questions of government-corporate impact upon the land and lives he purports to reveal has been borne more by some weird sort of ignorance or unwillingness to face facts than by a politically motivated desire to obfuscate certain fundamental truths. All of this *might* be believable, were it not for the fact that he has occasionally ventured into the domain of overt political content. Here, he tips his hand in ways which refute any possible disclaimer.

This goes to his willingness to depict, sometimes at great length and always in a manner both devoid of contextualization and framed in the most viciously demeaning and inaccurate ways, the politics of indigenous resistance to colonial rule. Take, for example, *Talking God*. Hillerman opens with perhaps the finest chapter he has ever written, having a young mixed-blood Navajo who works for the Smithsonian Institution, weary of fruitless arguments against the museum's practice of desecrating Indian graves and "collecting" the skeletal remains therein, make his point by digging up the curator's grandparents and shipping them to her in a box. The administrator is properly appalled at the turnabout. The message seems clear and entirely appropriate to the situation. But, having thus entered the credentials of his understanding in the matter, Hillerman devotes much of the rest of the book to administering a raft of punishment to the Indian, whom he plainly considers guilty of a deep transgression against institutional order and authority.

The character is developed as being tragically confused about his identity, a weak and pathetic creature desperately grasping for a cause, and ultimately one of the villains. In the end, we are left to conclude there was nothing actually wrong with the Smithsonian's systematic grave robbery, all protests by similarly misguided "wannabe" Indians notwithstanding. "Real" natives like Jim Chee, who helps track the boy down, are unconcerned with such things. In fact, Hillerman has Chee explain at one point, the Navajos—afflicted as they are with a host of rather sublime superstitions about the dead—might actually *prefer* that the bones of their ancestors be gathered up and warehoused in remote Euroamerican facilities like the Smithsonian. Consequently, what becomes inappropriate and offensive in this thinly-veiled polemic is the "arrogance" and "wrongheadedness" of real-life Indian "militants" attempting to challenge the colonial order's self-proclaimed "right" to take from native people whatever it desires at any given moment.[86]

Listening Woman provides an even better example (or a worse one, depending on your point of view). Here, we find Hillerman busily deploying an imaginary "splinter group" of the American Indian Movement derived from a 1976 FBI counterintelligence operation designed to discredit "Indian radicals." Known as the "Dog Soldier Teletypes," the disinformational documents involved were secretly leaked to the press by the Bureau's "media liaisons" as a means of establishing the public impression that AIM was a supremely bloodthirsty outfit, a portion of which was preparing to commit all manner of gratuitously violent acts against a random sample of innocent non-Indians. FBI Director Clarence M. Kelley was subsequently forced to admit under oath that there was "not one shred" of evidence supporting this characterization of any known element of the movement. The whole thing was nothing more than an elaborate and highly illegal hoax perpetrated by the Bureau as a means to garner popular support for the lethal campaign of political repression its agents were waging against the movement at the time.[87]

Having been so thoroughly and publicly debunked, one would think this particularly malignant lie might have been left to wither away into the nothingness it obviously warrants. Perhaps things would even have worked out that way, had Tony Hillerman not elected to utilize his rising popularity as a platform upon which to lend it new life in somewhat amplified form. In the resuscitated, retooled and revitalized—but hardly disguised—version developed for *Listening Woman*, the AIM Dog Soldier fable once again cloaks native activism in the garb of "terrorism."[88] To this end, the author deploys a character, referred to throughout as "gold-rims," to recruit a strange assortment of misfits for an absurdly postulated "program" entailing the kidnapping and murder of more-or-less randomly selected whites. The numbers of intended victims correspond to the casualties recorded as having been sustained by various Indian peoples in massacres occurring a hundred years and more ago.[89]

As it turns out, gold-rims himself has never believed for a moment in the bizarre conception of justice to which he attracts others. To the contrary, Hillerman has him using his depraved adherents as mere cannon fodder in a cynical scheme to enrich himself. Plainly, folk of his ilk are unworthy of support by anyone, Indian or non-Indian.[90] Equally clearly, the author wishes to lead his readers to the conclusion that a public service was performed through the extermination visited upon these mad dogs by Joe Leaphorn at the end of the book. From there, it is an easy step to applying the same rule to the *real* AIM members who have suffered the same fate at the hands of the *real* Indian police.[91] Indian radicalism, when it is not utterly mercenary, Hillerman's message reads, has its head mired hopelessly and irrationally in the past, its adherents are little more than psychotic killers bent on visiting retribution upon innocent people for "tragedies" occurring generations hence.[92]

The man is nothing if not consistent. Without exception, American Indian resistance to conquest and colonization, whether active or passive, signifies that which is evil and therefore to be overcome in Hillerman's books, just as "Communism" once did in Spillane's, and "labor agitation" did in some of Hammett's earliest work. Indigenous compliance with the colonial system is always good, and direct participation in or service to it is even better. The "best" among his Indian characters no longer even require direction from their Euroamerican overlords; they simply enforce colonialism's dictates against themselves. Indeed. And it follows that if the Vichy French who worked with the Gestapo were heroes, the partisans they tortured and murdered were of necessity villains.[93]

What is right rests in Hillerman's schema, naturally and perfectly, with the power of the colonial status quo; what is wrong and defective is reposited among the relatively powerless colonized. America's New World Order is not simply to be accepted or condoned, it is to be embraced, supported and applauded. That which impairs the functioning of that Order will be destroyed by any and all available means, not merely as a matter of grudging necessity, but unquestioningly, as a stimulus response, with the confidence and pleasure which comes with acting in accordance with some Higher Law.[94] It is all as inevitable as glaciation and that fact alone serves to reconcile and justify whatever it is that "must be done" as a means to "move things along."[95]

Ultimately, despite all the superficial and misleading distinctions with which he has been so careful to imbue his image, there is no incongruousness in Tony Hillerman's presence among the peculiar roster of personalities making up detective fiction's list of noted authors. Fundamentally, there is no difference whatsoever, all superficialities of style and presentation aside, between the logic and meaning of a Hillerman and that of a Mickey Spillane. The end is the same, and for precisely the same reasons, no matter whether the main protagonist is an enthusiastically efficient practitioner of torture and homicide like Mike Hammer or a better-natured cop like Jim Chee who must always fumble for the gun locked in his glove compartment.

And, if the way in which Spillane has Hammer impose order upon the disorderly oppressed can be properly termed "reactionary and sadistic," how much *more* sadistic is it for Hillerman to dispense with Hammer altogether? The maneuver changes nothing other than to exonerate the colonizers of direct participation in the sheer ugliness of the colonial process by eliminating their figurative representative as a key player. Much crueler in its subtle way is Hillerman's tactic of imparting willing complicity—often even full responsibility—to the colonized for the fact, continuation and perfection of their own colonization.

Spillane at least was more-or-less open about who he was and why, as were Hammett and Chandler before him. Hillerman's charade of not only providing but *being* their opposite number, capturing as it does the loyalties of a much broader contemporary audience, is far less honest. It is also much more sophisticated, efficient and dangerous, the logical next step in a popular literary progression reflecting the culminating phase of America's imperial pretensions. When all is said and done, one need not be a master detective to solve the "mystery" of why the Jim Chee/Joe Leaphorn novels have received such accolades from establishment reviewers. Both because the context of U.S.-Indian relations he has been canny enough to address and rationalize is of such absolutely vital importance to maintenance of the status quo, and because he holds the requisite writerly proficiency to make the project work, Tony Hillerman has been anointed to a position at the very crest of his chosen genre. It follows that his books lack even the slightest connection to liberatory literature. They are instead the very quintessence of modern colonialist fiction in the United States.

Notes

1. All of Hillerman's Leaphorn/Chee novels except *Sacred Clowns* have been published by Harper & Row. The latter was published by HarperCollins.

2. The quotes are taken from the dust jacket of *A Thief of Time*.

3. Ibid.

4. Poe, who suffered from chronic depression and hallucinations, never managed a booklength effort. Further, many of his stories, written between 1837 and 1849, would be more properly classified as horror than detective fiction. For the literary output, see *Complete Stories and Poems of Edgar Allen Poe* (Garden City, NY: Doubleday, 1966). Biographically, see Daniel Hoffman, *Poe Poe Poe Poe Poe Poe* (New York: Houghton-Mifflin, 1972).

5. Collins' *The Moonstone*, first published in 1868, is generally credited as being the first "real" detective novel, although others, such as William Goodwin's *Things as They Are; or, The Adventures of Caleb Williams* (London, 1794) were written earlier. Conan Doyle's four novels and 56 short stories featuring Sherlock Holmes and Watson, written in a stream which encompassed the last quarter of the nineteenth century and first quarter of the twentieth, established detective fiction as a viable form in its own right. For the complete works, see William S. Barring-Gould, ed., *The Annotated Sherlock Holmes*, 2 vols. (New York: Clark N. Pottinger, 1967). For context, see Audrey Peterson, *Victorian Masters of the Mystery: From Wilkie Collins to Conan Doyle* (New York: Frederick Ungar, 1984).

6. G.K. Chesterton, "A Defense of Detective Stories," in his *Twelve Types* (London, 1902). See generally, Dudley Barker, *G.K. Chesterton: A Biography* (New York: Stein & Day, 1973).

7. The best firsthand account of the *Black Mask* days is Frank Guber's *The Pulp Jungle* (Los Angeles: Sherborne Press, 1967). A fine sampling of the material published therein will be found in Herbert Ruhm, ed., *The Hard-Boiled Detective* (New York: Vintage, 1977). Ample bibliographical information is available in E.R. Hageman's *Comprehensive Index to* Black Mask, *1920–1951* (Bowling Green, OH: Bowling Green University Popular Press, 1982).

8. The films were based on Hammett's *The Maltese Falcon* (New York: Alfred A. Knopf, 1930) and Chandler's *The Big Sleep* (New York: Alfred A. Knopf, 1939). For an overview of the emergence of the cinematic detective genre, see Jon Tuska, *The Detective in Hollywood* (Garden City, NY: Doubleday, 1978).

9. See, e.g., David Madden, ed., *Tough Guy Writers of the Thirties* (Carbondale: Southern Illinois University Press, 1968). Also see Richard Laymon, *Beams Falling: The Art of Dashiell Hammett* (Bowling Green, OH: Bowling Green University Popular Press, 1979); Dorothy Gardiner and Katherine S. Walker, eds., *Raymond Chandler Speaking* (New York: Houghton-Mifflin, 1962).

10. On Hammett's history as a Pinkerton, his alcoholism, his smoking and tuberculosis, see Richard Lyman, *Shadow Man: The Life of Dashiell Hammett* (New York: Harcourt, Brace, Jovanovich, 1981); William F. Nolan, *Hammett: A Life at the Edge* (New York: Congden & Weed, 1983); Diane Johnson, *Dashiell Hammett: A Life* (New York: Random House, 1983).

11. For the character he imbued most heavily with his own persona, see Hammett's *The Thin Man* (New York: Alfred A. Knopf, 1934); *A Man Named Thin* (New York: Ferman, 1932). MGM based six movies on this character, beginning with *The Thin Man* (1936) and ending with *The Song of the Thin Man* (1947). The next in question is Joe Goes's *Hammett* (New York: G.P. Putnam, 1975).

12. The NBC *Mike Hammer* series, starring Darren McGavin, ran from 1958 through the 1960 season, following in the footsteps of such gumshoe groundbreakers as *Martin Kane, Private Eye* (NBC: 1949–53, 1957), *Man Against Crime* (CBS: 1949–53, 1956), *The Adventures of Ellery Queen* (NBC: 1950–54), *The Thin Man* (NBC: 1957–60), *Richard Diamond, Private Detective* (CBS: 1957–59; NBC: 1960), and *Perry Mason* (CBS: 1957–67). It appeared in the midst of an outright glut of TV detective series, including such staples as *Peter Gunn* (NBC: 1959–60, 1962), *Hawaiian Eye* (ABC: 1959–62), *Surfside Six* (ABC: 1960–63), and *The Defenders* (CBS: 1961–65). When viewed in the context of private eye also-rans, reruns of Hollywood movies and a similar wave of tough-guy cop shows—*Dragnet* (NBC: 1951–59, 1967–71), *Highway Patrol* (NBC: 1956–60), *State Trooper* (ABC: 1957–60), *M-Squad* (NBC: 1957–61), *The Line-Up* (CBS: 1954–60), *The Naked City* (ABC: 1957–63) and *The Untouchables* (ABC: 1959–63)—airing along with a number of failed efforts in the police genre at the same time, the full dimension of public conditioning to accept an essentially and brutally lawless sort of "order" can be appreciated. For further detail, see Richard Meyers, *TV Detectives* (London: Tantivy Press, 1981).

13. For trenchant analysis, see Ella Showhat and Robert Stam, *Unthinking Eurocentrism: Multuculturalism and the Media* (New York: Routledge, 1994).

14. Explication of the principles involved will be found in Jacques Ellul, *Propaganda: The Formation of Men's Attitudes* (New York: Alfred A. Knopf, 1968).

15. Julian Symons, *Mortal Consequences: A History from the Detective Story to the Crime Novel* (New York: Harper & Row, 1972) pp. 214–5.

16. See, e.g., Elizabeth Janeway, *Man's World, Woman's Place* (New York: Delta, 1971); Susan Brownmiller, *Against Our Will: Men, Women and Rape* (New York: Simon & Schuster, 1975); Joan Smith, *Misogynies: Reflections on Myth and Malice* (New York: Ballantine, 1989); Lynn A. Higgins and Brenda R. Silver, eds., *Rape and Representation* (New York: Columbia University Press, 1991).

17. The rhetoric accrues from speeches by Himmler to the SS leadership ("Gruppenführer") during the fall of 1943; quoted in Helmut Krausnik, Hans Buchheim, Martin Broszat and Hans-Adolf Jacobsen, *Anatomy of the SS State* (New York: Walker, 1968) pp. 334–9. Also see the quotes in Roger Manville and Heinrich Frankle, *Heinrich Himmler* (New York: Mentor, 1965) p. 163; Richard Breitman, *The Architect of Genocide: Himmler and the Final Solution* (New York: Alfred A. Knopf, 1991) pp. 242–3.

18. Quoted in Krausnik, et al., *op. cit.* Himmler made numerous statements to the same effect in his personal correspondence. See, e.g., the quotes in Heinz Höhn, *The Order of the Death's Head: The Story of Hitler's SS* (New York: Coward-McCann, 1969) pp. 364–5.

19. Ellul, *op. cit.* Also see William Graeber, *The Engineering of Consent: Democracy and Authority in Twentieth-Century America* (Madison: University of Wisconsin Press, 1987).

20. Höhn, *op. cit.*, Chap. 7 (inclusive), esp. pp. 151–5. For outcomes, see, e.g., Bruce Quarrie, *Hitler's Teutonic Knights: SS Panzers in Action* (Wellingborough, UK: Patrick Stephens, 1986). Overall, see George L. Mosse, *Nazi Culture: Intellectual, Cultural and Social Life in the Third Reich* (New York: Schocken, 1981).

21. An interesting, albeit oblique, treatment of this dynamic will be found in Howard Haycraft's *Murder for Pleasure: The Life and Times of the Detective Story* (New York: Carroll & Graf, [3rd ed.] 1984).

22. On Vietnam, see, e.g., the summary of evidence of the 1967–68 International War Crimes ("Russell") Tribunal provided by Arlette El Kaïm Sartre in Jean-Paul Sartre's *On Genocide* (San Francisco: Ramparts Press, 1968). On the Highway of Death and other Persian Gulf horrors, see, Ramsey Clark, et al., *War Crimes: A Report on United States War Crimes Against Iraq* (Washington, D.C.: Maisonneuve, 1992).

23. These and dozens of comparable quotations from U.S. military personnel in Southeast Asia will be found in Richard Boyle's *Flower of the Dragon: The Breakdown of the U.S. Army in Vietnam* (San Francisco: Ramparts Press, 1975). A classic illustration of the "dead gook rule" was reported in the *New York Times* on June 5, 1965: "As the Communists withdrew from Quangngai last Monday, United States jet bombers pounded the hills into which they were headed. Many Vietnamese—one estimate is as high as 500—were killed by the strikes. The American contention is that they were Vietcong soldiers. But three out of four patients seeking treatment in a Vietnamese hospital afterwards for burns from napalm, or jellied gasoline, were village women." Brigadier Patton is the namesake of his much more famous father, the legendary tank commander called "Old Blood and Guts" during World War II.

24. See, e.g., George Cheney, " 'Talking War': Symbols, Strategies and Images," *New Studies on the Left*, Vol. 14, No. 3, 1991; Eric Hoogland, "The Other Face of War," in Cynthia Peters, ed., *Collateral Damage: The New World Order at Home and Abroad* (Boston: South End Press, 1992) pp. 181–95.

25. For an incisive view of the English social milieu in which the detective fiction arose, see Colin Watson, *Snobbery with Violence: English Crime Stories and Their Audience* (London: Eyre Methuen, [2nd ed.] 1979).

26. A good overview is provided in the latter chapters of Sidney Lens, *The Forging of the American Empire: From the Revolution to Vietnam, a History of American Imperialism* (New York: Thomas Y. Crowell, 1971). Also see Paul A. Varg, *America: From Client State to World Power* (Norman: University of Oklahoma Press, 1990).

27. This is a theme well-developed in another connection by Richard Slotkin in his *Regeneration Through Violence: The Mythology of the American Frontier* (Middletown, CT: Weslyan University Press, 1990).

28. Symons, *op. cit.*, p. 214.

29. Slotkin, *op. cit.* Another useful interrogation of the psychology involved will be found in David R. Williams' *Wilderness Lost: The Religious Origins of the American Mind* (London: Associated Universities Press, 1987).

30. This shines through, perhaps despite the author's intentions, in Frederick Merk's classic text, *Manifest Destiny and Mission in American History: A Reinterpretation* (New York: Alfred A. Knopf, 1963). Another excellent analysis, especially useful in the thematic context of this essay, is Reginald Horsman's *Race and Manifest Destiny: The Origins of American Racial Anglo-Saxonism* (Cambridge: Harvard University Press, 1981).

31. Nolan, *op. cit.*, p. 60. For further elaboration, see his "The End of the Trail: The American West of Dashiell Hammett and Raymond Chandler," *Western Historical Quarterly*, Oct. 1975.

32. Quoted in Howard Zinn, *A People's History of the United States* (New York: Harper & Row, 1980) p. 248. For context, see John M. Reilly, "The Politics of Tough Guy Mysteries," *University of Dayton Review*, No. 10, 1973.

33. For personal recountings of how the process worked, see Bud Schultz and Ruth Schultz, *It Did Happen Here: Recollections of Political Repression in America* (Berkeley: University of California Press, 1989). A supreme irony was that no less than Dashiell Hammett himself was caught up in the witch-hunt and sentenced to six months for the "contempt" of refusing to testify before the House Committee on Un-American Activities; William F. Nolan, *Dashiell Hammett: A Casebook* (Santa Barbara, CA: McNally and Loftin, 1969). A personal account is provided by Lillian Hellman, Hammett's partner, in her *Scoundrel Time* (Boston: Atlantic, Little-Brown, 1976). Probably the best single volume covering the entire sweep of "McCarthyism" is David Caute's *The Great Fear: The Anti-Communist Purge Under Truman and Eisenhower* (New York: Simon & Schuster, 1978).

34. For a detailed overview of what went on under the rubric of COINTELPRO—and what continues to occur as part of its legacy—see my and Jim Vander Wall's *The COINTELPRO Papers: Documents from the FBI's Secret Wars Against Dissent in the United States* (Boston: South End Press, 1990).

35. A concise account of CIA operations during the entire period will be found in William Blum's *The CIA: A Forgotten History* (London: Zed Books, 1986).

36. Actually, the first known example of the form is probably James Fenimore Cooper's failed novel, *The Spy*, published in 1821. The genus of literary merit attending any spy fiction did not occur until publication of Erskine Chambers' *The Riddle of the Sands* in 1903. Joseph Conrad tried his hand at spies in *Secret Agent* (1907) and *Under Western Eyes* (1911). This was followed by John Buchanan's *The Thirty-Nine Steps* (1915). Occasional forays were made over the next two decades by noted writers like Eric Ambler in *The Dark Frontier* (1936) and *Epitaph for a Spy* (1938), Graham Greene in *The Confidential Agent* (1939), Geofrey Household in *Rogue Male* (1939), and Michael Innes in *The Secret Vanguard* (1940), but basically the embryonic genre languished (especially in comparison to detective and western fiction). Things really began to move only with the advent of the Cold War and publication of Ian Fleming's first James Bond novel, *Casino Royale*, in 1953. Graham Greene then weighed in with *The Quiet American* (1955) and was followed by a spate of books by John Le Carré (David John Moore Cornwell), notably *The Spy Who Came in from the Cold* (1963) and *The Looking Glass War* (1965), and Len Deighton with *The Ipcress File* (1963) and *Billion-Dollar Brain* (1966). By the mid-1960s, the spy thriller was nearly as well established as sleuth and cowboy yarns in both potboiler and serious literary modes. And, of course, Hollywood capitalized quickly on the new popular format.

37. For details on the Legion of Justice, see Margaret Jayko, ed., *FBI on Trial: The victory in the Socialist Workers Party suit against government spying* (New York: Pathfinder, 1988).

38. On the SAO, see Michael Parenti, *Democracy for the Few* (New York: St. Martin's, 1980) p. 24.

39. Quoted in Guenter Lewy, *America in Vietnam* (New York: Oxford University Press, 1978) p. 278.

40. This theme is developed rather well in William Ruelmann's *The Saint with a Gun: The Unlawful American Private Eye* (New York: New York University Press, 1974).

41. Tony Hillerman and Ernie Bulow, *Talking Mysteries: A Conversation with Tony Hillerman* (New Mexico: University of New Mexico Press, 1991).

42. Hillerman's reference to Chandler's influence upon his writing occurs in ibid., p. 27; he also acknowledges significant debts to Eric Ambler and Graham Greene.

43. Ross Macdonald began his Lew Archer series in the late 1950s and continued it until rather recently. Some of his earlier efforts, such as *The Zebra-Striped Hearse* (1964), hold up favorably in comparison to Chandler. He was, however, unable to sustain such quality and degenerated into something

of a formula writer. Willeford, creator of the Hoke Mosely series, is probably best known for his 1984 *Miami Blues*. He has several better efforts, including *New Hope for the Dead* (1985).

44. S.S. Van Dine (Willard Huntington Wright) is known for having written the Philo Vance detective series during the 1920s. Leslie Chartiris (Leslie Charles Boyer Yin) created the "Saint" series during the 1930s. Earl Stanley Gardiner write the Perry Mason series of nearly 120 books, selling upwards of 150 million copies in all. Rex (Todhunter) Stout launched his Nero Wolf series, beginning with *Fer-de-Lance* in 1934. "Ellery Queen," supposed author of an unending series of stories and short novels about his own cases, and editor/publisher of a crime magazine bearing his name, is actually the invention of a pair of writers, Nelson Lee and Patrick Dannay.

45. A good analysis is provided by Paul Joseph in his *Cracks in the Empire: State Politics and the Vietnam War* (Boston: South End Press, 1980).

46. The best overall explication may be Noam Chomsky's and Edward S. Herman's *The Political Economy of Human Rights, Vol. 2: After the Cataclysm—Postwar Indochina and the Reconstruction of Imperial Ideology* (Boston: South End Press, 1979). Also see Michael T. Klare, *Beyond the "Vietnam Syndrome": U.S. Interventionism in the 1980s* (Washington, D.C.: Institute for Policy Studies, 1981).

47. Quoted in the introduction to David Willis McCullough's anthology, *City Sleuths and Tough Guys: Crime Stories from Poe to the Present* (New York: Houghton-Mifflin, 1989) pp. xv-xvi. For further perspectives on the shift in public sensibility, see Robin W. Winks, ed., *A Colloquium on Crime* (New York: Scribner's, 1986).

48. Marvin is quoted in Meyers, *op. cit.*, p. 43.

49. *The Mod Squad* (ABC: 1968–73) starred Clarence Williams II, Peggy Lipton and Michael Cole. A "reunion" movie, entitled *The Return of the Mod Squad*, was aired in 1979.

50. Paretsky's V.I. Warshawski, portrayed by Kathleen Turner a few years back in a rather dismal movie of the same name, does follow standard female stereotypes in that she solves cases by intuition rather than logic (see, e.g., the story "Skin Deep," in McCullough, *op. cit.*, at p. 461). Sue Grafton's Kinsey Milhone, on the other hand, is more of a "tried-and-true granddaughter of Marlowe and Spade," demonstrating that in the new American sensibility, it's sometimes okay for women (but never men) to comport themselves like macho thugs (see "The Parker Shotgun" in ibid. at p. 425). Unlike their tough-guy predecessors, both female detective characters indulge themselves amply in such approved yuppie pastimes as jogging.

51. Although Dave Brandstetter, the central figure in Joseph Hansen's novels from 1970 onward, was not the first example of a gay detective character—that dubious honor goes to George Baxt's "Pharaoh of Love" in *A Queer Kind of Love* (1966)—he was the earliest to find general public acceptance. For a sample of Hansen/Brandstetter, see "Election Day," in McCullough, *op. cit.*, at p. 398.

52. Roger Simon's depiction of Moses Wine, the imaginary Jewish student radical turned private sleuth, has worked quite well in this respect. A more extreme example, Ernest Tidyman's John Shaft, a black detective based in Harlem, ultimately failed, not on racial grounds, per see, but because he was projected as being a sort of Afroamerican Mike Hammer; *Shaft* (New York: Macmillan, 1970).

53. Simon's Moses Wine fits this mold to a certain extent. Willeford's character, Hoke Mosely, however, is the very epitome of the genre's new white male detective figure. He is of middle age, pudgy, and wears false teeth, white socks, and polyester leisure suits. His wife has left him to move in with a wealthy pro baseball player, but continues to "assert herself" by compelling him to spend an appreciable part of his meager police salary underwriting the costs of dental work for the eldest of their two daughters. He lives in a sleazy hotel room in the wrong part of town, drives a battered old clunker of a car, and experiences almost continuous self-doubt concerning his own worth as a human being. This is obviously a far cry from the sorts of characters created by Hammett, Chandler and Spillane.

54. For example, in *The Big Fix*, while driving his children around in his Volkswagen bug during a visit permitted by his estranged wife (who has moved in with a brainy therapist), Moses Wine is stopped for a routine traffic violation. After disclosing to the cop that there is a licensed but never used .38 revolver in the glove compartment, Wine is ordered to produce it for inspection. It turns out to be rusty, minus its cylinder, its barrel filled with the children's crayons. The cop threatens to arrest Wine for "abuse of a weapon." One can be sure Mike Hammer would never be found in anything resembling these circumstances.

55. The process is examined quite thoroughly by Noam Chomsky in his *Necessary Illusions:Thought Control in Democratic Societies* (Boston: South End Press, 1989).

56. For cogent analysis of the *comprador* phenomenon within the African American community, see Joy James, *Transcending the Talented Tenth: Black Leaders and American Intellectuals* (New York: Routledge, 1996). Among Mexican Americans, see Rudolfo Acuña, *Occupied America: The Chicano's Struggle for Liberation* (San Francisco: Canfield Press, 1972). Perhaps the best explanations of the psychological process at work may be found in Frantz Fanon's *Black Skin, White Masks* (New York: Grove Press, 1966) and Albert Memmi's *The Colonizer and the Colonized* (New York: Orion, 1965).

57. This was conceded by the federal government itself; U.S. Department of Interior, Indian Claims Commission, *Final Report* (Washington, D.C.: 96th Cong., 1st Sess., U.S. Government Printing Office, 1979); U.S. Department of Interior, Public Land Review Commission, *One-Third of the Nation's Land* (Washington, D.C.: 91st Cong., 2d Sess., U.S. Government Printing Office, 1970).

58. See, e.g., Ronald L. Trosper, "Appendix I: Indian Minerals," in American Indian Policy Review Commission, *Task Force 7 Final Report: Reservation and Resource Development and Protection* (Washington, D.C.: U.S. Government Printing Office, 1977); U.S. Department of Interior, Bureau of Indian Affairs, *Indian Lands Map: Oil, Gas and Minerals on Indian Reservations* (Washington, D.C.: U.S. Government Printing Office, 1978).

59. For a seminal articulation of the relevance of the concept of internal colonialism to U.S./Indian relations, see Robert K. Thomas, "Colonialism: Classic and Internal," *New University Thought*, Vol. 4, No. 4, Winter 1966–67. Also see Jimmie Durham, "Native Americans and Colonialism," *The Guardian*, March 28, 1979; and my own "Indigenous Peoples of the U.S.: A Struggle Against Internal Colonialism," *The Black Scholar*, Vol. 16, No. 1, February 1985.

60. See David Boldt, *Gurkhas* (London: Weidenfield & Nicholson, 1967) and Amiya Barat, *The Bengal Native Infantry* (Calcutta: Firma K.L. Mukmopashyay, 1962). It should be noted that earlier, and quite successfully, British experiments along this line had been conducted using Highland Scots as guinea pigs. See, e.g., Philip Howard, *The Black Watch* (London: Hamish Hamilton, 1968); Christopher Sinclair-Stevenson, *The Gordon Highlanders* (London: Hamish Hamilton, 1968); Douglas Sutherland, *The Argyll and Sutherland Highlanders* (London: Leo Cooper, 1969); L.B. Oats, *The Highland Light Infantry* (London: Leo Cooper, 1969). Overall, see Patrick MacRoy, *The Fierce Pawns* (Philadelphia: J.B. Lippencott, 1966).

61. John Robert Young, *The French Foreign Legion* (New York: Thames & Hudson, 1984). A broad history of the use of troops from colonized or otherwise oppressed social sectors will be found in Cynthia Enloe's *Ethnic Soldiers: State Security in a Divided Society* (Baltimore: Penguin, 1980).

62. On the "Public Safety Program," see A.J. Langguth's *Hidden Terrors:The Truth About U.S. Police Operations in Latin America* (New York: Pantheon, 1978).

63. See James Van Hise, *Who Was that Masked Man? The Story of the Lone Ranger* (Las Vegas: Pioneer Books, 1990). For a succinct summary of the matrix of violence inherent to any true liberatory dynamic, see B. Marie Perinbaum, *Holy Violence:The Revolutionary Thought of Frantz Fanon* (Washington, D.C.: Three Continents, 1982).

64. The psychology is handled well in Albert Memmi, *Domination* (Boston: Beacon Press, 1969). Also see Fanon, *Black Skin, White Masks, op. cit.*; Memmi, *Colonizer and Colonized, op. cit.*

65. This was precisely the outcome pursued as a matter of formal Indian policy by the federal government from at least as early as the 1880s onward; Frederick E. Hoxie, *A Final Promise:The Campaign to Assimilate the Indians, 1880–1920* (Lincoln: University of Nebraska Press, 1985).

66. The whole thrust of "multiculturalism"—increasingly peddled over the past twenty years as a challenge to rather than reinforcement of the present eurocentric status quo—is bound up in realization of this very premise. See, e.g., the selections of essays included in James C. Stone and Donald P. DeNevi, eds., *Teaching Multicultural Populations* (New York: Van Nostrand, 1971) and Liza Fiol-Matta and Mariam K. Chamberlain, *Women of Color and the Multicultural Curriculum: Transforming the College Classroom* (New York: Feminist Press, 1994). For the specific rhetoric deployed, see Werner Sollors, *Beyond Ethnicity* (New York: Oxford University Press, 1985).

67. On literary representation, see Robert F. Berkhofer, *The White Man's Indian: Images of the American Indian from Columbus to the Present* (New York: Alfred A. Knopf, 1978). In terms of cinema, see Ralph and Natasha Friar, *The Only Good Indian. . . The Hollywood Gospel* (New York: Drama Book

Specialists, 1972). Overall, see Raymond William Stedman, *Shadows of the Indian: Stereotypes in American Culture* (Norman: University of Oklahoma Press, 1982).

68. See generally, William T. Hagan, *Indian Police and Judges: Experiments in Acculturation and Control* (New Haven, CT: Yale University Press, 1966).

69. With respect to the juridical doctrines at issue, see Sidney L. Harring, *Crow Dog's Case: American Indian Sovereignty, Tribal Law, and United States Law in the Nineteenth Century* (Cambridge: Cambridge University Press, 1994).

70. Robert Clark, ed., *The Killing of Chief Crazy Horse* (Lincoln: University of Nebraska Press, 1976); Stanley Vestal, *Sitting Bull: Champion of the Sioux* (Norman: University of Oklahoma Press, 1957).

71. See, e.g., Oliver Knight, *Following the Indian Wars* (Norman: University of Oklahoma Press, 1960).

72. On the IRA and its functioning, see Vine Deloria, Jr., and Clifford M. Lytle, *The Nations Within: The Past and Future of American Indian Sovereignty* (New York: Pantheon, 1984).

73. This is covered in depth in my and Jim Vander Wall's *Agents of Repression: The FBI's Secret Wars Against the Black Panther Party and the American Indian Movement* (Boston: South End Press, 1988). Also see Peter Matthiessen, *In the Spirit of Crazy Horse* (New York: Viking, [2nd ed.] 1991); Rex Weyler, *Blood of the Land: The U.S. Government and Corporate War Against the American Indian Movement* (Philadelphia: New Society, [2nd ed.] 1992).

74. For details on the life of the man whose very name has come to be synonymous with treason, see Paul M. Hayes, *Quisling: The Career and Political Ideas of Vikdun Quisling, 1887–1945* (Bloomington: Indiana University Press, 1972).

75. A good analysis of the Vichy regime as seen through the lens of its nominal head will be found in Geoffrey Warner's *Pierre Laval and the Eclipse of France* (London: Macmillan, 1968).

76. The poem is included in *Rudyard Kipling's Verse: Definitive Edition* (London: Macmillan, 1954). For analysis, see J. McClure, *Kipling and Conrad: The Colonial Fiction* (Cambridge, MA: Harvard University Press, 1981). For contextualization, see Edward Said, *Orientalism* (New York: Pantheon, 1978).

77. The construction holds up irrespective of whether the venue is fictive or ostensibly nonfictional. See the essays included in Chris Tiffin and Alan Lawson, eds., *De-scribing Empire: Postcolonialism and Textuality* (New York: Routledge, 1994); Robert Young, *White Mythologies: Writing History and the West* (New York: Routledge, 1990).

78. Such depictions are essentially no different than the sorts of distortive, offensive and officially sanctioned portrayals of native culture which have infested textbooks and other curricular materials in the United States throughout the twentieth century; Joann S. Morris, "Indian Portrayal in Teaching Materials," in James R. Young, ed., *Multicultural Education and the American Indian* (Los Angeles: UCLA American Indian Studies Center, 1979). On certain of the actualities involved, see the essays compiled in Deward E. Walker, Jr., and David Carrasco, eds., *Witchcraft and Sorcery of the American Native Peoples* (Moscow: University of Idaho Press, 1989). For useful interrogations of the origins of this aspect Euroamerica's entrenched anti-Indianism, see Norman Cohn, *Europe's Inner Demons: An Inquiry Inspired by the Great Witch-Hunt* (New York: Basic Books, 1975); Richard Drinnon, *Facing West: The Metaphysics of Indian-Hating and Empire-Building* (Minneapolis: University of Minnesota Press, 1980); Ioan P. Couliano, *Eros and Magic in the Renaissance* (Chicago: University of Chicago Press, 1987); Anthony Pagden, *The Fall of Natural Man: The American Indian and the Origins of Comparative Ethnology* (Cambridge: Cambridge University Press, [rev. ed.] 1986).

79. Good readings in this connection include the earlier-cited works by Frantz Fanon, Albert Memmi and Edward Said, as well as A.L. Epstein's *Ethos and Identity* (London: Tavistock, 1978) and Nimmi Hutnick's *Ethnic Minority Identity: A Social Psychological Perspective* (Oxford: Clarendon Press, 1991).

80. See, e.g., Bulow's introduction to *Talking Mysteries, op. cit.*

81. In this sense, Hillerman's thematics might best be understood as strictly conjunctive to other reactions against perceived erosions of eurosupremicist hegemony, whether "liberal" (e.g., Arthur Schlesinger's *The Disuniting of America: Reflections on a Multicultural Society* [New York: W.W. Norton, 1992]) or "conservative" (e.g., Dinesh D'Sousa's *Illiberal Education: The Politics of Race and Sex on Campus* [New York: Free Press, 1991]).

82. The ideological process of "criminalization" and its social functions are handled brilliantly at

the theoretical level by Michel Foucault in his *Discipline and Punish: Birth of the Prison* (New York: Pantheon, 1977). For a range of more concrete and topical representations, see the essays collected in my and J.J. Vander Wall's *Cages of Steel: The Politics of Imprisonment in the United States* (Washington, D.C.: Maisonneuve, 1992).

83. In general, see "Geographies of Sacrifice: The Radioactive Colonization of Native North America," in my *Struggle for the Land: Native North American Resistance to Genocide, Ecocide and Colonization* (Winnipeg: Arbiter Ring, [2nd Ed.], 1998).

84. See "Genocide in Arizona? The 'Navajo-Hopi Land Dispute' in Perspective"; ibid. Also see Jerry Kammer, *The Second Long Walk: The Navajo-Hopi Land Dispute* (Albuquerque: University of New Mexico Press, 1980); Anita Parlow, *Cry, Sacred Ground: Big Mountain, USA* (Washington, D.C.: Christic Institute, 1988).

85. For a good exposition on the rules—or tricks—of Hillerman's journalistic trade, see Michael Parenti, *Inventing Reality: The Politics of the News Media* (New York: St. Martin's Press, 1993). A handy tool for applying what is learned therein is the "Doublespeak Dictionary" published by Edward S. Herman in his *Beyond Hypocrisy: Decoding the News in an Age of Propaganda* (Boston: South End Press, 1992).

86. This is a standard subterfuge on the part of anthropologists and other culture vultures, as well as government officials. No matter what their offense, or how bitterly it is protested by indigenous people, the offenders are always able to subvert some native or another into opining that the offense is not only inoffensive, but desirable. He or she is then promoted by the offenders as being a "representative Indian spokesperson." This is of course as opposed to "malcontents" who are thus by definition "unrepresentative" as well as "irresponsible" and, often enough, cast as not being "real" Indians at all (subverted Indians are usually relied upon to advance the latter charge). See generally, Patricia Penn Hilden, *When Nickels Were Indians: An Urban Mixed-Blood Story* (Washington, D.C.: Smithsonian Institution Press, 1995).

87. The text of the main Dog Soldier Teletype and excerpts from Kelley's testimony are included in *The COINTELPRO Papers, op. cit.*, pp. 275–80.

88. For a detailed examination of the application of such disinformation techniques against AIM, see my "Renegades, Terrorists and Revolutionaries: The Government's Propaganda War Against the American Indian Movement," *Propaganda Review*, No. 4, Spring 1989. More broadly, see Edward S. Herman's *The Real Terror Network: Terrorism in Fact and Propaganda* (Boston: South End Press, 1982). It should be noted that, in the literary venue, Hillerman's portrayal of Indian militancy closely parallels that of paleoconservative writer Tom Clancy, whose *The Sum of All Fears* (New York: Berkley, 1991) includes a character, "Marvin Russell," cast as an ultra-hardcore AIMster who hooks up with outfits like a the PFLP and German RAF to plant a nuclear device at the Super Bowl.

89. Thus are the uncomfortably topical issues confronted by AIM and related groups—things like the uranium contamination, water depletion and compulsory relocation Hillerman so deftly ignores in his books—completely voided in the minds of readers. In constructing his fictional version of an "AIM agenda" along these lines, Hillerman dovetails his script with the standard anti-Indianist drivel about how indigenous activists, and native people more generally, are always "dwelling in the past," even—or perhaps especially—when we are attempting to put a stop to offenses occurring here and now. A subtext to this may be that in asserting native rights as a current reality we are by definition seen by our critics as being preoccupied with "ancient history" because only in the past do they believe us to be possessed of any rights at all.

90. There is an unfortunate element of truth in this characterization of an "AIM leader," at least insofar as Clyde Bellecourt, one of the real movement's founders, is concerned. Be it noted, however, that even in Bellecourt's case, the activities in question had nothing to do with terrorism. Rather, his offense was to violate the trust inhering in his position to peddle drugs in the Minneapolis Indian community; Gerald Vizenor, *Manifest Manners: Post-Indian Warriors of Survivance* (Hanover, NH: Wesleyan University Press, 1994) pp. 154–8.

91. Fostering such sentiment has become standard practice to the extent that a whole category of police operative, the *agent provocateur*, has long since been developed as an expedient to generating the necessary public (mis)impressions of activists/movements targeted for neutralization; see, e.g., Gary T. Marx, "Thoughts on a Neglected Category of Social Movement Participant: The *Agent Provocateur* and

Informant," *American Journal of Sociology*, No. 80, Sept. 1984; Alex Constantine, *Blood, Carnage and the Agent Provocateur* (Los Angeles: Constantine Reports, 1993). More broadly, see Robert Justin Goldstein, *Political Repression in Modern America, 1870 to the Present* (New York: Shenkman, 1978).

92. In the midst of this uninterrupted string of stale banalities—endlessly repeated by "Good Americans" everywhere—the question of their self-proclaimed perpetual "innocence" bears examination. People who don't just support but celebrate the processes of rape, pillage and plunder going into the conquest of America, and who don't just willingly but insistently benefit in material terms from the ongoing colonial/neocolonial degradation not only of Native America, but of the entire Third World, are anything but *innocent*. To the contrary, they are directly complicit, just as "Good Germans" were once complicit in the crimes of nazism. Put simply, one cannot cheer and tie yellow ribbons in public places to endorse the bombing of Iraqi children in Baghdad and at the same occupy a place of innocence vis-à-vis the resultant carnage. Those who exult in the systematic slaughter of others really have no valid complaint when visited with a few random doses of the same. Two good readings which bear heavily on these points are John Duffett's *Against the Crime of Silence: Proceedings of the International War Crimes Tribunal* (New York: Clarion, 1970) and Daniel Jonah Goldhagen's *Hitler's Willing Executioners: Ordinary Germans and the Holocaust* (New York: Alfred A. Knopf, 1996).

93. The partisans were certainly cast in such terms by the nazis and their French collaborators. See H.R. Kedward, *Resistance in Vichy France: A Study of Ideas and Motivations* (New York: Oxford University Press, 1978).

94. These are themes well explored by Noam Chomsky in his *Year 501: The Conquest Continues* (Boston: South End Press, 1992) and *World Orders, Old and New* (New York: Columbia University Press, 1996). Also see *Necessary Illusions, op. cit.*

95. Another mindless banality, endlessly repeated. In simplest terms, the Western conception of "progress"—invariably cast as a sort of immutable natural process rather than as the product of human consciousness and resulting but entirely alterable priorities—reduces to a systematically phased destruction of the natural world as a whole (each element of it being replaced by something of human design along the way). Regardless of how they cast their denials—and there are almost infinite variations on the theme—those who embrace the concept must necessarily accept the genocide and ecocide which are obviously integral to it. See Frederick Turner, *Beyond Geography: The Western Spirit Against the Wilderness* (New York: Viking, 1980).

A Little Matter of Genocide

Colonialism and the Expropriation of Indigenous Spiritual Tradition in Contemporary Academia

> They came for our land, for what grew or could be grown on it, for the re-
> sources in it, and for our clean air and pure water. They stole these things
> from us, and in the taking they also stole our free ways and the best of our
> leaders, killed in battle or assassinated. And now, after all that, they've come
> for the very last of our possessions; now they want our pride, our history, our
> spiritual traditions. They want to rewrite and remake these things, to claim
> them for themselves. The lies and thefts just never end.
>
> —Margo Thunderbird
> 1988

The exploitation and appropriation of Native American spiritual tradition is nothing new. In many ways the process began the moment the first of Columbus' wayward seamen washed up on a Caribbean beach, returning home with wondrous tales of "*los in Dios.*"[1] And it has been functioning in increasingly concerted fashion, under rationales ranging from the crassly commercial to the "purely academic," ever since. Over the past two decades, the ranks of those queueing up to cash in on the lucre and luster of "American Indian Religious Studies" have come to include a number of "New Age" luminaries reinforced by a significant portion of the university elite.

The classic example of this has been Carlos Castaneda, whose well-stewed borrowings from Timothy Leary, the Yogi Ramacharaka, and Barbara Myerhoff were blended with a liberal dose of his own turgid fantasies, packaged as a "Yaqui way of knowledge," and resulted not only in a lengthy string of bestsellers but a Ph.D. in anthropology from UCLA. So lacking was/is the base of real knowledge concerning things Indian within academia that it took nearly a decade for Castaneda to be apprehended as "the greatest anthropological hoax since Piltdown Man," and one still encounters abundant instances of *The Teachings of Don Juan* and *Journey to Ixtlan* being utilized in courses and cited (apparently in all seriousness) in ostensibly scholarly works as offering "insight" into American Indian thought and spiritual practice.[2]

Then there is "Dr. Jamake Highwater," an alleged Cherokee/Blackfeet from either Montana or Canada (the story varies from time-to-time), born by his own accounts in several different years. In an earlier incarnation (*circa:* the late sixties), this same individual appeared as "J Marks," a non-Indian modern dance promoter in the San Francisco area whose main literary claim to fame was in having penned an "authorized biography" of rock star Mick Jagger. Small wonder that the many later texts of "Dr. Highwater" on Native American spirituality and the nature of "the primal mind" bear more than passing resemblance to both the lore of Grecian mythos and the insights of hip-pop idiom à la magazines like *Rolling Stone.* Still, Highwater's material consistently finds itself required reading in undergraduate courses and referenced in supposedly scholarly fora. The man has also received more than one hefty grant to translate his literary ramblings into "educational" PBS film productions.[3]

Then again, there was Ruth Beebe Hill whose epic potboiler novel, *Hanta Yo*, set certain sales records during the late seventies via the expedient of depicting the collectivist spirituality of the nineteenth-century Lakota as nothing so much as a living prefiguration of her friend Ayn Rand's grossly individualistic cryptofascism. In the face of near-universal howls of outrage from the contemporary Lakota community, Hill resorted to "validating" her postulations by retaining the services of a single aging and impoverished Sioux man, Alonzo Blacksmith (a.k.a.: "Chunksa Yuha"), to attest to the book's "authenticity." Before dropping once again into a well-deserved obscurity, Blacksmith intoned—allegedly in a "dialect" unknown to Siouxian linguistics—that what Hill had written was true because "I, Chunksa Yuha, say so, say so." This ludicrous performance was sufficient to allow a range of professors to argue that the controversy [was] really just "a matter of opinion" because "*all* Indians are not in agreement as to the inaccuracy of *Hanta Yo.*" Such pronouncements virtually insured that sales would remain brisk in supermarkets and college book stores, and that producer David Wolper would convert it into a TV miniseries entitled *Mystic Warrior* during the mid-'80s.[4]

And, as if all this were not enough, we are treated to the spectacle of Lynn Andrews, an airhead "feminist" yuppie who once wrangled herself a weekend in the company of a pair of elderly Indian women of indistinct tribal origin. In her version of events, they had apparently been waiting their entire lives for just such an opportunity to unburden themselves of every innermost secret of their people's spiritual knowledge, immediately acquainted her with such previously unknown "facts" as the presence of kachinas on the Arctic Circle and the power of "Jaguar Women," charged her with serving as their "messenger," and sent her forth to write a series of books so outlandish in their pretensions as to make Castaneda seem a model of propriety by comparison. Predictably, the Andrews books have begun to penetrate the "popular literature" curriculum of academe.[5]

To round out the picture, beyond the roster of such heavy-hitters circle a host of also-rans extending from "Chief Red Fox" and "Nino Cochise" (real names and ethnicities unknown) to Hyemeyohsts Storm, David Seals and scores of others, each of whom has made a significant recent contribution (for profit) to the misrepresentation and appropriation of indigenous spirituality, and most of whom have been tendered some measure of credibility by the "certified scholars" of American universities.[6]

One result is that at this juncture, scarcely an Indian in the United States has not been confronted by some hippie-like apparition wishing to teach crystal-healing methods to Navajo grandmothers, claiming to be a pipe-carrier reincarnated from a seventeenth-century Cheyenne warrior, and with an assumed "Indian name" such as "Beautiful Painted Arrow" or "Chief Piercing Eyes." Needless to say, this circumstance has in turn spawned a whole new clot of hucksters such as the late "Sun Bear" (Vincent LaDuke, a Chippewa) who—along with his non-Indian consort *cum* business manager, "Wabun" (Marlise James)—was able to make himself rather wealthy by forming (on the basis of suitable "membership fees") what he called "the Bear Tribe," and the selling of ersatz sweat lodge and medicine wheel ceremonies to anyone who wanted to play Indian for a day and could afford the price of admission.[7]

As the Lakota scholar Vine Deloria, Jr., put it in 1982, "the realities of Indian belief and existence have become so misunderstood and distorted at this point that when a real Indian stands up and speaks the truth at any given moment, he or she is not only unlikely to be believed, but will probably be publicly contradicted and 'corrected' by the citation of some non-Indian and totally inaccurate 'expert.' More, young Indians in universities are now being trained to view themselves and their cultures in the terms prescribed by such experts *rather than* in the traditional terms of the tribal elders. The process automatically sets the members of Indian communities at odds with one another, while outsiders run around picking up the pieces for themselves. In this way, the experts are perfecting a system of self-validation in which all semblance of honesty and accuracy are lost. This is not only a travesty of scholarship, but it is absolutely devastating to Indian societies."[8]

Pam Colorado, an Oneida academic, goes further: "The process is ultimately intended to supplant Indians, even in areas of their own customs and spirituality. In the end, non-Indians will have complete power to define what is and is not Indian, even for Indians. We are talking here about an absolute ideological/conceptual subordination of Indian people in addition to the total physical subordination they already experience. When this happens, the last vestiges of real Indian society and Indian rights will disappear. Non-Indians will then 'own' our heritage and ideas as thoroughly as they now claim to own our land and resources."[9]

A Little Matter of Genocide

Those who engage in such activities usually claim to do so not for the fame and fortune (real or potential) involved, but for loftier motives. Many of Castaneda's defenders, for example, have argued that despite the blatant misrepresentation of Yaqui culture in which he has engaged, his books nonetheless articulate valid spiritual principles, the "higher truth value" of which simply transcend such "petty criticism" as demanding at least minimal adherence to facts.[10] Similar themes have been sounded with regard to Highwater, Andrews, and others. Within academia proper, such thinking has led to the emergence of a whole new pseudodiscipline termed "ethnomethodology" in which inconvenient realities can be simply disregarded and allegorical "truth" is habitually substituted for conventional data. Harold Garfinkle, a founder of ethnomethodology at UCLA has contended that such an approach represents "the pursuit of knowledge in its purest form."[11]

At another level, the poet Gary Snyder, who has won literary awards for the penning of verse in which he pretends to see the world through the eyes of an American Indian "shaman," has framed things more clearly: "Spirituality is not something which can be 'owned' like a car or a house," says Snyder. "Spiritual knowledge belongs to all humanity equally. Given the state of the world today, we all have not only the right but the obligation to pursue all forms of spiritual insight, and at every possible level. In this sense, it seems to me that I have as much right to pursue and articulate the belief systems developed by Native Americans as they do, and arguments to the contrary strike me as absurd."[12]

Indeed, the expression of such proprietary interest in native spiritual tradition is hardly unique to Snyder. For instance, at a 1986 benefit concert staged to raise funds to support the efforts of traditional Navajos resisting forcible relocation from their homes around Big Mountain, Arizona, one non-Indian performer took the opportunity between each of her songs to "explain" one or another element of "Navajo religion" to the audience. Her presumption in this regard deeply offended several Navajos in attendance and, during an intermission, she was quietly told to refrain from any further such commentary. She thereupon returned to the stage and announced that her performance was over and that she was withdrawing her support to the Big Mountain struggle because the people of that area were "oppressing" her through denial of her "right" to serve as a self-appointed spokesperson for their spirituality. "I have," she said, "just as much right to spiritual freedom as they do."[13]

Those who hold positions of this sort often go beyond assertion of their supposed rights to contend that the arguments of their opponents are altogether lacking in substance. "What does it hurt if a bunch of people want to believe they're the personification of Hiawatha?" asks the manager of a natural foods store in Boulder, Colorado. "I will admit that things can get pretty silly in these circles, but so what? People have a right to be silly if they want to. And it's not like the old days when Indians were being killed left and right. You could even say that the attention being paid to Indian religions these days is sort of flattering. Anyway, there's no harm to anybody, and it's good for the people who do it."[14]

The traditional Indian perspective is diametrically opposed. As Barbara Owl, a White Earth Anishinabe, has put it, "We have many particular things which we hold internal to our cultures. These things are spiritual in nature, and they are for *us*, not for anyone who happens to walk in off the street. They are *ours* and they are *not* for sale. Because of this, I suppose it's accurate to say that such matters are our 'secrets,' the things that bind us together in our identities as distinct peoples. It's not that we never make outsiders aware of our secrets, but *we* — not *they* — decide what, how much, and to what purpose this knowledge is to be put. That's absolutely essential to our cultural integrity, and thus to our survival as peoples. Now, *surely* we Indians are entitled to *that*. Everything else has been stripped from us already."[15]

"I'll tell you something else," Owl continued, "a lot of things about our

103

spiritual ways may be secret, but the core idea never has been. And you can sum up that idea in one word spelled R-E-S-P-E-C-T. Respect for and balance between all things, that's our most fundamental spiritual concept. Now, obviously, those who would violate the trust and confidence which is placed in them when we share some of our secrets, they don't have the slightest sense of the word. Even worse are those who take this information and misuse or abuse it for their own purposes, marketing it in some way or another, turning our spirituality into a commodity in books or movies or classes or 'ceremonials.' And it doesn't really matter whether they are Indians or non-Indians when they do such things; the non-Indians who do it are thieves, and the Indians who do it are sellouts and traitors."[16]

American Indian Movement (AIM) leader Russell Means not only concurs with Owl's assessment, but adds a touch of terminological clarity to her argument. "What's at issue here is the same old question that Europeans have always posed with regard to American Indians, whether what's ours isn't somehow theirs. And, of course, they've always answered the question in the affirmative. When they wanted our land they just announced that they had a right to it and therefore owned it. When we resisted their taking of our land they claimed we were being unreasonable and committed physical genocide upon us in order to convince us to see things their way. Now, being spiritually bankrupt themselves, they want our spirituality as well. So they're making up rationalizations to explain why they're entitled to it."[17]

"We are resisting this," Means goes on, "because spirituality is the basis of our culture; if it is stolen, our culture will be dissolved. If our culture is dissolved, Indian people *as such* will cease to exist. By definition, the causing of any culture to cease to exist is an act of genocide. That's a matter of international law; look it up in the 1948 Genocide Convention.[18] So, maybe this'll give you another way of looking at these culture vultures who are ripping off Indian tradition. It's not an amusing or trivial matter, and its not innocent or innocuous. And those who engage in this are not cute, groovy, hip, enlightened, or any of the rest of the things they want to project themselves as being. No, what they're about is cultural genocide. And genocide is genocide, regardless of how you want to 'qualify' it. So some of us are starting to react to these folks accordingly."[19]

For those who would scoff at Means' concept of genocide, Robert Davis and Mark Zannis, Canadian researchers on the topic, offer the following observation:

If people suddenly lose their 'prime symbol,' the basis of their culture, their lives lose meaning. They become disoriented, with no hope. A social disorganization often follows such a loss, they are often unable to insure their own survival. . . .The loss and human suffering of those whose culture has been healthy and is suddenly attacked and disintegrated are incalculable.[20]

Therefore, Davis and Zannis conclude, "One should not speak lightly of 'cultural genocide' as if it were a fanciful invention. The consequence in real life is far too grim to speak of cultural genocide as if it were a rhetorical device to beat the drums for 'human rights.' The cultural mode of group extermination is genocide, a crime. Nor should 'cultural genocide' be used in the game: 'Which is more horrible, to kill and torture; or remove [the prime cultural symbol which is] the will and reason to live?' *Both* are horrible."[21]

Enter *Mother Earth*

The analysis advanced by Means, Pam Colorado and other American Indians was substantially borne out by developments during the second half of the 1980s, as the line separating appropriation of the forms of indigenous spiritual tradition from the outright expropriation of that tradition has evaporated. Over the past few years, a major intellectual enterprise among New Age adherents has been the "demystification" of precontact Native America. Although the variants of this effort vary widely, they take as a common objective the "reinterpretation" of one or more positive aspects and attainments of autonomous indigenous society, "proving" that they never existed. Inevitably, the conclusion is reached that whatever is under discussion was "actually" introduced to the hemisphere by European invaders at some point after 1500.[22]

Hence, we find "radical ecologists" such as George Weurthner arguing in the pages of the supposedly progressive journal *Earth First!* that, far from having achieved spiritual traditions predicated in an understanding of natural harmony and balance, ancient American Indians were really the "first environmental pillagers." This flat reversal of even the most elementary meanings of Native tradition is then "explained" as Weurthner wanders through a consistently self-contradictory and wildly convoluted monologue in which he saddles North American indigenous societies with everything from the extinction of the wooly mammoth to desertification of the Sonora.[23] That he must abandon logic, known fact and even plain common sense to make his "case" does nothing to deter his stream of bald assertion.

Predictably, from this contrived springboard he is able to contend with superficial plausibility that the conceptualization now termed "ecology" did not—as is popularly imagined—spring from traditional Native American practice. Rather, in Weurthner's more "informed" view, it stems from the fertility of advanced brains such as his own. It follows that he feels compelled to demand that American Indians abandon the "myth and falsity" of their own belief structures in favor of the outlook he and his colleagues have expropriated from them.[24]

In a more public vein, the thinly veiled racism of Weurthner's sort of theorizing set the stage for the celebrated environmentalist author (and Earth First! guru) Edward Abbey to launch himself full tilt into avowals of an imagined "superiority of northern European culture" worthy of Josef Goebbels and Alfred Rosenberg.[25] Perhaps more pragmatically, it simultaneously laid the basis for Earth First! political leader Dave Foreman to declare Indian peoples a "threat to the habitat" and urge both ecologists and New Agers to actively resist our land and water rights claims.[26] All of this might be to some extent dismissable as the ravings of an irrelevant lunatic fringe were it not for the fact that, as usual, such ideas are finding their way into the realm of mainstream academia where they are being sanctioned and codified as "knowledge, truth and scholarship." The interlock and continuity between the expropriation of the physical resources of Native America on the one hand, and the expropriation of its spiritual/conceptual traditions on the other, could not be more clearly revealed.

Comes now Sam D. Gill, a non-Indian professor of Religious Studies at the University of Colorado/Boulder, and alleged specialist in Native American spirituality. In all fairness, it should be noted that Gill has heretofore been known primarily not so much on the grounds of his theses on Indian religion as for his advocacy of a rather novel approach to teaching. In essence, this seems to be that the crucial qualification for achieving university-level faculty status is to admittedly know little or nothing of the subject matter one is supposed to teach. As he himself put it in an essay contained in *On Teaching,* a 1987 anthology of "teaching excellence":

> In my classes on Native American religions I found I could not adequately describe the roles of women in Native American cultures and religions.... To begin to resolve my *ignorance* about Native American women and to pursue research ... I finally offered a senior-level course on Native American women and religions.... This course formally *initiated* my long-term research on Mother Earth [emphasis added].[27]

One might have been under the impression that filling a seat as a professor at a major institution of higher learning would imply not "ignorance," but rather the having of some pre-existing body of knowledge about or from which one is prepared to profess. Similarly, it might be thought that the offering of an advanced course in a particular content area might imply some sort of relationship to the *results* of research rather than the "initiation" of it. At the very least, one might expect that if a course needs to be taught for canonical reasons, and the instructor of record finds him/herself lacking in the knowledge required to teach it, s/he might retain the services of someone who *does* have the knowledge. Not so within the preferred pedagogy of Dr. Gill. Instead, he posits that "student questions and concerns" are most important in "shaping" what he does. Another way to say this might be: "pitch your performance to the crowd."

In any event, it was in this interesting commentary on the application of Harold Garfinkle's principles of attaining "pure knowledge" that Gill announced he had "a book in the process of being published by the University of Chicago Press. It is entitled *Mother Earth: An American Story*." He had thus assigned himself the task of articulating the "truth" of what is possibly the most central of all Native American spiritual concepts. Worse, he went on to remark that in order to "encourage my expeditious writing of the book, I committed myself to a presentation of it as a portion of a summer course entitled 'Native American Goddesses' to be offered the second five-week summer session. With that incentive I completed the writing by July 15 and was able to present the manuscript to this senior and graduate-level class. The manuscript was quickly revised based in part upon student responses and sent off to press."[28] Again, Gill's students (the vast bulk of whom are non-Indian) inform the teacher (also a non-Indian) of what they want to hear, he responds by accommodating their desires, and the result becomes the stuff which passes as "proper understanding" of Indians in academe.

News of this incipient text induced a certain rumbling among Denver-area Indians, complete with letters of outrage from community leaders. The institutional response was that Gill, regardless of the merits of anything he may have said or written, was protected within the rubric of "academic freedom." Wallace Coffey, a Comanche who directed the Denver Indian center, summed up community feeling at the time by observing that while the university was no doubt correct in claiming Gill's activities should be covered by academic freedom guarantees, "It's funny that every time a non-Indian wants to say something about Indians, no matter how outlandish or inaccurate, they start to talk about academic freedom. But every time an Indian applies for a faculty job, all they can talk about are 'academic standards.' I guess I'll be forgiven for saying it seems to me somebody's talking out of both sides of their mouth here. And I don't mind saying that I think this situation has a lot to do with why so few Indians ever get to teach in the universities in this state."[29]

Unsurprisingly, given the circumstances and overall context of its creation, when *Mother Earth* was eventually released it extended the thesis that it's subject had never been a bona fide element of indigenous tradition at all. Instead, its author held that the whole idea had been inculcated among American Indians by early European colonists, and had been developed and perfected since the conquest. With deadly predictability, he went on to conclude that insofar as any special rights to North America accrue to a belief in Mother Earth, they must accrue to everyone, Native and Euroamerican alike (one is left a bit unclear as to Gill's views on the proprietary interests of Afro and Asian Americans on the continent). Thus, *Mother Earth* is *An American* (rather than Native American) *Story.*[30]

A Discussion with Sam Gill

Shortly after his book's release, I called Sam Gill on the phone. After a few moments of conversation, he asked whether I was upset by what he'd written. I replied that I was indeed quite upset and responded to his query as to why this might be with a long and somewhat disjointed discourse on the nature of cultural imperialism, the fact that he'd quoted material I'd ghost-written for others quite out of context, and my impression that he'd quite deliberately avoided including *any* American Indians directly in the research process by which he'd reached conclusions about them so profoundly antithetical to their own. "I think we had better meet in person," he said.

To his credit, Gill kept the appointment, arriving as scheduled at my office. In response to his request to go deeper into some of the issues I'd raised on the phone, I explained that I felt there was probably validity to the idea he'd articulated in *Mother Earth* that the interpretation and reinterpretation of the Mother Earth concept by succeeding generations of Euroamericans (such as Gill himself) had blocked any broad understanding of the original indigenous meaning of it. I also acknowledged that this additive phenomenon had, over the years, no doubt carried the popular notion of Mother Earth very far from any indigenous meaning. However, with that said, I stressed that nothing in either postulation precluded there having already been a well-developed indigenous Mother Earth concept operant in North America before contact. Further, I emphasized he'd brought out nothing in his book which precluded an *ongoing* and autonomous Native American conceptualization of Mother Earth, divorced from popular (mis)understandings, exactly like traditionalist Indians presently claim.

"Well," he said, "this is interesting. I quite agree with you, and I think that's pretty much what I said in the book. Have you read it?" Taken by surprise, I reached across my desk for a copy and read an excerpt from page 6:

> As I have come to know it, the story of Mother Earth is a distinctively American story. Mother Earth, as she has existed in North America, cannot be adequately understood and appreciated apart from the complex history of the encounter between Native Americans and Americans of European ancestry, nor apart from comprehending that *the scholarly enterprise that has sought to describe her has had a hand in bringing her into existence, a hand even in introducing her to Native American peoples* [emphasis added].

Without looking up, I skipped to page 7: "... *Mother Earth has come into existence in America largely within the last one hundred years....* When her story is told, it becomes clear how all Americans, whatever their heritage, may proclaim Mother Earth to be the mother of us all ...[emphasis added]." And again, almost at random, from page 157: "Mother Earth is also mother to the Indians. This study has shown that *she has become so only recently,* and then not without influence from Americans ...[emphasis added]." With the third quote, I indicated I could go on but figured the point had been made. At this juncture Gill suggested that perhaps he'd not been as clear in the writing of the book as he'd intended. I countered that while I agreed the text suffered certain difficulties in exposition, these particular passages seemed quite clear, in line with his overall treatise as I understood it, and lacking only in possible alternative interpretations. "Oh well" he said with a small shrug, "I never intended this as a book on religion anyway. I wrote it as a study in American history. Are you planning to review it?"

When I replied that, yes, I was, and as widely as possible, he said, "Then I'd very much appreciate it if you'd treat it as an historical work, not in the framework of religious studies. Fair enough?" Surprised again, I agreed.

Gill's Historiography

There are a number of points of departure from which one might begin to assess Sam Gill's historical project, none of them as telling as the way in which he defines the object of his quest. On the very first page he declares that, "Mother Earth is not only a Native American *goddess* but a *goddess* of people the world over . . .[emphasis added]." Two things are striking here:

- First, Gill seems from the outset to simply disregard the obvious literal meanings of statements by three different American Indians—the nineteenth century Wanapum leader Smohalla, contemporary Navajo politician Peterson Zah, and AIM leader Russell Means—which he quotes on the same page. In each of these diverse utterances, the speaker refers to the earth *herself* as being "the mother." All allegorical references to human anatomy—e.g.: the soil as "skin," rocks as "bones"—are clearly extended *from* this premise in an effort to allow the (non-Indian) listener to apprehend the concept at issue. *No* attempt is being made to utilize the earth as an allegory by which to explain some humanesque entity.

- Second, Gill immediately insists upon precisely this reversal of polarities, quoting Edward Taylor to the effect that, "among the native races of America the Earth Mother is one of the great *personages* of mythology [emphasis added]." He then reinforces this by quoting Ake Hultkrantz, a major contemporary Swedish scholar on American Indian religions: "The belief in a *goddess,* usually identified with Mother Earth, is found almost everywhere in North America [emphasis added]."

This is what is commonly referred to as "setting up a straw man." By thus "establishing" on the opening page that the Native American conception of Mother Earth assumes the Eurocentric form of a "goddess"—rather than the literal "earth deity" embodied in the articulated indigenous meaning—Gill has contrived a false context for his historical examination which allows him to reach *only* the conclusions he desires: i.e., the notion of an "earth goddess" did not exist in Native North America prior to the European invasion. Therefore, ipso facto, it follows that Europeans had as much or more to do with the creation of the indigenous conceptualization of Mother Earth as did the Indians themselves.

The conclusions will be "true," of course, given the author's framing of the questions. But one could as easily decide that, insofar as the yin and yang principles of Taoism and Zen Buddhism embody female and male principles, they too "must" signify a god and goddess. Self-evidently, no amount of "historical scrutiny" will reveal the existence in these traditions of a goddess named Yin or a god named Yang. Not withstanding the fact that such god and goddess entities never had a place in the Buddhist or Taoist lexicons themselves, are we not bound by Gillian "logic" to conclude that neither the yin nor the yang principle ever had a place in the structure of either Taoist or Buddhist spiritual concepts? And, if we do manage to reach this absurd conclusion, does it not follow that since the terms yin and yang are now employed within the vernaculars of these traditions, they must have originated in the interaction between East and West, the concepts themselves "introduced" to the Orient by the Occident? To the extent that we can accept the whole charade up to this point, won't it follow that we are now entitled to consider Buddhism to be as much a part of our own non-Buddhist heritage (read: "property") as it is for the Buddhist Vietnamese, or even the Zen monks? Such questions tend to answer themselves.

In many ways, then, examination of Gill's historiography need go no further than this. A project as flawed at its inception as his offers little hope of reaching productive outcomes, a matter rendered all the more acute when an author exhibits as marked a propensity to manipulate his data, forcing it to conform to his predispositions regardless of the maiming and distortion which ensues, as does Gill. Examples of this last appear not only in the manner described with regard to the first page of *Mother Earth*, but in abundance—through the sins of both omission and commission—within the remainder of the book.

As concerns omission, one need only turn to a section entitled "The Triumph of Civilization over Savagism" (pages 30–39) to catch the drift. Here, we find Gill making much of the female Indian ("Mother Earth") iconography being produced in Europe and its North American colonies from roughly 1575 until 1765. It is not that he handles what he discusses with any particular inaccuracy. Rather, it's that he completely neglects to mention that there was a roughly equal proportion of male Indian iconography streaming from the same sources during the same period. Along the same line, and in the same section, he goes into the impact of Pocahontas (female Indian, "Mother Earth") mythology on the formation of Americana without even an aside to the existence of its Hiawatha (male Indian) corollary. The result of this sort of skewed presentation is to preclude the drawing of reasoned conclusions from the subject matter, and to block the book from serving as a useful contribution to the literature in any way at all.

In terms of commission, there is a small matter of Gill putting words (or meanings) into people's mouths. The clearest examples of this lie in Chapter 7 (pages 129–50), in which he sets out to "prove" that the adoption of a belief in Mother Earth has led contemporary American Indians away from their traditional tribal/cultural specificity and toward a homogeneous sort of "pan-Indianism" (this is a variation on the standard rationalization that Indian rights no longer exist as such because Indians in the traditional sense no longer exist). To illustrate this idea, he selects quotations from several individuals including Grace (Spotted Eagle) Black Elk, Sun Bear, and Russell Means.

Grace Black Elk is dead and can therefore no longer clarify or debunk the meaning Gill assigns her words. However, in my own (extensive) experience with her, she was always *very* clear that, while she strongly and unswervingly supported the rights of all indigenous peoples to pursue their traditional spirituality, she herself followed *only* what she described as "Lakota way." Further, she was consistently firm in her desire not to see the Lakota way diluted or "contaminated" by the introduction of other traditions. Such a position is obviously rather far from the somewhat amorphous, intertribal spiritual amalgam Gill claims she represented.[31]

Sun Bear was also quite clear, albeit in an entirely different way. Marketing aside, he stated repeatedly and for the record that the eclectic spiritual porridge he served up had "nothing to do with Indian religion," "pan" or otherwise. He also openly acknowledged that his adherents were composed almost exclusively of non-Indians; he admitted that he tended to steer well clear of Indians, because they would have "beat me up or kill[ed] me" due to the deliberately misleading marketing strategies he employed. *This* is the emblem of an "emerging pan-Indianism"?[32]

As concerns Russell Means, Gill quotes repeatedly from a single speech delivered at the 1980 Black Hills Survival Gathering. While assigning a pan-Indianist meaning to the passages he elects to use, he carefully destroys the context in which the words were spoken. This includes categorical statements, toward the end of the speech, that Means does *not* consider or intend himself to be a "leader" in the pan-Indian sense, and that his thinking and actions are guided by a view of himself as "an Oglala Lakota patriot."[33] Again, it is difficult to conceive a much clearer statement of tribally specific orientation and motivation—and rejection of pan-Indianism—than this.

Ultimately, the reviewer is left with the feeling that he should replay in paraphrase a scene from the film, *Apocalypse Now*. Sam Gill (playing Col. Kurtz; Marlon Brando) asks: "Do you find my methods to be unsound?" The reviewer (playing Capt. Willard; Martin Sheen) replies: "Frankly, sir, I can't find any valid method at all."

A Question of "Revisionism"

The point has been made by Roger Echohawk, a Pawnee student at the University of Colorado, that even if Gill's historiography is lacking in certain important respects, there could still be a practical value and utility to his analysis of particular themes or subtopics.[34] The point is accurate enough on its face, if a bit strained, and is therefore worth pursuing at least to some extent. By way of example, we will concentrate on the first of the major historical occurrences dealt with in *Mother Earth*—Tecumseh's "Mother Earth statement"—negation of which serves as a linchpin for Gill's arguments throughout the rest of the book.

After a brief and reasonably accurate depiction of Tecumseh's diplomatic and military confrontations with the United States (pages 8–13), Gill sets out to prove that the great Shawnee leader never actually made a particular statement—"The earth is my mother, and on her bosom I will repose"—during negotiations with William Henry Harrison in 1810. On pages 13–14, he notes that he has discovered a total of 27 references to this statement in the literature of the nineteenth century, the first of these in an article in the *National Recorder* on May 12, 1821, by an anonymous author. The next, he says on page 15, comes in a little-read history written by Moses Dawson, a former aide to Harrison and eyewitness to the negotiations, published in 1824. Then came Henry Rowe Schoolcraft's *Travels in the Central Portions of the Mississippi Valley* in 1825. After that, there were a steady stream of references, several by other eyewitnesses.

The obvious conclusion to be drawn from all this is that so many people refer to the Tecumseh statement for the simple reason that this is what the man said. The difficulty for Gill in this proposition, however, is that Tecumseh's having said it would seriously unhinge a portion of the thesis presented in *Mother Earth*. Hence, he faces the need to demonstrate that the verbiage attributed to the Indian actually came from another, non-Indian source, and that all succeeding published references merely parroted what had been said before. The logical source in this scenario would be

Schoolcraft, given that he was far and away the most popular, accessible, and thus quotable of the writers in question. This is problematic insofar as both the 1821 and 1824 references were published prior to Schoolcraft's book. Gill "solves" this difficulty on page 15 by "suggesting" that for unexplained reasons Schoolcraft—who is not at all known for a tendency to write anonymous tracts, and who was a "name" any editor would have gladly afforded a byline—authored the unattributed *Recorder* article in 1821, unaccountably fabricating the Tecumseh statement.

An implication of this thoroughly unsubstantiated "historical discovery," never brought out in *Mother Earth*, is that for some equally unexplained reason Dawson must next have opted to deliberately falsify *his* historical record of the negotiations by borrowing this fictional quotation from an obscure three-year-old article which even Gill describes as "filler" in the back pages of a magazine.

After the date of Schoolcraft's book, of course, Gill is much freer to write off other eyewitness accounts as fabrications (at least with regard to the Tecumseh statement). This includes an account contained in Josiah Gregg's 1844 *Commerce of the Prairies* (covered on pages 21–22), and the accounts of Augustus Jones and Major Joseph M. McCormick, recorded by Lyman D. Draper of the State Historical Society of Wisconsin during the mid-1880s (covered on pages 23–24). All one need do is accept Gill's utterly unsubstantiated—and unlikely—initial speculations, and his subsequent chronology of systematic plagiarism works out splendidly.

Having thus dismissed standard history as nothing short of a sustained hoax involving everyone from participants to playwrights, Gill next sets out to "correct" the record. This he purports to accomplish by reference to a solitary eyewitness account, this time by a man named Felix Bouchie, published in the *Vincennes Commercial* on January 8, 1889 (covered on pages 25–27). Therein is found a recounting of an interchange between Tecumseh and Harrison which occurred on a bench (not on the ground), lasting every bit of five minutes during two full days of negotiations, and in which the Mother Earth statement (an utterance which would require less than five seconds) is not made. Bouchie does not state that Tecumseh did *not* make the Mother Earth statement; he is simply recounting something else, and does not bring it up.

Again, there are obvious conclusions to be drawn. For instance, it would seem likely—since there was ample time available—that both the bench episode *and* the Mother Earth episode might have occurred at different points, or even different days during the negotiations. Bouchie does not claim to have been present during the entirety of the sessions, and his account could be responsibly viewed as a valuable *addition* to the record. Gill, however, will have none of this. Rather, he insists that Bouchie's version of events "must" have occurred *instead of* the other 27 more-or-less harmonious versions. This, he says, constitutes his final (crushing?) "proof" that the extremely well-documented Tecumseh statement is a fiction.

One senior American Indian scholar (who wishes to remain anonymous), upon reviewing Gill's Tecumseh material, dismissed him as "a lunatic, not worth the time and energy to argue with."[35] In a less emotional and more constructive vein, Osage/Cherokee theologian George Tinker, offered a more thoughtful insight:

> You know, what we're confronted with here is not uniquely—and maybe at this point not even primarily—an American Indian issue. What this calls to mind more than anything is the sort of "historical revisionism" practiced by people like Arthur Butz and Richard Harwood, guys who use all sorts of pseudo-scholarly sleights-of-hand to "prove" the Holocaust never happened. Their stuff won't hold up to even minimal scrutiny, but they keep right on going because they're ideologically motivated.[36]

Precisely. And with that, there seems very little left to say concerning the possible value of Sam Gill's historical analyses.

Conclusion

And so the question naturally arises as to what sort of ideology might prompt an individual like Sam Gill to write a book lending itself to comparison with the sordid neonazi sentiments of an Arthur Butz.[37] Certainly he would recoil in horror at the suggestion of such linkage at any level. Likely, the same can be said for any of his cohorts from Castaneda to Highwater, from Sun Bear's ersatz Indians to the ecology movement (with the possible exception of the Earth First! Foreman/Abbey/Weurthner group, which seems to have found its preferred niche under the term "fascist").[38]

By and large, it appears just as probable that most of the above would express a vehement and heartfelt disavowal of the historical processes of physical genocide and expropriation visited upon Native Americans by the federal government. In their own minds, they are typically steadfast opponents of all such policies and the ideologies of violence which undergird them. At some level they are no doubt sincere in their oft and loudly repeated professions of being true "Friends of the Indian."[39] There can be no question but that they've convinced themselves that they are divorced completely from the ugly flow of American history, and it would be worse than dubious to suggest that they might be inclined to muster forth the 7th Cavalry to work their will.

Yet, demonstrably, as much as any missionary, soldier or government bureaucrat who preceded them, those of the New Age have proven themselves willing to disregard the rights of American Indians to any modicum of cultural sanctity or psychological sanctuary. They too willfully and consistently disregard the protests and objections of their victims, speaking only of their own "right to know" and to victimize. They too have exhibited an ability to pursue courses of conduct bearing arguably genocidal implications, to shrug off the danger, and to argue only that genocide couldn't be genocide if they are the perpetrators of it.[40] They too have persistently shown themselves willing to lie, distort, fabricate, cheat and steal in order to accomplish their agenda. The salient queries may thus be reduced to "why?" and "what are they after?"

The answers, in a real sense, are as simple as the facts that they are here and that they fully plan to stay. While the New Age can hardly be rationally accused of performing the conquest of the Americas, and its adherents go to great lengths in expressing their dismay at the methods used therein, they have clearly inherited what their ancestors gained thereby, both in terms of resources and in terms of relative power. The New Agers, for all their protestations to the contrary, aren't about to give up any of either.[41]

Their task, then, is that of simultaneously hanging on to what has been stolen while separating themselves from the *way* in which it was stolen. It is a somewhat tricky psychological project of being able to "feel good about themselves" (that ultimate expression of the New Age) through "legitimizing" the maintenance of their own colonial privilege. The project is essentially ideological. As Martin Carnoy has explained it:

> The legitimation of the colonist's role requires the destruction of the [colonized's] sense of culture and history, so the colonized is removed [or excluded] from all social and cultural responsibility.[42]

Albert Memmi adds:

> In order for the legitimacy to be complete, it is not enough for the colonized to be a slave [or thoroughly dispossessed and disenfranchised], he must also accept his role. The bond between colonizer and colonized is thus [both] destructive and creative.[43]

Within the context of our immediate concern, these insights add up to the circumstance where Native Americans are marginalized or barred from participation in the generation of "knowledge" concerning their histories, cultures and beliefs. The realties at issue are then systematically supplanted, negated and reconstructed to suit the psychological needs of the current crop of colonizers, and the result reproduced as "truth" among both the oppressors and oppressed. As early as 1973, Jamake Highwater was telling us that, "[truth] is not simply a matter of getting the facts wrong, but of developing a credible falsehood."[44] In 1984, he went further:

> The final belief is to believe in a fiction, which you know to be a fiction. There being nothing else, the exquisite truth is to know that it is a fiction and that you believe in it willingly.[45]

In its final manifestation, the mythology which is forged ("created") in this process *always* assumes the form of an "inclusive" doctrine, legitimizing the present colonial status quo. The invaders' "contributions," however invented they may be, inevitably "entitle" them to superior status; there may have been a problem once, but it's in the past so forget it; we're all in this together now, so let's move forward (with me in the lead); I'm okay, you're okay (so long as you stay in your place and don't upset me with questions of or challenges to my privilege), and so on. We can now name the ideology which motivates the Sam Gills of America. It is called "New Age," but as Russell Means once remarked in an another connection, it represents only "the same old song of Europe."[46] And, in the contemporary United States, its codification has rapidly become an academic growth industry.

Hence, the living fabric of Indian society is to be destroyed as its youth are "educated" to view their heritage in exactly the same way as those who seek to subsume it. This is no rupture with, but rather a continuation and perfection of the twin systems of colonization and genocide which have afflicted Native America for the past 500 years. From this vantage point, false as it is from start to finish, the scholarly disgrace which constitutes *Mother Earth* really *is* "an American story."

Notes

1. See, e.g., Michael Hilger, *The New Golden Land: European Images of America from the Discoveries to the Present* (New York: Pantheon, 1975); Robert F. Berkhofer, Jr., *The White Man's Indian: Images of the Indian from Columbus to the Present* (New York: Alfred A. Knopf, 1978).

2. See Richard de Mille, *Castaneda's Journey: The Power and the Allegory* (Santa Barbara, CA: Capra Press, 1976); also see pp. 27-65 of this volume.

3. The best material on J Marks/Jamake Highwater is Hank Adams' *Cannibal Green* (Olympia, WA: Survival of American Indians, 1984). The biography is J Marks, *Mick Jagger: The Singer, Not the Song* (New York: Curtis Books, 1973). It should be noted that Adams conclusively identified a still earlier Highwater incarnation as being that of experiental filmmaker Gregory Markopoulis, the son of Greek immigrants. So much for his purported identity as an "American Indian," asserted most polemically in his "Second Class Indians," *American Indian Law Journal*, No. 6, 1980.

4. Vine Deloria, Jr., "*Hanta Yo*: Super-Hype," *CoEvolution Quarterly*, Vol. 5, No. 4, 1979; Beatrice Medicine, "*Hanta Yo*: A New Phenomenon," *The Indian Historian*, Vol. 12, No. 2, 1979; Ward Churchill, "Ayn Rand and the Sioux—Tonto Revisited: Another Look at *Hanta Yo*," *Lakota Eyapaha*, Vol. 4, No. 2., 1980.

5. Andrews has lately promoted herself to the station of "Master Shaman" in an interview posted on the worldwide web. Interestingly, while a considerable array of similar promotional materials also appear therein, and are readily accessible, server access has been blocked to all entries critical of either the "shaman" or her published writings. Putting up such roadblocks along the information superhighway must, of course, be the work of "Red Dog" or some other of the malevolent male spirits Andrews depicts as inhabiting the native cosmos (certainly she herself would never stoop to such tactics).

6. William Red Fox, *The Memoirs of Chief Red Fox* (New York: Fawcett, 1972); Nino Cochise, *The First Hundred Years of Nino Cochise* (New York: Fawcett, 1972); Hyemeyohsts Storm, *Seven Arrows* (New York: Ballantine, 1972); David Seals, *The Pow Wow Highway* (Denver: Sky Press, 1984).

7. For one of the slimiest imaginable overviews of these folk and others of their ilk, see Stephen Harrod Buhner's *one spirit, many peoples: a manifesto for earth spirituality* (Niwot, CO: Roberts, Rinehart, 1997). For a taste of the real deal, check out Sun Bear and Wabun, *The Medicine Wheel: Earth Astrology* (Englewood Cliffs, NJ: Prentice-Hall, 1980).

8. Vine Deloria, Jr., talk at the University of Colorado at Boulder, June 1982 (tape on file).

9. Pam Colorado, letter to Ward Churchill, Jan. 19, 1984.

10. See, e.g., Philip Staniford, "I Come to Praise Carlos, Not to Bury don Juan," in Richard de Mille, ed., *The Don Juan Papers: Further Castaneda Controversies* (Santa Barbara, CA: Ross-Erikson, 1980). p. 151.

11. For a good taste of Garfinkle's theory, see his *Studies in Ethnomethodology* (New York: Prentice-Hall, 1967). On his role in the development of ethnomethodological theory and technique, see John Heritage, *Garfinkle and Ethnomethodology* (New York: Polity Press, 1984).

12. Gary Snyder, talk at the Naropa Institute, Boulder, CO, June 1983.

13. The event was conducted at the Rocky Mountain Peace Center, Boulder, CO.

14. The store, now defunct, was called "Crystal Market."

15. Interview with Barbara Owl, Apr. 17, 1987 (tape on file).

16. Ibid.

17. Interview with Russell Means, Oct. 12, 1989 (tape on file).

18. The reference is to the United Nations 1948 Convention on Prevention and Punishment of the Crime of Genocide (U.S.T._____, T.I.A.S._____, 78 U.N.T.S). The full text of the Convention will be found in Ian Brownlie, ed., *Basic Documents on Human Rights* (Oxford: Clarendon Press, [3rd ed.] 1992) pp. 31-4.

19. Means interview, op. cit.

20. Robert Davis and Mark Zannis, *The Genocide Machine in Canada: The Pacification of the North* (Montréal: Black Rose Books, 1973) p.20.

21. Ibid.

22. There is a startling confluence in this regard between New Age "progressives" on the one hand and some of the most reactionary sectors of anthropological orthodoxy on the other. A good sampling of the latter will be found in James A. Clifton, ed., *The Invented Indian: Cultural Fictions and Government Policies*

(New Brunswick, NJ: Transaction Books, 1990). For critique, see pp. 121-36 of this volume.

23. George Weurthner, "An Ecological View of the Indian," *Earth First!*, Vol. VII, No. VII, 1987. Again, the confluence with ideas prevalent in the reactionary anthropological circles is striking. See, e.g., Paul S. Martin and H.E. Wright, eds., *Pleistocene Extinctions: The Search for a Cause* (New Haven, CT: Yale University Press, 1967).

24. Weurthner, "Ecological View," op. cit.

25. See, e.g., Abbey's "Letter to the Editor," published in the April-May 1986 edition of *Bloomsbury Review*. For related views on Latinos—that they are "ignorant, unskilled, and culturally-morally-generically impoverished people"—see his *One Life at a Time, Please* (New York: Henry Holt, 1987) p. 43. As to Abbey's being an Earth First! "guru," it should be noted that his novel *The Monkey Wrench Gang* (Salt Lake City: Dream Garden Press, 1985 reprint of 1975 original) provided the organization's formative inspiration; see Dave Foreman and Bill Haywood, *Ecodefense: A Field Guide to Monkeywrenching* (Tucson: Ned Ludd Books, [2nd ed.] 1987). Also see Susan Zakin, *Coyotes and Town Dogs: Earth First! and the Environmental Movement* (New York: Viking, 1993) pp. 133-4.

26. Foreman also openly adopted a "let them starve" posture during the Ethiopian famine of the 1980s, as an expedient to reducing overpopulation of African blacks. As he himself explains it, he comes from "a deeply entrenched racist tradition" that "gives little thought to exploiting...people of color," a matter that "undoubtedly affects [his] politics and organizing"; Steve Chase, ed., *Defending the Earth: A Dialogue Between Murray Bookchin and Dave Foreman* (Boston: South End Press, 1991) pp. 125, 89. It should be noted that Earth First! leader Christopher Manes went rather further than Foreman. Writing under the psuedonym "Miss Ann Thropy," he enthusiastically embraced the AIDS epidemic, not only in central Africa and the Caribbean, but among North American gays, as a mechanism of reducing the planet's surplus population of humans ("Population and AIDS," *Earth First!*, Vol. VII, No. VI, 1987).Manes is author of *Green Rage: Radical Environmentalism and the Unmaking of Civilization* (Boston: Little, Brown, 1990). For more of the wit and wisdom of Dave Foreman, see his *Confessions of an Eco-Warrior* (New York: Crown, 1991).

27. Sam Gill, "The Continuity of Research and Classroom Teaching, or How to Have Your Cake and Eat It Too," in Mary Ann Shea, ed., *On Teaching* (Boulder: University of Colorado Teaching Excellence Program, 1987) p. 68.

28. Ibid.

29. Wallace Coffey, "Letter to the Editor," *Camp Crier*, Mar. 11, 1988.

30. Sam D. Gill, *Mother Earth: An American Story* (Chicago: University of Chicago Press, 1987).

31. For a sample of Grace Black Elk's views, see her statement in Jane Katz's *I Am the Fire of Time: Voices of Native American Women* (New York: E.P. Dutton, 1977).

32. Sun Bear was emphatic on these points during a 1984 meeting in Denver between him, Colorado AIM leader Glenn T.Morris and myself arranged by his daughter, Winona LaDuke, to discuss exactly such points.

33. Russell Means, "The Same Old Song," in my *Marxism and Native Americans* (Boston: South End Press, 1983) pp. 19-34.For the record, I'm the person referred to on the first page of the piece referred to as having written it.

34. Echohawk's comments were made during a roundtable on *Mother Earth* at the University of Colorado/Boulder, Apr. 19, 1988.

35. It can at this point be revealed that the senior scholar was Vine Deloria, Jr., who made his observation during a conversation over coffee during the spring of 1989.

36. George Tinker, letter to Ward Churchill, May 3, 1988. His reference is to the neonazi Institute for Historical Review, a California-based entity devoted to publishing materials purportedly proving that the Holocaust never occurred. On this and related matters, see Pierre Vidal-Niquet, *Assassins of Memory: Essays on the Denial of the Holocaust* (New York: Columbia University Press, 1992); Deborah Lipstadt, *Denying the Holocaust: The Growing Assault on Truth and Memory* (New York: Free Press, 1993).

37. The two books Tinker apparently had in mind were Arthur Butz's *The Hoax of the Twentieth Century: The Case Against the Presumed Extermination of European Jewry* (Torrance, CA: Institute for Historical Review, 1977) and Richard Harwood's *Did Six Million Really Die?* (Richmond, Surrey, UK: English Historical Review Press, 1974). It is noteworthy that Harwood's real name is Richard Verrall.

38. Actually, "ecofascist." Murray Bookchin is credited with originating the term in an article titled "Social Ecology versus Deep Ecology," although he subsequently retracted it; Chase, *Defending the Earth*, op. cit., p. 124. Also see Bill Devall, "Deep Ecology and Its Critics," *Earth First!*, Vol. VII, No. VI, 1987; Warwick Fox, *Towards a Transpersonal Ecology* (Boston: Shambhala, 1990) p. 49.

39. For insights into an earlier iteration of the same mentality, see Francis Paul Prucha, ed., *Americanizing the American Indian: Writings of the "Friends of the Indian," 1800-1900* (Lincoln: University of Nebraska Press, 1973).

40. This is exactly the position taken by Stephen Harrod Buhner in his *one spirit, many peoples*, op. cit.

41. For extended analysis, see "Indians 'R' Us? Reflections on the Men's Movement," in my *Indians Are Us? Culture and Genocide in Native North America* (Monroe, ME: Common Courage Press, 1994) pp. 207-72.

42. Martin Carnoy, *Education as Cultural Imperialism* (New York: David McKay, 1974) p.62.

43. Albert Memmi, *The Colonizer and the Colonized* (Boston: Beacon Press, 1965) p. 89.

44. Marks, *Singer*, op. cit., p. 134.

45. Jamake Highwater, *Words in the Blood* (New York: New American Library, 1984) p. ix

46. Means, "Same Old Song," op. cit., p.26.

The New Racism

A Critique of James A. Clifton's *The Invented Indian*

> Here come the anthros,
> Better hide your past away.
> Here come the anthros,
> On another holiday.
>
> —Floyd Westerman
> *Here Come the Anthros*

In a lecture delivered at the University of Colorado's Boulder campus in 1987, black liberation movement leader Kwame Turé (Stokely Carmichael) observed that, "In the struggles of the 1960s, we confronted a defining characteristic of American life which was as old as the republic itself. This was a racism which stood proud and defiant, which strutted its stuff in hoods and robes by the light of burning crosses, a racism that ruled through Jim Crow, backed up by the lyncher's rope. We confronted this racism and it's fair to say we defeated it in open battle. The evidence of this is that by the 1970s we witnessed racism in retreat and disarray. For the first time in American history, racism was forced to become a whimpering thing, scurrying timidly from shadow to shadow, slinking about the recesses of white consciousness." He then proceeded to describe what happened next:

> Here, we made a fundamental error. Having succeeded in driving racism underground, we became comfortable and complacent, falsely believing this hidden creature was dead or dying. Instead of going forward and driving our stake through the heart of the monster, we relaxed and enjoyed ourselves, allowing racism time and space in which to recover from its wounds, to regroup, refit and reenter the fray. And so now it is back, vibrantly resurgent, having analyzed and digested the lessons of its temporary losses in the '60s. Consequently, it is a new and far more sophisticated form of racism which we must confront in the '80s. . . . Racism today, and this will undoubtedly be the case throughout the '90s, no longer travels the road of Lester Maddox, Bull Connor and the Ku Klux Klan. Where the old racism was overt, frankly announcing its hatred and opposition to all peoples of color, the new racism smiles and insists it is our friend.

Where the old racism ruled through physical violence, racism in its new form asserts its dominance through sheer mendacity. Racism has become covert in its expression, hiding behind a mask of calm and reason. The key to understanding racism today is that it inevitably parades itself about, cloaked in the garb of antiracism. It is therefore far more dangerous, powerful and difficult to combat than ever before.

The book at hand fits neatly into such an assessment. *The Invented Indian: Cultural Fictions and Government Policies* (Transaction Books, New York, 1990), a collection of essays assembled and edited by University of Wisconsin anthropologist James A. Clifton, purportedly seeks, according to its jacket notes, to help American Indians by utilizing "passion, wit and sound scholarship" to inject a "healthy dose of realism" into both popular and academic non-Indian understandings of us.[1] This is a noble purpose, since only through such realism can the debunking of myths and stereotypes, and the correction of more "scientifically" erroneous information, can relations between culturally distinct peoples be bettered. This is especially true in situations such as Indians and Euroamericans now find themselves, where one group has come to completely dominate the other. Unfortunately, the jacket blurbs lie. The function of *The Invented Indian* is to attempt a repeal of virtually every glimmer of truth about Native America which has emerged since 1970, reasserting in their stead the full range of reactionary fables long advanced by proponents of the white supremacist colonialism in which Indians are presently engulfed.

Setting the Stage

The tone of what will follow is established by Clifton himself on the first page of his introduction, "Memoir, Exegesis," in a passage where he acknowledges a personal lack of interest in "Indians per se."[2] As he explains it in the next several paragraphs, he got into the Indian business as a student, by accident, and only because of the splendid opportunity to engage in clinical observation of a process of radical "social transformation" afforded by the government-mandated termination and dissolution of the Klamath Nation during the 1950s. One is left with the queasy feeling that the editor/author's view is that indigenous societies exist only to serve as a series of "valuable case studies" edifying the curiosities of "skilled researchers" such as himself. Generous whiffs of the aromatic mentality described by Robert Jay Lifton in *The Nazi Doctors* drift through more than a few of Clifton's initial passages.[3]

Nor do things improve thereafter. Throughout the introduction and in the book's first chapter—"The Indian Story: A Cultural Fiction," also written by the editor—it is argued in effect that acknowledging anything positive in the native past is an entirely wrongheaded proposition.[4] This is so, he argues with no substantiation whatever, because no genuine Indian accomplishments have ever "really" been substantiated. Stripped of its pseudoacademic trappings, however, Clifton's position is entirely political, a matter he tacitly admits when he announces that what is at issue in his book is not mere "scholarly truth," but "deadly serious twentieth-century business."[5]

Reduced to simplest form, his thesis is that recognizing precontact indigenous attainments contributes to unseemly measures of pride and hope for the future on the part of modern Indians, a combination which retards their necessary and inevitable disappearance as culturally identifiable human groups. The rightful role of scholarship, he implies, is to assist in the process of cultural genocide, perfecting a Eurospecific hegemony designed to exclude American Indians from history and, ultimately, from existence itself. Noting that the then-approaching quincentennial of Columbus' arrival in the Americas provides a perfect arena for such counterproductive activities, Clifton announces that the intended function of *The Invented Indian* itself is to help restrain the general public from being "bamboozled" by such unhelpful sentiments as guilt or remorse into assisting native people in bettering their current lot.[6] 1992, it is suggested, should instead be the year in which "the vanishing native" finally vanishes, once and for all.

A major impediment to realization of this lofty goal, the editor makes clear, has been that far too many Indians and "sympathetic" non-Indians have been lately allowed to present their case. While gratuitously dismissing as "unfounded" such learned and widely respected material as the works of Vine Deloria, Jr., Francis Jennings' *The Invasion of America*, Russell Thornton's *American Indian Holocaust and Survival*, Steven Cornell's *Return of the Native*, James Axtell's *The Invasion Within*, Dee Brown's *Bury My Heart at Wounded Knee*, Jack Weatherford's *Indian Givers*, and other "volumes . . . draped with footnotes, statistical tables, and flow charts,"[7] Clifton demonstrates his own near-perfect ignorance of such subject matter by predicting that his conclusions will by attacked by such "Red McCarthyite" publications as *The Indian Historian*, a scholarly journal which had at the time been defunct for approximately ten years.[8]

Predictably, the antidote Clifton selects as appropriate to counteract the severe problems he sees streaming from contemporary American Indian studies is adoption of the methodological approach advocated by Werner

Sollors in his guidebook to the new racist intellectualism, *Beyond Ethnicity*.[9] This is to say that all work done about Indians by Indians—or by non-Indians, but with which Indians are known to agree—should, no matter what its presentation or documentation, be disregarded out of hand as "partisan . . . intellectual atrocities."[10] "Sound scholarship" requires that all such material be (re)interpreted by "responsible" Euroamerican academics who, above all else, embody the necessary "distance" and "objectivity" necessary to arrive at "realistic" determinations about any people of color (by the same token, of course, this would mean only people of color possess the neutrality and perspective needed to analyze and assess Euroamerica, but this truism seems never to have dawned on either Sollors or Clifton).

The Invented Indian is thus composed, exclusively and intentionally, of articles authored by non-Indians, most of them eager to go on record as "rethinking" one or another positive characteristic attributed to native people. Most of them appear to be motivated primarily by a desire to engage in public one-upsmanship with colleagues who they perceive as having snubbed them professionally at one time or another. Four of the contributors, including Clifton himself, are rather candid about having personal axes to grind with Indians in general. In several cases, they seem to have been further commended to the editor by nothing so much as their complete and utter incompetence to address the topics assigned them.

Charlatans and Shams

For instance, there is Temple University anthropologist Elizabeth Tooker, an alleged "leading authority on the culture and history of Northern Iroquoians."[11] Her essay, "The United States Constitution and the Iroquois League," supposedly refutes the "myth" that the six nations Haudenosaunee confederacy was a model of governance which significantly influenced the thinking of the founding fathers in the process of conceiving the U.S. republic.[12] Tooker has spent several years vociferously repeating her theme in every possible forum, and has actively attacked the credibility of scholars such as Don Grinde and Bruce Johansen, the results of whose research have reached opposite conclusions.[13] Yet, when questioned closely on the matter in a recent academic conference, this "expert" was forced to admit she had not only ignored all Iroquois source material while forming her thesis, but that she is quite unfamiliar the the relevant papers of John Adams, Thomas Jefferson, Benjamin Franklin, Tom Paine, and others among the U.S. founders themselves.[14]

Tooker is joined in her endeavor by Leland McDonald, a University of Victoria anthropologist who confesses to spending much of his own research time "refreshing [his] soul bird-watching or observing the fauna of tide-pools."[15] This would, of course, be commendable for someone working in ornithology or marine biology, but McDonald's project—elaborated in a piece titled "Liberty, Justice, Fraternity: Was the Indian Really Egalitarian?"—is to deny the generally recognized democratic content, not only of the Haudenosaunee, but of other indigenous North American societies as well.[16] In doing so, he not only rejects detailed information tendered by native people themselves, but by such notable non-Indian scholars as Lewis Henry Morgan and Franz Boas. Tellingly, he approaches the Herculean task of overturning a fundament of his discipline on the basis of a paucity of personal field work and a total of twenty-one end notes, nine of them lacking any citation whatsoever.

Then there is University of Colorado Religious Studies Professor Sam Gill, a self-annointed authority on native spirituality. In *The Invented Indian*, he brings forth the contention that a core concept of many indigenous traditions, the sense of earth as feminine entity, did not exist until Europeans came along to teach it. His essay, "Mother Earth: An American Myth," is a capsulized recycle of his earlier *Mother Earth: An American Story*, a book already exposed as one of the shoddier historiographical exercises in living memory.[17] At least one of Gill's supposed sources in preparing his Mother Earth thesis has gone on record calling him an out-and-out liar, while others have said as much in less public fashion.[18]

Next, we are treated to a pontification by David Henige, whose credentials in addressing an American Indian technical topic consist of being a bibliographer in *African* Studies at the University of Wisconsin. In his "Their Numbers Become Thick: Native American Historical Demography as Expiation," Henige claims to refute the arithmetic of such researchers as Lesley B. Simpson, Sherburn F. Cook, Woodrow Borah, Carl O. Sauer and Henry Dobyns, whom he dubs collectively as being "High Counters."[19] Although he never quite gets around to saying what he thinks the precontact native population of North America actually was, one is left to conclude that he seeks to negate any estimates going beyond the initial "conservative" projections advanced by James Mooney and Alfred L. Kroeber—whose own methodological abuses are by this point notorious, a matter about which Henige remains conspicuously silent—during the first half of this century.[20]

Reinforcement of suspicions that this is a goal of *The Invented Indian* comes in the form of a smug assertion advanced without so much as a pretense of support by French sociologist Jean-Jacques Simard in his essay, "Ghosts and Shadows: The Reduction of North American Natives": "The [less than two million] people today enumerated as Indian and Inuit in the United States and Canada now total about the same as the estimated population of the continent when Columbus arrived."[21]

Insights and Obfuscations

The question of indigenous agriculture is also raised. In this connection, an essay by the late Lynn Ceci, an anthropologist whose undistinguished career seems to have consisted primarily of questioning whether Indians ever engaged in *any* sort of human enterprise, is deployed. In the course of her lengthy tenure at SUNY, the author developed into an able if tedious tactician, as her posthumous contribution to the present volume readily indicates. Unable to nullify the obvious altogether, Ceci's "Squanto and the Pilgrims: On Planting Corn 'in the manner of the Indians'" instead belabors the weighty question of whether native planters along the eastern seaboard really used fish as fertilizer in the way described by early European colonists.[22] The idea appears to be that if the author can establish that this bit of Americana is incorrect, at least in part, then the whole notion that many Indian peoples were essentially farmers rather than "hunter-gatherers" can be drawn into question. As with most things, the process of deconstructing reality proceeds one step at a time.

Ceci's effort is accompanied by an even more trivial piece by Carol I. Mason who, like Clifton, is a University of Wisconsin anthropologist. In "A Small Sweet Something: Maple Sugaring in the New World," Mason fails even in her own terms to disprove that Indians utilized this substance (along with honey and other sweets) as an integral dietary component in precontact times, or that they passed along knowledge of it to the first European explorers: "[H]ow can independent testing procedures verify or not verify the conclusions drawn from the documents?. . . The promise of archaeological verification for problems of this kind is too often still but a promise."[23] Nonetheless, she goes on to conclude authoritatively that, "The Indian as aboriginal sugar maker is a projection of the state of dietary affairs in seventeenth-century England, a clearly ethnocentric interpretation of what constitutes an appropriate human diet."[24]

Another article mining the veins of banality, albeit with a non-agricultural focus, is "Pride and Prejudice: The Pocahontas Myth and the Pamunkey" by Christian F. Feest, a University of Vienna anthropologist who doubles as curator of North and Middle American collections at the Museum für Völkerkunde in the same city.[25] Feest's first essay—he has two, the second of which will be addressed below—is not so much offensive as it is irrelevant, showing as it does that a given indigenous people has undergone culture change over the past three centuries, and that the nature of this change has included incorporation of aspects of other cultures with which it has interacted. The intent may have been to demonstrate that the Pamunkey are no longer "really Indian" from a perspective which defines "Indianness" in terms of contemporary looking and acting exactly as they did in 1607, but all that is ultimately accomplished is to show that native North American cultures are neither static nor less adaptable than any other.

Perhaps ironically, *The Invented Indian* does contain three relatively good articles, written by Alice B. Kehoe, Richard de Mille, and Feest, respectively. In "Primal Gaia: Primitivists and Plastic Medicine Men," Kehoe, an anthropologist at Marquette University, does an excellent job of illuminating the fraudulent nature of "New Age Indianists" of both the genetically Indian (i.e.: Vincent "Sun Bear" LaDuke, "Rolling Thunder," Dhyani Ywahoo, Hyemeyohsts Storm and Wallace Black Elk) and of the non-Indian (i.e.: Adolf "Hungry Wolf" Gutohrlein, J "Jamake Highwater" Marks, Gary Snyder, Hilda Neihardt Petri, "John Redtail Freesoul," Lynn Andrews and José Arguelles) varieties.[26] A major problem with her piece, however, is that it is largely redundant, merely echoing public denunciations of these same individuals and practices advanced by native organizations as prominent and diverse as the North American Circle of Elders, American Indian Movement, National Indian Youth Council, and Northwest Indian Women's Circle beginning at least as early as 1980.[27] The author not only fails to acknowledge or reference the positions already adopted by indigenous traditionalists, she attributes the term "plastic medicine men" to "an Austrian Friends-Of-The-Indian group" when it actually originated in the Colorado AIM chapter.[28] The resulting impression conveyed is that Indians typically support ersatz shamanism, while it is left to smart white folks like herself to save the day by seeing through it.

Far and away the most honest and accurate item included in *The Invented Indian* is "Validity Is Not Authenticity: Distinguishing Two

Components of Truth," a reprint of an essay written by Richard de Mille for his earlier *The Don Juan Papers*.[29] The author vigorously disassembles the various lies about the Yaqui and other indigenous peoples injected into both the scholarly and popular arenas by Carlos Aranja (aka Carlos Castaneda), whom de Mille accurately describes elsewhere as being "the greatest anthropological hoax since Piltdown Man."[30] To his great credit, de Mille makes it absolutely clear that the Castaneda problem is a specifically Eurocentric rather than Native American phenomenon, and spends the bulk of his time analyzing the ways in which the discipline of anthropology churns out what might be best described as "disinformation specialists." Taken most broadly, his is a message many of the contributors to the present volume would do well to heed in the context of their own misbegotten twistings of reality.

Feest, too, does an adequate job in his second essay, "Europe's Indians," in which he unmasks the spurious foundations of Old World conceptions of Indianness elaborated by hack writers such as Karl May.[31] Taken together, these last three pieces might have formed the basis for a useful and informative book. Unfortunately, given the setting in which their authors have allowed them to be published, they serve now more as a brush with which to tar genuine indigenous spiritual traditions than as a mechanism by which the assorted phoneys preying upon these traditions might be exposed for who and what they are. They are simply insufficient in themselves to offset the thrust of the rest of the collection.

The Real Agenda

This is all the more true when one considers the cluster of essays which comprise the core of *The Invented Indian*, laying bare the sort of bedrock issues which prompted editor Clifton to collect and publish it. Put bluntly, this central material devolves on themes intended to preclude any public perception of legitimacy in Indian land claims (or reserved land rights, for that matter), efforts to assert control over their own affairs, or attempts to speak the truth of what is being done to them. The package is presented as being "of benefit" to Indians insofar as their acceptance of it might foster "improved interracial relations." The rest of the volume may be assessed as having been orchestrated more-or-less to provide "background," adding an appearance of academic credibility to this more nuts-and-bolts body of highly politicized verbiage.

Leading the pack in this regard is Allan van Gestel, an attorney whose main qualification as a contributor is having unsuccessfully defended non-Indian interests against the 1985 Oneida Land Claim in New York State. Titling his essay "When Fictions Take Hostages," the author asserts that individual non-Indian property owners within Indian land claim areas are victimized both by having their titles clouded during litigation, and by facing potential eviction from their homes whenever Indians win.[32] The individuals at risk, he declares (accurately enough), are largely innocent of personal wrongdoing, and should thus not be made to bear the burden of redressing native grievances. Indians' persistence in filing suits to recover lands taken from them in contravention of both U.S. and international law is, he contends, tantamount to their taking these bystanders "hostage" as an expedient to forcing state or federal governments into land restoration actions they would likely not otherwise undertake.[33] It is incumbent upon Indians, he argues, to cease such provocative endeavors lest the rage of the hostages eventually vent itself upon their captors.[34] No mention is made of the possibility that the Euroamerican governments might bear a certain responsibility to resolve the problem by ending their blanket refusal to return territory they demonstrably—and often admittedly—took from indigenous people through other than legal means.

Although he claims juridical expertise, van Gestel inverts the entire tradition of English Common Law, in which U.S. codes are anchored, by suggesting that non-Indians holding deeds within Indian treaty areas are somehow inherently entitled to keep the property, no matter if it can be shown to be stolen, merely by virtue of having "acted in good faith" in acquiring it. He is plainly playing to a crowd of non-Indians who seek peace of mind in their property investments rather than following legal logic. The latter holds clearly and as a matter of fundamental principle that stolen property must be returned to its rightful owners wherever these can be found. Those who receive stolen property are *never* entitled to keep it, even though they they may have had no participation in or knowledge of the theft, and may even have honestly purchased the property from the thief or thieves. Such persons *are* entitled to be compensated for their losses by the thieves, in this case the government, *not* the Indians.

Were he truly concerned with promoting interracial harmony based in sound legal posture, van Gestel might advocate that Indians and the non-Indians unite in a common effort to bring government in line with its own laws. Instead, he strives to affix blame where it isn't, set one group of victims against the other, and allow the only guilty parties in the whole mix to walk away unblemished.

Apparently aware of the intrinsic irrationality of the stance he's assumed, the author hurriedly scuttles to the task of amending it. This is done by asserting that Indians possess no legitimate standing from which to press claims that anything, including land, was ever stolen from them. Native peoples were never, he says, " 'distinct, independent, political communities' qualified to exercise powers of self-governance and having other prerogatives by virtue of their . . . sovereignty." In fact, they weren't even "tribes," in his view.[35] Exactly what he thinks the indigenous form of sociopolitical existence *was* (herds? packs? coveys? gaggles?) is left unstated as he plunges ahead, decreeing that the "notion of an Indian 'tribe' or 'nation' is a . . . fiction" contrived by Euroamerican jurists and politicians to allow them to go about acquiring legal title to much of North America through an orderly process of bilateral and multilateral treaty negotiations with a number of indigenous groups.[36] Now that the desired acreage has been obtained, as well as most of that reserved by Indians for themselves as part of the treaty process, the "fiction" has outlived its usefulness and should be discarded without further ado. Indians would thus become what van Gestel insists they always were— nonentities—and nonentities, to be sure, have no legal standing. Hence, no thieves, no stolen property, and no problem.

Leaving aside the peculiar readings of history with which he accompanies his theoretics, the author has deliberately avoided several other major issues:

- First, and most important, there is the fact that *all* nations—not least that renegade republic known as the United States—as well as the sovereignty thereof are "legal fictions" in the sense van Gestel employs the term. Indigenous nations are no different than any other in this respect. Moreover, behind his careful abstractions there are real human beings who have, for the benefit of others, been dispossessed of the real land which is their real birthright. They experience real loss and feel real pain as a result. They are collectively entitled to, but have been systematically denied, very real human rights of collective self-determination.

- Second, the United States Constitution is quite clear in its first article, requiring that treaty relationships be entered into by the federal government *only* with other fully sovereign national entities. This means, whether van Gestel likes it or not, that each time the Senate ratified a treaty with an Indian people, as it did at least 371 times, it simultaneously bestowed formal U.S. recognition of the other party as a sovereign nation in the most unequivocal legal sense.

- Third, neither the Constitution, nor international custom and convention, allow for the United States to legally "unrecognize" a nation that is already recognized. To the contrary, any such action would likely violate the "crimes against the peace" provisions of the Nuremburg Doctrine—formulated by the United States itself—and a number of other elements of international law.

- Fourth, the legitimacy of U.S. title to its territoriality within the 48 contiguous states derives exclusively—the United States having officially renounced rights of conquest by 1790—from the treaty agreements reciprocally guaranteeing specific territorialities to signatory indigenous nations. Abrogation of the treaties would nullify U.S. title to all territory within its main landmass, with ownership reverting entirely to the original inhabitants under the Doctrine of Discovery.

Fifth, and conclusively, the entire cynically manipulative approach van Gestel suggests as appropriate for U.S. participation in treaty relations is quite literally Hitlerian in both its mode and its moral content. The magnitude of malicious falsity involved in his reasoning is staggering. It is plainly not justice he seeks, but *lebensraum*. That, and a rationalization leading to some psychic consolidation of a white supremacist empire. Thankfully, he is in no position to implement his malignant vision.

Additional Polemics

Still, he is hardly alone in his cryptofascist sentiments, as is witnessed by the submission of Stephen E. Feraca, a deeply imbittered non-Indian employee of the Bureau of Indian Affairs who went into retirement as quickly as possible after that agency began to exercise Indian hiring preferences. In his essay, "Inside the BIA: Or, 'We're Getting Rid of All These Honkies,'" the author first paints what can only be an intentionally misleading portrait of how sensitively and with what steel-trap efficiency the Bureau served the interests of native people in the days before "they" came aboard in large numbers.[37] To do this, of course, he must ignore the BIA's characteristic penchant for using its "trust" control over Indian affairs to force the long-term, low-cost leasing of every possible acre of reservation land to non-Indian interests. Similarly, he fails to mention the Bureau's chronic pattern of negotiating mining contracts—which typically lacked even minimal safety and land reclamation provisions, and which seldom pay the BIA's indigenous "wards" more than 15 percent of market rates on extracted minerals—with major corporations desiring to operate on reservation lands. And again, he is silent concerning the large numbers of Indian women involuntarily sterilized while availing themselves of Bureau-coordinated "health services."

The reasons for Feraca's neglect of the facts is quite simple. His purpose is to bemoan—through a lengthy stream of personal anecdotes in which no names are named, and which rely upon a grand total of two end notes for substantiation—the "reverse racism" of Indian preference policies,[38] and the "severe damage" to the BIA's beneficent programming which he claims has resulted therefrom.[39]

In a perverse way, he is correct. Indian preference *is* a belated and rather insufficient response to more than a century of unremitting "whites only" policies which have excluded Indian participation from all meaningful participation in the decisions most directly affecting them. Further, whatever else may be said of the congregation of native bureaucrats ("apples" is their conventional descriptor) now haunting the Bureau's hallowed halls, they *have* made headway in halting or at least curtailing some of the BIA's worst practices. In a nutshell then, Feraca's sour grapes reduce to nothing other than a demand that, "in fairness," Indian Affairs should be returned to its historical status as a medium of white careerism, and to its service as an instrument through which the absolute, unhampered non-Indian control over residual native land, lives and resources may be extended.

The icing is put on the cake by the late John A. Price, yet another in the seemingly unending roster of anthropologists contributing to *The Invented Indian*. Described as "an authority on the native peoples of Canada, and on advocacy groups and development programs concerning them," the author devotes much of his article—entitled "Ethnic Advocacy Groups Versus Propaganda: Canada's Indian Support Groups"—to explaining how "preferentially" indigenous people are treated under Canadian law.[40] As an example, he observes that "Indians are exempt from federal and provincial taxation on reserve land, personal property on reserve land, and income derived while working on reserve land." Such a situation, he says, is unfair "to the citizenry at large."[41] Worse, Price contends, it stems from "new interpretations of old treaties," never mentioning that these new interpretations represent a substantial diminishment of the native rights original indigenous signatories intended the treaties to secure.[42]

The author then moves on to consider the "ungrateful" response of indigenous people and their supporters to various aspects of Canadian Indian policy. Taking a series of block quotes drawn from several publications, each of which provides a cogent assessment of the topic it treats, he dismisses them as part of "an implicit political strategy, which is propagandistic in design and execution."[43] His method of analysis in arriving at this conclusion is not so much faulty as inexplicable. For instance, he offers the following illustration of commentary on Canada's dual standard of justice:

> In one highly publicized case, Donald Marshall, a Micmac wrongly served eleven years in prison for murder before the White man, Roy Ehsanz, who committed the crime, confessed, and Marshall was released. "In contrast to Marshall's life sentence for second degree murder, Ehsanz got one year for manslaughter."[44]

Price makes no claim that this is untrue. To the contrary, he seems to accept the veracity of what is said. Hence, it becomes apparent that what he really seeks is to categorize *any* native criticism of the status quo, no matter how well founded, as "propaganda." Following this definition, the only non-propagandistic observations Indians and their supporters can make—and thus the only legitimate "advocacy" posture open to us—would be those which, no matter how inaccurately, serve to support and endorse official conduct. That adhering to such "standards" would place native people in the role of actively seeking our own demise is precisely the point.

The articles prepared by van Gestel, Feraca and Price ultimately form a tidy triad: 1) *any* recognition of indigenous land rights in North America is "unfair to the broader population," 2) *any* genuine Indian control over our own affairs is "racist" and therefore "unfair to non-Indians," and 3) *any* native comment or complaint concerning losses of basic rights and resources may be dismissed *a priori* as mere "political gimmickry." To these might be added a fourth element, representing most of the rest of the book, holding that any historical/anthropological interpretations of fact leading to conclusions that American Indians ever comported themselves as bona fide human beings—readings which might serve to make the main three premises seem unconscionable—are "grossly inaccurate." The theoretical stage for a "final solution of the Indian problem" is thus amply set.

Conclusion

"Propaganda," says Price on the first page of his essay, "typically uses stereotyping for political or commercial ends. The presentations are too biased, too selective to tell the whole truth. Emotional appeals may be substituted for a fully reasoned, balanced analysis of issues. One result is that even honest, ethical, and reasoned [positions which go in the same direction] become tainted by association with the propaganda of fanatic proponents of any cause. . . Such problems occur when advocates abandon fundamental principles of serious research. . .[presenting] only that evidence and information which supports the position they are endorsing."[45] All in all, this observation may be accepted as an adequate depiction of his own material and much of the rest of the book in which it finds its home.

James Clifton has assembled an odyssey into historical revisionism, not in the admirable sense originally connoted by the work of Alice and Staughton Lynd, Howard Zinn and others, but in the more recent and thoroughly squalid sense exemplified by those like Arthur Butz who seek to "debunk the myth" that the Third Reich perpetrated genocide against the Jews.[46] It is bad enough that we have such minds festering within contemporary society. The problem is made far worse by the willingness of supposedly reputable publishers to present such pseudoscholarship in the guise of legitimate academic exposition. If there is any utility at all to the release of *The Invented Indian*, it lies in the open self-identification of a whole cast of North American neonazis. Now we know beyond any reasonable doubt where they stand. All those involved should be accorded the degree of disgust they have so richly earned.

Notes

1. James A. Clifton, ed., *The Invented Indian: Cultural Fictions and Government Policies* (New Brunswick, NJ: Transaction Books, 1990).

2. The introduction spans the pages 1–28.

3. Robert Jay Lifton, *The Nazi Doctors: Medical Killing and the Psychology of Genocide* (New York: Basic Books, 1986).

4. Clifton's essay falls at pp. 29–48.

5. Ibid., p. 26.

6. Ibid., p. 27.

7. Ibid., p. 41. The books at issue are Francis Jennings, *The Invasion of America: Indians, Colonialism, and the Cant of Conquest* (Chapel Hill: University of North Carolina Press, 1975); Russell Thornton, *American Indian Holocaust and Survival: A Population History Since 1492* (Norman: University of Oklahoma Press, 1988); Steven Cornell, *Return of the Native: American Indian Political Resurgence* (New York: Oxford University Press, 1987); James Axtell, *The Invasion Within: The Contest of Cultures in Colonial North America* (New York: Oxford University Press, 1985); Dee Brown, *Bury My Heart at Wounded Knee: An Indian History of the American West* (New York: Holt, Rinehart & Winston, 1971); and Jack Weatherford, *Indian Givers: How the Indians of the Americas Transformed the World* (New York: Crown, 1988). Clifton also seems to take particular exception to Deloria's *Custer Died For Your Sins: An Indian Manifesto* (New York: Macmillan, 1969) and *God Is Red* (New York: Grossett & Dunlap, 1973).

8. Clifton, *op. cit.*, p. 26.

9. Werner Sollors, *Beyond Ethnicity: Descent and Consent in American Literature* (New York: Oxford University Press, 1985).

10. Clifton, *op. cit.*, p. 41.

11. Ibid., p. 378.

12. Tooker's essay appears at pp. 107–28.

13. Tooker is particularly unctuous about Grinde's *The Iroquois and the Founding of the American Nation* (San Francisco: Indian Historian Press, 1977) and Johansen's *Forgotten Founders* (Ipswich, CT: Gambit Publishers, 1982), as well as Jose Barriero, ed., "Indian Roots of American Democracy" (*Northeast Indian Quarterly*, Ithaca, NY: Cornell University, 1988). Her polemics seem designed, at least in part, as an attempt to block publication of Grinde's and Johansen's *Exemplar of Liberty* (UCLA, 1990).

14. For detailed analysis, see Donald A. Grinde, Jr., "The Iroquois Political Concept and the Genesis of the American Government: Further Research and Contentions," *Northeast Indian Quarterly*, Vol. 6, No. 4, Winter 1989.

15. Clifton, *op. cit.*, p. 376.

16. McDonald's essay appears at pp. 145–67.

17. Gill's essay falls at pp. 129–44. The book in question was published by the University of Chicago Press in 1987. For criticism, see the special section devoted primarily to Gill in *Bloomsbury Review*, Summer 1988.

18. See the interview with Russell Means in *Bloomsbury, op. cit.*

19. Henige's essay may be found at pp. 169–91. His title is a play upon Henry F. Dobyns, *Their Numbers Become Thinned: Native American Population Dynamics in Eastern North America* (Nashville: University of Tennessee Press, 1983). He focuses his attack upon Sherburn F. Cook and Leslie B. Simpson, "The Population of Central Mexico in the Sixteenth Century (*Ibero-Americana*, No. 31, Berkeley: University of California Press, 1948); Woodrow W. Borah, "The Historical Demography of Aboriginal and Colonial America: An Attempt at Perspective" (in William E. Denevan, ed., *The Native Population of the Americas in 1492* (Madison: University of Wisconsin Press, 1976); and Borah's "America as Model: The Demographic Impact of European Expansion Upon the Non-European World" (in *Actos y Memorias del XXXV Congreso International de Americanistas* (Mexico City: Instituto Nacional de Antropología, 1964).

20. Henige seems especially attracted to Mooney's estimates, published as *The Aboriginal Population of America North of Mexico* (John R. Swanton, ed., Smithsonian Miscellaneous Collections, LXXX, No. 7, Washington, D.C., 1928), and Kroeber's subsequent downward revision published in his *Cultural and Natural Areas of Native North America* (Berkeley and Los Angeles: University of California Publications in

American Archeology and Ethnology, XXXVIII, 1939). The demographies of both men are definitively exposed as fraudulent in Jennings, *op. cit.*, pp. 16–31.

21. Simard's essay falls at pp. 333–69 of Clifton, *op. cit.*, the quote at pp. 340–1.

22. Ibid., pp. 71–9.

23. Mason's essay may be found at pp. 91–105, the quote at p. 103.

24. Ibid., p. 103.

25. Feest's essay appears at pp. 49–70.

26. Kehoe's essay may be found at pp. 193–209.

27. Texts of these denunciations are reproduced in my *Critical Issues in Native North America, Volume II* (Copenhagen: International Work Group on Indigenous Affairs, 1990).

28. Ibid., p. 199.

29. De Mille's essay appears at pp. 227–54. It is reprinted from *The Don Juan Papers: Further Castaneda Controversies* (Belmont, CA: Wadsworth, 1990).

30. The description is taken from Richard de Mille, *Castaneda's Journey: The Power and the Allegory* (Santa Barbara, CA: Capra Press, 1976).

31. Feest's second essay comes at pp. 313–32.

32. Van Gestel's essay is at pp. 291–312.

33. Ibid., p. 298.

34. Ibid., p. 294.

35. Ibid., pp. 300–2.

36. Ibid., p. 300.

37. Feraca's essay falls at pp. 271–90.

38. Ibid., p. 281.

39. Ibid., p. 286

40. Price's essay may be found at pp. 255–70, the description of his pedigree at p. 378.

41. Ibid., pp. 260–1.

42. Ibid., p. 259.

43. Ibid., p. 269.

44. Ibid.

45. Ibid., p. 255.

46. See, for example, Arthur D. Butz, *The Hoax of the Twentieth Century: The Case Against the Presumed Extermination of European Jewry* (Torrance, CA: Institute for Historical Review, 1977).

Beyond Ethnicity?

Werner Sollors' Deepest Avatar of Racism

> [Q]uite suddenly, with little comment or ceremony, ethnicity is a ubiquitous presence.
>
> —Ronald Cohen

The question of "ethnicity" has long been one of the more perplexing challenges confronting students of American literature. Issues begin with controversy over proper definition of the term itself, and extend into concerns as to who might be legitimately viewed as an ethnic writer, the influence of ethnic-specific work on the evolution of the American writing tradition, and the impact of such influence upon the whole of American letters today. Serious debate centers even on who might be said to be qualified to evaluate the increasingly complex situation. The result, of course, is an incredible intellectual muddle.

Comes now Werner Sollors, a literary scholar of no small repute, offering to inject order and clarity into the confusion. Tellingly entitled *Beyond Ethnicity*, Sollors' sweeping study draws immediately upon its subtitle, positing a potentially powerful analytical method hinging on the interaction of what its author describes as streams of "consent" (subjectively chosen group identification) and "descent" (objectively "born" or inherited identification) common to all elements of ethnic differentiation in American culture. Further, to obtain the desired depth of insight into the facts and functions of ethnicity in writing, he rejects mere topical scrutiny, choosing instead to apply his dialectical mechanism of examination across the historical spectrum of appropriate literatures, from the output of colonial times through the present.

Such an exploratory paradigm, inherently nuanced and comprehensive as it appears, promises much in terms of unraveling the primary characteristics marking the various pools of literary ethnicity prevailing in America. It also holds out the prospect of a coherent explanation of the individuated streams flowing from these pools in tempering, defining and sometimes merging with what has come to be seen as an ethnically pluralistic American literature. From such a rich and multifaceted handling of the subject matter, a range of accurate and incisive overall conclusions might reasonably be expected to be reached.

The "Confusing Category" of Race

Having so aptly prescribed a methodological approach to the problem he purports to treat, however, Sollors promptly busies himself with a dramatic undercutting of its innate utility. Early in the text, while attempting to counter what he believes to be M.G. Smith's "erroneous" proposition that "race [is] a special 'objective' category that cannot be meaningfully discussed under the heading 'ethnicity' " (p. 36), Sollors announces his own alignment with Harold Abramson's argument that, while "race is the most salient ethnic factor, it is still only one of the larger cultural and historical phenomenon [sic] of ethnicity" (p. 36). This would have been all well and good had Sollors not then proceeded to demote Abramson's "most salient ethnic factor" for his own purposes, reducing it to being just "one aspect of ethnicity" (p. 39), with no special emphasis at all.

The author attempts to defend his marginalization of the issue of race by professing concern with hypotheticals such as ". . . in the complicated ethnic scene today, are Cuban immigrants or Japanese-Americans races or ethnic groups?" (pp. 38–39). The contradiction is strikingly evident: Such "either/or" dichotomies are precisely in line with the very Smithian postulation Sollors had already categorically rejected, rather than Abramson's "both at once, with emphasis on race" formulation which he clearly claims to "have sided with" (p. 36). Utilization of the latter principle would, to be sure, have destroyed the author's superficially ambiguous straw man a priori.

Nonetheless, he insists upon having it both ways as an expedient to concluding that, "I think it most helpful not to be confused by the heavily charged term 'race'. . ." (p. 39), and thereupon drops the entire concept of racial differentiation as a factor of ethnicity. At this point, both the theses and content of Beyond Ethnicity have been forced drastically out of sync with its auspicious beginnings. Still, the situation might have been salvaged, at least to some extent.

At one level, all of this abstract playing of both ends against the middle could be considered as no more than a somewhat deceptive and exceedingly sloppy way of circumscribing the scope of what Sollors had determined to be an overly ambitious project. This would be true if he followed up by matching his self-imposed methodological constraints by restricting subsequent practical considerations to the play of ethnical factors within a given racial group. And, indeed, in some ways it seems he sets out to follow such a course of post hoc consistency by erecting a "typology of ethnicity" for the New World based entirely upon tenets of biblical interpretation, with reference to the European migration (likened, of course, to the Jewish exodus from Egypt). Puritan New England, which Sollors follows Hans Kohn in describing as "the first example of modern nationalism" (p. 56), thus quickly becomes his benchmark of "ethnicization" or "ethnification" (terms borrowed from Andrew Greeley; p. 57).

He goes on to lay out the polarities of discussion as residing in, on the one hand, the "melting pot" thesis posited in 1909 via an Israel Zangwill play of the same title and, on the other hand, later opposing contentions surfaced in such sociological works as Glazer and Moynihan's *Beyond the Melting Pot* (1963) and Michael Novak's *The Rise of the Unmeltable Ethnics* (1975). In this contestation, Sollors sets forth his affinity to the Zangwillian notion, ultimately assigning modern American ethnic distinctions status as a semiological preoccupation, i.e., signifying the continuation of socially useful codes of symbology rather than the living of concrete daily realities. As he puts it on page 35, "modern ethnic identification works by external symbols rather than by continual activities which make demands upon people who define themselves as 'ethnic.' " Or, on page 39:

> I propose that for purposes of investigating group formation, inversion, boundary construction and social distancing, myths of origins and fusions, cultural markers and empty symbols, we may be better served, in the long run, by the vocabulary of kinship and cultural codes than by the cultural baggage that the word "ethnicity" contains.

In the main, Sollors attempts to accomplish a proof to this proposition within the remainder of his text by undertaking a relatively systematic analysis of the thematics of succeeding generations of European immigrants, from roughly the point of the English invasion of North America onward. As promised during its methodological exposition, the study's exemplary selections include not only such pillars of literary effort in colonial New England as Cotton Mather and Michel-Guillame-Jean de Crevecoeur (a.k.a.: J. Hector St. Joan), but their late twentieth-century successors such as Jack Kerouac and Norman Mailer. This temporal gamut is amply fleshed out with other luminaries as diverse as Ralph Waldo Emerson, Henry David Thoreau, James Fenimore Cooper, Harriet Beecher Stowe, Mark Twain, Vachel Lindsay, Francis Parkman and even Woody Allen.

Various strains of Euroamerican ("white") literary ethnicity are accorded their interactive moment(s), some at considerable length, as with the deployment of Ludwig Lewishohn (German [and Jewish] American), John Brougham (Irish-American), Ole E. Rolvaag (Norwegian-American), Mary Antin (Russian [and Jewish] American), Mario Puzo and Emanuel Carnevali (Italian-American), Abraham Cahan and Horace M. Kallen (Jewish American) and so on. Attention is also paid to argumentation as to whether writers such as Carl Sandburg, Eugene O'Neill, Nelson Algren, Nathanael West and Vladimir Nabokov should rightly be considered figures of ethnic literature at all.

Summatively, Sollors arrives at the conclusion that the functionality of ethnicity in American writing rests in what might be paradoxically called "the homogeneity of heterogeneous existence." As he himself puts it, "Embracing a regional or group identity in voluntary defiance (as in Faulkner's 'I don't hate it, I don't hate it!') allows Americans to steer a Joycean middle course between ancient narrowness and vulgar monotony. By creating new, not traditionally anchored, group identities and by authenticating them, they may represent individuality and American identity at the same time" (pp. 206–207). Further, "popular contrasts with the ethnically homogeneous and hierarchically structured old worlds are often melodramatically overdrawn" (p. 260).

In other words, according to Sollors, the melting pot has done its work to the point where America, the land of ethnic diversity, has become as ethnically homogeneous as the old world, at least at the practical level. Ethnicity now serves the social function of allowing the expression of creative individuality as "[f]reedom from the fetters of descent was achieved while other forms of descent were literally thought of as deserving fetters . . . Enough ethnic distinctions have emerged in the United States to put the theory of old world survivals to rest" (p. 260). In this vein, "The language of consent and descent has been flexibly adapted to the most divergent kinds of ends and has amazingly helped to create a sense of Americanness among the heterogeneous inhabitants of this country . . . [t]he ways in which stories have helped to create the rites and rituals which can impart to the diverse population of the United States a shared sense of destiny are impressive" (p. 259).

At this juncture, it seems appropriate to suggest that Sollors has produced a viable, if not necessarily definitive analysis of the "mainstream" experience in America, at least as apprehended within its literary tradition. He spells out compellingly how a seemingly disparate array of European migrations were able to resettle to this hemisphere and transcend their initial particularities, becoming in the end an overarching racially/culturally identified "we" or "us," regardless of residual and often contrived "ethnical" proclivities. Had this been all there was to it, despite its early difficulties in theoretical formulation and a marked tendency toward an overblown language of universalization, *Beyond Ethnicity* might safely be considered a generally successful, useful and informative book. Matters, however, are not so simple.

The Real "Melting Pot"

The problem which prevents such a positive assessment begins when, on page 11, Sollors notes that there are certain recalcitrants abroad in the land who have "seldom fully appreciated their texts in the context of the newer theories of ethnicity [e.g., the author's own conception of consent-dominated ethnic identification]." On the same page, he goes on to observe that, rather than "understanding their texts as [semiotic] codes for a socialization into ethnic groups and into America, readers have overemphasized and exaggerated the (frequently exoticized) ethnic particularities of the works [of non-whites] . . . belief is widespread among critics who stress descent at the expense of consent [again, mainly non-whites] that only biological insiders can understand and explicate the literature of race and ethnicity." One can almost feel the author recoiling in horror as he concludes this passage by recounting how Richard Gilman has even "suggested a general moratorium on white critics [such as Sollors] reviewing black writers." He sets out to counter, and there follows the long and convoluted polemical ending in his determination that it is "most helpful" to utterly eliminate the "confusing" category of race from the analytical lexicon.

This decision to ignore questions of the functionality of racial designations in America was not, however, coupled to a corresponding restraint in dealing with multiracial authors and literatures. To the contrary, having smugly vaulted away the essential force and motivation of many (or most) non-white writers, Sollors consistently engages himself throughout the remainder of his book in trotting out carefully selected references to and quotations of them. Severed intentionally and completely from the sociocultural consciousness which generated them, these quotations/citations are interwoven at will by the author with the overwhelmingly more extensive material he has gleaned from Euroamerican sources. In each instance, the non-white selections are used in such a way as to appear directly subordinate to the "broader" Euroamerican literary context Sollors is describing and, in this way, are utilized as mere tokens, props by which the author reinforces his major goal of establishing the primacy of consent in contemporary ethnic identification.

He is rather astute in his choices of those he abuses in this way, deploying as he does representatives from each non-white racial group and including at least mention of writers typically considered as "radicals" on the issue of race. Those descended from the various Asian ethnicities will find passing references to Frank Chin (Chinese-American), and Hisaye Yamamoto (Japanese-American), as well as a brief quotation from the verse of Diana Chang (Chinese-American). Chicanos are included by virtue of mention accorded Gaspar Perez de Villagra, Luis Valdez and Richard Rodriguez, while a brief synopsis is provided concerning the work of Jose Garcia Villa. Native Americans will find the names (no more) of N. Scott Momaday (Kiowa), Leslie Marmon Silko (Laguna) and Hyemeyohsts Storm (ersatz Cheyenne) on page 254.

Blacks—on whose literature and circumstances Sollors, head of the Afro-American Studies Department at Harvard University, apparently considers himself an expert—receive relatively heavy exposure in the form of mention or quotation from Frederick Douglass, Booker T. Washington, Jean Toomer, Richard Wright, James Weldon Johnson, Phyllis Wheatley, Amiri Baraka/LeRoi Jones, Nat Turner, Malcolm X, Elijah Muhammad, Martin Robeson Delaney, Marcus Garvey, Lincoln Steffens and Ishmael Reed, among others. Nevertheless, it must be said that, among Blacks, only the work of W.E.B. DuBois is afforded even a pretense of examination in depth.

The object of this somewhat elaborate exercise in orchestration is to manipulate into apparent existence a circumstance wherein everyone—white and non-white alike—fits into what Sollors wishes to project as a single, holistic "American" sociocultural matrix based upon a mutuality of consent among all concerned. Hence, there can be no attempt in *Beyond Ethnicity* to come to grips with even the most fundamentally obvious multiracial questions, such as how an American Black (or any other non-white) is supposed to transcend his/her inherited, genetic, racial darkness (i.e., the determinate factor of his/her "descent") in order to "consent" to join the racially exclusivist white ethnic mainstream of the United States.

Such concerns are the purview of "archaic" theories of ethnicity, Sollors implies; *he* is occupied with meatier issues such as "[h]ow an Italian-American academic picks up an Afro-American militant gesture and uses it for his own purposes" (p. 14). Besides, serious address of such matters would tend to disturb the teleological tidiness of the author's purposeful extrapolation of Euroamerican realities to cover everybody else, and so he blocks with one of his yanked-from-context quotations (this one a tired banality from Nathan Huggins): "Contrary to what one might suspect, an Afro-American and the grandson of a Polish immigrant will be able to take more for granted among themselves than the former could with a Nigerian or the latter with a Warsaw worker" (pp. 13–14).

"Interpretations"

Perhaps as telling as the misappropriation of non-white literature in which Sollors engages, is that which he excludes while developing subject matter entirely relevant to it. For example, although the issue is mentioned on page 8, the author doesn't bother to articulate exactly how he validates his novel idea that the ethos of consensual ethnic merging evidenced by Europe's voluntary transplants to America would, or even could be shared by those American Indians whose lands and lives the newcomers usurped (and continue to usurp). Rather, he falls back on Michael Novak's inane suggestion that, "Given a grandparent or two, one chooses to shape one's life by one history rather than another" (p. 33) before blithely launching into a drawn-out process of having Euroamerican writers speak for the Indian.

A total of 146 pages and two full chapters—"Romantic Love, Arranged Marriage and Indian Melancholy" and "Interlude: From Indian to Urban"—are devoted to Euroamerican "interpretation" of the meaning of "Indianness" in the American melting pot, all without a single Native American voice being heard. The implications of this sort of handling present themselves most clearly when, on pages 132–3, Sollors purports to decipher the differences between American interethnic humor and, say, German anti-Jewish or Turkish anti-Armenian jokes. The distinction, he claims, is that the latter two examples "served to support genocidal policies," and the reader is left to ponder what—precisely—an at least 95 percent reduction in American Indian population by the end of the nineteenth century signifies if not genocide.

Similarly, there is no explanation as to why the author is unable to detect a whiff of the same aroma in U.S. slave and segregation policies.

Both crucial breaches of dialectical method—the deliberate miscasting of non-white writing within antithetical contexts, and its deliberate exclusion from contexts which were made to concern it—were, of course, perfectly avoidable on their face. This does not hold, however, given the predetermined conclusions and consequent structure of discourse Sollors set out to achieve. Had the real weight of Amiri Baraka's or Ishmael Reed's writing been set loose inside the author's carefully controlled study, the result could only have been a more-than-metaphoric undoing of his thesis of the dominance of ethnic consent. The same could be said for any number of black literary figures—Alice Walker, Maya Angelou, Tony Morrison, Melvin Van Peebles, Erika Huggins, Eldridge Cleaver, Angela Y. Davis and Bobby Seale among them—made conspicuous by their very absence from the pages of *Beyond Ethnicity*.

By the same token had Leslie Marmon Silko been allowed off the leash which extended only as long as her name, she could have communicated a sense of "otherness" so profound as to completely unhinge Sollors' neatly crafted illusion of consensual ethnic interchange with Euroamerica. Inclusion of Vine Deloria, Jr.'s *God Is Red* (1973) or even his subsequent *Metaphysics of Modern Existence* (1979) would have broken beyond all repair the idea of an hegemonic Judeochristian ideal (i.e., Puritanism) governing the evolution of American ethnicity along cross-racial lines. Allowing other prominent Indian literary voices—such as those of James Welch, Simon J. Ortiz, Wendy Rose, John Trudell and Joy Harjo—to be heard would simply have completed the overall job of demolition. Ultimately, then, the author had no real alternative but to play his hand as he did.

Because of this, *Beyond Ethnicity* must stand as far worse than a failed promise. Its underlying premises were never tenable, its real trajectory never so much explanatory as deliberately obfuscatory and fringing on fantasy. Whatever real utility it might have yielded in terms of a better understanding of ethnic interplay in Euroamerica is lost in its devious insistence upon having that particular cultural milieu exercise a domination which even Sollors describes as being "expressed in the power to define" (p. 193) everyone else's reality. At bottom, then, this is an extremely deceitful book and dangerous, not so much for the wildly Eurocentric perspective it exhibits, as for the gloss of rationality, balance and academic objectivity under which it was written.

The Deepest Avatar of Racism

In the end, we are left to speculate as to why a scholar of Werner Sollors' undeniable abilities should have reduced himself to such a level, maiming beyond all redemption what might otherwise have stood as a solid and respectable little study. For what purpose does he go to such lengths in attempting to deny descent differentiations which even his own illustrational material often tacitly conjures up? To what end does he persist in a peculiar form of intellectual masochism, pretending to miss points which even academic amateurs will find easy and all but self-evident? Why does he insist upon repeatedly trying to slam round pegs into square holes? The answers, perhaps, rest in the tenderness with which he reacted to Richard Gilman's suggested critical moratorium, and Sollors' subsequent observation that:

> This attitude is quite common in ethnic studies today. It is based on the assumption that experience is first and foremost ethnic. Critics should practice cultural relativism and stick to their own turfs (based, of course, on descent), since an unbridgeable gap separates Americans of different ethnic backgrounds and most especially all white Anglo-Saxon Protestants (acronymically known as WASPS) from all non-WASPs (p. 12).

This is much more than a casual point or one observation among many. A nerve has been struck here, and struck hard. Sollors is himself a WASP (i.e., of Germanic Anglo-Saxon Protestant descent) who has fashioned himself an academic career upon the enterprise of purporting to define and explain non-WASPs—most especially non-whites—to themselves. To this degree at least, he is functioning well within one of the most hallowed institutional corridors of the WASPishly conceived "white man's burden." Assertions, such as Gilman's, that non-whites may well be better prepared and able to explain things for themselves seem, not unnaturally, to appear both personally threatening to Sollors, and deeply subversive to his sense of the established propriety of things.

In any event, his defensive reaction to the perceived unruliness presently pervading ethnic studies has been to emit the cry of the wounded WASP, scurrying to restore a certain ethnocentric order to the situation. This is first and always to demonstrate (i.e., reassert) the inherent preeminence of WASP culture in America, mythologically lodged as it is in Puritan New England. Secondly, it must be shown that all subsequent migrations from Europe to the New World first revolved around this culturally integral mass and then were gradually allowed to merge with it. And finally, "proof" must be offered that all non-white groups in the United States are currently in the same sort of orbit previously experienced by, say, the Irish, and are seeking admission to the ethnic status quo.

Once this scenario for intercultural/interracial historiography and aesthetics has been rendered viable—"by any means necessary," to use a quotation from Malcolm X in the manner Sollors might have, had he bothered—the situation is saved. The author, as a WASP insider, is in the ideal position to rejoin Gilmanesque upstarts with the observation that, not only is he as qualified to review non-white writing as any non-white critic, he is more so, given that he is already what they are aspiring to become. Sollors must be experiencing a truly sublime satisfaction in having been able to lick his psychic wounds in such fashion, putting his antagonists "in their place" so publicly. This is no doubt all the more true, given that the publisher of his atavistic excursion is no less than Oxford University Press, that citadel of academic excellence into whose pages so few dissident thinkers "of color" have managed to find their way.

In the final analysis, however, it will be for naught. It is difficult to conceive a book which could have done more to reinforce the basis for the attitudes Sollors decries within ethnic studies than his own. He has greatly strengthened rather than diminished the credibility of those he sees as opponents. The ultimate irony, moreover, is not to be found at this level, but rather in the observation of the French philosopher Jean Baudrillard that:

> The deepest avatar of racism is to think that an error about [other] societies is politically or theoretically less serious than a misinterpretation of our own world. Just as a people who oppresses another cannot be free, so a culture that is mistaken about another must be mistaken about itself.

The bottom line is that Werner Sollors misunderstood nothing so much as he misunderstood the WASP . . . and himself.

Sources

Abramson, Harold J., *Ethnic Diversity in Catholic America* (New York, London, etc.: John Wiley, 1973).

Baudrillard, John, *The Mirror of Production* (St. Louis, MO: TELOS Press, 1975).

Cohen, Ronald, "Ethnicity: Problems and Focus in Anthropology," *Annual Review of Anthropology*, Vol. 7 (1978), pp. 379–403 (quote from p. 379).

Deloria, Vine Jr., *God Is Red* (New York: Delta Books, 1973).

_____, *Metaphysics of Modern Existence* (New York: Harper & Row, 1979).

Glazer, Nathan and Daniel Patrick Moynihan, *Beyond the Melting Pot: The Negroes, Puerto Ricans, Jews, Italians and Irish of New York City* (Cambridge: MIT Press, 1963).

Greeley, Andrew M., *Ethnicity in the United States: A Preliminary Reconnaissance* (New York, London, etc.: John Wiley, 1974).

Huggins, Nathan I., "Afro-American National Character and Community," *Center Magazine* (July/August 1974), pp. 51–66.

Kohn, Hans, *The Ideal of Nationalism* (New York: Macmillan, 1945).

Novak, Michael, *The Rise of the Unmeltable Ethnics: Politics and Culture in the Seventies* (New York: Macmillan, 1975).

Smith, M.G., "Ethnicity and Ethnic Groups in America: The View From Harvard," *Ethnic and Racial Studies 5* (1982), pp. 1–22.

Zangwill, Israel, *The Melting Pot* (New York: Macmillan, 1909 [Arno Press edition, 1975]).

In the Service of Empire

A Critical Assessment of Arnold Krupat's
The Turn to the Native

> [A]ccepting the role of being a colonizer means agreeing to be a non-legitimate person, that is, a usurper. To be sure, a usurper claims his place and, if need be, will defend it with every means at his disposal. . . He endeavors to falsify history, he rewrites laws, he would extinguish memories — anything to succeed in transforming his usurpation into legitimacy.
>
> — Albert Memmi
> *The Colonizer and the Colonized*

In the final essay of his most recent book, *The Turn to the Native: Studies in Criticism and Culture*, self-styled "ethnocritic" Arnold Krupat wonders aloud whether, through his interpretive activities, he hasn't become a "leftist colonizer" of the very sort critiqued so scathingly by Tunisian revolutionary theorist Albert Memmi more than three decades hence (p. 126).[1] This worthy query, which seems to have been posed mainly as a rhetorical device allowing its author to absolve himself of the charge — he shortly concludes that, simply by being "someone who reads and writes about Native American literatures," he has made himself "useful without vanity," and that he is therefore merely "a nice Jewish boy among the Indians" (p. 130) — is plainly deserving of a rather deeper and less self-interested interrogation.

Leaving aside the obvious element of personal vanity imbedded in the decision by any writer to publish an autobiographical piece, and the question of the perspective from which Krupat's work might be judged useful — on the book's flyleaf, its publisher, the University of Nebraska Press, announces that *The Turn to the Native* has been "long-awaited," but neglects to mention by whom or why — this thin volume contains no shortage of material upon which to base a more detached and scrupulous sort of analysis (indeed, one might fairly describe it as a kind of treasure trove in this respect). Predictably, any close reading of the text leads unerringly to an understanding of the author's sentiments radically at odds with the carefully contrived air of innocence and good intentions he adopts toward its end.

Actually, one need venture no further than the opening pages of the first essay, a smug little ditty entitled "Criticism and Native American Literature," to gain an appreciation of both the magnitude of Krupat's anti-Indian bias and the lengths to which he is prepared to go in alternately defending and denying it. In this single twenty-nine-page endeavor, he manages not only to "debunk" virtually every indigenous author who has lately contributed significantly to the field of literary/cultural criticism—a roster extending alphabetically from Sherman Alexie to Robert Allen Warrior—but to openly align himself with positions assumed by many of the dominant society's worst appropriationists: Michael Castro, Sam Gill, Jerry Mander and Werner Sollors, to name a few.[2] Along the way, he offers a tacit endorsement of such unabashedly Indian-hating diatribes as those compiled by James Clifton in *The Invented Indian* (p. 11), a collection with which he seems quite unfamiliar, since he not only fails to cite it directly but seriously misstates the thrust of its major argument.[3]

Ultimately, one is left with the distinct impression that there is hardly a white "interpreter" of Native America Krupat is not prepared to support in one way or several, scarcely an indigenous writer he is not prepared to manipulate, misrepresent or degrade. Take, for example, his casual dismissal of several detailed native critiques of the material put forth by "James Clifton, Werner Sollors, and Sam Gill, among others" as "ad hominem attacks." This altogether cavalier and misleading depiction is offered on the very same page where he himself opines, after barely a sentence of analysis and no quotations at all, that remarks critical of a "prominent non-Native scholar," made in 1992 by Lakota poet/essayist Elizabeth Cook-Lynn, were "racist" (p. 11).[4] *The Turn to the Native* is littered from start to finish with similarly transparent polemical distortions.

The motives underlying this squalid performance, which on its surface resembles nothing so much as a genteel "intellectual" recasting of the script for the recent movie *Falling Down*, with Krupat assuming the role played by Michael Douglas in the film, are not especially mysterious. His own preferred station in life—"the work that now names me," as he puts it with typical mock eloquent self-flattery (p. 127)—is to serve as one of Euroamerica's "leading practicioners [of] Native American studies" (flyleaf). By this, it is meant that he excels at reconnoitering the terrain of indigenous reality and then "explaining" it, not least to the natives themselves, in a manner which affirms the propriety, or at least the inevitability, of their collective place in the prevailing politicoeconomic structure.[5] He is in effect rewarded, both materially and in terms of the social privileges and prestige attending his professorial posting, solely because of his facility in rendering hegemonic reinforcement to the status quo.[6]

This of course raises the question of the nature of the order to which Krupat has been harnessed (or has harnessed himself). Here, there should be no controversy, since even he readily admits, as part of a caveat about why he considers "postcolonial" an inappropriate descriptor of American Indian literature, that the position of indigenous people in contemporary North America remains one of "internal colonial" subordination to a system of "domestic imperialism" (p. 30).[7] It follows that the function of his role as a settler culture "translator" and "teacher" of things native is best illuminated with an insight offered by Martin Carnoy:

> There are two very important points here: First, the colonizer needs the poverty and degradation of the colonized to justify his own place in the society. After all, where would he be without the colonized? He would not be able to do as well economically, since the colonial system exploits the colonized to the profit of the colonizer. He would also lose much of his self-importance if he were simply one of many among his own kind. Second, the colonial situation manufactures colonists, just as it manufactures the colonized. It is not just the predisposition to become a colonizer or colonized that produces these roles. . .but the colonial situation itself. The colonizer comes with power into the colonial context: he has the economic and military might of the metropole behind him. The colonized has no power. If he attempts to fight, he is physically conquered. The colonized is not free to choose between being colonized or not. The colonizer can enforce his usurpation with great punishment. The colonized adjusts to the situation by developing those traits with which the colonizer characterizes him. . . . Many of these traits are incompatible with each other, but that doesn't bother the colonizer, because the general traits are designed to destroy any culture or history that the colonized brings to the relationship.[8]

"The history which is taught [the colonized] is not his own," adds Memmi. "At the base of the entire construction, one finds a common motive; the colonizer's economic and basic needs, which he substitutes for logic, and which shapes and explains each of the traits he assigns to the colonized."[9]

> In order for the colonizer to be a complete master, it is not enough for him to be so in actual fact, but he must also believe in its legitimacy. In order for that legitimacy to be complete, it is not enough for the colonized to be a slave, he must also accept his role. The bond between colonizer and colonized is thus destructive and creative. It

destroys and recreates the two partners of colonization into colonizer and colonized. One is disfigured into an oppressor, a partial, unpatriotic and treacherous being, worrying only about his privileges and their defense; the other into an oppressed creature, whose development is broken and who compromises by his defeat.[10]

Is such an assessment too harsh (an "ad hominem attack," as it were)? Do Krupat's main positions really conform to the specification that they shore up the material/cultural/psychological structure of U.S. internal colonial domination in the manner described by Carnoy, Memmi and others? Whatever else may be said of colonialism, and there is much, it devolves only initially upon a forcible preemption of the sovereign standing of the colonized nation/people. It is maintained thereafter, not primarily by physical force, but through an increasingly complex and systematic indoctrination of colonizer and colonized alike to believe that any genuine resumption of sovereignty by the latter is not simply "undesirable," but "unrealistic" and "impossible."[11] The critical lens through which any work emanating within a colonial context must be examined, if its true utility is to be apprehended, can be located with precision in the stance of its author concerning the rights of the colonized to political and economic self-determination.[12]

On this score, Krupat is quite straightforward. After noting that a reassertion of sovereignty is indeed a legitimate aspiration of American Indians (p. 14), he waxes momentarily humble, conceding that it "is not for [him] to say what should or might happen between the federal government and [native nations] in these regards," before proceeding immediately to do just that: "I think it is, however, reasonable to say that whatever happens, it is unlikely that Native American nations, in any foreseeable future, will possess sovereignty in anything like the literal dictionary definition of the word" (p. 15). From there, he becomes more specific. The idea that indigenous nations might achieve a restoration of their status as territories existing as independent states is "inappropriate . . . inasmuch as even nineteenth-century [federal] proposals for the creation of an Indian state never assumed that this state would be any more independent (i.e., a *nation*-state) of the federal government than were any of the existing states" (p. 15).

Having thus firmly embraced and advanced the colonizer's own limits on the parameters of "reasonable" and "appropriate" discussion, Krupat quickly applies the finishing touches to his negation not only of native hopes, but the most fundamental requirements of international law.[13] In the end, *any* tangible form of genuine native sovereignty—he lists the possibilities, only to reject them, each in turn—are sloughed off as "hardly realistic likelihoods" (p. 15). With that said, he next presumes to describe, ostensibly on the basis of the vast expertise he's obtained through a reading of a single book, the "proper" standing of indigenous nations vis-à-vis the United States.[14] This, essentially, is as an aggregate "third level" of the federal government itself (pp. 15–16).

Unmentioned is the fact that the recipe—formal incorporation of indigenous governments into the United States as subparts of the federal system—is identical to that recently formulated by the Senate Select Committee on Indian Affairs as an expedient to perfecting America's internal colonial structure.[15] This is rationalized in Krupat's handling by resort to the kind of obfuscatory "logic" referred to above by Memmi:

> Lest this seem to denigrate Native Americans' desires in these regards, it should be said that in the present moment of transnational capitalism, no state or nation has sovereignty in the strong sense of the dictionary definition. Even the United States is subject to the requirements of international corporatism, as, for example, in the instance of American economic policy toward Mexico, a policy largely determined by the need to bail out Citibank. Mexican "sovereignty," meanwhile, like the "sovereignty" of the developing nations, is thoroughly compromised by the demands of the World Bank and the International Monetary Fund (p. 15).

While this is certainly true enough, it is also irrelevant unless it is meant to imply that there is no practical difference between the political standing of the United States on the one hand, and Third World countries on the other. If so, then the argument could be deployed with equal validity to redeem not only the U.S. domination of Native North America, but the French colonization of Algeria and Indochina, the British of India and Kenya, or even the nazi regime in Poland.[16] Subordinator or subordinated, colonizer or colonized, occupier or occupied, it makes no difference, since the sovereignty of all countries is mediated and constrained by one factor or fifty.

> In this regard, legal sovereignty and cultural sovereignty—to get to this matter at last— although they may seem to be digital (on/off, either/or, you have it or you don't), they are in fact more nearly analogue (loud/soft, hot/cold, more or less). Both political sovereignty and cultural sovereignty are meaningful only contextually and conjecturally. In the first instance, sovereignty is the material outcome of negotiations on a variety of levels between Native American tribes or nations and a multiplicity of non-Native institutions and governmental entities. In the second instance, sovereignty is yet again the result of complex negotiations and encounters between traditional cultural practices and the practices, impossible to circumvent or ignore, of Euramerican cultures (p. 16).

Put bluntly, this is pure nonsense. Political sovereignty does *not* accrue from negotiations or encounters, no matter how pervasive and complex. Rather, as virtually all thoughtful commentators on the topic concur, it is an inherent and immutable characteristic of any entity through which it is manifested (indeed, the whole concept of sovereignty originates in an idea of powers bestowed by divinity, not humanity). This is the principle firmly articulated in political philosophy and the laws of nations, not the "contextual and conjectural" equivocation Krupat spoons up.[17] While it is true that the *exercise* of sovereignty can be, and usually is, mediated by the processes to which he refers, the legitimacy of resulting constraints is entirely dependent upon their voluntary acceptance by all parties to the negotiation or encounter. Imposition by one nation of what it intends to be a permanent abridgment of sovereign rights upon another, as is the case in any colonial setting, is illegitimate by black letter international legal definition.[18]

The same pertains to what Krupat calls "cultural sovereignty" (by which he apparently means cultural autonomy), a matter inseparably linked with the exercise of national sovereignty.[19] While it is certainly true that cultures tend to be interactive and acquisitive, perhaps intrinsically so, the real question is whether each entity involved in a process of cultural exchange remains in control of the terms of its own participation, trading and adapting cultural/intellectual property in accordance with emic perceptions of need and interest, however dynamic and evolving these may be.[20] Should one party to the "encounter" directly impose itself upon another, however, especially when it does so with the express intent of negating the other culture and assimilating its members (as the United States has done to American Indians for well over a century), an altogether different situation presents itself.[21]

Under such circumstances, indicative as they are of advanced colonial systems, the struggle to restore cultural autonomy must be seen as not only integral to but in some ways spearheading efforts by the colonized to achieve more tangible forms of decolonization. Of necessity as well as inclination, this entails in the first instance a conscious and deliberate strategy to heal the cultural rupture precipitated through colonial intervention by affirming the traditions of their precolonial past. As Ella Shohat has observed, this "assertion of culture prior to conquest forms part of the fight against continuing forms of annihilation."[22] From there, the object is to utilize the reclaimed sense of national culture, not as an end in itself, but as a basis upon which to integrate those elements of the colonizer's imposition which may be employed, ju jitsu-style, to further the broader liberatory project.

It is at this juncture that Krupat digs in most deeply to defend the status quo. Ridiculing the very notion that there is—or even could be—anything resembling an emergent body of authentically autonomous native intellectuality, he insists that whatever of literary/theoretical consequence is produced by indigenous writers/scholars "ought to be included in the [American] canon . . . so that they might illuminate and interact with the texts of the dominant, Euramerican culture, to produce a genuinely heterodox national canon" (p. 19). At base, this is the equivalent of arguing that material produced by Vietnamese and Algerian resistance figures during the 1950s should be categorized as French literature in order that France might reflect a proper heterodoxy in *its* national canon.[23] It also dovetails nicely, at the cultural level, with the government's current plan to finalize its absorption of Native America into the U.S. politicoeconomic/territorial corpus.

The crux of Krupat's contention, he claims, is both "linguistic" and "conceptual": because indigenous writers rely upon English as our main vehicle of expression and communication, our claim to offer a "uniquely American Indian perspective" is, ipso facto, invalid. If, on the other hand, we generate material in our own languages, we are invalidated because our work is textually rendered—Krupat erroneously believes print to be a Eurospecific or exclusively Euroderivative presentational format (p. 17)—and because it is self-consciously offered as a literature corresponding to "Western" classifications of content.[24]

> "Native American philosophy" is a Western category, and so is "Native American literature." So too "Native American religion" and "Native American art" are Western categories. Traditional cultures abound in philosophical thought, powerful verbal and visual expression, and deeply felt relations to the divine or supernatural. But traditional cultures neither conceptualize or articulate the generalized abstract categories of philosophy, literature, and religion (p. 17).

Hence, to "consider . . . native thinkers as 'autonomous,' 'unique,' 'self-sufficient,' or 'intellectually sovereign'—as comprehensible apart from Western intellectualism—is simply not possible" (p. 18). By the same definition, of course, Italian cuisine cannot be considered Italian, since the idea of pasta (noodles) was brought back by Marco Polo from East Asia, while both tomatoes and peppers originated in the Americas; may we assume, therefore, that Krupat expects to order spaghetti in a Chinese restaurant or to find a good recipe for marinara sauce in a guidebook to American Indian cookery?

For that matter, given the nature of the "logic" he applies so gratuitously to Indians, one is entitled to wonder wherein he finds a basis for the existence of "Western culture" itself. Surely he is aware that many of its essential ingredients were acquired elsewhere: gunpowder, that fundament of European weapons technologies, came from China (although the English sought to attribute its invention to Roger Bacon), as did many "Western" astronomical/geographical/cartographical methodologies; the West's mathematics, engineering and architectural principles, its medical practices, even its understanding of Greek philosophy were "borrowed," without anything approaching proper attribution, from Islam (i.e., "the East"); most of the vegetal foodstuffs that laid the foundation for modern "Western" agriculture came from the New World, along with pharmacology and much else.[25]

Such an itemization could be extended to great length. This makes it quite possible—nay, inevitable for anyone willing to adopt Krupat's brand of "reasoning"—to arrive at the diametrical opposite of his own preferred conclusion: nothing at all is really comprehensible in conjunction with Western intellectualism because that tradition is in itself merely a mirage-like composite of elements, none of which can be understood apart from some other intellectual tradition. But, then, none of these other traditions have meaning apart from . . . Eventually, like the proverbial college sophomore, we are left with little but a vacuum of incomprehensibility.

Before wandering off into this absurd realm, it might be well to inquire as to whether there haven't been more constructive interpretations of the linguistic/conceptual/cultural phenomena Krupat purports to address. Consider, for instance, Memmi's observation that an imposed colonial language can, if approached correctly, be used in juxtaposition with native language to afford the colonized a "second tool" of liberation.[26] Or take the remarks of Kenyan novelist Ngugi wa Thiong'o, partially quoted by Krupat (p. 19), to the effect that all weapons—linguistic, cultural and otherwise—are appropriately deployed in the struggle to "decolonize the minds" of oppressed and oppressor alike. Perhaps most germane are the reflections of Frantz Fanon, French-speaking and -educated black Martiniqais theorist of the Algerian revolution.

> We believe that the conscious and organized undertaking by a colonized people to reestablish the sovereignty of that nation constitutes the most complete and obvious cultural manifestation that exists. It is not alone the success of the struggle which afterward

gives validity and vigor to culture; culture is not put into cold storage during the conflict. The struggle itself in its development and in its internal progression sends culture along different paths and traces out entirely new ones for it. The struggle for freedom does not give back to national culture its former value and shapes; the struggle which aims at a fundamentally different set of relations between men cannot leave intact either the form or the content of the people's culture. After the conflict there is not only the disappearance of colonialism but also the disappearance of colonized man.[23]

This, it seems to me, sums up the understandings and objectives of the American Indian intelligentsia rather admirably. None of us seek the circumscribed, static and reified cultural constructs to which Krupat would consign us in the name of our identities, nor do we accept that to be anything other than what he defines as legitimately native is to become synonymous with our colonization. Rather, as Shohat has noted, we are "obliged by circumstances to assert, for [our] very survival, a lost and even irretrievable past" in order to attain a new synthesis between what was and what is, creating thereby what can be: the resurrection of our cultures, and thus our nations, as vibrant, living entities, evolving and participating fully in the real world.[28] This is true, whatever our differences, whether one's point of reference is to me or to Robert Allen Warrior, to Elizabeth Cook-Lynn or to Vine Deloria, to Jimmie Durham or to Wendy Rose, Terry Wilson, John Mohawk, Leslie Marmon Silko, Sherman Alexie or any of the scores of others, named and unnamed, who are discounted in *The Turn to the Native*. All of us, each in his or her own way, has cast off the lot of compromise and oppression described by Memmi. We are not creatures broken by our defeat(s). On the contrary, we will speak our own history, create our own realisms and possibilities, define for ourselves the nature of a relations to others, forge the future of our generations in our own terms.

As to Arnold Krupat, he answers, by virtue of the various sophistries he employs in seeking to deny us our autonomy and our integrity, and in trying to retain his imagined position of primacy over us, the question he is quoted as posing at the outset of this critique. Far from being "nice," he is indeed a colonizer, a "usurper," a "partial, unpatriotic and treacherous being, worrying only about his privileges and their defense." Krupat and the colleagues to whom he refers so often and approvingly, not only those already mentioned, but others like Brian Swann, Alan Velie, Marvin Harris, Jerome Rothenberg, Gary Snyder and Armand Schwerner, are useful only to the colonial order, never to the colonized they profess to serve.

Notes

1. Arnold Krupat, *The Turn to the Native: Studies in Criticism and Culture* (Lincoln: University of Nebraska Press, 1996). His reference, uncited, is to Albert Memmi's *The Colonizer and the Colonized* (Boston: Beacon Press, 1965).

2. For detailed analysis of work produce by Castro, Gill, and Sollors, see the relevant essays contained in this volume. On Mander, see my *Indians Are Us? Culture and Genocide in Native North America* (Monroe, ME: Common Courage Press, 1994).

3. Krupat, whose annotation is for the most part exceedingly vague, in this instance references my own analysis of James A. Clifton's *The Invented Indian: Cultural Fictions and Government Policies* (New Brunswick, NJ: Transaction, 1990), in this volume. However, he goes on to describe Clifton's book as "an intense critique of Indian self-identifications," a characterization which would come much closer to fitting the latter's *Being and Becoming Indian: Biographical Studies of North American Frontiers* (Chicago: Dorsey Press, 1989). The salient argument presented in *The Invented Indian* is that Native Americans do not, and have never, really existed in any form at all.

4. According to *Webster's Ninth New Collegiate Dictionary*, "ad hominem" means either to "[appeal] to a person's feelings or prejudices rather than his intellect" or "marked by an attack on an opponent's character rather than to answer his contentions." Neither usage is in any way accurate or appropriate in describing a twenty–page, point-by-point, quote-laden dissection of a book. On the contrary, deliberate misapplication of the term to such a critique—no matter how strongly one disagrees with its premises or conclusions—is itself an ad hominem attack. In any event, Krupat's handling of Cook-Lynn fits within the definition quite admirably.

5. For a fullblown elaboration of the phenomenon at hand, albeit in another context, see Edward Said's magnificent study, *Orientalism* (New York: Random House, 1978). Also see John Tomlinson, *Cultural Imperialism* (Baltimore: Johns Hopkins University Press, 1991).

6. Perhaps the best explication of the concept of hegemony in the sense intended here will be found in Walter L. Adamson's *Hegemony and Revolution: A Study of Antonio Gramsci's Political and Cultural Theory* (Berkeley: University of California Press, 1980).

7. Even while conceding the accuracy of the terms, Krupat seeks to blunt their implications, quoting his colleague, Alan Velie, to the effect that "not all Native Americans are 'victims' enmeshed in a 'culture of poverty'" because there are a "great many oil-rich natives" in Oklahoma and that, "in Connecticut, the Mashantucket Pequots number among the super-rich" (p. 31). This caveat, paraphrasing such deep and liberatory thinkers as Ronald Reagan and Andy Rooney, is no more relevant to understanding the impact of U.S. internal colonialism on American Indians than are comparable references, made by other apologists, to the wealth accumulated within a few elite sectors of those Latin American countries subjected to U.S. neocolonial domination; see, e.g., Section V of Andre Gunder Frank's *Capitalism and Underdevelopment: Historical Studies of Chile and Brazil* (New York: Monthly Review Press, [2nd ed., rev.] 1969) pp. 219–318.

8. Martin Carnoy, *Education as Cultural Imperialism* (New York: David McKay, 1974) p. 61.

9. Memmi, *op. cit.*, pp. 105, 83. For further elaboration, see Robert Young, *White Mythologies: Writing History and the West* (London: Routledge, 1990).

10. Memmi, *op. cit.*, p. 89.

11. Ibid.; Carnoy, *op. cit.* A very good overview of the process, drawn from a range of settings, will also be found in Patricia Williams and Laura Chrisman, eds., *Colonial Discourse and Post-Colonial Theory* (New York: Columbia University Press, 1994).

12. For further methodological details, see, e.g., the selection of readings assembled by Chris Tiffin and Alan Lawson, eds., *De-Scribing Empire: Post-colonialism and Textuality* (London: Routledge, 1994).

13. Under provision of the United Nations Charter (1946), it is required that all colonial powers inscribe their colonies on a U.N.-administered list of "Non-Self-Governing Territories," subject to internationally supervised decolonization procedures. The principles enshrined therein are amplified in the 1960 Declaration on the Granting of Independence to Colonial Countries, an instrument which pronounces unequivocally that the "right of all peoples to self-determination" is fundamental, and prescribes the very *complete* independence of colonized peoples Krupat calls "unrealistic" as the sole legal remedy to colonialism. See, e.g., Nannum Hurst, *Autonomy, Sovereignty and Self-Determination*

(Philadelphia: University of Pennsylvania Press, 1990).

14. "My understanding of the issue of political sovereignty for Native Americans derives substantially from Vine Deloria, Jr. and Clifford Lytle's 1984 study, *The Nations Within: The Past and Future of American Indian Sovereignty*" (New York: Pantheon); Krupat, *op. cit.*, p. 13.

15. Krupat seeks to disguise the direction he is leading readers by referencing his argument to Vine Deloria's famous observation that indigenous nations are, at worst, entitled to stand "on the same footing with respect to the United States as does Monaco toward France, San Marino toward Italy, and Liechtenstein toward Switzerland and Austria," rather than to the Senate Select Committee (p. 15); Deloria and Lytle, *op. cit.*, p. 329. What is avoided in the process is that Deloria was/is seeking to establish concrete markers by which indigenous peoples can utilize self-governance as a route to the reassertion of a much broader range of sovereign prerogatives—affirming their status as entities related to but distinct from the United States—while the Senate initiative is a subterfuge designed to legally foreclose on sovereignty by institutionalizing native governments as part of the federal apparatus itself. Krupat's overall treatment of the sovereignty question reveals quite clearly which of these two perspectives he is aligned with.

16. In actuality, this has been a standard line of imperialist polemic during the latter phases of colonialism; see generally, Stewart C. Easton, *The Rise and Fall of Western Colonialism: A Historical Survey from the Early Nineteenth Century to the Present* (New York: Praeger, 1964); Raymond F. Betts, *Europe Overseas: Phases of Imperialism* (New York: Basic Books, 1968); Franz Anspringer, *The Dissolution of Colonial Empires* (London: Routledge, 1989).

17. A succinct overview will be found in Vine Deloria, Jr.'s "Sovereignty," in Roxanne Dunbar Ortiz and Larry Emerson, eds., *Economic Development in American Indian Reservations* (Albuquerque: University of New Mexico Native American Studies Center, 1979). More broadly, see Carl Schmitt's *Political Theology: Four Chapters on the Concept of Sovereignty* (Cambridge, MA: MIT Press, 1985); Wilfred C. Jencks, *Law in the World Community* (New York: Oxford University Press, 1967).

18. Hurst, *op. cit.* Also see W. Ofuatey-Kodjoe, *The Principle of Self-Determination in International Law* (Hamden, CT: Archon Books, 1972); Cristescu Aureliu, *The Right to Self-Determination: Historical and Current Developments on the Basis of United Nations Instruments* (U.N. Doc. E/CN.4/Sub.2/404 Rev.1 (1981)); Michla Pomerance, *Self-Determination in Law and Practice* (The Hague: Marinus Nijhoff, 1982). For application of these principles specifically to the circumstance of America's indigenous peoples, see Michael D. Gross, "Indian Self-Determination and Tribal Sovereignty: An Analysis of Recent Federal Policy," *Texas Law Review*, No. 56, 1978.

19. "One [cannot] speak of cultural identity without reaffirming the fundamental concepts of national sovereignty and territorial independence. . . [We declare] that cultural autonomy is inseparable from the full exercise of sovereignty"; UNESCO, *Final Report of the World Conference on Cultural Policies: Mexico City* (Paris: UNESCO, 1982) pp. 22, 61.

20. For a thorough explication, see Raymond Williams, *Culture* (London: Fontana, 1981).

21. U.S. assimilation policy combined both elements in roughly equal measures; indigenous cultural practices were universally criminalized towards the end of the nineteenth century while native children were subjected en masse to a compulsory "educational" process designed explicitly to indoctrinate them with the cultural values and orientation of their colonizers; see, e.g., David Wallace Adams, *Education for Extinction: American Indians and the Boarding School Experience, 1875–1928* (Lawrence: University Press of Kansas, 1995). Although some of the more virulent practices have been abandoned, probably because they are seen as having long since accomplished their objectives, the goal of "mainstreaming" Indians remains a predominating aspiration of American pedagogy to the present day.

22. Ella Shohat, "Notes on the Post-Colonial," *Social Text*, Vol. 31, No. 2, 1992, p. 110.

23. The analogy is hardly farfetched. In the case of Algeria, France actually maintained that the colony was part of its "home" territoriality in much the same manner that the United States claims Native America as part of itself; see, e.g., Joseph Kraft, *The Struggle for Algeria* (New York: Doubleday, 1961). Those wishing to object that Algeria was "different" because of its separation from France by a body of ocean water should consider the circumstance of Native Hawaiians; see, e.g., Haunani-Kay Trask, *From a Native Daughter: Colonialism and Sovereignty in Hawai'i* (Monroe, ME: Common Courage Press, 1993).

24. "In 1403 the Koreans produced the first metal type known to history," establishing that the basis for a printing system may have been in use in China and Japan as well as Korea by the time of Johann

Gutenberg's "belated discovery in Europe" a half-century later; Will Durant, *Our Oriental Heritage* (New York: Simon & Schuster, 1935) p. 730. The idea of the text is even less "Western." Indeed, several forms of textual production in Native America are known to have predated the European invasion. In any event, a contemporary American Indian writer availing him/herself of print technology to produce texts is no more inherently "un-Indian" than was a seventeenth-century native hunter who traded for steel traps and knives, or a nineteenth-century warrior who appropriated guns and ammunition with which to defend his people. It is also extremely dubious that the system of classification at issue is even "Western" in origin. More likely, it was pioneered by the Egyptians, worked out by the Greeks, and subjected to considerable refinement by Islamic scholars before being acquired by Europe's comparatively primitive intellectual establishment somewhere around 1300 A.D.; see, e.g., Hichem Djait, *Europe and Islam: Cultures and Modernity* (Berkeley: University of California Press, 1985) pp. 105–14.

25. On the attribution of gunpowder to Bacon, see Will Durant, *The Age of Faith* (New York: Simon & Schuster, 1950) p. 1015. Concerning the origins of "modern" astronomical/geographical methods — evident in China as early as 2400 B.C., not adopted in Europe until the sixteenth century — see Kenneth C. Davis, *Don't Know Much About Geography* (New York: Morrow, 1992) pp. 64–8. Regarding the massive influence of Islam in the formation of European intellectuality, see Djait, *op. cit.* On Native American agriculture, etc., see Jack Weatherford, *Indian Givers: How the Indians of the Americas Transformed the World* (New York: Fawcett Columbine, 1988).

26. Memmi, *op. cit.*, p. 107.

27. Frantz Fanon, *The Wretched of the Earth* (New York: Grove Press, 1966) pp. 245–6.

28. Shohat, *op. cit.*, p. 110.

"Interpreting" the American Indian?
A Critique of Michael Castro's Apologia for Poetic Racism

> Repression works like a shadow, clouding memory and sometimes even to blind, and when it is on a national scale, it is just not good. . . . It was a national quest, dictated by economic motives. Europe was hungry for raw material, and America was abundant forest, rivers, land.
>
> —Simon J. Ortiz
> *From Sand Creek*

The relationship between indigenous realities and their interpretation by external observers, particularly by those who profess sympathy or even commonality with the native, has always been an important consideration for indigenous activists and thinkers. This is especially true in countries such as Australia, New Zealand, South Africa and virtually all the nations of the Americas, places where the form assumed by nineteenth-century European imperialism was that of "the settler state." In such areas, colonization of indigenous populations was such that the natives were subsumed within or permanently subordinated to an in-place "replacement population" imported from the colonizing country. This is as opposed to the more classic model of colonialism where the mother country merely dispatched military and administrative cadres to occupy and manage its new "possession."

It is a given in any colonial situation that the colonizing power presumes, on the basis of social darwinism if nothing else, that its culture is inherently superior to that of the colonized. Hence, it assumes the right, the obligation and "civilizing mission"—the "White man's burden," as it were—to explain this to its subjects, rendering the colonized ever more accommodating to the "natural condition" of their domination by the colonial master, ever more compliant to the inevitability of material exploitation by the colonizer. Such has been a clear historical utilization of interpretation of indigenous cultures by their conquerors. Still, within the structure of such a schema, there remains a clear distinction between the colonizer and the colonized, a more-or-less pure "them/us" dichotomy allowing ongoing cultural integrity (albeit in diluted form) to both parties.

Within the context of advanced settler-state colonization however, things become rather more complex and confusing. Here, members of the dominant culture are unable to retain their sense of distance and separation from that which they dominate. Instead, over a period of generations, they increasingly develop direct ties to the "new land" and, consequently, exhibit an ever-increasing tendency to proclaim *themselves* as "natives." This, of course, equals a quite literal negation of the very essence and existence of those who are truly indigenous to the colonized locales. The famed anti-colonialist psychiatrist Frantz Fanon has termed this process "the final liquidation, indeed the digestion of the native." What is at issue in this instance is thus not simply systematic resource expropriation (with all the concomitant human misery that implies), but genocide. It is genocide of an extremely sophisticated type, to be sure, but it is genocide nonetheless.

As Albert Memmi, a noted literary figure of the Algerian revolution, has observed: this process of genocide assumes the form of an appropriation of the identity of the colonized by the colonizer. Stripped of the particularities of its identity, the colonized people ultimately dissolves and is absorbed whole by the corpus of a newly homogenized "master culture." Insofar as such a process is primarily intellectual rather than physically oriented, interpretation of indigenous sensibilities and worldview for consumption by the non-indigenous constitutes a key element of its operant technique. Interpretation in this sense bespeaks not the repression of indigenous cultures prevalent under classical colonial conditions, but the repackaging and even promotion of native perspectives as a means to facilitate their incorporation into the dominant culture. This, in turn, empowers the non-native to begin to view him/herself totalistically, as a new hybrid embodying "the best of both worlds."

Psychically, the process tends to be self-validating, justified at a certain level by a desire to ease the degree of tension and discord between colonizer and colonized. Hence, the leading practitioners of identity appropriation are often motivated by sincere empathy and a genuine will to open viable channels of communication between oppressor and oppressed. However, the very real power dynamics of colonialism preclude even the best and most sensitive of such efforts from doing other than reinforcing and enhancing the structure of domination at play.

In the United States, where settler-state colonialism is currently most developed, the desired "fusion" of indigenous realities (albeit in often grossly distorted configurations) with the dominant consciousness is generally accommodated by the mass media, what Theodor Adorno labeled "the culture industry" and which is intended as an expression to cover all genuinely popular communications formats from television to mass-distributed reading material. As such, it might seem more appropriately the topic for sociological consideration than for literary criticism. However, as Walter Benjamin long ago pointed out in his *Illuminations*, the content and methods of the culture industry itself are mediated and tempered by more rarefied artistic forms: literature, dance, the plastic arts, drama, music and—perhaps most allegorically of all—poetry. A concrete linkage between the arts and the much more overtly propagandistic functions of the mass media can neither be truthfully denied nor rightly ignored.

Michael Castro, in his recent book *Interpreting the Indian*, takes up the important question of the appropriation of indigenous identity by non-Indian poets in the twentieth-century United States. In this, the first attempt at an overall and coherently formulated study of the subject matter, he is confronted with a situation rife with opportunity for exploration and development of in-depth analysis into that which is discovered. The book could well have been a landmark. Unfortunately, the author fails to achieve a particularly satisfactory posture, either as an explorer or as an analyst.

The book starts well enough. In his all-too-brief introductory section, Castro offers an overview of the evolution of Indian thematics in American literature, taking pains in the limited space he allows himself to bring out the relationship between the literary examples he employs and the phases of colonial development with which they correspond (e.g., his citation of Melville on page xv linking "the brutish savage stereotype" to "the genocidal hand of government, as it cleared the way to America's manifest destiny").

A similar sort of promise is extended in the quotation with which he opts to lead his first chapter, a passage from Mary Austin's *American Rhythm* in which the poet neatly encapsulates the pathos of identity appropriation by stating, ". . .when I say that I am not, have never been, nor offered myself, as an authority on things Amerindian, I do not wish to have it understood that I may not, at times, have succeeded *in being an Indian* [emphasis added]." As if to demonstrate compellingly that Austin's arrogance was not a peculiar or isolated phenomenon within the context of his study, but rather represents sentiments integral to an accelerating pattern of appropriative progression, Castro leads his second chapter with the observation from William Carlos Williams' *In the American Grain* that, "I do believe the average American to be an Indian. . . ."

Between these astutely selected of telling quotations, however, the author falls flat. Rather than following his own lead in examining the meaning of such postulations within the broader historical socioeconomic context (which, after all, has been reasonably well chronicled), he chooses to treat each, biographically and aesthetically, as the manifestation of the individuated consciousness of its author. That such an idealized understanding of artistic creation, particularly that of the twentieth-century European/Euroamerican variety, has for some time been exposed as nonsensical goes without saying. One need not demand emulation of Arnold Hauser to expect art to be situated in social circumstance by any serious historian or critic.

Castro at least tacitly acknowledges such problems, and the necessity of locating his subjects somewhere beyond the immediate confines of their individual consciousness, when he goes to the trouble of attempting to define them in terms of emergent trends in American literature. Such a method holds the possibility of providing a plausible, if superficial, closure while avoiding the obvious political volatility of coming to grips with broader contextual matters. But even at this level Castro sidesteps substance and meaning. Rather than building a nuanced examination of the range of poets topically mining the veins of "Indianness" during the periods he purports to investigate, the author resorts to compiling representative lists of materials published during various decades. Hence, he often reduces himself from the level of aesthetic criticism to that of vulgar journalism. Simultaneously, he opens up legitimate questions as to whether he was in fact even conversant enough with his topic to presume writing a book on it.

Throughout the reading of *Interpreting the Indian*, one is struck by the paucity of mention afforded secondary or tertiary poets within the genre at hand, as well as of reference to contemporaneous criticism. Nowhere is this thin treatment more in evidence than the single (final) chapter Castro devotes to consideration of Native American poetry. Very important voices, such as those of Peter Blue Cloud, Wendy Rose and Joy Harjo are included only by virtue of their mention in a list. Others, such as Mary Tall Mountain, William Oandasan and Linda Hogan do not appear at all. Nor is there so much as a reference given to critical efforts such as Karl Kroeber's *Studies in*

American Indian Literature project at Columbia University, an effort which is rather influential and relatively well known. While such a listing of defects might be extended at length, the examples should speak for themselves.

To the extent that Castro's handling yields any explanatory power at all, it is of a clearly evasive and apologetic sort. While ignoring the more significant implications of the positions and utterances of his various protagonists (it is as if the nineteenth-century Indian policies he brings out in his introduction mysteriously disappear in the twentieth), he seems forever in search of ways and means to mitigate them, to render them sympathetically and to tidy up the ugliness of the colonial ramifications of their poetics. The result is an "I'm okay, you're okay" sort of sentimentality.

Thus, to pick but one example, the author is able to indicate in his chapter on Gary Snyder that the poet has fashioned a career on the basis of excursions into other peoples' cultures, always to return as a primary medium of expression for that culture (first he fancied himself an articulator of the inner visions of Japanese Zen Buddhism, and then won a Pulitzer elaborating an "American Indian" perspective on North America), without ever drawing a conclusion on what this peculiar state of affairs might mean. Of course, it is noted that Snyder has been (justly) criticized for having "borrowed" a bit too freely from other cultures without having come to grips with the meaning of his own heritage, but Castro then lets the thought die as if it is too uncomfortable a revelation to be dealt with further. The treatment of Snyder is therefore left quite vacuously to hinge upon the man's undeniably great technical skills in the poetic craft.

All in all, Michael Castro's book can only be viewed as a failed promise. It is abundantly lacking in analytical force, and is far too scanty to suggest itself as a survey text. The portraits it offers of given poets and their psychic relationships to American Indians (real or imagined) are much too narrowly "balanced" to offer real insight into their individual motivations and characters. There are no thematics, beyond the title concept, tying the book together which would even seem particularly appropriate for future development elsewhere. Castro's effort might more aptly have been dubbed "interpreting the interpreters in a sympathetic light." Still, in going to press with his title, the author may be viewed as having opened the formerly closed door on his subject matter simply by calling attention to it at long last. That he follows with a thoroughly inadequate text serves to compellingly demonstrate how very much work must be done before we have an articulation/

understanding corresponding to the title. For showing us all graphically how not to accomplish this, we all owe Michael Castro a backhanded thanks.

Fantasies of the Master Race
The Cinematic Colonization of American Indians

> Now those movie Indians wearing all those feathers can't come out as human beings. They're not expected to come out as human beings because I think the American people do not regard them as wholly human. We must remember that many, many American children believe that feathers grow out of Indian heads.
>
> —Stephen Feraca
> Motion Picture Director
> 1964

The cinematic depiction of indigenous peoples in America is objectively racist at all levels. This observation encompasses not only the more than two thousand Hollywood movies featuring or at least touching upon such subject matters over the years, but the even greater number of titles made for television.[1] In this, film is linked closely to literature of both the fictional and ostensibly nonfictional varieties, upon which most scripts are based. It is thus both fair and accurate to observe that all modes of projecting images and attendant conceptualizations of native people to the "mainstream" public fit the same mold.[2] Moreover, it is readily observable that within the confines of this mold are included only the narrowest and most negative range of graphic/thematic possibilities.[3]

While the same points might undoubtedly be made with respect to the celluloid portrayals accorded any/all "primitive" peoples, or even people of color per se, the vast weight, more than forty-five hundred productions in all, has fallen upon American Indians.[4] On balance, it seems no overstatement to suggest that throughout the twentieth century audiences have been quite literally saturated with very specific and repetitive dramatic characterizations of Indians. It follows, as with anything pursued with such intensity, that these characterizations themselves have been carefully contrived to serve certain ends.[5]

It would be well, then, to come to grips with the manner in which Indians have been displayed on both tube and silver screen, as well as the motivations underlying it. And, since the former may be easily divided into several distinct but related categories of stereotyping—indeed, it virtually divides itself in this way—it seems appropriate to take each in turn, using the whole as a basis upon which to explore the question of motive(s).

Indians as Creatures of a Particular Time

Nothing, perhaps, is more emblematic of Hollywood's visual pageantry than scenes of Plains Indian warriors astride their galloping ponies, many of them trailing a flowing headdress in the wind, thundering into battle against the blue-coated troops of the United States. By now, more than five hundred feature films and half again as many television productions have included representations of this sort.[6] We have been served such fare along with the tipi and the buffalo hunt, the attack upon the wagon train and the ambush of the stagecoach until they have become so indelibly imprinted upon the American consciousness as to be synonymous with Indians as a whole (to non-Indians at any rate and, unfortunately, to many native people as well).[7]

It's not that the technical inaccuracies in such representations are what is most problematic, although these usually are many and often extreme. Rather, it is the fact that the period embodied in such depictions spans barely the three decades running from 1850 to 1880, the interval of warfare between the various Plains peoples and the ever-encroaching soldiers and settlers of the United States.[8] There is no "before" to the story, and there is no "after." Cinematic Indians have no history before Euroamericans come along, and then, mysteriously, they seem to pass out of existence altogether.[9]

So it has been since the earliest experimental flickers like *Buck Dancer* and *Serving Rations to the Indians* in 1898. Never, with the exception of the sublimely ridiculous *Windwalker* (1980), has an effort been made to produce a movie based on the life of Native North Americans a thousand years or more before Columbus, a timeframe corresponding rather favorably to that portrayed in such Eurocentric epics as Robert Wise's *Helen of Troy* (1955), or Cecil B. DeMille's extravagant remake of *The Ten Commandments* (1924; 1956). Nowhere will one find a Native American counterpart to *Quo Vadis?* (1912; 1951), *The Robe* (1953), *Ben Hur* (1907; 1926; 1959), *Spartacus* (1960), *Cleopatra* (1917; 1934; 1963) or any of scores of less noteworthy releases set deep in what Euroamerica takes to be its own heritage.[10]

Much the same vacuum pertains to depictions of things Indian after conclusion of the so-called "Indian Wars" (they were actually settlers' wars throughout).[11] While a relative few films have been devoted to, or at least include, twentieth-century Native Americans, they have largely served to trivialize and degrade us through "humor." These include such "classics" as Busby Berkeley's *Whoopee!* (1930), the Marx Brothers' *Go West* (1940) and the W.C. Fields/Mae West hit *My Little Chickadee* (1940), as well as Abbott and Costello's *Ride 'Em Cowboy* (1942).[12] Other heavy hitters include the Bowery Boys' *Bowery Buckaroo* (1947), Bob Hope's *Paleface* (1948), *Son of Paleface* (1952) and *Cancel My Reservation* (1972), not to mention Lewis and Martin's *Hollywood or Bust* (1956).[13]

As Daniel Francis comments, Euroamericans "did not expect Indians to adapt to the modern world. Their only hope was to assimilate, to become White, to cease to be Indians. In this view, a modern Indian is a contradiction in terms: Whites could not imagine such a thing. Any Indian was by definition a traditional Indian, a relic of the past."[14] For "real" or "serious" Indians, then, it was necessary to look back upon the "vanishing" species of the nineteenth century, a theme diligently pursued in early documentaries like Edward S. Curtis's perversely titled *In the Land of the Headhunters* (1913-14) and Robert Flaherty's *Nanook of the North* (1922), and subsequently picked up in commercial movies like *The Vanishing American* (1925), *Eskimo* (1930), *The Last of the Redman* (1947), *Last of the Comanches* (1953), *The Last Frontier* (1955), *The Last Hunt* (1956), *The Apache's Last Battle* (1966) and, most recently, the Academy Award-winning *Dances With Wolves* (1990), *The Last of the Mohicans* (1992) and *Last of His Tribe* (1995).[15] All the while, untold thousands of doomed savages have been marched off to the oblivion of their reservations at the end of literally hundreds of lesser films.

In its most virulent form, Hollywood's famous "disappearing Indian" trick was backdated onto the nineteenth century's "crimsoned prairie" itself, rendering native people invisible even there. One will look in vain for any sign of an indigenous presence, even as backdrop, in such noteworthy westerns as *High Noon* (1952), *Shane* (1953), *Gunfight at the OK Corral* (1957), *Warlock* (1959), *Pat Garrett and Billy the Kid* (1973), *Heaven's Gate* (1981) and *Tombstone* (1994). It's as if, observes Cherokee artist/aesthetician/cultural theorist Jimmie Durham, at "some point late at night, by the campfire, presumably, the Lone Ranger ate Tonto. By the time Alan Ladd becomes the lone ranger in *Shane*, his Indian companion has been consumed."[16]

When not being depicted as drunken buffoons, as in *Flap* (1970), or simply as buffoons, as in the 1989 "road" movie *Powwow Highway*, modern Indians have been mostly portrayed in a manner deriving directly from the straightjacket of temporal stereotype.[17] The ways in which this has been accomplished are somewhat varied, ranging from 1950s war stories like *Battle Cry* and *Never So Few* to monster flicks like *Predator* (1988) and *Deep Rising* (1998), and they have sometimes been relatively subtle, as in *One Flew Over the Cuckoo's Nest* (1975), but the rule nonetheless applies.

Creatures of a Particular Place

Constricting the window of Native America's celluloid existence to the mid-nineteenth century has, because it was then the locus of Indian/white warfare, had the collateral effect of confining natives to the geographic region known generically as the "West." In truth, the area is itself subdivided into several distinct bioregional locales, of which Hollywood selected two, the Plains and the Upper Sonoran Desert region of New Mexico and Arizona (often referred to as the "Southwest"), as being representative. It follows that the bulk of tinseltown's filmstock would be expended in setting forth images of the peoples indigenous to its chosen domain(s).[18]

The Plains of filmdom are inhabited primarily by "Sioux" (Lakotas) to the north, Cheyennes in the center and Comanches to the south. Not infrequently, smaller peoples like the Arapahos and Kiowas make appearances, and, every now and again, Pawnees and Crows as well (usually as scouts for the army).[19] Leaving aside a host of glaring inaccuracies otherwise conveyed by filmmakers about each of these cultures, it can be said that they at least managed (or bothered) to get the demographic distribution right.

Not so the Southwest. Although the "empty desert" was/is filled with a host of peoples running the gamut from the Hopi, Zuni and other "Puebloans" to the Pima, Maricopa, Cocopah, Yuma, Yaqui and Navajo, anyone taking their ethnographic cues from the movies would be led rapidly to the conclusion that there was but one: The Apaches.[20] In fact, more films have been dedicated to supposedly depicting Apacheria than the domain of any other native people, the "mighty Sioux" included.[21]

The roster began with silent movies like *Apache Gold* (1910; remade in 1965), *The Curse of the Red Man* (1911), *On the Warpath* (1912) and *A Prisoner of the Apaches* (1913), was continued with talkies like *Bad Lands* and *Stagecoach* in the 1930s, and has most recently included Cherokee actor Wes Studi playing the title role in the third remake of *Geronimo* (1990; earlier versions appeared in 1939 and 1962). Along the way, there have been *Apache Trail* (1942) and *Apache Chief* (1949), *Apache Warrior* (1957) and *Apache Woman* (1955), *Apache War Smoke* (1952) and *Apache Uprising* (1965), *Apache Country* (1953) and *Apache Territory* (1958), *Apache Rifles* (1965) and *Fury of the Apaches* (1965), *The Battle at Apache Pass* (1952), *Stand at Apache River* (1953), *Rampage at Apache Wells* (1966) and *40 Guns to Apache Pass* (1966). On and on and on. The count at this point is nearly six hundred titles and rising, plus an untold number of skits made for TV.[22]

The reasoning here is true to form. The people of Victorio and Geronimo, Mangus and Cochise sustained their resistance to Euroamerican invasion longer, and in a proportionately more effective fashion, than any group other than the Seminoles (who, fortunately or unfortunately for them, depending on one's point of view, did their fighting in the wrong place/time to fall much within the bounds of proper cinematography).[23] Give the duration and intensity of their martial interaction with whites, Apaches could be seen as "consequential," and therefore worthy of an equal intensity of cinematic attention.

There is a certain consistency to this prioritization, albeit a patently objectionable one. Things really become confusing, however, when one considers the approach taken by John Ford, perhaps the most esteemed director of the entire western movie genre. Simultaneously fixated on the beadwork, buckskins and feather heraldry of Plains Indians and the breathtaking desert geography of the Southwest's Monument Valley, both for what he described as "aesthetic reasons," Ford exercised his "artistic license" by simply combining the two. Still, he and his publicists proudly, loudly and persistently proclaimed his "unparalleled achievement" in capturing an "authentic" flavor in visually evoking the "Old West."[24]

Ford won Academy Award nominations for two of the seven pictures he shot in Monument Valley between 1939 and 1964, all of which received substantial critical acclaim.[25] Meanwhile, in *Stagecoach* (1939), *The Searchers* (1956) and *Cheyenne Autumn* (1964), two generations of American moviegoers were brought to understand that western Kansas looks just like northern Arizona, and, consequently, the environments of the Comanches and Cheyennes were indistinguishable from that of the Apaches. As Lakota scholar Vine Deloria, Jr. explains, "It's the same as if Hollywood were claiming to have made the most realistic movie ever about the Cossacks, and it turned out to have been filmed in fishing villages along the Irish coast, or with the Matterhorn as a backdrop. It makes a difference, because culture and environment are pretty intimately connected."[26]

The situation was even more muddled by the fact that before 1965, an era in which location-shooting was beyond the budgets of all but the most prestigious directors, the very same Plains topography was represented in literally hundreds of B-movies and TV segments via the Spahn Movie Ranch and similar sets scattered across southern California.[27] By the seventies, when increasing attention began to be paid to the idea that films might be "validated" by way of the technical accuracy of their physical details, the damage had long since been done. American Indians, already denied any sort of genuinely autochthonous history in the movies, had been thoroughly divorced from material reality as well.

Seen One Indian, Seen 'em All

The space/time compression imposed by Hollywood upon Native America has generated other effects, to be sure. "You would think," writes Cherokee law professor Rennard Strickland, "if you relied on the Indian films, that there were no [peoples] east of the Mississippi, none but the Plains Indians [and Apaches], except possibly the Mohawks, and that the country was unoccupied throughout the entire Great Lakes and central region except for an occasional savage remnant, perhaps a stray Yaqui or two who wandered in from the Southwest. We almost never have a Chippewa or a Winnebago or a . . . Hopi or even a Navajo on the screen."[28]

In the few instances filmmakers decided, for whatever reason, to make a movie about native people in the East, the results have usually been bizarre. A prime example used by Strickland is that of *Seminole Uprising* (1955), in which we "see Florida Everglades-dwelling Seminoles wearing Plains feathered bonnets and battling bluecoated cavalry on desert buttes."[29] The same principle pertains in somewhat less blatant form to the attire displayed in four other films—*Distant Drums* (1951), *Seminole* (1953), *War Arrow* (1954) and *Yellowneck* (1957)—made about the Seminoles during the same period.[30]

Nor is the displacement of Plains Indian attributes onto other peoples the end of it. The Plains cultures themselves have become distorted in the popular conception, often wildly so, by virtue of a succession of cinematographers' obsessions with conjuring up "great images" out of whatever strikes their fancy. Perhaps the best (or worst) example will be found in *A Man*

Called Horse (1970), a movie prefaced with a scrolled testimonial from the Smithsonian Institution's chief "ethnohistorian," Wilcomb Washburn, that it was "the most authentic description of American Indian life ever filmed."[31]

In actuality, borrowing its imagery willy-nilly from the full body of George Catlin's graphic survey of northern Plains cultures during the 1830s,[32] director Eliott Silverstein's staff had decided that the Lakotas allegedly depicted in the film should wear an array of hairstyles ranging those typical of the Assiniboin to those of their mortal enemies, the Crows. Their tipi design and decoration is also of a sort unique to Crows. About the only thing genuinely "Sioux" about these supposed Sioux is the name, and even then there is absolutely no indication as to which Sioux they are supposed to be. Oglalas? Hunkpapas? Minneconjous? Secungus (Brûlés)? Bohinunpas (Two Kettles)? Ituzipcos (Sans Arcs)? Sihasapas (Blackfeet; not to be confused with the indigenous nation of the same name). The Lakotas, after all, were/are a populous people, divided into seven distinct bands, at least as different from one another as Maine Yankees are from Georgia Crackers.[33]

Probably the most repugnant instance of transference in *A Man Called Horse* occurs when Silverstein has his "Sioux" prepare to conduct a Sun Dance, their central spiritual ceremony, in a domed below-ground structure of the sort unknown to Lakota culture but which were habituated by Mandans along the Missouri River. The ritual itself is then performed in a manner more-or-less corresponding to Catlin's description of the Mandan, *not* the Lakota practice of it.[34] Finally, the meaning of the ceremony, sublimely reverential for both peoples, is explained as being something akin to medieval Europe's macho tests of courage, thence "manhood," by the ability to unflinchingly absorb pain.

Surveying the ubiquitousness of such cinematic travesties as "Delawares dressed as Sioux" and "Indians of Manhattan Island . . . dwelling in tipis," even an establishmentarian like Alanson Skinner, curator of the Department of Anthropology at the American Museum of Natural History, prefigured Deloria. Condemning such things as "ethnographically grotesque farces" in the pages of the *New York Times*, he posed the obvious question: "If Indians should stage a white man's play, and dress the characters in Rumanian, Swiss, Turkish, English, Norwegian and Russian costumes, and place the setting in Ireland, would their pleas that they thought all Indians alike save them from arousing our ridicule?"[35]

Skinner might also have inquired as to the likely response had Indians portrayed High Mass as a Protestant Communion, interpreted the wine and wafers as symbolic cannibalism, and then implied that the whole affair was synonymous with Satanism. It matters little, however, since until very recently no Indians—with the momentary exception during the 1930s of Will Rogers, a Cherokee—have ever been in a position to make either plays or films in which they could personify themselves accurately, much less parody their white tormentors.[36]

A major reason the "seen one Indian, seen 'em all" attitude had become quite firmly entrenched among the public by the end of the fifties was that the public was literally seeing no Indians at all in Hollywood's endless renderings of things native. Aside from Molly Spotted Elk, a Penobscot cast as the lead in *Silent Enemy* (1930), and Rogers, who filled the same bill in several comedies during the thirties, no Indian appeared in a substantial film role prior to 1970.[37] The same can be said with respect to directors and scriptwriters.[38]

Instead, pleading that it just couldn't find Indians capable of playing themselves on screen "convincingly," Hollywood consistently hired whites to impersonate native people in a more "believable" manner. As a consequence, the history of American cinema is replete with such gems as the 6'4" blond, blue-eyed former professional baseball pitcher, Chuck Connors, being cast as the swarthy, 5'3", obsidian-eyed title character in *Geronimo* (1962). And, if this "makes about as much sense as casting Wilt Chamberlain to play J. Edgar Hoover," as one native actor lately put it, there are plenty of equally egregious examples.[39]

Take Victor Mature being cast as the great Lakota leader in *Chief Crazy Horse* (1955). Or Gilbert Roland and Ricardo Montalban as the no less illustrious Dull Knife and Little Wolf in *Cheyenne Autumn* (1946). Or Jeff Chandler cast as Cochise, an Apache of comparable stature, in *Broken Arrow* (1950). Or Rock Hudson cast in the title role of *Taza, Son of Cochise* (1954). Or Burt Lancaster as the Sac and Fox super-athlete in *Jim Thorpe—All American* (1951).[40] Or J. Carol Naish as *Sitting Bull* (1954). Or Tony Curtis cast as Pima war hero Ira Hayes in *The Outsider* (1961). Or Robert Blake in the title role of *Tell Them Willie Boy Is Here* (1969). Or how about Robbie Benson playing Lakota Olympic gold medalist Billy Mills in *Running Brave* (1983)? The list could obviously be extended to include thousands of such illustrations.[41]

Women? Try Debra Paget as Cochise's daughter in *Broken Arrow*. How about Mary Pickford as "the little Indian maiden [who] Paid Her Debt of

Gratitude" to the White Man with sex in *Iola's Promise* (1912)? Or Delores Del Rio in the title role of *Ramona* (1928)? Or Linda Darnel as the "Indian" female lead in *Buffalo Bill* (1944)? Or Jennifer Jones as the sultry "half-breed" in *Duel in the Sun* (1946)? May Wynn as a nameless "Indian maiden" in *They Rode West* (1954)? Donna Reed as Sacajawea in *The Far Horizons* (1955)? And then there's Julie Newmar, complete with a pair of designer slacks, as the indigenous sex symbol in *McKenna's Gold* (1969). Again, the list might go on for pages.[42]

We should perhaps be grateful that John Wayne was never selected to play Red Cloud, or Madonna as Pocahontas, but given Hollywood's overall record—Wayne *was* cast as the Mongol leader Genghis Khan in a 1956 release entitled *The Conqueror*—such things seem more a matter of oversight than of design.[43]

Even when Indians were deployed on-screen, usually as extras—a job Oneida actor/comedian Charlie Hill likens to serving as a "prop" or, more accurately, "a pop-up target to be shot full of holes by cowboys and cavalry-men"[44]—little concern was ever given to accuracy. John Ford, for instance, habitually hired Navajos to impersonate the peoples of the Plains with no apparent qualms about the groups being as physically dissimilar as Swedes and Sicilians.[45] Cumulatively, Hill describes the results of Hollywood's and the television industry's imaging as the creation of "a weird sort of Indian stew" rather than anything resembling a valid apprehension of indigenous realities.[46]

Peoples Without Culture

The emulsification of native cultural content by Hollywood amounted, in essence, to its negation. As Rennard Strickland points out, "In the thousands of individual films and the millions of frames in those films, we have few, if any, real Indians . . . who have individuality or humanity. We see little, if any, of home or village life, of the day-to-day world of Native Americans or their families."[47] Creation of this vacuum has, in turn, allowed filmmakers to figuratively reconstruct native culture(s) in accordance with their own biases, preconceptions or sense of expediency and convenience.

Mostly, they elected to follow the quasiofficial script traditionally advanced by the Smithsonian Institution, that Native North Americans were, until Euroamericans came along to "civilize" us, typically brutish stone-age savages, maybe a million primitives wandering nomadically about the landscape, perpetually hunting and gathering our way along the bare margins of subsistence, devoid of all that might be called true culture.[48] An astonishing example of such (mis)perceptions at play will be found in the 1954 film *Apache*, in which the sullen southwesterners are taught to cultivate corn by a group of displaced southeasterners, Cherokees, who supposedly picked up the "art" from their benevolent white neighbors in Georgia.[49]

Never mind that it is an established fact that corn was hybridized from grass by indigenous Americans centuries before an Italian seaman, now revered as a "Great Navigator," washed up on a Caribbean beach half-a-world away from where he thought he was. Never mind that, like corn, two-thirds of the vegetal foodstuffs now commonly consumed by humanity were undeniably under cultivation in the Americas and *nowhere else* at the time of the "Columbian landfall."[50] Never mind that, as a matter of record, American military commanders from John Sullivan to Anthony Wayne, even Kit Carson, had to burn off miles of native croplands in order to starve Indians onto reservations where we could be "taught to farm."[51]

Agriculture is indicative of civilization, not savagery, and so, ipso facto, Indians could not have engaged in it, no matter how self-evident the fact that we did, or how extensively so.[52] In its stead, the Smithsonian, and therefore Hollywood, bestowed upon us an all-consuming and wholly imaginary "warrior mystique," that is to say, a certain propensity to use force in stealing from others that which, in their telling, we had never learned to do or make for ourselves. Thus were the relational roles of Indian and white in American history quite neatly and completely reversed so that those who stole a continent might be consistently portrayed as the victims of their victims' wanton and relentless "aggression."[53]

Such themes have always been exceedingly difficult to apply to the East where it had taken Europe fully two centuries of armed conflict with masses of native people to "win the day." How to explain that we who were supposedly so few had managed, generation after generation, to field so many in the course of our resistance? And how, once our real numbers were to some extent admitted, to explain either where we went, or how we'd been able to sustain ourselves for all those thousands of years before "the coming of the white man" supposedly endowed us with the miracle of growing our own food?[54]

To be fair, Hollywood *has* tried to incorporate such matters into its master narrative, especially during its formative years. From 1908 to 1920, not less than twenty-eight feature films and perhaps a hundred one-reel shorts purported to deal with Indian/white relations during the sixteenth, seventeenth and eighteenth centuries.[55] The task proved impossible, however, or nearly so, and thereafter the number of such pictures declined steadily, centering mainly in the above-mentioned "Seminole" movies and periodic remakes of James Fenimore Cooper's "Leather Stocking" fables.[56]

Thus, by 1935 movieland had locked in upon the final round of wars in the West as its interpretive vehicle. The choice carried obvious advantages in that it placed Indians within a geography remote from, and thus alien to, the vast majority of non-Indians residing east of the Mississippi (and, later, along the west coast). It seemed reasonable to expect that the people inhabiting the area might seem equally alien and remote. Also helpful was the fact that western lands did/do not appear suitable for farming, and that the events ostensibly depicted occurred at the very point when the native population, already reduced by some 90 percent and suffering severe dislocation from its traditional ways of life, was fighting most frantically to stave off being liquidated altogether.[57]

Having attained such utter decontextualization, filmmakers were free to indulge themselves—and their audiences—almost exclusively in fantasies of Indians as warriors. Not just any warriors, mind you, but those of a most hideously bestial variety. This is exemplified in John Ford's *Stagecoach*, where the director uses techniques common to monster movies of the era, building a tremendous sense of dread long before any Indian is allowed to appear. Then, late in the movie, when the "Apaches" finally materialize, they are portrayed in an entirely dimensionless and inhuman fashion.[58]

Some directors went Ford one better, hiring actors known mostly for their portrayals of actual cinematic monsters to play native people. Bela Lugosi, for instance, who would later gain fame as the vampire in *Dracula*, was cast as Uncas in a 1922 German-made version of *Last of the Mohicans* which was received quite well in the United States.[59] Cecil B. DeMille selected Boris Karloff, already famous as the creature in *Frankenstein*, to play an Indian in his 1947 movie *Unconquered*.[60] "Wolfman" Lon Chaney, was also cast repeatedly in such roles, most notably in *The Pathfinder and the Mohican* (1956), *Along the Mohawk Trail* (1956) and *The Long Rifle* (1964), a ghastly trilogy pasted together from episodes of the *Hawkeye and the Last of the Mohicans* TV series (CBS; 1957-58).[61]

In other instances—Robert Mulligan's *The Stalking Moon* (1968) comes to mind—things are put even more straightforwardly. Here, a fictional Apache named "Salvaje," is withheld from view for most of the movie (à la *Stagecoach*) as he tracks a terrified Gregory Peck and Eva Marie Sainte across two states. Towards the end of the film Salvaje is finally revealed, but always from a distance and garbed in a strange and very un–Apachean set of "cave man" furs conveying the distinct impression that he is actually a dangerous form of animal life.[62]

Hundreds of movies and television segments follow more-or-less the same formula. If they don't revolve around the notion of individual Indians being caught up in the fulltime job of menacing usually unoffending whites, it's because they have us being far too busy attacking the same victims in "swarms," howling like "wolves," slaughtering and mutilating the innocent or carrying them away as captives upon whom we can work our animalistic wills at leisure.[63] And believe it or not, those, for Hollywood, are our *good* points.

The "down" side is that, even as warriors, we are in the end abysmally incompetent. Witness how gratuitously we expend ourselves while riding our ponies around and around the circled wagons of our foes (time after time after time). Watch as we squander our strength in pointless frontal assaults upon the enemy's most strongly fortified positions (again and again and again).[64] Worst of all, observe that we don't even know how to use our weapons properly, a matter brought forth most clearly in *A Man Called Horse*, when scriptwriter Jack DeWitt and director Silverstein team up to have an Englishman, played by Richard Harris, teaching his "Sioux" captors how best to employ their bows and arrows when repelling an attack by other Indians.[65]

Small wonder, given our continuous bombardment with such malignant trash, that by the 1950s, probably earlier, American Indian children had often become as prone as anyone else to "root for the cavalry" in its cinematic extermination of their ancestors (and, symbolically, themselves).[66] "After all," asked a native student in one of my recent film classes (by way of trying to explain the phenomenon to her non-Indian peers), "who wants to identify with such a bunch of losers?" Yes, who indeed?

The Only Good Indian . . .

"The only good Indians I ever saw," General Phil Sheridan famously observed in 1869, "were dead."[67] Filmmakers, for their part, brought such sentiments to life on the screen with a vengeance, beginning at least as early as D.W. Griffith's *The Battle of Elderbush Gulch* in 1913.[68] By the mid-'30s, native people were being symbolically eradicated in the movies at a truly astounding rate, often with five or six of us falling every time a single bullet was fired by gallant white men equipped with what were apparently fifty-shot six-shooters.[69] The celluloid bloodbath by no means abated until a general decline of public interest in westerns during the mid-to-late 1960s.[70]

So fixated was Hollywood upon images of largescale Indian-killing by the military during the late nineteenth century that it transplanted them to some extent into western Canada, where nothing of the sort occurred. Apparently preoccupied with the possibility that the red coats of the North West Mounted Police (NWMP; now the Royal Canadian Mounted Police, RCMP) might look better on screen than U.S. Army blue, directors simply shifted the Mounties into the roll traditionally filled by the cavalry and cranked away.[71]

The first such epic, *The Flaming Forest*, appeared in 1926 and has the NWMP putting down the first Métis rebellion (1868) fully five years before the force ever appeared in the West. In 1940, DeMille made a picture entitled *North West Mounted Police*, about the second Métis rebellion (1885). Three features—*Fort Vengeance* (1953), *Saskatchewan* (1954) and *The Canadians* (1961)—were then produced on the theme of Mounties battling Sitting Bull's Lakota refugees during their brief Canadian sojourn in the late 1870s.[72]

> In the style of the shoot-'em-up western, Indians in the Mountie movies attacked wagon trains, burned settler's cabins and roasted captives at the stake, all things that never took place in the Canadian West. The Canadian frontier had its problems: the illicit trade in alcohol, the disappearance of the buffalo, the spread of disease. But these were not the problems moviegoers saw. Rather the Mountie movie provided another opportunity for the Hollywood dream machine to act out its melodramatic fantasies about the American Wild West.[73]

Meanwhile, another sort of "good" Indian was being cultivated. Based archetypally on Fenimore Cooper's Chingachgook and/or Daniel DeFoe's Friday in *Robinson Crusoe*, the character is exemplified by Tonto—the word literally means "fool, dunce or dolt" in Spanish—, "faithful Indian companion" of *The Lone Ranger* radio program's masked white hero from 1933 onward.[74] By the 1938, the formula had proven so popular that it was serialized by moviemakers as Saturday matinée fare. The serial was condensed into a 1940 feature entitled *Hi-Ho Silver* before mutating into a longrunning ABC TV series in 1948.[75] Back in theater venues with *The Lone Ranger* (1956) and *The Lone Ranger and the City of Gold* (1958), the Masked Man and Tonto did not make their final big screen appearance (to date) until a 1979 remake of the 1956 film.[76]

As Cherokee analyst Rayna Green explains, the "good Indian [embodied in Tonto] acts as a friend to the white man, offering . . . aid, rescue, and spiritual and physical comfort even at the cost of his own life or status and comfort in his own [nation] to do so. He saves white men from 'bad' Indians, and thus becomes a 'good' Indian."[77] Or, to quote Canadian author Daniel Francis, the "good Indian is one who stands shoulder to shoulder" with whites in their "settlement" of the continent, serving as "loyal friends and allies" to the invaders who were committing genocide to fulfill their self-assigned "Manifest Destiny" of possessing *all* native land and resources.[78] It is "their antiquated, stoic acceptance" of their own inherent inferiority to Euroamericans and of "their individual fate and of the ultimate demise of their people that endeared these noble savages to white [audiences]."[79]

By 1950, the stereotype had been perfected to a point that director Delmer Daves was prepared to deploy it as the centerpiece of his *Broken Arrow*, usually considered to be the first major motion picture to attempt a "sympathetic" depiction of Indians.[80] Based loosely on the real life interaction during the 1870s between Cochise, a principle Chiricahua Apache leader, and a white scout named Tom Jeffords, the entire story is presented through the voice-over narrative of the latter while the former is reduced in the end to a Kiplingesque parody of himself.[81] So edifying was Daves' treatment to mainstream viewers that the film received a special award from the thoroughly non-Indian Association of American Indian Affairs and Jeff Chandler, the then-unknown white actor cast as Cochise, was nominated for an Academy Award. Television quickly cashed in when NBC cloned a *Broken Arrow* TV series which ran for several seasons.[82]

Every cinematic good guy must, of course, be counterbalanced by a "heavy."[83] In *Broken Arrow*, the requirement is met by the film's handling of Geronimo, another important Chiricahua leader. Where Cochise's "virtue" is manifested in the lengths to which he is prepared to go in achieving not just peace but cordiality with whites—at one point Daves even has him executing another Apache to ensure the safety of his friend Jeffords—Geronimo's "badness" is embodied in the adamance of his refusal to do the same. In essence, capitulation/accommodation to aggression is defined as "good," resistance as "evil."[84] As S. Elizabeth Bird has framed the matter, wherever plot lines devolve upon "constructive" figures like *Broken Arrow*'s fictionalized Cochise:

> [T]he brutal savage is still present in the recurring image of the renegade... These Indians have not accepted White control, refuse to stay on the reservation, and use

violent means to combat White people, raiding farms and destroying White property. Although occasion lip service is paid to the justness of their anger, the message is clear that these warriors are misguided. [Enlightened whites] are frequently seen trying to persuade the friendly Indians to curb the ["hostiles'"] excesses. The renegades are clearly defined as deviant, out of control, and a challenge to the ["Good Indian"] who suffers all indignities with a stoic smile and acknowledgment that really there are many good, kind White people who wish this had never happened.[85]

The dichotomy of indigenous good and evil thus concretized in Daves' historically distortive juxtaposing of Cochise and Geronimo was almost immediately hammered home in *Taza, Son of Cochise*, another vaguely historical film in which one of the long-suffering Apache's two sons, Tahzay, who followed his father onto the San Carlos Reservation and ultimately succeeded him as principle Chiricahua leader, is employed as the vehicle for depicting native virtue. He is framed in harsh contrast to his brother, Naiche, a "recalcitrant" who was a noted figure in Geronimo's protracted resistance struggle. [86]

From there, such scenarios became something of an industry standard. As early as 1951, in *Across the Wide Missouri*, MGM cast Clark Gable in a role quite similar to James Stewart's portrayal of Tom Jeffords in *Broken Arrow*.[87] In 1952, the same studio had a youthful Charlton Heston playing an oddly Cochise-like Sioux in *The Savage*. In *Drum Beat* (1954), it was Alan Ladd's turn to emulate Stewart's performance, although no suitable counterpart to Cochise materialized. Other period films attempting more-or-less the same thematics included *The Big Sky* (1952), *The Great Sioux Uprising* (1953), *The Last Wagon* (1956), *Walk the Proud Land* (1956), *The Redmen and the Renegades* (1956), *The Oregon Trail* (1959), *The Unforgiven* (1960), *The Long Rifle and the Tomahawk* (1964), *Last of the Renegades* (1966) and *Frontier Hellcat* (1966).[88]

Although the drop in the number of westerns produced after 1966 has resulted in a corresponding diminishment in the number of such "statements" by Hollywood, there is ample evidence that the Good Indian genre remains alive, well and firmly entrenched. Prime examples will be found in the parts assigned Squamish actor Dan George in such acclaimed films as *Little Big Man* (1970) and *The Outlaw Josey Wales* (1976), Lakota AIM leader *cum* actor Russell Means in the latest version of *Last of the Mohicans*, Graham Greene, an Oneida, in *Thunderheart* (1991), Eric Schweig as *Squanto* (1994), and, most recently, the character portrayed by Cree actor Gordon Tootoosis in *Legends of the Fall* (1996).[89]

Television also followed up on the early success enjoyed by ABC's *Broken Arrow* with a CBS effort, *Brave Eagle* (1955-56) and NBC's dismal *Hawkeye* series. In 1957, ABC weighed in again with *Cheyenne*, staring *Yellowstone Kelly's* Clint Walker as a part-Indian cowboy/scout obviously inclined towards his "better" genetics (the series was highly popular and ran until 1963). NBC finally scored in 1959 with *Law of the Plainsman*, an utterly incongruous saga in which a fourteen-year-old Apache boy "about to scalp a wounded army captain, inexplicably relents and nurses the soldier back to health. The captain adopts the supposedly nameless boy, christening him Sam Buckhart. Sam eventually goes to Harvard, then becomes a lawman in New Mexico [serving] the larger society in trying to calm angry natives."[90]

So well was the latter theme received that ABC countered in 1966 with *Hawk*, a series starring part-Seminole actor Burt Reynolds as a contemporary New York police lieutenant of mixed ancestry. There being no Indian uprisings to quell in the Big Apple, the program folded after only three months, only to be replaced in 1974 with *Nakia*, a series focused on a Navajo, played by stock Indian stand-in Robert Forster, who hires on as a rural New Mexico deputy sheriff in furtherance of his struggle to "bridge" himself from the anachronism of his own society to the "modern world" of Euroamerica.[91]

The latest in television's seemingly endless variations on the "Good Indian" theme came with CBS's *Dr. Quinn, Medicine Woman* in 1992. A transparent genuflection to the "postmodern" mainstream sensibilities of the nineties, the series' predominantly white cast is peopled by "several strong, independent women; a male population of bigots and weaklings, who receive their comeuppance from Dr. Quinn on a weekly basis; and one African-American couple, who provide opportunities for Dr. Quinn to display her progressive fervor."[92] An interesting setting is provided by a nearby "Cheyenne village" whose mostly anonymous inhabitants, although the show is set in Colorado during the very period when the territorial government was waging what it itself called an outright campaign of extermination against them, engage themselves for the most part in looking perfectly serene and "natural."[93]

The main Indian character is "Cloud Dancing," a supposed traditional healer played by Larry Sellers who spends most of his time alternately passing his secrets to and trying to learn from the *real* "Medicine Woman"—who is of course a white M.D.—all the while looking sad and, most of all, being "friendly." He is "a calm, noble person who never fights back and is grateful for the attentions of heroic White individuals."[94] As the series progresses, Cloud Dancing loses an unborn child because of his wife's malnutrition (caused by white buffalo hunters' killing off the Cheyennes' main food supply); his adult son is killed while saving Dr. Quinn's life; forty-five members of his village die hideous deaths due to the whites' distribution of typhus-infested blankets; finally, he suffers the butchery of the remainder of his people, including his wife, first during the 3rd Colorado Volunteers' infamous Sand Creek Massacre of 1864 and then at the at the hands of Custer's cavalry during the 1868 Washita Massacre. The handling of the last incident is indicative of the rest:

> While Sand Creek has received only passing mention, [the] Washita was finally addressed in an episode broadcast late in the 1994–1995 season. The episode was revealing in the characteristic way in which it showed the massacre—not as a catastrophe for the Cheyenne, but as a trauma for Michaela Quinn. She fails to talk Custer out of attacking and she and Sully [her boyfriend], along with Cloud Dancing, come upon the village, completely wiped out, with everyone dead. Cloud Dancing's wife, Snowbird, dies in his arms. Everything from then on continues from Michaela's point of view. She withdraws from her family, blames herself for the massacre, and goes into a depression. Finally, Cloud Dancing comes to her and assures her that it was not her fault, then spends several days passing on his medical skills to her, before leaving for South Dakota. Michaela returns to her family, and happiness reigns again.[95]

At another point, after Sully professes to being "sorry for everything my people are doing to yours," Cloud Dancing replies that the "spirits tell me anger is good [but] hate is not. There are good men, there are bad men. You're a good man, Sully. You're still my brother."[96] Every Indian-focused segment of *Dr. Quinn* is salted with comparable gestures of absolution and forgiveness from victim to victimizer. The "role of the Cheyenne is to provide an exotic, attractive backdrop for the heroes and, subtly, to suggest that they are willing to fade away in the face of White [superiority]. Part of that role is to die, sometimes in great numbers, in order to move the plot along and showcasing Michaela and Sully. The show has a knack for touching on some of the most horrific episodes in the history of Indian-White relations, yet nevertheless suggesting that everything really came out all right."[97]

What a wonderful tonic for a body politic beset during the Great Columbus Quincentennial Controversy of the early '90s by flickerings of doubt about the honor and even the legitimacy of "The American Heritage."[98] Small wonder, all things considered, that *Dr. Quinn* became the most popular new TV series of the 1992-93 season.[99] Someone out there has clearly found it expedient to ignore the response of a character played by Creek actor Will Sampson after being made the butt of Tonto jokes one too many times by his white partner in the 1977 CBS television movie *Relentless*: "Hey ... Buck," sighs Sampson. "That's enough. ... No more."[100]

Voices of the Voiceless

All of this is, to be sure, pure nonsense. Real Indians—as opposed to Reel Indians—even of the Tonto variety, would never actually have said/done what Hollywood has needed us to say and do. Occasional snatches of autonomous dialogue such as that of Sampson's quoted just above make this abundantly clear. Hence, it has been necessary to render us either literally voiceless, as with the "Chief Broom" character Sampson played in *One Flew Over the Cuckoo's Nest*, or effectively so.

A standard means to the latter end ties directly to the more general nullification of indigenous culture addressed earlier. This takes the form of a pretense that native "tongues," despite their typically being just as intellectually refined and expressive as European languages—often more so; Micmac, for instance, evidences much more semantic precision and contains five times as many words as English[101]—are extraordinarily crude or "primitive." A classic example of how this is accomplished will be found in *The Way West* (1967), where director Andrew McLaglen has a "Sioux chief" wearing a Mohawk haircut and a woman's shawl address a group of whites with a string of Lakota terms selected seemingly at random (translated, they make up a meaningless word salad).[102]

One director went further, presenting his audiences with English language recordings played in reverse to signify the exotic sounds of spoken "Indian." Most often, however, filmmakers have simply followed historian Francis Parkman's notoriously ignorant comment that the word "How!" constitutes "a monosyllable by which an Indian contrives to express half the emotions of which he is susceptible."[103] Or, in fairness, they have elected to enrich Parkman's vocabulary by adding "Ugh," "Ho," and a smattering of guttural grunts. To this has been added a weird sort of pidgin English best described by Raymond Stedman as comprising a "Tonto School of Communication."[104] Consider as sufficient illustration the following four consecutive lines delivered by the faithful Indian companion during a *Lone Ranger* program aired on June 30, 1939.

Who you?
Ugh.
You see-um him?
Me want-um him.[105]

With Indians thus rendered functionally mute in our own right, however, it remained nonetheless necessary that audiences often be informed as
to exactly how they should understand many of the celluloid savages' otherwise inexplicable on-screen actions. This problem was solved when, early in
Broken Arrow, Delmer Daves has James Stewart peremptorily announce that
"when the Apaches speak, it will be in our language."[106] From that point on,
everything is explained "through the eyes of"—which is to say, from the
point-of-view and *in the voice of*—Stewart's white character.

The same can be said of Audie Murphy's John Clum in *Walk the Proud
Land*, the Britton Davis character in the latest remake of *Geronimo*, or any of
a host of other real life soldiers, settlers and frontiersmen whose memoirs, letters and diaries have been used as the basis for scripts purportedly telling
"Indian" stories.[107] Completely fictional variants of the same device have also
been used with such regularity over the past fifty years as to establish a cinematic convention. Sometimes it is adhered to in unorthodox ways, as when
John Ford gratuitously appended a white female schoolteacher to the body
of fleeing Indians in *Cheyenne Autumn*, but inevitably there is a central white
character to "tell the story of the Indians" in a manner familiar and ultimately
comfortable to Euroamerican audiences.[108]

This is as true of *Soldier Blue* and *Little Big Man*, the so-called "revision-
ist" or "protest" flicks of 1970, and their successors like *Dances With Wolves*, as
it is of the most blatantly reactionary John Wayne western.[109] Indeed, it may
well be more so. John Wayne movies, after all, don't pretend to be *about*
Indians, or even sympathetic to us. Rather, they are for the most part
unabashed celebrations of our "conquest" and, in that sense at least, they are
honest enough.[110] The subgenre of "protest" or "progressive" films *do*, on the
other hand, purport to be about native people, and sympathetically so. To this
extent, they are fundamentally *dis*honest, if for no other reason than because
the whole purpose of their persistent injection of non-Indian narrators into
indigenous contexts amounts to nothing so much as a way of creating the illusion of sympathetic *white* alternatives to Wayne's triumphalist status quo.

The most topical examples undoubtedly reside among the ever-so-
enlightened and sensitive Euroamerican leads of *Dr. Quinn*. In fact, as S.

185

Elizabeth Bird has observed with regard to the male character in particular, "Sully's ongoing role is to stand in for the Cheyennes, so that their culture can be represented, while they as a people can be pushed into the background. After all, he is a better Indian than the Cheyenne, as is made abundantly clear in the opening scene of one episode, when he beats Cloud Dancing at a tomahawk-throwing contest."[111] The principle applies equally to all such figures, from Dustin Hoffman's Jack Crabbe in *Little Big Man*, to Richard Harris's Lord Morgan in *A Man Called Horse*, to Kevin Costner's Lieutenant Dunbar in *Dances With Wolves*, to Daniel Day-Lewis's Hawkeye in the most recent iteration of *Last of the Mohicans*.

Having thus contrived to substitute whites for Indians both verbally and to some extent physically as well, filmmakers have positioned themselves perfectly, not just to spin their yarns in whatever manner strikes their fancy at a given moment but to make them appear to have been embraced by all sides, native and non-native alike. Hence, white story or Indian story, they become indistinguishable in the end, following as they do a mutual trajectory to the same destination within the master narrative of an overarching "American Story."[112]

Those Cavaliers in Buckskin

The ways in which this has been accomplished have plainly undergone a significant metamorphosis through the years. In the "bad old days" of unadulterated triumphalism, plotlines invariably orbited around the personas of noble and heroic white figures, whether ostensibly real or admittedly invented, with whom it was intended that audiences identify. Such projections were never as easily achieved as it may seem in retrospect, usually entailing a wholesale rewriting of history.

Irrespective of the false and degrading manner in which native people were depicted, it was still vitally important that cinematic whites be portrayed in ways which posed them as embodying diametrically opposing "traits." This was no mean feat when it came to things like the 1890 Wounded Knee Massacre, still a vividly current event during the movies' early days, where the U.S. troops had slaughtered some three hundred fifty unarmed Lakota prisoners, overwhelmingly composed of women, children and old men.[113]

The problem of how such behavior might come to be perceived was addressed, experimentally, by a group calling itself the Colonel W.F. Cody (Buffalo Bill) Historical Picture Company in 1914. Retaining General

Nelson A. Miles, renowned as a expert Indian-fighter, to verify the accuracy of their endeavor in much the same fashion Wilcomb Washburn would authenticate *A Man Called Horse* more than a half-century later, they produced a film entitled *The Indian Wars Refought*. In it, the "Battle of Wounded Knee" was reenacted in such a way as to show how the defenseless Lakotas had themselves "picked a fight" with the hundreds of well-armed soldiers surrounding them. The Indians had thus brought their fate upon themselves, so the story went, the troopers having "had no choice" but to defend themselves with Hotchkis machine guns.[114]

Heavily promoted by its makers for use in and widely adopted by the nation's schools as a medium of "truth," the film set the "standard" for much of what would follow.[115] Within a few years, the reversal of reality was complete: the massacre at Wounded Knee was popularly understood to have been a "battle" while the 1876 annihilation of a portion of "General" (actually Lt. Colonel) George Armstrong Custer's 7th Cavalry Regiment in open combat was habitually described as a "massacre."[116] Indians were "killed" by whites while whites were always "murdered" by Indians; Indians "committed depredations" while whites "defended themselves" and "won victories."[117]

The same sort of systematic historical falsification was of course brought to bear on the records of individual whites, notably Custer himself. This was epitomized in director Raoul Walsh's casting of Hollywood's premier swashbuckling glamour boy, Errol Flynn, to play "the boy general" in *They Died With Their Boots On* (1941). Here, Custer—whose pedigree included demonstrable cowardice in the face of the enemy and being court-martialed and relieved of his command for desertion, and whose main claim-to-fame as an Indian-fighter rested in having perpetrated the Washita Massacre—is presented in an altogether different light.[118]

Actually, Walsh saw to it that neither the court martial nor the Washita were so much as mentioned, while Flynn's Custer was quite literally backlit with a Christ-like halo at various points in the film. Meanwhile, the man who broke the 1868 Fort Laramie Treaty with the Lakotas, Cheyennes and Arapahos by leading an 1874 expedition into the Black Hills, the very heart of their homeland, was presented as its staunchest defender.[119] Similarly, although Custer personally instigated the war of conquest against these same peoples in which he was killed two years later—a gambit meant to further his own presidential ambitions—he is depicted as having gallantly sacrificed himself and his men to prevent just such a war.[120]

And so it went, from Edward Sedgwick's *The Flaming Frontier* (1926) to DeMille's *The Plainsman* (1936), from Michael Curtiz's *The Santa Fe Trail* (1941) to Charles Marquiz Warren's *Little Big Horn* (1951), from Ernest Haycox's *Bugles in the Afternoon* (1952) to Joseph H. Lewis's *Seventh Cavalry* (1956), from Lewis R. Foster's *Tonka* (1958) to Sidney Salkow's *The Great Sioux Massacre* (1965). As late as 1967, director Robert Siodmak cast the dashing Irish actor Robert Shaw in the lead role when making his conspicuously Walsh-style *Custer of the West*.[121]

Although paleohistorians like Robert Utley persist to this day in describing the wretched Custer as a "cavalier in buckskins,"[122] the preferences of an appreciable portion of the U.S. viewing public had begun to undergo a sea change by the time Siodmak released his movie. Horrified at the prospect of being conscripted to serve as fodder in Vietnam, and taking their cue from the military's own references to enemy-held territory there as being "Indian Country," millions of young whites began, increasingly, as a part of their own resistance, to compare the ongoing carnage in Southeast Asia to that of the Indian Wars and to revile the leaders presiding over both processes.[123]

Sensing that the potential for a vast audience was bound up in the desire of America's baby boomers to emotionally/figuratively distance themselves from the status quo, hip directors like Arthur Penn and Ralph Nelson were quick to cash in. In catering to the new "countercultural" sensibility, Penn opted to display the Custer of *They Died With Their Boots On* in virtual reverse image. Where the Walsh/Flynn approach decreed Custer's intrinsic nobility, hence that of the tradition he was mustered to represent, the characterization offered in *Little Big Man* was that of a vulgarly egotistical psychopath.[124] Nelson followed suit in *Soldier Blue*, albeit using a somewhat amorphous representation of Colonel John Chivington, the infamous commander at Sand Creek, to make his point.[125]

Chivington had previously received such cinematic packaging under the name "Colonel Templeton" in a slightly pioneering Arthur Hiller movie, *Massacre at Sand Creek* (1956), and he would again, as "Colonel Schemmerhorne," in a TV miniseries made from James Michener's *Centennial* during the late '70s. As for Custer, he has continued to be portrayed primarily in accordance with the negative model established by Penn, most recently in 1995, in the earlier-discussed episode of *Dr. Quinn*.

While *Little Big Man* and *Soldier Blue* certainly punched large holes in the triumphalist stereotype, as critics Ralph and Natasha Friar observed shortly after the films were released this merely signified that Hollywood had shifted from glorifying the extermination of native people to "excusing genocide by attributing it to the whims of a few unbalanced people, i.e., General Custer."[126] More precisely, by making such attribution filmmakers were both acknowledging the obvious—admitting that genocidal events had occurred in the course of American history and that they were wrong—and presenting them as something abnormal and therefore exceptional.

When this was combined with sympathetic white characters like Hoffman's Jack Crabbe in *Little Big Man*, those played by Candice Bergen's Christa Lee and Peter Strauss's Honis Gant in *Soldier Blue*, Costner's Dunbar in *Dances With Wolves*, or Michaela Quinn and Sully in *Dr. Quinn*, the appearance of a fundamental polarity within Euroamerican society itself is created. This serves a very useful purpose, especially when stirred in with the Good Indian (friendly)/Bad Indian (hostile) stereotypes already discussed. As Elisabeth Bird explains:

> [While] *Dr. Quinn* goes along with notions of White guilt, it equally clearly allows White audiences to see the destruction of Indian culture as both inevitable and as somehow accidental. The show holds on to the "renegade" image, for example, because it helps assuage guilt: After all, some of the Indians drove us to it, helping to bring about their own destruction. Thus there were good and bad guys on both sides, and the bad things happened because bad guys like Custer and the renegades, but good guys like Michaela and Sully are who *we* are [emphasis added].[127]

Thus, psychologically at least, genuinely sympathetic white figures, who did exist but who were historically anomalous in the extreme, are rendered normative in terms of audience identification.[128] Conversely, men like Custer and Chivington, who were in fact normatively expressive of public sentiment—virtually the entire citizenry of Denver *did* turn out to cheer when the "Bloody Third" returned from Sand Creek, parading its scalps, genitalia and other anatomical "trophies"; Custer *was* an extraordinarily popular public figure after the Washita; bounties on Indian scalps *were* proclaimed in *every* state and territory of the continental United States at one time or another—become the anomalies.[129]

The result is in no sense a transformation but instead a much more potent reconfiguring of the Euroamerican status quo. What Penn, Nelson and their colleagues accomplished was to find a means to let the "protest generation" of the 1960s off the hook of its own professed dissidence. What they provided was and is a convenient surrogate reality allowing whites to symbolically disassociate themselves from the intolerable ugliness of "Custerism" (whether in the Wild West or Vietnam), thereby "feeling good about themselves" even while continuing to participate in and benefit from the very socioeconomic order Custerism has produced.[130]

This "reconstitution of imperial ideology" as a "friendlier" form of fascism has been expressed in a variety of ways, both on-screen and in the real world, but nowhere more clearly than in an exchange between Sully and Michaela's young son, Brian, during a special two-hour episode of *Dr. Quinn* broadcast during the 1993-94 season.[131] Toward the end, having just listened to a thoroughly triumphalist explanation of why the Cheyennes were being exterminated, the boy asks whether these weren't lies. Sully, the "White Indian," responds: "I'm afraid so, Brian; they lie to themselves. But this is still the best country in the world. . . ."[132]

Although the style of delivery is obviously different, such lines might easily have been uttered by John Wayne at the conclusion of any John Ford western. In fact, it seems no stretch at all to suggest that the Duke would have been proud to pronounce them. So much for the alleged "critical distinctions" between films like *Little Big Man* or *Dances With Wolves* on the one hand, and *They Died With Their Boots On* or *Custer of the West* on the other. "Meet the new boss," as Pete Townsend of The Who once put it with admirable succinctness, "same as the old boss."[133]

Ravages by Savages

As Eldridge Cleaver brilliantly explained in *Soul on Ice*, the structure of sexual relations imposed by Euroamerica upon African Americans can be understood as a metaphor for the broader relational matrix of domination and subjugation defining the social positions of whites and blacks respectively. In this formulation, white men are accorded a self-assigned status as "Omnipotent Administrators," primarily cerebral beings who, by presuming to monopolize the realm of thought itself, have assigned black men the subordinate status of mindless "Ultramasculine Menials."[134]

To complete the figurative disempowerment of the latter, and thus to signify their own station of unimpeachable supremacy, the Administrators proceed first to constrain and then to preempt the Menials in that most crucial of all physical arenas, their sexuality. Black men are, by white male ordination, categorically denied sexual access to white women while, concomitantly, white men grant themselves unrestricted rights to the black female "Booty" deriving from their posture of domination. Black men are thereby reduced to a degraded status as "social eunuchs" while black women, transformed into sexual commodities, are dehumanized altogether, and white women, consigned to serve as desexualized objects adorning the omnipotence of their men, fare little better.[135]

The great fear for the Administrators, according to Cleaver, is that the Menials might somehow discover a means of breaking the psychic bounds of their oppression, that is, of liberating themselves from their state of emasculated debasement by allegorically turning the tables and violating the "purity" of white womanhood.[136] So deep-seated was this dread that it assumed the form of an outright cultural psychosis leading, among other things, to the ubiquitousness of a myth that black men are imbued, innately and insatiably, with a "need" to rape white women. Several thousand lynchings were carried out in the United States between 1889 and 1930, mainly to deter black men from acting upon this supposed compulsion.[137]

With only minor transpositions, the paradigm can be as readily applied to Euroamerica's perception of its relationship to native people as to imported African chattel. Indeed, the evidence strongly suggests that the transposition occurred in reverse order; the model was developed with respect to Indians, then modified to some extent for application to blacks. In any event, preoccupation with the idea that native men were animated by the "darkest" desires vis-à-vis white women can be traced back to the earliest writings of the New England Puritans.[138] By the end of the nineteenth century, the theme had long been a staple of American literature and drama, both high-brow and low.[139]

Once movies became a factor, the situation was exacerbated substantially. In 1913's *The Battle at Elderbush Gulch*, for example, only the timely arrival of the cavalry saved a trembling Lillian Gish from a "mercy slaying" meant to save her from a "fate worse than death" at the hands of surrounding savages.[140] The scene was repeated with some regularity over the next forty years, most prominently in Ford's *Stagecoach*. By the early fifties, white women were accorded a bit more autonomy, as when director Anthony Mann has James Stewart hand actress Shelley Winters a weapon in *Winchester '73* (1953) so that she may participate in their mutual defense. "Don't worry," she assures him, "I understand about the last [bullet]."[141] Better death than "suffering ravage by a savage," as Charlie Hill puts it.[142] In *Fort Massacre* (1969), Joel McCrea's wife goes everybody one better by killing not only herself but her two children rather than allow any of them to be taken captive by Apaches.

Despite a veritable mountain of evidence that rape was practiced in few if any native societies, a diametrically opposed "truth" was presented in hundreds of Hollywood westerns.[143] "Did you ever see what Indians do when they get a *white* woman?" asks a seasoned scout portrayed by James Whitmore in *Chato's Land* (1972). "Comanches," another scout explains to an army captain trying to figure out whether it was they or the Apaches who had perpetrated a massacre, in *A Thunder of Drums* (1961), "rape their own women" rather than whites, "so it was likely Apaches." "If we stop now," one beleaguered cavalry officer tells another in *The Gatling Gun* (1971), "all those women have to look forward to is rape and murder."[144]

"You *know* what Indians do to women," declaims a trooper at the beginning of *Soldier Blue*. "They're going to rape me Soldier Blue, and then they're going to kill you," Candice Bergen clarifies to a horrified Peter Strauss after the pair are captured by Kiowas later in the same film. "They're going to rape me, Jack," explains Crabbe's older sister in *Little Big Man*, shortly after they'd been taken home by a Cheyenne who'd happened upon the two children after their family had been massacred by Pawnees.[145] Most recently, in a 1994 episode of *Dr. Quinn*, Cloud Dancing's son proves that he, like his father, is a "Good Indian" by sacrificing himself to save the white heroine from being raped and murdered by "Dog Soldier renegades."[146]

In both *The Searchers* and *Ulzana's Raid* (1972), white women are depicted as having been "raped into insanity" by Indians.[147] In *Land Raiders* (1969), Apaches attack a town and, despite the ferocity of the fighting and the severity of their casualties, still find time to rape white women. In *The Deserter* (1970), the hero's wife is not only raped but skinned alive and left for her husband to kill.[148] Who could blame white men for having responded to such unrelenting horror by exterminating those responsible?

Often the rescue of white women taken by Indians comprises the entire plot of a movie, or a substantial part of it. Such is the case with *Iona, the White Squaw* (1909), *The Peril of the Plains* (1911), *The Pale-Face Squaw* and *The White Squaw* (both 1913), *Winning of the West* (1922), *Northwest Passage* (1940), *Ambush* (1950), *Flaming Feather* (1951), *Fort Ti* (1953), *The Charge at Feather River* (1953), *Comanche* (1956), *Comanche Station* (1960), *The Last Tomahawk* (1965) and *Duel at Diablo* (1966), among scores of others.[149] Sometimes, as in *Two Rode Together* (1961), the idea is handled with at least a semblance of sensitivity.[150] The worst of the lot is Ford's *The Searchers*, in which John Wayne is scripted to track down his abducted niece so he can kill her because she's been so irredeemably "soiled" by her experience.[151]

Even where the intended fate of the "rescued" is not so grim, it is often made plain that the purpose of their recovery is not so much to save *them* as it is to deny Indians the "spoils" they represent. Just as the effrontery of having "known" a white woman constitutes a death sentence for a native man and frequently his entire people, so too does the fact of her "fall from grace" license punishment of the woman herself. The scorn of townspeople visited upon the former "Indian's woman" portrayed by Barbara Stanwyck in *Trooper Hook* (1957), for example, forces her to live outside *any* society, white *or* native. Much the same principle applies to Linda Cristal's character in *Two Rode Together*, that of Eva Marie Sainte in *The Stalking Moon*, and many others.[152]

The only occasion prior to 1975's *Winterhawk* in which the American cinema had a native male actually marrying a white female was in the 1909 short, *An Indian's Bride*. The reasons for this glaring bias were none too subtle.

> Zane Grey originally published his novel, THE VANISHING AMERICAN (1925), as a magazine serial in 1922 in THE LADIES HOME JOURNAL, a Curtis publication. . . . At the conclusion, Grey had his heroine, a blonde-haired, blue-eyed schoolteacher marry his full-blood Navajo hero. This set off such an outraged reaction among the magazine's readers that, henceforth, Curtis publications made it a stipulation that Indian characters were never again to be characterized and Harper's refused to publish the novel until Grey agreed to have the Navajo die at the end.[153]

The second ending, of course, was the one used in the movie. Probably the most ridiculous contortion undertaken with respect to this squalid convention came in Lambert Hillyer's *White Eagle* (1932). In this oat-burner, the hero, played by Buck Jones, is supposedly a full-blooded Bannock pony express rider who falls head over heels for a white woman. Just before the movie ends, "Buck's father tells him the truth: he is white! He was stolen from his family as a child. This permits Buck, without violating the color line, to embrace the heroine."[154]

Native women, of course, are another matter entirely. Not uncommonly they are depicted as appropriate objects of Euroamerican sexual aggression; the James Whitmore line quoted above was uttered to justify the fact that two white men were busily raping an Indian woman just off screen.[155] Apache actress Sacheen Littlefeather was able to fashion something of a cinematic career for herself only by her willingness to portray indigenous rape victims, as she did in *Winterhawk*, in one movie after another.[156] The same pertained, albeit to a lesser extent, to her contemporaries, women like Dawn Little Sky, Princess Lois Red Elk, and Pablita Verde Hardin.[157]

At the same time, Indian women have been consistently limned as suffering a hopeless, usually fatal, attraction to the omnipotence of white men. It's a story as old as the legend of *Pocahontas* (1908) coined by John Smith in 1624,[158] and has been repeated on the big screen hundreds of times, beginning with films like *An Indian Maiden's Choice* and *The Indian Girl's Romance* (both 1910), *Love in a Tepee* (1911), *Broncho Billy and the Navajo Maid* (1912) and *The Fate of the Squaw* (1914), and continuing right up to the present moment with such fare as *Captain John Smith and Pocahontas* (1953), *Fort Yuma* (1955), *Fort Bowie* (1958), *Oklahoma Territory* (1960), *Wild Women* (1970) and, of course, Disney's 1992 animated version of *Pocahontas*.[159]

Such romantic yearnings were doomed from the outset, or, more properly, the female characters who expressed them were. It was one thing for white men to gratify themselves sexually at the expense of native women, not only by raping them but, sometimes more tenderly, by cohabiting; it was quite another for "mere squaws" to be accorded the dignity of actually marrying one of their racial/cultural "betters." The consequence of Pocahontas's wedding an Englishman was, after all, her death by smallpox.[160] Fenimore Cooper made it even plainer: the only possible outcome of such romantic entanglements was death.[161] Although the theme was first explored in *The Indian Maiden's Sacrifice* (1910), it is *The Squaw Man* (1913, 1918, 1931) which really served as the cinematic prototype for all that would follow.

> Based on Edwin Milton Royce's very successful stage play of 1905, the film concerns an English noble, falsely accused of a crime his brother actually committed, who ventures into the American west in an effort to clear his name. He falls in love with an Indian maiden of the Pocahontas stereotype variety and they have a child. Years pass and his brother, on his death bed, makes a confession exonerating the hero. . . . The hero, now able to return to England and claim his title, accidentally shoots the Indian maiden (in the play she is a suicide); she dies in his arms, happy, because, as she tells him, she knows white culture to be superior and their child need not be held back because of her primitive ways.[162]

And so it went. Debra Paget, as James Stewart's Apache bride in *Broken Arrow*, dies tragically, the victim of an ambush by "Bad Whites." In *Drum Beat*, "Marisa Pavan, among the noble savages, has a crush on the white hero, Alan Ladd. Ladd sets her straight: she must marry within her own people.

Then he pays court to the white heroine while Pavan, apparently in despair, loses her life trying to save his."[163] Linda Darnel does herself in when she can't ride off into the sunset with *Buffalo Bill*; Marie Elena Marques does pretty much the same in *Across the Wide Missouri*. Even Donna Reed's Sacajawea considers it when she realizes she'll never fit into the world of Charlton Heston's William Clark in *The Far Horizon*.[164]

All told, then, the panorama of Indian/white sexuality presented in movies has always been far more akin to what one might have expected from the Marquis de Sade than from anything socially constructive or redeemable.[165] Foundationally, there is little to distinguish even the best of Hollywood's productions from *Jungle Blue* (1978), *Sweet Savage* (1979), *Kate and the Indians* (1979), *Deep Roots* (1980) and other such X-rated, Indian-themed filth spewing from America's thriving porn-video industry.[166]

Lust in the Dust

Carnality, whether packaged as rape or love, "true" or unrequited, inevitably results in offspring. When the progenitors are of different races, such progeny will obviously be endowed with an interracial admixture of "blood" and thence, presumably, of culture as well. Hollywood, as much as the dominant society of which it is a part, has from the first exhibited an abiding confusion as to how it should respond to the existence of such creatures, especially since their numbers have tended to swell at rates much greater than those of any "purer breeding stock" throughout the course of American history.[167]

At one level, it might be argued, as it has been by American thinkers like Thomas Jefferson and Henry Lewis Morgan, that a "touch of Indian" in the country's then preponderantly caucasian makeup might serve create a hybrid superior to the original strain (even as it diluted native gene stocks to the point of extinction and beyond).[168] On another level it has been argued, and vociferously, that any such process of "mongrelization" results only in a dilution and consequent degradation of the "white race" itself.[169]

The best of both worlds or the worst? That is the question, never resolved. Typically, filmmakers have followed the lead set by D.W. Griffith in *Birth of a Nation* (1914), his aesthetically groundbreaking cinematic celebration of the Ku Klux Klan.[170] By and large, children of mixed parentage have been consigned either to their mother's society rather than their father's— movies figuring upon the spawn of unions between native men and white women having for reasons discussed above been exceedingly rare—or to drift in anguish through an existential netherworld located somewhere between.

Such has been the case, certainly, with films like *The Halfbreed*, first released in 1916, and then remade as *The Half Breed* in 1922 and *The Half-Breed* in 1952. And so it has been with *The Dumb Half-Breed's Defense* (1910), *The Half-Breed's Atonement* (1911), *Breed of the North* and *Bred in the Bone* (both 1913), *Indian Blood* (1914), *The Ancient Blood* and *The Quarter Breed* (1916), *The Great Alone* and *One Eighth Apache* (both 1922), *Call Her Savage* (1932), *Wagon Wheels* (1934), *Daughter of the West* and *Colorado Territory* (both 1949), *The Hawk of Wild River* (1952), *The Proud and the Profane* (1956), *Nevada Smith* (1966) and well over a hundred others.[171]

Most frequently, those of mixed heritage have been depicted as a sort of antimiscegenist's incarnation of evil, as in *The Halfbreed*, *The Half Breed* and *The Half-Breed*. Films produced using this motif have included *Half Breed's Treachery* (1909, 1912), *The Half-Breed's Way* (1912), *Bring Him In* (1921), *The Heritage of the Desert* (1924), *The Verdict of the Desert* (1925), *Hawk of the Hills* (1927), *Pony Soldier* (1952), *Reprisal* (1956), *War Drums* (1957) and *Last Train from Gun Hill* (1959). Sometimes the "breeds" turn out wrong because of the influences of dubious white men, as in *Broken Lance* (1954). On other occasions, our malignity is even explained as having been precipitated by white atrocities, as in the *Centennial* miniseries' (mis)representation of Charlie Bent and his brothers.[172] But the resulting impression is essentially the same.

Breeds are bad, as is explained in *The Barrier of Blood* (1913) and *The Apache Way* (1914), because we "naturally" incline towards our "Indian side." Nowhere is this brought out more clearly than in the "wholesome family entertainment" provided by cinematic adaptations of Mark Twain's *Tom Sawyer* and *The Adventures of Huckleberry Finn*, books in which the most malevolent character, a half-breed called Injun Joe, readily explains that his evil deeds are due to the fact that his "Injun blood ain't in me for nothing."[173]

The Unforgiven, a film that remains arguably the most venomously racist of all Hollywood's treatments of native people, was anchored by exactly this premise. A few lines from the 1957 Alan LeMay novel upon which it was based should prove sufficient to carry the point.

> This is one thing I know. The red niggers are no human men. Nor are they beasts, nor any kind of earthly varmint, for all natural critters act like God made them to do. Devil-

spirits, demons out of red kill, these be, that somehow, on some evil day, found a way to clothe themselves in flesh. I say to you, they must be cleansed from the face of this earth! Wherever one drop of their blood is found, it must be destroyed! For that is man's most sacred trust, before Almighty God.[174]

This transparently Hitlerian statement is made to a young woman played by Audry Hepburn, presumably a child captive brought up by the Kiowas and then recovered by whites, who is mortally afraid that she might in fact be of mixed ancestry. Her self-protective response is to try and sound even worse. At one point, when queried by her adoptive white mother about the people in the village where she was raised, she replies: "There weren't any *people* there, Mama. Those were Indians."[175]

Ironically, it is this very same DNA structure, deemed so dangerous by Griffith and his ilk, which has been seized upon by more "progressive" filmmakers to project mixed-bloods as being good, or at least better than native "fullbloods," simply by way of inclining us towards our "white side."[176] This countering interpretation was manifested in all four versions of *Ramona* (1910, 1914 [reissue], 1916, 1928, 1936), as well as such early releases as *Red Wing's Constancy* and *Red Wing's Loyalty* (both 1910), *An Indian Hero* (1911), *The Half-Breed's Sacrifice* (1912), *The Half-Breed Parson* and *The Half-Breed Sheriff* (both 1913).[177]

By the 1960s, Hollywood was even prepared to cast actual mixed-bloods like Elvis Presley in such roles, once in the passable *Flaming Star* (1960) and again in *Stay Away Joe* (1968), a movie "so bad that one is tempted to shout: 'John Wayne, where are you now that we need you?'"[178] Things have improved little in portrayals of mixed-bloods in the 1990s, as is witnessed by Val Kilmer's role in the idiotic *Thunderheart* and the even more recent characterization offered in the *Walker, Texas Ranger* TV series.[179]

Regardless of whether they've been oriented towards the notion of "breeds" as good, or convinced that we're inherently bad, however, one thing most directors seem to have been able to agree upon is that, as the fruit of illicit matings, we're somehow sexy.

The screen almost burst into flames with Jennifer Jones as half-breed Pearl Chavez. Her sultry walk captured the eye of Gregory Peck in *Duel in the Sun* (1946), a film one sharp-tongued critic called "Lust in the Dust." . . . Dimitri Tiomkin recalls creating the musical score. . . . He rewrote and rewrote it. Finally, in a meeting with [David O.] Selznik he said he had done all he could or would do. In desperation, he asked the producer what he really wanted. "I want it to sound like an orgasm," [Selznik replied].[180]

And it's not just women. As Peter van Lent has lately pointed out, "In current popular culture the exoticism of the Native male is always carefully controlled. For example, most of the heroes of the Indian romance novels are of mixed blood— 'half-breeds.' This convention provides a safety net against several sexual pitfalls. First, it checks the exotic image from being too alien and keeps it within the bounds of 'tall, dark and handsome.' Second, it avoids any sqeamishness about miscegenation on the part of the reader. Since the hero is half-white, the romantic-sexual bond is not truly interracial and . . . 'the half-breed's' appearance can be quite comfortably Caucasian. In the words of one romance author: 'Bronson could pass as a white man.' "[181]

Van Lent, while correct in the main, is wrong about mixed-bloodedness quelling qualms among Euroamerican readers about miscegenation. In the same novel he quotes—Fabio's *Comanche*—the plot line devolves upon a white wife's rejection of her husband once she discovers the truth of his gene code.[182] The book is a bestseller in its niche, likely to be made into a movie, at least for consumption on TV. Moreover, it is but one among scores of comparable tracts lining bookstore shelves and grocery store checkout lanes across the country.[183] The more things "change," the more they stay the same.

Cowboys and . . .

"From 1913 to the present, Hollywood has produced thousands of feature films on cowboys and Indians," wrote native documentary producer Phil Lucas in 1980. "These films, coupled with a preponderance of supportive literature (dime novels, poems, books, essays, journals, and plays), art, and more recently, television and advertising erase the varied cultural and ethnic identities of over four hundred distinct . . . nations of the original inhabitants of the Americas, and have successfully replaced them with a fictional identity . . . the Hollywood Indian."[184]

The process began much earlier than either cinema or the twentieth century. Robert Berkhofer, for one, dates its inception from the earliest writings by Europeans about Indians.[185] Daniel Francis, a more visually oriented analyst, finds the point of origin somewhere among the renderings of George Catlin, Karl Bird King, Karl Bodmer and their Canadian counterparts like Paul Kane.[186] Extending Susan Sontag's observation that "to photograph is to appropriate the thing photographed" to cover painting, drawing and, ultimately, cinema, Francis concludes that when "they drew the Indians or took their photographs, artists . . . were taking possession of the Indian image. It was [then] theirs to manipulate and display in any way they wanted."[187]

> When . . . cultures meet, especially cultures as different as those of western Europe and indigenous North America, they inevitably interpret each other in terms of stereotypes. At its best, in a situation of equality, this might be seen as a phase in a longer process of familiarization. But if one side in the encounter enjoys advantages of wealth or power or technology, then it will usually try to impose its stereotypes on the other. That is what occurred in the case of the North American encounter between European and aboriginal. We have been living with the consequences ever since.[188]

"Images have consequences in the real world," Francis sums up, "ideas have results. The Imaginary Indian does not exist in a void. In their relations with Native people over the years, non-Native[s] have put their image of the Indian into practice."[189] This is true, whether the image is that of Cassily Adams' famously howling hordes in Budweiser's "Custer's Last Stand" poster, or the nobly vanishing savage of James Fraser's equally famed 1914 sculpture, "The End of the Trail."[190] Both are false, and have the effect of dehumanizing those thus depicted, one no less than the other.

One consequence has been that, while Native North Americans have today been consigned to a degree of material destitution and attendant physical degradation comparable to that evident in most areas of the Third World, hardly a glimmer of concern emanates from the vast settler population benefitting from both our historical decimation and dispossession and the current regime of impoverishment imposed upon us. Why, after all, should those conditioned to see us as less or other than human, or even at some level to believe us nonexistent, care *what* happens to us?[191]

Euroamerican cinema's defending aestheticians have typically sought to skirt such issues by asserting, as Robin Wood did in 1971, that however erroneous and "unpleasant" the dominant society's portrayals of Indians, they are nonetheless defensible in "mythic terms."[192] On this score, one can do no better than to quote Jon Tuska's rejoinder that, "To put it bluntly, what apologists mean by a 'mythic' dimension in a western film is that part of it which they know to be a lie but which, for whatever reason, they still wish to embrace."[193]

Other comers have tried to varnish such polemics with a patina of belated "balance" or "equity," as when John H. Lenihan attempted to justify Delmer Daves' extravagantly inaccurate and anti-Indian *Drum Beat* on the basis that since the director had already "presented the Indian's point of view in *Broken Arrow*," it was necessary for him "to offer the settler's side of the story" in the later film (as if a couple thousand movies already doing exactly that weren't enough to "offset" Daves' single "pro-Indian" picture).[194]

Somewhat more sophisticated have been the superficially critical arguments advanced by Jack Nachbar and others, holding that it is time for Hollywood to transcend the "appealing but shallow concepts of right and wrong" altogether, offering instead "a new synthesis of understanding" in which, historically speaking, Indian or white, "ain't none of us right."[195] While such suggestions undoubtedly resonate quite favorably with social elites increasingly desirous of decontextualized "I'm okay/you're okay" historical constructions,[196] and a mainstream saturated with cinematic dramatizations of how the disempowered poor tend to victimize the rich and powerful, they plainly beg more than a few significant points.

Foremost in this regard is the fact that if Wood/Lenihan/Nachbar-style prescriptions were to be applied equally to all sets of historical relations it would be "necessary" that the Holocaust, for example, be depicted in such a way as to show that nobody was right, nobody wrong. The SS, as much as the inmates at Auschwitz, would be cast as victims; the Jews and Gypsies as much aggressors as the SS.[197] Having told "the Jewish side of the story" for so long, Hollywood would "need" at last to "balance" its record by representing "the nazi side."[198] In such an endeavor, filmmakers could reply on the "mythic terms" advanced by Julius Streicher and others of Germany's more noteworthy antisemitic publicists as plot devices.[199]

Contra Nachbar and his colleagues, it should "be required of filmmakers, if they expect their films [not to be] classed as a form of racist propaganda, to be truthful not only to the period and the place [they depict] but to the people as well."[200] Nothing of the least positive value "will become possible until screenwriters and filmmakers generally are willing to present audiences with historical reconstructions, until there is a legitimate historical reality informing both the structure and the characters in a western film."[201]

"If 'Indians' are not to be considered as victims of colonial aggression," Jimmie Durham once queried, "how are we to be considered" at all?[202] And since, as Sartre insisted, the meaning of colonial aggression can only be fully understood in its effect as a mode of genocide,[203] American Indians must be viewed as being on the receiving end of both. There are to be sure clearcut dimensions of right and wrong in any realistic appraisal of both historical and topical circumstance, dimensions that are not ultimately reducible to the superficialities of good guys and bad.

As more than one native analyst has commented in this connection, "you can look at somebody like Custer as an evil person, but the fact [is] that it was a deliberate policy . . . these things were [and remain] institutional."[204] As Indians have heretofore been portrayed by Hollywood, and as we would continue to be portrayed in Nachbar's "new synthesis," we serve as both the simulacra and the simulacrum by which Euroamerica has been best able to hide the truth of itself from itself in order that it can continue to do what it does in "all good conscience."[205]

The Song Remains the Same

One of the very few genuinely poignant and meaningful non-Indian movies ever made about modern native life is *Geronimo Jones* (1970), the story of a youngster agonizing over whether to keep an old Indian medal, his only inheritance from his grandfather, or to trade it for a new TV. Decision made, he lugs the tube home, gathers his family, and turns it on. The first image appearing on the screen is that of a savage "redskin" in an old Hollywood western.[206]

There have been a few other such efforts, as with the superbly well-intentioned *Journey Through Rosebud* (1972) and the Canadian *Fish Hawk* (1980), but, overwhelmingly, non-Indian filmmakers have opted to pursue the formula advanced in *Indian in the Cupboard* (1995), a children's movie implying that to be an Indian man even in the contemporary era is still "naturally" to be a warrior. This is the case, obviously, with the fictional native characters, invariably dubbed "Chief," routinely included in the World War II all-American platoons of films like *Battle Cry* (1955) and *Never So Few* (1959), and with Tony Curtis's supposedly more factual Ira Hayes in *The Outsider*.[207] Figuratively, the rule might also be applied to Burt Lancaster's *Jim Thorpe* and Jack Palance's boxer in *Requiem for a Heavyweight* (1962).

Most assuredly, it registers as well on the mixed-blood former Green Beret karate expert turned ersatz native traditionalist/friend of flower-power character in *Billy Jack* (1971), *The Trial of Billy Jack* (1974) and *Billy Jack Goes to Washington* (1977).[208] The same can be said of the Indians cast more recently as members of elite military units, Sonny Landham's "Billy" in *Predator* (1987) being a case in point. Wes Studi's character in *Deep Rising* (1998), although technically a civilian, fits into very much the same mold.

Probably the clearest, and most asinine, example of such thematics will be found in director Franc Roddams' *War Party* (1989), in which three young Blackfeet get themselves killed in the best John Ford manner while trying to "become" their nineteenth-century ancestors.[209]

Other non-Indian pictures have gone in the already-discussed direction embodied in 1990s releases like *Dances With Wolves*, *Last of the Mohicans*, *Geronimo* and TV's *Dr. Quinn*. These include Turner Network Television productions like *Son of the Morning Star* (1991), *The Broken Chain* (1993), *Lakota Woman* (1994) and *Crazy Horse* (1996)[210]—somewhat more sensitive and marginally more accurate, but aesthetically very flimsy—as well as such quincentennial epics as *Christopher Columbus—The Discovery* and *1492: The Conquest of Paradise* (both 1992).[211]

Television did much better than most big-screen filmmakers with its *Northern Exposure* series (1990–97), the ensemble cast of which included two native actors, Elaine Miles and Darren E. Burrows, who portrayed contemporary indigenous Alaskans as fully dimensional human beings. Nonetheless, the show was a disaster in terms of its cultural characterizations.

> Despite the variances among real Alaskan Natives, *Northern Exposure* dilutes native identity to one generic form. Marilyn [Miles] comes simply from "Marilyn's tribe," and Ed [Burrows] comes from "Ed's tribe," which for four years remained anonymous. Although refusing to name the cultural base for Cicely [the town in which it is set], *Northern Exposure* has nevertheless progressively appropriated a Tlingit culture. Since the premier episode, the town has featured totem poles, which are found only among the Tlingits and the Haidas, and various artwork and artifacts in the Tlingit black, form-line style. However . . . all geographic references since the premier have put Cicely north of Anchorage . . . in the Alaskan interior, home primarily to Athabascans in real life. . . . By the 1994–1995 season, Cicely had shifted west and seemed very close to being in an Inupiat Eskimo area. Creating a Tlingit identity for an Alaska interior village is akin to fabricating a Canadian town in Mexico or identifying New Yorkers as the majority population of Louisiana: It is ridiculous.[212]

Hence, while it can be said that Geronimo Jones might do somewhat better in the late '90s than he did during the early '70s, tuning his new TV to *Northern Exposure* or its superior Canadian counterpart, *North of 60*, rather than watching endless reruns of *The Searchers* and *The Stalking Moon*, the improvement is hardly sufficient to warrant the metaphorical exchange of his heritage for the device his swap implied.

From Reel to Real

Probably the only white-constructed cinema to date which represents a genuine break with convention in its handling of Indian themes have been the films of such offbeat writer/directors as Sam Shepard, whose independently produced *Silent Tongue* (1994) is at points too surreal to allow coherent analysis. Somewhat better was Frank Perry's *Rancho Deluxe* (1975) which features Sam Waterson as a young mixed-blood prone to parodying Hollywood stereotypes with sardonic suggestions that he and his cattle rustler partner go out to "rape and pillage" during moments of boredom. Television has also had its avant-garde moments in this connection during the 1980s, each time Michael Horse put in an appearance as the enigmatic Deputy Hawk in David Lynch's eccentric series, *Twin Peaks*.[213]

The most promising efforts have come from Canada, as with Richard Bugajski's *Clearcut* (1991), a deliberately ambiguous tale tracing the desublimation of guilt-ridden understandings in a white liberal lawyer presuming to help his native clients obtain a modicum of justice in modern Euroamerican society.[214] Best of all is undoubtedly Jim Jarmusch's *Dead Man* (1997), featuring Gary Farmer and Johnny Depp in a well-crafted and accessibly surrealistic black & white travelogue across late nineteenth-century North America, replete with biting literary metaphors and analogies to contemporary circumstance.[215]

While such films demonstrate that at least some Euroamericans are capable of producing worthwhile films on the theme of Indian/white relations, a greater potential would seem to reside in a still embryonic native filmmaking scene, pioneered by actors like Will Sampson and Chief Dan George, which has been slowly gathering steam since 1970. Although the truly accomplished acting of men like Graham Greene and Gary Farmer, and to a somewhat lesser extent women like Tantoo Cardinal, Sheila Tousey and Irene Bedard, remains definitive of the milieu, indigenous documentarists, scriptwriters, producers and directors have recently asserted an increasing presence.[216]

Evidence of this came as early as 1969 with Duke Redbird's *Charley Squash Goes to Town*, a breakthrough followed by George Burdeau's *Buffalo, Blood, Salmon and Roots* (1976). In 1982, Creek director Bob Hicks came out with *Return of the Country*, a film produced through American Film Institute in Los Angeles which hoists Hollywood on its own petard by satirizing "almost every cliché of the Indian in film, from the over-heated love sequence by wig-bedecked white actors to the elaborate musical dance sequences and the late-night talk-show promotion."[217]

> A brilliant, ironic perspective dominates the sequences, done as if in a dream. *Return of the Country* turns the tables, with an Indian President of the United States and the formation of a Bureau of Caucasian Affairs, which is instructed to enforce policies to help little Anglo boys and girls into the mainstream of Indian culture. The performances of Native American actors offset the old Hollywood stereotype of emotionless players incapable of deep, varied, and mature performances. Actor Woodrow Haney, a Seminole-Creek musician and tribal elder, infuses his role as a Native American leader with both humanity and dignity.[218]

Hicks's comedy followed close behind a five-part series put together by native producer Phil Lucas for Seattle television station KCTS/9 in 1980 and covering much of the same ground in documentary fashion. Entitled *Images of Indians* and narrated by Will Sampson, the series' segments include "The Great Movie Massacre," "Heathen Indians and the Hollywood Gospel," "How Hollywood Wins the West," "The Movie Reel Indians" and "War Paint and Wigs." To call it a devastating indictment is to substantially understate the case.[219]

Another such short film, Chippewa novelist/postmodern critic Gerald Vizenor's *Harold of Orange* (1984), with Charlie Hill cast in the lead role, gores the ox of the federal funding agencies upon which Indians have been rendered dependent. Still another, the late Chris Spotted Elk's *Do Indians Shave?* (1974), "uses the man-on-the-street-interview technique to probe the depth of stereotypes about Native Americans; of what one reviewer called the 'potpourri of inane myths, gross inaccuracies, and inadvertent slander . . . used to justify genocide, and the mindless indifference . . . that makes possible the continuing oppression of Indian people.' "[220]

More serious still was Spotted Elk's *The Great Spirit in the Hole* (1983), a compelling look at "the efficacy of Native American religious practices in rebuilding the lives of a group of Indian [prison] inmates. This is a significant film that shows how cinema can be used as a powerful tool for displacing negative stereotypes. A number of courts and prison boards have been persuaded by this film to allow religious . . . freedom to Native [prisoners] in using their traditional sweatlodges."[221] Other fine work has been done by individuals like George Horse Capture (*I'd Rather Be Powwowing*, 1981). Arlene Bowman (*Navajo Talking Picture*, 1986) and Victor Massayesva, Jr. (*Hopiit*, 1982; *Itam Hakim, Hopiit*, 1985; *Hopi Ritual Clowns*, 1988; and others), as well as collectively: the Creek Nation's *Green Corn Festival* (1982), for example, and the American Indian Theater Company's *Black Elk Speaks* (1984).[222]

Strong as some of these films are, however, they are of the sort shown mainly at indigenous confabs like Oklahoma City's Red Earth Festival, in film and native studies courses, and occasionally on the Discovery Channel or PBS. They thus have little or no possibility of attracting and influencing a mass audience. To do that, it is necessary for native filmmakers to penetrate the cost-intensive venue of commercial feature films, a realm from which a combination of Hollywood's history of anti-Indian bias and their own community's endemic poverty have always served to exclude them.

This has been understood all along, of course, and attempts have been made to address the issue. In 1972, for instance, Kiowa author N. Scott Momaday managed to organize the filming of his Pulitzer Prize-winning novel, *A House Made of Dawn*, casting Harold Littlebird as the lead. Completed on a veritable shoestring budget, the film "captured a real sense of Indianness. Unfortunately, it did not receive the support and promotion necessary to reach the audiences that the quality of production warranted."[223] The same could be said for Will Sampson's independently produced *Pieces of Dreams* (1970) and others.

It was not until 1996 that Indians finally got on the commercial feature map, albeit through the side door, when the Home Box Office (HBO) cable channel came out with *Grand Avenue*, a beautifully constructed picture, the screenplay for which was adapted by Pomo/Miwok writer/UCLA professor Greg Sarris from a volume of his own short stories bearing the same title.[224] Coproduced by Sarris along with Paul Aaron of the Sundance Institute— Robert Redford served as executive producer—*Grand Avenue* featured uniformly excellent performances by native actors like Sheila Tousey and Irene Bedard, received the highest viewer ratings of any HBO program for the season, and was described in the *New York Times* as "a giant step toward offering a gritty and unsparing depiction of urban Indian life."[225]

In 1998, this auspicious beginning was followed by Chris Eyre's *Smoke Signals*, released by Miramax, the first major motion picture directed by an American Indian. Eyre, an Arapaho, also coproduced the film with Spokane author Sherman Alexie, who developed the screenplay from the short stories contained in his *The Lone Ranger and Tonto Fistfight in Heaven*.[226] Although hardly as challenging as *Grand Avenue*, *Smoke Signals* is a nonetheless a well-crafted film, highlighted by the solid lead acting of Adam Beach and Evan Adams, both slotted in such roles for the first time, as well as fine support work by Tantoo Cardinal, Irene Bedard and Gary Farmer.

At present, *Smoke Signals* appears to be as well-received as *Grand Avenue*, perhaps better, a matter harkening the prospect of other such productions in the future. This is all the more true in that these movies' success has attracted the attention of the Mashantucket Pequots, a small but suddenly very wealthy people in Connecticut—their revenues derive from a casino operation established during the mid-1980s—who have expressed interest in underwriting big screen ventures by other native filmmakers.[227] The degree of indigenous autonomy embodied in such a proposition tends to speak for itself.

Given these current developments, it may be that things may yet be turned around, that, to borrow a phrase from African American critic bell hooks, people like Chris Eyre and Greg Sarris can still transform Indians from "reel to real" in the popular imagination.[228] It's true that the thousands of films already devoted to creating the opposite impression constitutes a tremendous barrier to overcome, but maybe, just maybe, like Chief Broom in *One Flew Over the Cuckoo's Nest*, the sleeping giant of Native North America can still reawaken, crushing Hollywood's time-honored fantasies of the master race beneath the heel of a different future. But, as they say in tinseltown, that's another story. . . .

Notes

1. Elizabeth Weatherford and Emelia Seubert, *Native Americans in Film and Video*, 2 vols. (New York: Museum of the American Indian, 1981, 1988). Also see the excellent 830-title filmography in Michael Hilger's *The American Indian in Film* (Metuchen, NJ: Scarecrow Press, 1986).

2. A number of works analyze this connection. Two of the better efforts are Hugh Honour's *The New Golden Land: European Images of America from the Discoveries to the Present Time* (New York: Pantheon, 1975) and Raymond F. Stedman's *Shadows of the Indian: Stereotypes in American Culture* (Norman: University of Oklahoma Press, 1982).

3. For exploration of this point in a number of facets, see Lester D. Freidman, ed., *Unspeakable Images: Ethnicity and the American Cinema* (Urbana: University of Illinois Press, 1991).

4. Most comprehensively, see Allen L. Wald and Randall H. Miller, *Ethics and Racial Images in American Film and Television: Historical Essays and Bibliography* (New York: Garland, 1987). On African Americans in particular, see Donald Bogel's *Toms, Coons, Mulatoes, Mamies and Bucks: An Interpretive History of Blacks in American Films* (New York: Viking, 1973) and Thomas Cripps' *Making Movies Black: The Hollywood Message Movie from World War II to the Civil Rights Era* (New York: Oxford University Press, 1993). On Latinos, see George Hadley-Garcia, *Hispanic Hollywood: The Latins in Motion Pictures* (New York: Carol Publishing-Citadel Books, 1993). On Asian Americans, see Jun Xing, *Asian America Through the Lens: History, Representations and Reality* (Walnut Creek, CA: AltaMira Press, 1998).

5. For a brilliant exposition on precisely this point, see Peter Biskind, *Seeing Is Believing: How Hollywood Taught Us to Stop Worrying and Love the Fifties* (New York: Pantheon, 1983).

6. Weatherford and Seubert, *Native Americans in Film and Video*, Vol. 2, op. cit.

7. A poignant reflection on the ramifications of this situation will be found in Patricia Penn Hilden's *When Nickels Were Indians: An Urban Mixed-Blood Story* (Washington, D.C.: Smithsonian Institution Press, 1995).

8. Ralph Andrist, *The Long Death: The Last Days of the Plains Indian* (New York: Macmillan, 1964).

9. Such treatment is hardly reserved for Indians nor restricted to film. Rather, it is how the "West" has increasingly tended to treat all "Others" since medieval times. See Eric R. Wolf, *Europe and the People Without History* (Berkeley: University of California Press, 1982).

10. The case could of course be made that events transpiring 2-3,000 years ago in Egypt and the Near East have little or nothing to do with the heritage of Europe, which remained as yet remained uninvented. The point is, however, that in synthesizing itself Europe *claimed* these events as antecedents to its own tradition. Additionally, films such as *Cleopatra* do not devolve upon Egyptians so much as upon Roman interactions with Egyptians, and the Romans, to be sure, *were* antecedent Europeans. Thus, one might observe that Hollywood's handling of ancient Egypt is essentially the same as its handling of Indians: The people or culture involved has interest/meaning only insofar as Europeans are present to inject it. On the creation of what has become known as Europe, *circa* 800 C.E., Philippe Wolff, *The Awakening of Europe: The Growth of European Culture from the Ninth Century to the Twelfth* (New York: Penguin, 1968); Richard Hodges and David whitehouse, *Mohammed, Charlemagne and the Origins of Europe* (Ithaca, NY: Cornell University Press, 1983).

11. Alan Axelrod, *Chronicles of the Indian Wars from Colonial Times to Wounded Knee* (New York: Prentice-Hall, 1993).

12. The Abbott and Costello flick was originally scheduled to be titled *No Indians Please*; Rennard Strickland, "Tonto's Revenge, or, Who Is That Seminole in the Sioux Warbonnet? The Cinematic Indian!" in his *Tonto's Revenge: Reflections on American Indian Culture and Policy* (Albuquerque: University of New Mexico Press, 1997) p. 29.

13. Ibid. The list presented here does not include several gambits by the Three Stooges.

14. Daniel Francis, *The Imaginary Indian: The Image of the Indian in Canadian Culture* (Vancouver, BC: Arsenal Pulp Press, 1992) p. 59.

15. Bill Holm and George Irving Quimby, *Edward S. Curtis in the Land of the War Canoes: A Pioneer Cinematographer in the Pacific Northwest* (Seattle: University of Washington Press, 1980); Ann Fienup-Riordan, *Freeze Frame: Alaskan Eskimos in the Movies* (Seattle: University of Washington Press, 1995). It should be noted that films such as *Nanook* and *Land of the Headhunters* dovetailed perfectly with the literary sensibility of the day. See, e.g., B.O. Flower, "An Interesting Representative of a Vanishing Race,"

Arena, July 1896; Simon Pokagon, "The Future of the Red Man," *Forum*, Aug. 1897; William R. Draper, "The Last of the Red Race," *Cosmopolitan*, Jan. 1902; Charles M. Harvey, "The Last Race Rally of Indians," *World's Work*, May 1904; E. S. Curtis, "Vanishing Indian Types: The Tribes of the Northwest Plains," *Scribner's*, June 1906; James Mooney, "The Passing of the Indian," *Proceedings of the Second Pan American Scientific Congress, Sec. 1: Anthropology* (Washington, D.C.: Smithsonian Institution, 1909-1910); Joseph K. Dixon, *The Vanishing Race: The Last Great Indian Council* (Garden City, NY: Doubleday, 1913); Stanton Elliot, "The End of the Trail," *Overland Monthly*, July 1915; Ella Higginson, "The Vanishing Race," *Red Man*, Feb. 1916; Ales Hrdlicka, "The Vanishing Indian," *Science*, No. 46, 1917; J.L. Hill, *The Passing of the Indian and the Buffalo* (Long Beach, CA: n.p., 1917); John Collier, "The Vanishing American," *Nation*, Jan. 11, 1928. Overall, see Christopher M. Lyman, Brian W. Dippie, *The Vanishing American: White Attitudes and U.S. Indian Policy* (Middletown, CT: Wesleyan University Press, 1982); Christopher M. Lyman, *The Vanishing Race and Other Illusions* (New York: Pantheon, 1982).

16. Jimmie Durham, "Cowboys and…" in his *A Certain Lack of Coherence: Writings on Art and Cultural Politics* (London: Kala Press, 1993) p. 176. The descriptive phrase used is taken from S.L.A. Marshall's *Crimsoned Prairie* (New York: Scribner's, 1972).

17. *Flap* is based on a novel by Claire Hussaker entitled *Nobody Loves a Drunken Indian* (1993 Buccaneer reprint of 1964 original). For its part, *Powwow Highway* is based upon a self-published novel of the same title written by an alleged Abenaki named David Seals and widely condemned by the native community as, at best, a travesty. While it does have the distinction of being one of the few movies that is far better than the book from which it originates—see, e.g., George Bluestone, *Novels Into Film: The Metamorphosis of Fiction Into Film* (Berkeley: Unviersity of California Press, [2nd ed.] 1973)—even a fine performance by Oneida actor Gary Farmer is insufficient to save it from being a waste of resources which might have been more usefully devoted to a worthy project.

18. It seems not to have occurred to Hollywood that the West also includes the Intermountain Desert of Utah/Nevada as well as the Great Basin of Idaho and eastern Washington/Oregon, and that peoples like the Utes, Paiutes, Shoshones, Bannocks and others were always available for depiction, even within movieland's self-imposed spatial/temporal constraints. The explanation for this, of course, rests in the relative absence of Indian/white warfare in these areas. Indeed, the only significant exception to the subregional blackout comes with *I Will Fight No More Forever* (1979), a television tragedy focusing on the 1877 attempt by Idaho's Nez Perces to escape into Canada after fighting a brief defensive action against an overwhelming number of U.S. troops; Merril D. Beal, *"I Will Fight No More Forever": Chief Joseph and the Nez Perce War* (Seattle: University of Washington Press, 1963).

19. It is unclear exactly what geocultural disposition is supposed to be occupied by the Indians portrayed in "mountain man" films like *Yellowstone Kelly* (1959) and *Jeremiah Johnson* (1972). Apparently, they are consider to be of the "Plains type," or close enough to be treated as such.

20. In their thematic listing of major film releases through 1970, Ralph and Natasha Friar show a total of sixteen films focusing on Navajos, eight on Hopis, one on Zunis, eight on other Pueblos, one on the Yumas and none at all on Maricopas or Cocopahs. The Pimas are represented to some extent by a filmic biography of Marine war hero Ira Hayes; *The Only Good Indian… The Hollywood Gospel* (New York: Drama Books, 1972) pp. 317-9.

21. The Friars list 122 major films focusing specifically on Apaches, 100 on the Sioux; ibid., pp. 313-4. For more comprehensive listings reflecting more or less the same proportionality, see Weatherford and Seubert, *Native Americans*, op. cit.

22. Wall and Miller, *Ethics and Racial Images*, op. cit.

23. The first U.S. war against the Seminoles was waged in 1816-17 to "clear" Florida of its remaining native population. It was indecisive. A second was launched in 1835, but for "every two Seminoles who were sent West, one soldier died—1,500 in all. The war cost the federal government $20 million, and it ended in 1842 not through any victory on either side, but because the government simply stopped trying to flush out the remaining Seminoles who had hidden themselves deep in the Everglades." A third war was fought with these remnants from 1855 to 1858, with even less conclusive results; Axelrod, *Indian Wars*, op. cit., pp. 146-7. On the protracted and almost equally costly nature of U.S. campaigns against the western Apaches, see E. Leslie Reedstrom, *The Apache Wars: An Illustrated Battle History* (New York: Sterling, 1990).

24. See generally, Ronald L. Davis, *John Ford: Hollywood's Old Master* (Norman: University of Oklahoma Press, 1995).

25. The nominations were for *Stagecoach* (1939) and *The Searchers* (1956). The other Monument Valley films were *My Darling Clementine* (1946), *Fort Apache* (1949), *She Wore a Yellow Ribbon* (1949), *Wagon Master* (1950) and *Cheyenne Autumn* (1964); J.A. Place, *The Western Films of John Ford* (Seacaucus, NJ: Citadel Press, 1974). It should be noted that Ford actually won four Academy awards for best picture or best director. These were for *The Informer* (1935), *Grapes of Wrath* (1940) *How Green Was My Valley* (1940) and *The Quiet Man* (1952); Davis, *John Ford*, op. cit.

26. Vine Deloria, Jr., talk at the University of Colorado/Boulder, June 1982 (tape on file). For more on the geocultural distortions involved in Hollywood westerns, see Jon Tuska, *The Filming of the West* (Garden City, NY: Doubleday, 1976).

27. Virtually all of the serial westerns coming out of the studios the 1930s and '40s were set in this fashion, among them the highly popular Gene Autry, Roy Rogers, Hopalong Cassidy, Lash Laroo, Sundown Carson, and Johnny Mac Brown movies. Among the top-rated weekly TV programs projecting the Plains to mass audiences in the same fashion during the 1950s and '60s were *Gunsmoke*, *Wagon Train*, *Wanted Dead or Alive*, *The Rebel*, *Cheyenne*, *Maverick*, *Rawhide* and *Have Gun, Will Travel*. See C.L. Sonnischen, *From Hopalong to Hud: Thoughts on Western Fiction* (College Station: Texas A&M Press, 1978); Phil Hardy, *The Western: A Complete Film Sourcebook* (New York: William Morrow, 1986); Michael R. Pitts, *Western Movies: A TV and Video Guide to 4200 Genre Films* (Jefferson, NC: McFarland, 1986).

28. Strickland, "Tonto's Revenge," op. cit., p. 20.

29. Ibid. In a weird kind of turnabout, albeit a very early one, the high plains-dwelling Lakotas are shown picking their way through a malaria-ridden subtropical swamp in *Ogallalah* (1912).

30. The Friars list another eight films on Seminoles as having been made between 1906 and 1911; one, *Ramshackle House*, in 1924; none in the thirties or forties; and one, *Johnny Tiger*, in 1966. None of been made since. The total number of films centering on Seminoles stands at fifteen; *The Only Good Indian...*, op. cit., p. 316. The count is not contracted by information in either Weatherford and Seubert, *Native Americans*, op. cit.; Wall and Miller, *Ethics and Racial Images*, op. cit.; or Hilger, *American Indian in Film*, op. cit.

31. For more on Washburn, see my "Friends of the Indian? A Critical Assessment of Imre Sutton's *Irredeemable America: The Indians' Estate and Land Claims*," *New Studies on the Left*, Vol. XIII, Nos. 3-4, 1988.

32. George Catlin, *Letters and Notes on the Manners, Customs and Conditions of the North American Indians* (New York: Dover, 1973 reprint of 1844 original). In fairness, Curtis used exactly the same technique as Silverstein, carrying with him a trunk full of "typical Indian garb" in which to dress many of the subjects of his renowned turn-of-the-century photoportraiture; Holm and Quimby, *Edward S. Curtis*, op. cit. For examples of the portraiture, see Edward S. Curtis, *Photos North American Indian Life* (New York: Promontory Press, 1972).

33. See generally, Richard Erdoes, *The Sun Dance People: The Plains Indians, Their Past and Present* (New York: Vintage, 1962).

34. Catlin, *Letters and Notes*, op. cit.

35. Skinner's query dates from 1914; quoted in Strickland, "Tonto's Revenge," op. cit., p. 32.

36. Rogers, already having established himself as a popular syndicated columnist and radio commentator, was allowed to produce and star in three reasonably successful films directed by John Ford—*Doctor Bull* (1933), *Judge Priest* (1934) and *Steamboat Around the Bend* (1935)—before his untimely death in an airplane crash in the latter year; Davis, *John Ford*, op. cit., p. 73.

37. Bunny McBride, *Molly Spotted Elk: A Penobscot in Paris* (Norman: University of Oklahoma Press, 1995) pp. 96-127.

38. It's not because none were available. James Young Deer, a Winnebago, directed several films. including the remarkable *Yacqui Girl* (1911), before setting out to make documentaries in France during World War I. Upon his return, he remained without assignment until the mid-'30s when he was finally picked up as a second-unit director on "poverty row." Similarly, Edwin Carewe, a Chickasaw, directed several noteworthy films, including *The Trail of the Shadow* (1917) and *Ramona* (1928), before being abruptly "disemployed" by the major studios. At about the same time Carewe was being pushed out of the industry, Lynn Riggs, a Cherokee, wrote a play entitled *Green Grow the Lilacs*. It served as the basis for Rogers and Hammerstein's *Oklahoma!*, although its author never received the praise, career boost and

financial rewards bestowed so lavishly on her Euroamerican counterparts; Strickland, "Tonto's Revenge," op. cit., pp. 33-4. Also see Phyllis Cole Braunlick, *Haunted by Home: The Life and letters of Lynn Riggs* (Norman: University of Oklahoma Press, 1988).

39. The comment was made by Oneida comic Charlie Hill during a game of chess at my home in 1982.

40. In his memoirs, native actor Iron Eyes Cody recounts how an aging Thorpe actually broke down and wept after being denied a chance to play his father in the film based on his own life; *Iron Eyes: my Life as a Hollywood Indian* (New York: Everest House, 1982) p. 154.

41. At pages 281-3 of *The Only Good Indian...* (op. cit.), the Friars provide a list of 350 white actors and actresses who've appeared in redface over the years. They do not, however, correlate the names to films or roles. An incomplete but nonetheless very useful resource in this connection is Roy Pickard's *Who Played Who on the Screen* (New York: Hippocrene Books, 1988).

42. Ibid. For further analysis, see several of the essays included by Gretchen M. Bataille and Charles L.P. Silet in their coedited volume, *The Pretend Indians: Images of American Indians in the Movies* (Ames: Iowa State University Press, 1980), as well as Michael T. Marsden's and Jack Nachbar's "The Indian in the Movies," in Wilcomb Washburn, ed., *Handbook of the North American Indians, Vol. 4: History of Indian-White Relations* (Washington, D.C.: Smithsonian Institution Press, 1988) pp. 607-616.

43. Damien Bona, *Starring John Wayne as Genghis Khan: Hollywood's All-Time Worst Casting Blunders* (Seacaucus, NJ: Citadel Press, 1996) pp. 30-1.

44. Hill conversation, op. cit.

45. Davis, *John Ford*, op. cit., pp. 184, 212, 224-5, 240.

46. Hill conversation, op. cit. It should be noted that where Indians were featured more prominently, as when Cherokee actor Victor Daniels (Chief Thunder Cloud) was cast in the mostly non-speaking role of *Geronimo* in 1939, he was required to don make-up so that he would resemble more closely the appearance of the white actors audiences were used to seeing portray Indians.

47. Strickland, "Tonto's Revenge," op. cit., p. 28.

48. This articulation is often thought to derive from anthropology. Actually, it predates the "discipline" itself, comprising as it does the core rationalization for Europe's exercise of self-defined "conquest rights" elsewhere on the planet from about 1650 onward. Anthropology was subsequently invented for the explicit purpose of conjuring up pseudoscientific justifications for the whole enterprise. See generally, Sharon Korman, *The Right of Conquest: The Acquisition of Territory by Force in International Law and Practice* (Oxford: Clarendon Press, 1996) pp. 56-66.

49. The real nature of the white/Cherokee relationship in the Southeast, and the true measure of Euroamerican "benevolence," can be found in the fact that the Indians had been forcibly removed from their homeland during the 1830s and dumped on lands belonging to other native people west of the Mississippi. The whites of Georgia then took over the Cherokees' rich agricultural complex; Gloria Jahoda, *The Trail of Tears: The Story of the Indian Removals* (New York: Holt, Rinehart & Winston, 1975).

50. Most accessibly, see Jack Weatherford, *Indian Givers: How the Indians of the Americas Transformed the World* (New York: Crown, 1988).

51. On the destruction of Seneca croplands in particular, see Frederick Cook, *Journals of the Military Expedition of Major General John Sullivan against the Six Nations of Indians in 1779* (Auburn, NY: New York Historical Society, 1887). On "Mad Anthony" Wayne's destruction of Shawnee corn fields extending an estimated fifty miles along the Ohio River, see Richard Drinnon, *Keeper of Concentration Camps: Dillon S. Myer and American Racism* (Berkeley: University of California Press, 1987) p. 23. On the destruction of the Navajo's extensive fields and orchards along the bottom of Cañon de Chelly, see Clifford E. Trafzer, *The Kit Carson Campaign: The Last Great Navajo War* (Norman: University of Oklahoma Press, 1982).

52. This polarity and its implications were well-explored by Roy Harvey Pierce in his seminal *Savagism and Civilization: A Study of the American Indian in the American Mind* (Baltimore: Johns Hopkins University Press, 1953), and again in *The Savages of America: A Study of the Indian and the Idea of Civilization* (Baltimore: Johns Hopkins University Press, 1965).

53. See, e.g., Jay P. Kinney, *A Continent Lost—A Civilization Won: Indian Land Tenure in America* (Baltimore: John Hopkins University Press, 1937).

54. The "controversy" about the size of North America's precolumbian population, and the lengths "responsible scholars" have gone to in falsifying evidence to support superficially plausible underestimates is well-handled in the chapter entitled "The Widowed Land" in Francis Jennings' *The Invasion of America: Indians, Colonialism and the Cant of Conquest* (Chapel Hill: University of North Carolina Press, 1975). Suffice it here to say that twentieth-century orthodoxy has decreed that the population of North America in 1492 numbered not more than a million, while the real figure was likely fifteen million or more.

55. Many of these are devoted to the reputedly "fierce" Mohawks and others of the Haudenosaunee, or Iroquois Six Nation Confederacy, as it is known. Examples include *Fighting the Iroquois* (1909), *A Mohawk's Way* (1910) and *In the Days of the Six Nations* (1911). A few later films—notably *Drums Along the Mohawk* (1939), *The Iroquois Trail* (1950) and *Mohawk* (1956)—were made following the same themes. Other significant exceptions to the rule include *Northwest Passage* (1940), *The Battles of Chief Pontiac* (1952) and *The Light in the Forest* (1958); Friar and Friar, *The Only Good Indian...*, op cit., pp. 305-6.

56. *The Deerslayer*, for example, was first filmed in 1911, again in 1913, and then twice more, in 1943 and 1957. *The Pathfinder* was shot in 1911 and 1952. *Leather Stocking* appeared as a feature in 1909, before being serialized in 1924. *The Last of the Mohicans*, aside from its 1932 serialization, has appeared five times, in 1911, 1914, 1920, 1936 and 1992; ibid.

57. See, e.g., the chapter entitled " 'Nits Make Lice': The Extermination of North American Indians, 1607-1996," in my *A Little Matter of Genocide: Holocaust and Denial in the Americas, 1492 to the Present* (San Francisco: City Lights, 1997) esp. pp. 209-45.

58. One is never allowed to see the "Other" early in such films, but is kept continuously aware that "it" is out there somewhere, lurking, just waiting for the chance to commit the unspeakable. The imagination takes over, conjuring a fear and loathing among viewers that no literal imagery ever could. Usually, when the monster or space alien (or Indian) actually appears on screen, the audience experiences a sense of collective relief since whatever is shown is seldom as horrifying as what they've created in their own minds; Carlos Clarens, *An Illustrated History of Horror and Science Fiction Films: The Classic Era, 1895-1967* (New York: De Capo Press, 1997).

59. Friar and Friar, *The Only Good Indian...*, op. cit., p. 134.

60. Ibid.

61. Ibid., p. 215.

62. Stedman, *Shadows*, op. cit., p. 116. The Indian as beast is a standard theme in American letters, analyzed very well by Richard Drinnon in his *Facing West: The Metaphysics of Indian-Hating and Empire Building* (Minneapolis: University of Minnesota Press, 1980). Mulligan's screenplay was based on Theodore V. Olson's *The Stalking Moon* (Garden City, NY: Doubleday, 1965).

63. Scalping and comparable forms of mutilation were actually primarily white practices, not Indian; "Nits Make Lice," op. cit., 178-88. As to Indians "slaughtering" large numbers of people, it was officially estimated in the 1890 U.S. Census that fewer than 5,000 whites had been killed in all the Indian Wars combined. The rape of female captives is another case composed largely of transference; see my "The Crucible of American Indian Identity: Native Tradition versus Colonial Imposition in Postconquest North America," *American Indian Culture and Research Journal*, Vol. 23, No. 1, 1999..

64. There are only a handful of incidents on record in which Indians attacked a wagon train in anything resembling the manner commonly shown in the movies, and none in which we engaged in an outright assault on a fort anywhere west of the Mississippi. In reality, the cases where large numbers of Indians attacked *anything* are few (the Fetterman Fight, Wagon Box Fight, Beecher's Island, Adobe Walls and the Little Big Horn are exceptional); Andrist, *The Long Death*, op. cit.

65. For more on this cinematic atrocity, see Jon Tuska, *The American West in Film: Critical Approaches to the Western* (Lincoln: University of Nebraska Press, 1988) p. 206. It should be noted that much the same device, that of having a white man supersede Indians at their own skills, is hardly uncommon. Witness the Hawkeye/Natty Bumppo/Nathaniel character of *Last of the Mohicans* and other Fenimore Cooper sagas, or Fess Parker's title characterization *Davy Crockett: King of the Wild Frontier* (1955). Or, for that matter, consider the characters portrayed by John Wayne in *Hondo* (1953) and Rory Calhoun in *Apache Territory* five years later (both films were based on Louis L'Amour novels published in 1953 and '57, respectively)

66. Rennard Strickland quotes his colleague, Oklahoma City University Professor Carter Blue Clark, as recalling such an experience during Saturday matinee in the heart of Sioux country during the 1950s ("Tonto's Revenge," op. cit., p. 18). I myself went through much the same thing at about the same time, albeit in a much more mixed-cultural setting, and have repeated the ordeal in several different localities since.

67. Quoted in Paul Andrew Hutton, *Phil Sheridan and His Army* (Lincoln: University of Nebraska Press, 1985) p. 180.

68. Scott Simmon, *The Films of D.W. Griffith* (Cambridge: Cambridge University Press, 1993) p. 9.

69. Actually, six-shooters aren't needed. In *The Comancheros* (1961), a little boy armed with a blunderbuss manages to down three Indians with his one shot. For context, see John G. Cawelti, *The Six-Gun Mystique* (Bowling Green, OH: Bowling Green University Popular Press, 1975); Will Wright, *Sixguns and Society: A Structural Study of the Western* (Berkeley: University of California Press, 1975).

70. For analyses of this erosion in popularity, see George N. Fenin and William K. Everson, *The Western: From Silents to the Seventies* (New York: Grossman, 1973); William T. Pilkington and Don Graham, eds., *Western Movies* (Albuquerque: University of New Mexico Press, 1979).

71. See generally, Pierre Berton, *Hollywood's Canada* (Toronto: McClelland & Stewart, 1975); A.L. Haydon, *The Riders of the Plains: A Record of the Royal North-West Mounted Police of Canada, 1873-1910* (Toronto: Copp Clark, 1912); Gerald Friesen, *The Canadian Prairies: A History* (Toronto: University of Toronto Press, 1984).

72. On the Métis rebellions, and the NWMP's role — or, more appropriately, non-role — in quelling them, see John Jennings, "The North West Mounted Police and Indian Policy after the 1885 Rebellion," in F. Laurie Barron and James B. Waldron, eds., *1885 and After* (Regina, Sask.: Canadian Plains Research Centre, 1986). On NWMP relations with the Lakota exiles, see Grant MacEwan, *Sitting Bull: The Years in Canada* (Edmonton, Alta.: Hurtig, 1973).

73. Francis, *The Imaginary Indian*, op. cit., p. 80. Canadian filmmakers have done somewhat better with Mountie/Indian themes, as in the 1975 *Dan Candy's Law*.

74. Friar and Friar, *The Only Good Indian…*, op. cit., p. 188. On the Robinson Crusoe connection, see Stedman, *Shadows of the Indian*, op. cit., pp. 52-4, 179, 260. It should be noted that the Lone Ranger/Tonto duet appeared in a series of pulp novels beginning in 1936, and as a comic book series a year later. During the 1960s, they also formed the basis of a short-lived animated TV series.

75. Tonto was portrayed by two different Indians with virtually identical pseudonyms in the radio series and movie serials. Chief Thundercloud (Scott T. Williams) handled the airwave chores, while Chief Thunder Cloud (Victor Daniels) appeared on the silver screen. Daniels' other credits include *Ramona*, the 1939 version of *Geronimo* and *I Killed Geronimo* (1950). The part in the TV series and 1950s films was handled Micmac actor Jay Silverheels, whose other credits include *Broken Arrow, The Battle at Apache Pass* and *Walk the Proud Land* (1956); Friar and Friar, *The Only Good Indian…*, op. cit., pp. 251-2.

76. Tonto was played in this instance by native actor Michael Horse, better known for his role in the 1980s David Lynch TV series *Twin Peaks*. Overall, see Lee J. Felbinger, *The Lone Ranger: A Pictorial Scrapbook* (Green Lane, PA: Countryside Advertising, 1988); James Van Hise, *Who Was That Masked Man? The Story of the Lone Ranger* (Las Vegas: Pioneer Books, 1990).

77. Rayna Green, *The Only Good Indian: Images of the Indian in American Vernacular Culture* (Bloomington: Indiana University, [Ph.D. Dissertation] 1974) p. 382.

78. Francis, *The Imaginary Indian*, op. cit., p. 167. If the formulation of Manifest Destiny sounds a bit Hitlerian, it should. The nazis modeled their *Lebensraumpolitik* (politics of living space) directly on the example of the "Nordics of North America, who had ruthlessly pushed aside an inferior race to win for themselves soil and territory for the future"; Norman Rich, *Hitler's War Aims: Ideology, the Nazi State, and the Course of Expansion* (New York: W.W. Norton, 1973) p. 8. Also see Frank Parella, *Lebensraum and Manifest Destiny: A Comparative Study in the Justification of Expansionism* (Washington, D.C.: Georgetown University, [M.A. Thesis] 1950).

79. Robert S. Tilton, *Pocahontas: The Evolution of an American Narrative* (Cambridge: Cambridge University Press, 1994) p. 56. On the notion of inherent racial inferiority bound up in the "Good Indian" stereotype, see Reginald Horsman, *Race and Manifest Destiny: The Origins of American Racial Anglo-Saxonism* (Cambridge, MA: Harvard University Press, 1981).

80. Fenin and Everson, for example, were still describing *Broken Arrow* as "a moving and sensitive film" a quarter-century later (*The Western*, op. cit., p. 281). Analyst Robert Baird also continues to hold the movie in high regard, but then he is so ignorant on the subject that he continuously refers to the people depicted therein as "Cheyennes"; see his "Going Indian: Discovery, Adoption, and Renaming Toward a 'True American,' from *Deerslayer* to *Dances with Wolves*, in S. Elizabeth Bird, ed., *Dressing in Feathers: The Construction of the Indian in American Popular Culture* (Boulder, CO: Westview Press, 1996) p. 201.

81. For comparison of Hollywood's stock treatments of American Indians with the handling of East Indians it borrowed from the Kipling tradition, see, as examples, *The Lost Patrol* (1934), *Lives of a Bengal Lancer* (1935) and *Gunga Din* (1939). For background, see, J. McClure, *Kipling and Conrad: The Colonial Fiction* (Cambridge, MA: Cambridge University Press, 1981).

82. Chandler had played Cochise twice more by 1954, as the Indian lead in *The Battle of Apache Pass*, and in a cameo at the beginning of *Taza, Son of Cochise*. Interestingly, the TV series cast Michael Ansara, an actor of actual native descent, in the same role; Friar and Friar, *The Only Good Indian...*, op. cit., p. 203; Stedman, *Shadows of the Indian*, op. cit., p. 218.

83. This is in the sense that virtually all westerns are at base simple moral plays; Wright, *Sixguns and Society*, op. cit., p. 3.

84. Stedman, *Shadows of the Indian*, op. cit., p. 209.

85. S. Elizabeth Bird, "Not My Fantasy: The Persistence of Indian Imagery in *Dr. Quinn, Medicine Woman*," in her *Dressing in Feathers*, op. cit., p. 249.

86. Stedman, *Shadows of the Indian*, op. cit., p. 211.

87. The main change-up in this drama was that Gable, as befit his standing as a romantic lead, relied on a comely female played by Marie Elena Marques rather than a dignified male as his native counterpart; ibid., p. 29.

88. Friar and Friar, *The Only Good Indian...*, op. cit., pp. 303-4.

89. *The Outlaw Josey Wales*, it should be noted, was based on a book of the same title written by "Forrest Carter," a purported part-Cherokee who turns out instead to be Asa Earl "Ace" Carter, a "Ku Klux Klan thug and virulent racist, author not only of western novels but also of anti-Semitic pamphlets and some of former Alabama governor George Wallace's strongest anti-Black speeches"; Francis, *Imaginary Indian*, op. cit., p. 110. Small wonder that his depictions of Indians appeal to white sensibilities, so much so that, despite the truth of his background now being public information, plans are currently underway to turn another of his yarns, *The Education of Little Tree*, into a movie.

90. Annette M. Taylor, "Cultural Heritage in *Northern Exposure*," in Bird, *Dressing in Feathers*, op. cit., p. 231.

91. The resemblance of the *Nakia* Indian character—it should actually be spelled *Nakai*—to that of Jim Chee in the novels of Tony Hillerman goes unremarked by Taylor; see "Hi-Ho Hillerman... (Away)," in this volume.

92. Bird, "Not My Fantasy," op. cit., p. 248. Also see John O'Connor, "It's Jane Seymour, M.D., in the Wild and Woolly West," *New York Times*, Feb. 4, 1993; Richard Zoglin, "Frontier Feminist," *Time*, Mar. 1, 1993.

93. For instance, during the program's opening credits, viewers are presented with a montage of close-ups portraiting Dr. Quinn and all other noteworthy characters. The Cheyennes, however, are depicted by a faceless group on horseback moving against a the majestic panorama of Colorado's front range landscape; Bird, "Not My Fantasy," op. cit., p. 248. On the extermination campaign, see David Svaldi, *Sand Creek and the Rhetoric of Extermination: A Case Study in Indian-White Relations* (Washington, D.C.: University Press of America, 1989).

94. Ibid., p. 249.

95. Ibid., p. 251. The "Washita was the second two-hour special that focused on the Cheyenne—an episode from the previous season had followed the same pattern. Again, the suffering of the Cheyenne functions mainly to contrast [Dr. Quinn's] nobility with the brutality of the U.S. army and townspeople. In this show, Black Kettle [a real historical personality who stands in here as Cloud Dancing's "chief"] has been involved in peace talks with the army and is persuaded to accept to accept gifts of food and blankets as part of a settlement. Dr. Quinn helps persuade the Cheyenne to take the blankets, which turn out to

be infested with typhus, and the Cheyenne begin to fall sick and die. This becomes a side issue, however, because Michaela's adopted son Matthew also has typhus. On learning this, she leaves the Indians and runs to Matthew, who of course survives. . . . By the end of the episode, forty-five Cheyenne are dead, yet somehow the show presents a happy ending, as the townspeople perform a pageant for George Washington's birthday"; ibid., p. 252. The program leaves the impression that the whole thing was probably an "unfortunate accident." On the realities of U.S. bacteriological extermination of native peoples, see my "Nits Make Lice," op. cit., pp. 151-6.

96. Quoted in Bird, "Not My Fantasy," op. cit., p. 258.

97. Ibid., p. 251.

98. See, e.g., John Yewell, Chris Dodge and Jan DeSirey, eds., *Confronting Columbus: An Anthology* (Jefferson, NC: McFarland, 1992).

99. Ibid., p. 246.

100. Quoted in Stedman, *Shadows of the Indian*, op. cit., p. 251. Sampson, a talented actor best known for his portrayal of Chief Broom in *One Flew Over the Cuckoo's Nest*, was habitually put in Tonto rolls. Probably the worst example came in a 1976 potboiler, *The White Buffalo*, in which he was cast as Crazy Horse opposite Charles Bronson's Wild Bill Hickock. Together, the pair battle and destroy the most sacred animal of the Lakotas—which is depicted as a gigantic pillaging monster rather than as a normal buffalo with unique pigmentation—becoming "brothers" in the process.

101. Geoffrey York, *The Dispossessed: Life and Death in Native Canada* (Toronto: Little, Brown Canada, 1990) p. 55.

102. Stedman, *Shadows of the Indian*, op. cit., pp. 217-8; Tuska, *American West in Film*, op. cit., p. 256. A clip of this scene is included in the excellent 5-part PBS series, *Images of Indians*, produced by Phil Lucas and narrated by Will Sampson.

103. Quoted in Stedman, *Shadows of the Indian*, op. cit., p. 72.

104. Ibid., p. 62.

105. Quoted in ibid., p. 71.

106. Quoted in ibid., p. 62.

107. Like *Broken Arrow*'s Jeffords, both Clum and Davis are actual historical figures who wrote about their experiences during the "Apache Wars" and after. See, e.g. Britton Davis, *The Truth About Geronimo* (Chicago: Lakeside Press, 1951 reprint of 1929 original).

108. The sheer absurdity of placing a white woman on a buckboard amidst the desperately fleeing Cheyennes of the 1878 Breakout could not have been lost on Ford, since his script was ostensibly based on Mari Sandoz's superb *Cheyenne Autumn* (New York: Avon, 1954). Moreover, the author herself was available to serve as a consultant, had he desired. Inclusion of the teacher, however, allowed him to soften considerably the genocidal implications of what was actually done to the Cheyennes, and so he proceeded.

109. Little Big Man, be it known, is the name not of a white youngster adopted by the Cheyennes, but of the Oglala Lakota traitor who pinioned Crazy Horse's arms, allowing an army private named William Gentles to bayonet the great warrior through the kidneys in 1877; Robert A. Clark, ed., *The Killing of Chief Crazy Horse* (Lincoln: University of Nebraska Press, 1976). The name's (mis)usage in the Arthur Penn film stems from author Thomas Berger's having decided it was "catchy," and therefore entitling himself to reassign it to the title character of his 1964 novel. For analysis of the social function of the "protest flicks" themselves, see Stewart Brand, "Indians and the Counterculture, 1960s-1970s," in *Handbook of the North American Indian*, op. cit., p. 570.

110. For "The Duke's" own views on the matter, see Randy Roberts and James S. Olson, *John Wayne: American* (Lincoln: University of Nebraska Press, 1995).

111. Bird, "Not My Fantasy," op. cit., p. 251. Probably the most extreme example of a white character being scripted to stand in for Indians will be found in *Hombre* (1967), a film in which no native people appear at all (other than in a montage behind the opening credits). Instead, their culture is represented exclusively by a white man taken captive as a child and raised among them. At the end of the film, the character, played by Paul Newman, even fulfills the role of Hollywood's "Good Indians" by sacrificing himself to save a white woman in distress.

112. It's not just movies. "Progressive" academics like Werner Sollors and Sam Gill, not to mention

the whole "New Age" movement, have been pushing exactly the same "inclusive" themes for nearly thirty years now. On Sollors, Gill and their counterparts, see the relevant essays in this volume. On New Agers, see "Indians 'R' Us? Reflections on the 'Men's Movement'," in my *From a Native Son: Selected Essays in Indigenism, 1985-1995* (Boston: South End Press, 1996) pp. 367-408.

113. On the realities of the Wounded Knee Massacre, see "Nits Make Lice," op. cit., pp. 244-5.

114. It should be noted that Wounded Knee was still officially designated as the site of a "battle" rather than a massacre until the mid-1970s. The myth of an Indian having fired the first shot still holds sway; Andrist, *The Long Death*, op. cit., pp. 351-2.

115. Strickland, "Tonto's Revenge," op. cit., p. 33. Worth noting is that early Lakota actor Chauncy Yellow Robe spent years trying to set the record straight with respect to the glaring inaccuracies so deliberately incorporated into *The Indian Wars Refought*.

116. As to the myth of Custer's being "massacred," it results in part from the unstinting efforts of his widow, Elisabeth Bacon Custer ("Libby"), to redeem his reputation during the remaining years of her lengthy life. In this, she was joined by an army establishment deeply humiliated that one of its crack cavalry regiments had been obliterated by mere "savages." The upshot was/is an absurd contention — repeated some 250 times in books and articles; this relatively incidental battle is far and away the most written-about engagement in U.S. military history — that Custer and the 211 men under his immediate command had been unfairly pitted against about 5,000 Indians. In truth, there were likely fewer than 1,500 poorly armed native fighters in the Little Big Horn Valley on June 25, 1876, against which Custer had available roughly 750 well-equipped and -supplied troopers. See generally, W.A. Graham, *The Custer Myth: A Source Book of Custeriana* (Lincoln: University of Nebraska Press, 1986 reprint of 1953 original); Brian Dippie, *Custer's Last Stand: The Anatomy of an American Myth* (Missoula: University of Montana Press, 1976).

117. The semantics involved were of course not new, finding their origins in the earliest European expositions on native people; see Honour, *The New Golden Land*, op. cit.; Berkhofer, *The White Man's Indian*, op. cit. Their impact in cinematic format, however, *was* something new and far more totalizing than what had come before; Andrew Tudor, *Image and Influence: Studies in the Sociology of Film* (New York: St. Martin's, 1975). The insidious persistence of such term usage is perhaps best illustrated by the ubiquitousness with which it appears in serious histories such as Stan Hoig's otherwise excellent *The Sand Creek Massacre* (Norman: University of Oklahoma Press, 1961).

118. Custer — who had been appointed acting major general during the Civil War, but whose actual rank was lieutenant colonel — was court-martialed after deserting his troops in the field towards the end of his unsuccessful 1867 summer campaign against the Cheyenne. Relieved of his command, he was reinstated in time for the 1868 winter campaign in which he won his "great victory" at the Washita only through the intervention of powerful friends like General Phil Sheridan. The triumph was marred, however, by Custer's military incompetence. Having failed to reconnoiter his target before attacking, he gleefully "pitched into" the noncombatant villagers of Black Kettle, thinking they were the only Indians at hand. The orgy of violence which followed — Custer ordered that even the Cheyennes' ponies should be slaughtered — was interrupted by the appearance of large numbers of warriors who had been encamped, unnoticed, a bit further up-river. Realizing at that point that he might have an actual fight on his hands, Custer turned tail and ran so quickly that he abandoned a detachment of troops under Major Joel Elliott (a fact that led to the near complete disintegration of moral among the officers of his regiment). Embarrassed, Sheridan and others who'd lobbied in his behalf covered up the sordid details. Walsh, for his part, leaves all of this unmentioned despite the fact that the information was readily available at the time he made his film. See generally, Frederick F. Van de Water, *Glory Hunter: A Life of General Custer* (New York: Bobbs-Merrill, 1934).

119. Donald Jackson, *Custer's Gold: The United States Cavalry Expedition of 1874* (Lincoln: University of Nebraska Press, 1966).

120. Although it is dubious that Custer's expedition actually discovered gold in the Black Hills, it is clear that the Custer himself, writing under a pseudonym, reported that it had in eastern newspapers. His purpose was to precipitate a gold rush into the sacred core of Lakota territory, a circumstance against which the Indians would have no alternative but to defend themselves. In the ensuing war, Custer reckoned to win another of his great victories, the glory of which he believed might prove sufficient to

propel him into the White House. It was all working out splendidly until he repeated the blunder he'd committed at the Washita by charging, full speed ahead, into an unreconnoitered native encampment he apparently believed to be filled mostly with noncombatants. Having compounded his error by dividing his regiment into three parts—flanking elements were sent out in both directions so that the quarry would be unable to escape—Custer found himself outmatched when it turned out that there were as many or more native fighters along the Little Big Horn as there were troopers in his 7th Cavalry. Custer, far from being the gallant center of the "last stand" depicted in the famous Budweiser poster copied by Walsh and so many other filmmakers, was more likely the very first man hit during his assault. There is also prima facie evidence that he either committed suicide, or was dispatched by one of his own men, once it was clear that all was lost. One further reason it turned out this way is that Major Marcus Reno and Captain Frederick Benteen, commanders of the two flanking forces and embittered friends of Major Elliott (fatally abandoned by Custer at the Washita), appear to have returned the favor by refusing to come to his assistance once he came under heavy attack. See generally, Van de Water, *Glory Hunter*, op cit.; Mari Sandoz, *The Battle of the Little Big Horn* (New York: Curtis Books, 1966).

121. Friar and Friar, *The Only Good Indian...*, op. cit., pp. 270-1; Tuska, *American West in Film*, op. cit., pp. 204-9. Also see Rita Parks, *The Western Hero in Film and Television: Mass Media Mythology* (Ann Arbor, MI: UMI Research Press, 1982).

122. Robert M. Utley, *Cavalier in Buckskin: George Armstrong Custer and the Western Military Frontier* (Norman: University of Oklahoma Press, 1988).

123. Tom Hayden, for example, now an apologetic California legislator but then a very prominent antiwar radical, used a quote from Sitting Bull as the title of one of his books: *The Love of Possessions is a Disease With Them* (New York: Holt, Rinehart & Winston, 1972). The sociocultural linkages between Vietnam and the Indian Wars were, however, brought out much better a bit later by Richard Drinnon in his *Facing West*, op. cit. On the problems experienced by Hollywood in attempting to package the war in Southeast Asia in its customary triumphalist manner, see Gilbert Adair, *Vietnam on Film: From the Green Berets to Apocalypse Now* (New York: Porteus Books, 1981).

124. Tuska, *American West in Film*, op. cit., p. 209.

125. Three separate federal investigations into Sand Creek concluded, although he was never tried for it, that Chivington had committed what would now be called crimes against humanity at Sand Creek; Hoig, *Sand Creek Massacre*, op. cit., pp. 177-92. He is nonetheless treated quite sympathetically by Reginald S. Craig in his *The Fighting Parson: A Biography of Col. John M. Chivington* (Tucson: Western Lore, 1994 reprint of 1959 original). Nelson's screenplay for *Soldier Blue* was based on Theodore V. Olsen's *Arrow in the Sun* (Garden City, NY: Doubleday, 1969).

126. Friar and Friar, *The Only Good Indian...*, op. cit., p. 213.

127. Bird, "Not My Fantasy," op. cit., p. 258.

128. This is hardly the only cinematic context in which such things hold true. For broader discussion, see John E. O'Connor and Martin A Jackson, eds., *American History/American Film: Interpreting the Hollywood Image* (New York: Ungar, 1979); George McDonald Fraser, *The Hollywood History of the World* (London: Harvill Press, 1996); Peter C. Collins, ed., *Hollywood as Historian: American Film in a Cultural Context* (Knoxville: University Press of Kentucky, [rev. ed.] 1998).

129. On the pervasiveness and durability of scalp bounties, see "Nits Make Lice," op. cit., pp. 178-88. More generally, see Drinnon, *Facing West*, op. cit.; Svaldi, *Rhetoric of Extermination*, op. cit.

130. Such "stabilizing" effects are examined in Tudor, *Image and Influence*, op. cit.

131. This was the program dealing with typhus-infected blankets described in note 95. For explication of the phrases quoted, see Noam Chomsky and Edward S. Herman, *After the Cataclysm: Postwar Indochina and the Reconstruction of Imperial Ideology* (Boston: South End Press, 1979); Bertram Gross, *Friendly Fascism: The New Face of Power in America* (Boston: South End Press, 1982).

132. Quoted in Bird, "Not My Fantasy," op. cit., p. 252. One question which is never posed is how a semiliterate frontiersman like Sully, who's plainly never been anywhere *but* the United States, might be in a position to hold an informed judgment as to which country is best. Extrapolating, the same would hold true today for all the Pittsburg hardhats and high school seniors who truly believe they know the answer. Important glimpses of the answer will be found in books like Jacques Ellul's *Propaganda: The Formation of Men's Attitudes* (New York: Alfred A. Knopf, 1965).

133. Or, to paraphrase by way of borrowing from Noam Chomsky, "enjoy the new order, same as the old"; *World Orders, Old and New* (New York: Columbia University Press, 1996).

134. Eldridge Cleaver, "The Allegory of the Black Eunuchs," in his *Soul on Ice* (New York: Ramparts Books, 1968), pp. 155-75.

135. Ibid. Much has been made by white feminist analysts over the past thirty years of the idea that Cleaver's articulation of this male-centered schematic is evidence of his own virulent sexism; e.g., Robin Morgan, *The Demon Lover: On the Sexuality of Terrorism* (New York: W.W. Norton, 1989) pp. 167, 177. Without denying that he may have been—nay, undoubtedly was—a sexist of the first order, I would argue that making the charge on this basis is absurd. Cleaver, after all, was by no means advancing his own notion of how things should be. Rather, he was describing, and quite accurately, how white men saw it, and thus what had been imposed upon blacks and white women alike. Moreover, his conclusion, clearly drawn, is that the whole arrangement is sick, leading to pathological behaviors which he describes with a great deal of precision (but not endorsement). A much better job of treating what is actually objectionable in Cleaver's writing is provided by Michelle Wallace in her *Black Macho and the Myth of the Superwoman* (London: Verso, 1990).

136. Again, Cleaver is describing a white male projection, not endorsing it. White feminists like Susan Brownmiller have wrongly accused him of "justifying" or even "advocating" rape as a "liberatory strategy"; see Brownmiller's *Against Our Will: Men, Women and Rape* (New York: Simon & Schuster, 1975) pp. 248-52. Rather, in describing his own resort to rape under the misimpression that it constituted a form of "insurrectionary activity," Cleaver was attempting to explain the kind of psychological *deformity* induced among black men by the structure of white male supremacy so that it might be understood and corrected through the formation of a genuinely viable liberatory praxis.

137. 3,724 lynchings were documented as having been carried out in the U.S. during this period; Arthur F. Raper, *The Tragedy of Lynching* (New York: Dover, 1970 reprint of 1933 original). To this tally must be added an unknown number, perhaps doubling the total, occurring between 1865 and 1889, undocumented lynchings occurring between 1889 and 1930, and a not insubstantial number occurring from 1931 onward. A reasonable estimate would thus be that roughly 8,000 black men have been murdered in an organized fashion by whites since the end of the Civil War, largely to deter their peers from even considering the "taking of liberties" with white women. And this does not speak to the thousands of others beaten, mutilated and/or falsely imprisoned for the same purpose. It is important to bear in mind that much more than literal rape, real or invented, is at issue here. A classic example is that of 14-year-old Emmett Till, beaten to death in 1955 for having *whistled* at a Mississippi white woman.

138. Actually, one can trace the set of relations at issue all the way back to the Spanish system in mid-sixteenth century Mexico; see, e.g., the section entitled "Notes on Genocide as Art and Recreation," in my *Little Matter of Genocide*, op. cit., pp. 104-6. In North America, it first evidences itself in the more generalized régime of sexual repression imposed by John Endicott, periodic governor of the Plymouth Plantation, beginning in 1628; Frederick C. Crews, *Sins of the Fathers* (New York: Oxford University Press, 1966). Also see G.E. Thomas, "Puritans, Indians and the Concept of Race (*New England Quarterly*, XLVIII, 1975) and Philip L. Berg, "Racism and the Puritan Mind (*Phylon*, XXXVI, 1975).

139. The first dramatization which might be said to conform in some ways to Cleaver's schematic was James N. Barker's *The Indian Princess; or, La Belle Sauvage*, which opened in Philadelphia in 1808. This was followed by such notable productions as John Augustus Stone's *Metamora; or, the Last of the Wampanoags* (1829), George Washington Parke Custis's *Pocahontas; or, the Settlers of Virginia* (1830), Louisa H. Medina's stage adaptation of *Nick of the Woods* (1838), John Brougham's *Po-Ca-Hon-Tas; or, the Gentle Savage* (1855), David Belasco's and Franklin Fyles' *The Girl I Left Behind Me* (1893), William C. De Mille's *Strongheart* (1905) and E.M. Royce's *The Squaw Man* (1905). On the literary front, there were Charles Brockden Brown's *Edgar Huntly; or, Memoirs of a Sleepwalker* (1799) and, of course, the Fenimore Cooper novels, beginning with *The Pioneers* (1823) and ending with *The Deerslayer* (1841). Meanwhile, Washington Irving had weighed in with *The Sketch Book* (1819) and his later trilogy of Indian-focused novels (1835-37), William Gilmore Simms published *The Yemasee* (1835) and Robert Montgomery Bird produced *Nick of the Woods* (1837). A few years later Henry Wadsworth Longfellow came forth with his epic *Song of Hiawatha* (1855). In 1860, the first of the Beadle dime novels (*Malaeska; the Indian Wife of the White Hunter*) was released. Following in the tradition of such early potboilers as *Frontier Maid; or, the Fall of Wyoming*

(1819) and *Ontwa, Son of the Forest* (1822), the overwhelmingly positive reception of *Malaeska* laid the groundwork for *The Red Hand; or, Buffalo Bill's First Scalp for Custer*, the initial production of the Colonel William F. Cody Theatrical Company in 1876. By 1882, there were a dozen such "Wild West Shows" touring the country. See generally, Albert Keiser, *The Indian in American Literature* (New York: Oxford University Press, 1933); Arthur Hobson Quinn, *Representative American Plays from 1767 to the Present Day* (New York: Appleton-Century-Crofts, 1953); Henry Blackman Sell and Victor Weybright, *Buffalo Bill and the Wild West* (New York: Oxford University Press, 1955); "Legend Maker of the West—Erastus Beadle," *Real West Annual*, 1970; Horace A. Melton, "King of the Dime Novels," *Western Frontier Annual*, No. 1, 1975.

140. Director D.W. Griffith appears to have lifted the scene whole from David Belasco's 1893 Broadway play, *The Girl I Left Behind Me*; Stedman, *Shadows of the Indian*, op. cit., p. 109.

141. Quoted in Tuska, *American West in Film*, op. cit., p. 239.

142. Hill conversation, op. cit.

143. Virtually all the early "captive narratives," such as that of Mary Rowlandson (1682), flatly denied that "threats to their chastity" had occurred. Some, like Isabella McCoy (1747), went so far as to assert that their own society's treatment of women was far worse than anything they'd experienced at the hands of Indians. Feminist analysts like Susan Brownmiller, in an effort to develop a transcultural "men = rape" paradigm, have sought to finesse this "problem" by claiming each woman with firsthand experience was likely to have falsified the record in order to avoid stigma upon returning to white society. While the idea is superficially plausible, it is belied by Brownmiller's own citation of anonymous narratives, where such potential consequences were not at issue, saying essentially the same thing. Hence, to make their model seem to work, feminists subscribing to Brownmiller's outlook have not only discounted the accounts of female captives but accepted the secondhand libidinal interpretations of Cotton Mather and others of the women's white male counterparts, tracts which more careful researchers like Richard Drinnon have described as being little more than "violence pornography." Frederick Drimmer, compiler of one of the better collections of captive narratives, has concluded that, for a variety of reasons ranging from "medicine" to commerce, indigenous men east of the Mississippi almost never raped anyone, native *or* white, an assessment shared by even so biased a writer as Richard Slotkin. Similarly, Morris Edward Opler, one more knowledgeable students of Chiricahua Apache culture, concludes that these "most vicious of Indians" in the West "were traditionally reticent in sexual matters. The raping of women when on raids was looked upon by Chiricahua[s] with extreme disfavor and rarely took place." See *The Narrative of the Captivity and Restoration of Mrs. Mary Rolandson* (Boston: Houghton-Mifflin, 1930 reprint of 1682 original) p. 71; "Isabella McCoy," in Frederick Dimmler, ed., *Scalps and Tomahawks: Narratives of Indian Captivity* (New York: Howard-McCann, 1961) p. 13; Brownmiller, *Rape*, op. cit., pp. 140-5; Drinnon, *Facing West*, op. cit., p. 61; Richard Slotkin, *Regeneration Through Violence: The Mythology of the Western Frontier* (Middletown, CT: Wesleyan University Press, 1973) p. 357; Morris Edward Opler, *An Apache Life-Way: The Economic, Social, and Religious Institutions of the Chiricahua Indians* (Chicago: University of Chicago Press, 1941) p. 228.

144. Quoted in Stedman, *Shadows of the Indian*, op. cit., p. 105; Tuska, *American West in Film*, op. cit., pp. 250, 246.

145. The Cheyennes do no such thing, but Arthur Penn has it that this is because the girl is too homely to arouse their desire rather than because they socially prohibit such conduct.

146. Bird, "Not My Fantasy," op. cit., p. 249.

147. See Jack Nachbar, "*Ulzana's Raid*," in Pilkington and Graham, *Western Movies*, op. cit.

148. Tuska, *American West in Film*, op. cit. pp. 256, 250.

149. The Friars list another sixty such films prior to 1971 without even touching upon the Leatherstocking Tales, serial westerns and the like; *The Only Good Indian...*, op. cit., pp. 304-5.

150. The film is based on Will Cook's novel, *Comanche Captives* (New York: Bantam, 1960), which is in turn based on one of the more celebrated of the real-life captive stories, that of Cynthia Ann Parker. Taken as a nine-year-old during a Comanche raid along the Texas frontier in May 1836, she was raised as a Quahadi and was plainly viewed as such (not least, by herself). As an adult, she married Pina Nacona, a principle leader of the band, and had two sons and a daughter by him. After being forcibly "restored" to white society in 1860—her husband and several friends were killed in the process—she wasted

steadily away and eventually died of what was described as a "broken heart"; Cynthia Schmidt Hacker, *Cynthia Ann Parker: The Life and the Legend* (El Paso: Texas Western Press, 1990).

151. The film is based on Alan LeMay's novel of the same title, published by Harper & Row in 1954. The book is also based, loosely, on the story of Cynthia Ann Parker. Although Wayne's Ethan Edwards, who seems to be based on Robert Montgomery Bird's revenge-crazed Nathan Slaughter in *Nick of the Woods*, ultimately spares the girl, it is obviously a close call.

152. About the only time it is judged "okay" for celluloid Indians to abscond with Euroamerican females comes in Burt Lancaster's *The Scalphunters* (1968), a complicated and rather weird film, the screenplay for which was written by William Norton. Here, a group of Kiowas end up, with the hero's blessing, in possession of an entire wagonload of white prostitutes. This outcome is possible, presumably, because the women are to be assessed as having already forfeited whatever virtue they might once have possessed. Consignment to the savages is thus an appropriate moral penalty.

153. Tuska, *American West in Film*, op. cit., p. 248.

154. Ibid.

155. This is another of those tidy inversions of reality at which Hollywood excels. As Leslie Feidler notes in his *The Return of the Vanishing American* (New York: Stein & Day, 1968, pp. 45-6), to whatever extent native men may finally have come to practice rape, it was plainly in retaliation for the habitual and often systematic molestation of Indian women by white males. Nor can Euroamerican women be classified, or classify themselves, as mere "innocent bystanders and victims" in all this. White women no less than white men were and remain avid in their rationalization/celebration of the conquest/subjugation of native people, a process to which the rape of native women was an integral feature. Often enough, such knowledge was/is explicit. The men of the 7th Cavalry, for example, including Custer himself, customarily raped their female prisoners. Indeed, it was common knowledge that Custer kept Monaseetah, the daughter of a slain Cheyenne leader, as his personal concubine for some months. Libby Custer not only knew it and turned a blind eye, but devoted her life to glorifying her husband's "accomplishments." While thus serving as the enabler in rape is not the same as being a rapist per se, it *is* to be complicit in the crime, and thus by no means "innocent" of it. On Custer, Monaseetah, etc., see Van de Water, *Glory Hunter*, op. cit.

156. Littlefeather (Marie Louise Cruz), is probably best known for having stood in for Marlon Brando at the Academy Awards ceremony in 1973, when he declined the Oscar for Best Actor as a protest of Hollywood's historical and ongoing misrepresentation of native people.

157. There were a total of six "American Indian-Speaking Females" listed by the Screen Actors Guild in 1971.

158. As is well known, love of the white man is supposed to have prompted Pocahontas to have thrown herself over the prostrate body of the English adventurer, John Smith, in order to prevent his being brained by her father's angry men after Smith had unprovokedly attacked them and gotten himself captured in the process. There is, however, no mention of this fabulous tale in Smith's original 1608 account of his exploits in the Virginia Colony. Rather, he appears to have fabricated it after the woman had already become a celebrity of sorts in England as the result of marrying another colonist, John Rolf, then taking up residence in London. His motive seems to have been, purely and simply, to enhance the salability, thence profits, of his *General History of Virginia, New England, and the Summer Isles*, published in 1624. From there, the story became a mythic staple of Americana, anchored firmly in J.N. Barker's highly successful 1808 stageplay, *The Indian Princess; or La Belle Sauvage*, and Custis's *Pocahontas* 22 years later (note 139). See generally, Rayna Green, "The Pocahontas Perplex: The Image of Indian Women in American Culture," *Massachusetts Review*, Vol. 16, No. 4, 1975; Tilton, *Pocahontas*, op. cit.

159. The Friars list nearly 200 such films under various headings; *The Only Good Indian...*, op. cit. pp. 309-11.

160. Tilton, *Pocahontas*, op. cit., p. 3.

161. In the latest remake of *Last of the Mohicans*, director Michael Mann supposedly "solves" the problems of racism and sexism embedded in Fenimore Cooper's formulation by having both Uncas and the younger Munro daughter die, he while trying to save her from Magua, the film's "Bad Indian," she by resulting suicide. Hawkeye ("Nathaniel") and the elder daughter, Cora, are, however, allowed to live. Not coincidentally, both are white. The time-honored message thus remains exactly as it was described in

other connections by Jon Tuska: "The ideology is simple: The races should not mix. When they do, the Indians are numerically the biggest losers, while an errant white may [expect] a penalty no less severe"; *American West in Film*, op. cit., pp. 240-1.

162. Ibid., pp. 239-40. "The film was so popular that a sequel was made titled *The Squaw Man's Son* (Famous Players, 1917). . . . The next year DeMille directed a remake of the original . . . and he even made a subsequent talking version twice as long as the 1918 remake. . . . An Indian actress named Redwing had played the Indian maiden in the original. Ann Little, who was not an Indian but who had played Sky Star in *The Invaders*, had the part in the remake and Lupe Valdez essayed the role in the talking version. In all three versions...the audience is reassured that Anglo-American culture is pre-eminent. Moreover, in vanishing, i.e., dying, the Indians give that culture their whole-hearted blessing and wish it well in a future which cannot include them"; ibid., p. 240.

163. Ibid., p. 244.

164. Probably the most duplicitous handling of the "issue" on record comes in *The Conquest of Cochise* (1953), when the Chiricahua leader, played by John Hodiak, is scripted to inform a young woman whom he desires that "Apache law" forbids her to marry a white army officer, Robert Stack, with whom she is in love. Thus is the white-imposed color line foisted off on the Apaches.

165. This is said despite Simone de Beauvoir's valiant effort to some extent rehabilitate de Sade in her "Must We Burn Sade?" *Les Temps Modernes*, Dec. 1951/Jan. 1952 (reprinted as an introduction to the 1966 Grove Press edition of Sade's *The 120 Days of Sodom and Other Writings*).

166. See Robert H. Rimmer, *The X-Rated Videotape Guide* (New York: Arlington House, 1984); *X-Rated Videotape Guide II: 1,200 New Reviews and Ratings* (Buffalo, NY: Prometheus Books, 1991).

167. It is credibly estimated that virtually all American blacks are to some extent genetically intermixed with whites at this point, and that more than a third are intermixed with Indians as well. By the same token, fewer than 10 percent of those identified as American Indians can make any sort of legitimate claim to being free of Euroamerican and/or Afroamerican admixture. Less remarked upon is what this implies with respect to the "purity" of whites. Plainly, the nomenclature of "race" has no applicability in contemporary North America other than via its utility as a Eurosupremacist ideological construction. See, e.g., Joel Williamson, *The New People: Miscegenation and Mulattoes in the United States* (New York: Free Press, 1980); Jack D. Forbes, *Black Africans and Native Americans: Race, Color and Caste in the Making of Red-Black Peoples* (London: Routledge, 1988); George M. Frederickson, *White Supremacy: A Comparative Study in American and South African History* (New York: Oxford University Press, 1981).

168. For a range of quotes by Jefferson to this effect, see Bernard W. Sheehan, *Seeds of Extinction: Jeffersonian Philanthropy and the American Indian* (Chapel Hill: University of North Carolina Press, 1973). Morgan's views are presented in Bernard J. Stern's *Lewis Henry Morgan: Social Evolutionist* (New York: Russell & Russell, 1931) and Carl Resek's *Lewis Henry Morgan: American Scholar* (Chicago: University of Chicago Press, 1960).

169. See, e.g., the quotes from phrenologist J.C. Nott and others in Berkhofer, *White Man's Indian*, op. cit., pp. 58-9. More broadly, see William Stanton's *The Leopard's Spots: Scientific Attitudes Towards Race in America, 1815-1859* (Chicago: University of Chicago Press, 1960). For analysis of contemporary applications, see Troy Duster's *Backdoor to Eugenics* (New York: Routledge, 1990).

170. Simmon, *Films of D.W. Griffith*, op. cit. Also see Wyn Craig Wade, *The Fiery Cross: The Ku Klux Klan in America* (New York: Simon & Schuster, 1987) 119-39.

171. The Friars list 108 films pursuing this theme by 1970; *The Only Good Indian...*, pp. 300-1.

172. Among the Cheyennes, there were the brothers George, Robert and Charlie Bent, sons of William Bent, a noted white trader, and his native wife. While each struggled for their people's rights in his own way — George, for instance, fought briefly against the white invaders and testified on three separate occasions against perpetrators of the Colorado militia's infamous 1864 massacre of noncombatant Cheyennes and Arapahos at Sand Creek — Charlie is the better example (or at least the most reviled among mainstream commentators). Accepted into the Cheyennes' élite Crazy Dog Society ("Dog Soldiers"), he acquired an almost legendary status because of his courage in physically defending his homeland. Ultimately, Charlie Bent gave his all, dying an agonizingly lingering death in 1868 of wounds suffered during a skirmish with Pawnees fighting for the United States. It is instructive that while William Bent and his son George are frequently referenced in the literature, there is virtually no mention of

Charlie. When his name comes up at all, it is almost invariably as a negative aside. Probably the best all-round study of the Bent family is David Lavender's *Bent's Fort* (Garden City, NY: Doubleday, 1954). On the Crazy Dogs, see, e.g., George Bird Grinnell, *The Fighting Cheyennes* (Norman: University of Oklahoma Press, 1956).

173. As Jerry Allen pointed out in his article "Tom Sawyer's Town" (*National Geographic*, July 1956), the real life personage upon whom Twain (Samuel Clemens) based the character was actually a man called "Indian Bill," a "kindly old rag-picker" in Hannibal, Missouri. There is of course no hint of this in such subsequent screen adaptation's of Twain's novels as *The Adventures of Huckleberry Finn* (1960; 1985), *Tom Sawyer* (1973), *The Adventures of Mark Twain* (1985), *The Adventures of Huck Finn* (1993), and *Tom and Huck* (1995).

174. Alan LeMay, *The Unforgiven* (New York: Harper & Bros., 1957); quoted in Stedman, *Shadows of the Indian*, op. cit., pp. 124-5. Nomination of the film as "most racist" was made by Will Sampson in *Images of the Indian*, op. cit. While I don't necessarily disagree with him, I feel the dubious distinction should be shared by *The Searchers*—also based on a LeMay novel—and perhaps *The Stalking Moon*.

175. Such lines were hardly a cinematic first. In *They Rode West* (1954), for instance, when the hero, an army captain, is told that there are "some people" moving around outside the fort, he responds: "*People? You mean Indians!*"

176. For an apt assessment of the schisms such racist value-loading has caused among Indians, see Hilden, *When Nickels Were Indians*, op. cit. Perhaps the most crushing indictment of the entire conceptual structure involved will be found in Ashley Montague's *Man's Most Dangerous Myth: The Fallacy of Race* (Cleveland: World, [4th ed.] 1964). Also see Steven Jay Gould's *The Mismeasure of Man* (New York: W.W. Norton, 1981).

177. The *Ramona* films are based on Helen Hunt Jackson's factually based novel of the same title (Boston: Little, Brown, 1921 reprint of 1884 original), a classic of turn-of-the-century "reformist" literature. In it, a mixed-blood girl first "goes Indian" by way of marriage, then returns to the fold after her husband is murdered by a white man.

178. Strickland, "Tonto's Revenge," op. cit., p. 21.

179. *Walker* premiered on Nov. 24, 1993. About the only thing observably "Indian" about the character is that he stops in, every episode, to visit with his "Uncle Ray," played by Floyd Westerman.

180. "Gregory Peck recalled that David O. Selznik delighted in the perversity of the casting. Jennifer Jones had recently won an Oscar as the saint in *Song of Bernadette* (1943) and Peck had just played a priest in *Keys to the Kingdom* (1944)"; Strickland, "Tonto's Revenge," op. cit., p. 27.

181. Peter van Lent, "'Her Beautiful Savage': The Current Sexual Image of the Native American Male," in Bird, *Dressing in Feathers*, op. cit., pp. 216-7.

182. Fabio, *Comanche* (New York: Avon, 1995). Van Lent himself notes the plot, but fails to draw the obvious conclusion.

183. See Peter G. Beidler, "The Contemporary Indian Romance: A Review Essay," *American Indian Culture and Research Journal*, Vol. 15, No. 4, 1991.

184. Phil Lucas, "Images of Indians," *Four Winds*, Autumn 1980.

185. Berkhofer, *White Man's Indian*, op. cit.

186. Francis, *Imaginary Indian*, op. cit., pp. 16-43. For background, see Robert J. Moore, Jr., *Native Americans, A Portrait: The Art and Travels of Charles Bird King, George Catlin, and Karl Bodmer* (New York: Stewart, Tabori & Chang, 1997); J. Russell Harper, ed., *Paul Kane's Frontier* (Toronto: University of Toronto Press, 1975). For specific applications, see Rennard Strickland, *Bodmer and Buffalo Bill at the Bijou: Hollywood Images and Indian Realities* (Dallas: DeGoyler Library, 1989).

187. Susan Sontag, *On Photography* (New York: Farrar, Straus & Giroux, 1977) p. 4; Francis, *Imaginary Indian*, op. cit., p. 43.

188. Francis, *The Imaginary Indian*, op. cit., p. 221.

189. Ibid., p. 194.

190. The poster, a major bit of Americana, derives from a painting entitled "Custer's Last Fight" and done on a tent fly by Cassily Adams, purchased by St. Louis beer magnate Adolphus Busch and displayed in a saloon in that city while a somewhat altered copy was produced. The latter, retitled "Custer's Last Stand," was then cloned into a massively reproduced advertising poster by the Anheuser-Busch

Corporation while the original was donated to the 7th Cavalry, who displayed it in their officer's club at Fort Bliss, Texas, until it was destroyed by a fire on June 13, 1846. Meanwhile, the poster was itself being imitated, most famously by Elk Eber, whose painting remains at present in the Karl May Museum in Dresden, Germany; Graham, *Custer Myth*, op. cit., pp. 22, 348.

191. As Russell Means once put it, "[W]ho seems most expert at dehumanizing other people? And why? Soldiers who have seen a lot of combat learn to do this to the enemy before going back into combat. Murderers do it before they commit murder. SS guards did it to concentration camp inmates. Cops do it. Corporation leaders do it to workers they send into uranium mines and to work in steel mills. Politicians do it to everyone in sight. And what each process of dehumanization has in common for each group doing the dehumanizing is that it makes it alright to kill and otherwise destroy other people. One of the Christian commandments is "thou shall not kill, at least other humans, so the trick is to mentally convert the victims into non-humans. Then you can proclaim violation of your own commandment to be a virtue"; "The Same Old Song," in my *Marxism and Native Americans* (Boston: South End Press, 1983) p. 22. On material/physical conditions, see Rennard Strickland, " 'You Can't Rollerskate in a Buffalo Herd Even If You Have All the Medicine': American Indian Law and Policy," in *Tonto's Revenge*, op. cit., pp. 53-4.

192. Robin Wood, "Shall We Gather at the River? The Late Films of John Ford," *Film Comment*, Fall 1971.

193. Tuska, *American West in Film*, op. cit., p. 237.

194. John H. Lenihan, *Showdown: Confronting Modern America in the Western Film* (Urbana: University of Illinois Press, 1980) p. 141. As Tuska observes in this connection, "A book such as Lenihan's, which was considered sufficiently well researched for him to earn a Ph.D. on the basis of it, actually does little more than extend the propaganda contained in the films themselves"; *American West in Film*, op. cit., p. 251.

195. Nachbar, "*Ulzana's Raid*," op. cit., p. 140. More extensively, see Jack Nachbar, *Focus on the Western* (New York: Prentice-Hall, 1974).

196. The phrase accrues from Thomas A. Harris's classic of "transactional analysis" (read: self-absorbed 1970s-style yuppism), *I'm OK—You're OK* (New York: Avon Books, 1973).

197. This is really not that far off when one considers the implications of Ronald Reagan's 1986 state visit to the German military cemetery at Bitburg, during which he laid a wreath near the graves of SS men whom, he said, "were victims, too." For various viewpoints on the meaning of Reagan's conduct, see Geoffrey Hartman, ed., *Bitburg in Moral and Political Perspective* (Bloomington: University Press of Indian, 1986); also see Ilya Levkov, ed., *Bitburg and Beyond: Encounters in American, German, and Jewish History* (New York: Shapolsky, 1987).

198. No less than Steven Spielberg has already taken the first significant step in this direction with his 1993 *Schindler's List*, a film explicitly devoted to a "good nazi." One still awaits an equally competent and compelling treatment of "bad nazis."

199. For examples of how this could work in practice, see David Stewart Hull, *Film in the Third Reich: A Study of German Cinema, 1933-1945* (Berkeley: University of California Press, 1969); Irwin Leiser, *Nazi Cinema* (New York: Macmillan Publishers, 1974); Eric Rentschler, *The Ministry of Illusion: Nazi Cinema and Its Afterlife* (Cambridge: Harvard University Press, 1996).

200. Tuska, *American West in Film*, op. cit., p. 258.

201. Ibid.

202. Durham, "Cowboys and…," op. cit., pp. 18-9.

203. Jean-Paul Sartre, "On Genocide," *Ramparts*, Feb. 1968; Jean-Paul Sartre, and Arlette El Kaim-Sartre, *On Genocide and a Summary of the Evidence and Judgments of the International War Crimes Tribunal* (Boston: Beacon Press, 1968).

204. Anonymous respondant, quoted in Bird, "Not My Fantasy," op. cit., p. 258.

205. On simulacra/simulacrum, see Jean Baudrillard, *Simulations* (New York: Semiotext(e), 1983). More accessibly, see J.G. Merquoir, *The Veil and the Mask: Essays on Culture and Ideology* (London: Routledge & Keegan Paul, 1979); Noam Chomsky, *Necessary Illusions: Thought Control in Democratic Societies* (Boston: South End Press, 1989).

206. Strickland, "Tonto's Revenge," op. cit., pp. 17-8.

207. For an excellent overview of the actual situations confronted by the men upon whom such

characters are ostensibly based, see Tom Holm, *Strong Hearts, Wounded Souls: Native American Veterans of the Vietnam War* (Austin: University of Texas Press, 1996).

208. See generally, Brand, "Indians and the Counterculture," op. cit.

209. Even so staid a reviewer as Leonard Maltin describes *War Party* as "an excuse for a cowboy and Indians movie" and "just another botched opportunity for Hollywood to shed light on the problems of the American Indian"; *Leonard Maltin's 1999 Movie & Video Guide* (New York: Signet Books, 1999) p. 1494.

210. *Son of the Morning Star* is based on Evan Connell's biography of Custer bearing the same title (San Francisco: North Point Press, 1984), but is too confused in its character development to classify. *The Broken Chain* is based in various biographies of the eighteenth-century Mohawk leader Joseph Brant as well as Francis Jennings' *The Ambiguous Iroquois Empire: The Covenant Chain Confederation of Indian Tribes with the New England Colonies* (New York: W.W. Norton, 1984), but is too thin to do its topic(s) justice. *Lakota Woman*, based very loosely on the already problematic autobiography of the same title authored by Richard Erdoes on behalf of Mary Crow Dog, is perhaps marginally more accurate than the usual Hollywood fare. *Crazy Horse* seems based more than anything on Mari Sandoz's *Crazy Horse: Strange Man of the Oglalas* (Lincoln: University of Nebraska Press, 1942). It is the best of the lot, but by no means good cinema; "TNT Film Chronicles Sioux Legend from Crazy Horse's Point of View," *The Sunday Oklahoman Television News Magazine*, July 7, 1996.

211. In an attempt to make it seem "progressive," the title of the last movie was consciously appropriated from Kirkpatrick Sale's benchmark study, *The Conquest of Paradise: Christopher Columbus and the Columbia Legacy* (New York: Alfred A. Knopf, 1990). It's content, however, was much closer to the same stale mythology found in Samuel Eliot Morison's *Admiral of the Ocean Sea: A Life of Christopher Columbus* (Boston: Little, Brown, 1942).

212. Taylor, "*Northern Exposure*," op. cit., p. 239.

213. On the series, see Kenneth C. Kaleta, *David Lynch* (New York: Twayne, 1993) pp. 133-55.

214. Unfortunately, most white viewers seem to walk away with the misimpression that the vicious Indian character played by Graham Greene is intended to be real rather than a figment of the white lawyer's imagination. Actually, the attorney, played by Ron Lea, conjures the Greene character up in his own mind as a signifier of how Indians seem (to him) entitled to respond to the kinds and severity of white transgression.

215. This is in some ways an extraordinarily complicated film; see, e.g., Gregg Rickman, "The Western Under Erasure: *Dead Man*," in Jim Kitses and Gregg Rickman, eds., *The Western Reader* (New York: Limelight Editions, 1998) pp. 381-404.

216. Some years ago at a film festival in Toronto, Greene, who'd recently received an Academy Award nomination as Best Supporting Actor for his role in *Dances With Wolves*, explained that he wouldn't figure he'd really "made it" in his profession until, and not before, he could be cast in non-Indian parts as readily as non-Indians have been historically cast as Indians. By this definition, he "arrived" in the 1995 action flick, *Die Hard With a Vengeance*, when he was hired to play a New York City police detective of no particular ethnicity. Farmer was also selected to play a non-ethnic role in the 1996 Canadian release, *Moonshine Highway*. It should be noted that, despite the inclusion of numerous secondary white actors, there are entries for neither Greene nor Farmer—nor even Will Sampson—in such standard cinematic references as *Leonard Maltin's Movie Guide* (op. cit.) and Ephraim Katz's *The Film Encyclopedia* (New York: HarperPerennial, [3rd ed.] 1998). See generally, Millie Knapp, "Graham Greene: Leading Man," *Aboriginal Voices*, Vol. 3, No. 2, 1996.

217. Strickland, "Tonto's Revenge," op. cit., p. 32.

218. Ibid.

219. See note 102.

220. Strickland, "Tonto's Revenge," op. cit., p. 35.

221. Ibid.

222. On Massayesva in particular, see the entry in Lori Zippay, ed., *Artists Video: An International Guide* (New York: Electronic Arts Intermix and Abbeville Press, 1991) p. 139. More broadly, see Weatherford and Seubert, *Native Americans in Film and Video*, op. cit.

223. Strickland, "Tonto's Revenge," op. cit., p. 36.

224. Greg Sarris, *Grand Avenue: A Novel in Stories* (New York: Penguin, 1994). Also see Alison Schneider, "Words as Medicine: Professor Writes of Urban Indians from the Heart," *Chronicle of Higher Education*, July 19, 1996.

225. The *Times* comment was made by Modoc author Michael Dorris, quoted in ibid., p. 43. Also see Miles Morrisseau, "Irene Bedard: In a Place of Being," *Aboriginal Voices*, Vol. 4, No. 4, 1997. It should be noted that despite its overwhelmingly positive reception by critics, Indians and general population viewers alike, *Grand Avenue* is not much rerun on HBO, and has never been released on video tape. Nor is there an entry for it in *Leonard Maltin's Movie Guide* (op. cit.)

226. Sherman Alexie, *The Lone Ranger and Tonto Fistfight in Heaven* (New York: Atlantic Monthly Press, 1993); *Smoke Signals* (New York: Hyperion, 1998).

227. The first Pequot award, in the amount of $700,000, was made to Valerie Red-Horse/Red-Horse Productions in August 1997 to support a film entitled *Naturally Native*. Starring Irene Bedard and *Northern Exposure's* Kimberly Norris Guerrero, *Naturally Native* was premiered at the 1998 Sundance Film Festival and expected to be in video release by early 1999; Millie Knapp, "A Fabulous First," *Aboriginal Voices*, Vol. 5, No. 3, 1998.

228. bell hooks, *Reel to Real: Race, Sex and Class at the Movies* (New York: Routledge, 1996).

And They Did It Like Dogs in the Dirt. . .

An Indigenist Analysis of Black Robe

> As we learned from movies like *A Man Called Horse*, the more "accurate" and "authentic" a film is said to be, the more extravagant it is likely to be in at least some aspects of its misrepresentation of Indians . . . the more "even-handed" or even "sympathetic" a movie is supposed to be in its portrayal of Indians, the more demeaning it's likely to be in the end . . . the more "sophisticated" the treatment of Indians, the more dangerous it's likely to be.
>
> —Vine Deloria, Jr.
> 1978

Perhaps the only honest way to begin a review of Bruce Beresford's *Black Robe* (Alliance Communications, 1991), is to acknowledge that, as cinema, it is a truly magnificent achievement. Beginning with Brian Moore's adaptation of his own 1985 novel of the same title,[1] the Australian director of such earlier efforts as *Breaker Morant, The Fringe Dwellers, Driving Miss Daisy* and *Mr. Johnson*, has forged yet another work of obvious beauty and artistic integrity, capturing a certain sense of his subject matter in ways which are not so much atmospheric as environmental in their nuance and intensity. In arriving at such an accomplishment, he has been assisted quite ably by cinematographer Peter James, whose camerawork in this instance genuinely earns the overworked accolade of being brilliant.[2] Tim Wellburn also excelled, attaining a nearly perfect editing balance of pace and continuity, carrying the viewer along through the movie's spare one hundred minutes even while instilling the illusion that things are stretching out, incorporating a scope and dimension which, upon reflection, one finds to have been entirely absent.[3] The score, a superbly understated ensemble created by Georges Delerue, works with subtle efficiency to bind the whole package together.

Set in 1634 in that portion of Canada then known as "New France" (now Québec), *Black Robe* purports to utilize the context of the period's Jesuit missionarism as a lens through which to explore the complexities of

Indian/White interactions during the formative phase of European colonialism in North America. The film is expressly intended to convey a bedrock impression that what is depicted is "the way it *really* was," and no pain has been spared to obtain this result. As the producers put it, "Finding locations that looked remote enough for the film, as well as a river that was wide enough to double as the St. Laurence, with no buildings or power lines in sight, was the job of Location Manager François Sylvester. [He] spent months flying up and down Québec rivers until he found the perfect site on the banks of the Saguenay and Lac St. Jean."[4] Thereafter, cast and crew spent eleven weeks under rugged conditions in the Canadian north pursuing the desired effect.

> Rushes show the cast paddling canoes in icy water (Beresford fell in twice), dragging canoes on slippery, icy snow along the riverbanks, stumbling through the forest, trudging through the brush. This is neither glamorous or comfortable. The landscape. . .is a mix of wide valleys and mountains; ice has choked some of the rivers into narrow channels, and the light is steely grey. . . . The look of the film [moves] from the amber of autumn to the grey/green of winter, with cold blues, and gradually moving into the contrast of black and white as the snow thickens. As Peter James sees it, the trees and rivers are as much characters as the people; they look brighter or bleaker, and they contribute to the mood.[5]

Similarly, Herbert Pinter's production design is authentic to the minutest detail: "Some people said to me, 'It's the 17th Century, so who's going to remember?', but that's not how I work. I'd say 99 per cent of what you see is accurate. We really did a lot of research. It's actually easier this way, because if you do your homework, you avoid silly mistakes."[6]

> Pinter fashioned rectangular shovels out of birch bark, used shoulder bones of a moose for another digging implement, bound stone axes with spruce roots, knitted ropes of fibre and used cedar bark (obtained free from a merchant in Vancouver, but costing $37,000 in transport) to build the outer walls of huts. . . . In the Huron village scene at the end of the film, Pinter created a strikingly authentic little chapel, lit only by candles waxed onto stones that are wedged into the fork of stag antlers.[7]

The many extras used to represent the indigenous peoples involved are actually Indians, many of them Crees from villages located in the general area of the shoot. Native languages are spoken throughout the movie, and the corresponding subtitles deployed do no particular damage to the content of the dialogue. The construction of both the Mohawk and Huron villages used as sets — each of which took about six weeks to complete — are accurate right down to the cloying smoke persistently drifting about the interior of buildings, a standard means by which Indians traditionally repelled insects. The inside of a Mohawk longhouse is adorned with scores of real rabbit and goose carcasses strung from racks, many of them slowly dripping blood which begins to coagulate as a scene wears on.

The entire stew was completed with deployment of an astutely selected combination of veteran and first-time actors. They are headed by Lothaire Bluteau, noted for his lead role in *Jesus of Montréal*, who plays Father LaForge, *Black Robe's* fictionalized protagonist. Bluteau also appears to have served as something of a "team captain" among the cast. As critic Andrew Urban observed after visiting the location of the work-in-progress:

> Bluteau is . . . the most dedicated actor I have ever seen on a set. Whether he is called or not, he is there, absorbing, watching—and discussing details with Beresford, or James. He wants to know every frame, and has a possessive view of the film. . . . He wants to know, and to agree with, all the major creative decisions. He wants it to be a film he endorses.[8]

Bluteau's devotion to his craft is ably complemented by that of the prolific August Shellenberg, who plays Chomina, a major Indian character. Several of the Indians who garnered support roles—Billy Two Bulls, Lawrence Bayne, Harrison Liu and Tantoo Cardinal among them—are also longtime professionals who brought their well-refined and not insignificant talents to bear. These seasoned pros appear to have established a momentum which allowed several cinematic novices to transcend themselves in the quality of their performances. This is particularly true of Adan Young, an eighteen-year-old Canadian-born actor picked up during a casual audition in Australia to play Daniel (the main European character behind LaForge), and Sandrine Holt, a seventeen-year-old Eurasian from Toronto who was cast as Annuka, the Indian female lead. All told, the competence in acting displayed throughout the film lends an essential weight and substance to the sheer technical acumen embodied in its production.

"More than Just a Movie"

It should be noted that production of *Black Robe* was made possible only by virtue of a formal treaty allowing for largescale cinematic collaboration between Canadian and Australian concerns. As Robert Lantos, whose Alliance Entertainment is the largest production and independent distribution house in Canada, put it, "We pursued, lobbied and pressured both governments to get it signed and we got good co-operation from Canada's Department of Communication."[9] This allowed the project to be under-written with a budget of $12 million (U.S.), the highest ever—by a margin of more than 20 percent—for a "Canadian" undertaking.[10]

Given the sort of deadly seriousness with which the making of *Black Robe* was approached by all concerned, it was predictable that it would be treated as something more than just another movie by analysts. Indeed, from the outset, the mainstream media have rushed to accept at face value the pro-nouncements of Australian producer Sue Milliken, that the film is meant as an important tool for the understanding of "[Canada's] social history,"[11] and Lantos, that, because *Black Robe* was intended to be at least as much a work of history as of art, no attempt had been made to to "tamper with its heart, its honesty."[12] Some papers have even gone so far as to enlist the services of professional historians to assess the picture on the basis of its historiography rather than its aesthetics.[13] Where this has not been the case, film critics themselves have postured as if they were suddenly possessed of an all-encom-passing and scholarly historical competence.

Jay Scott of the *Toronto Globe and Mail*, for instance, immediately hailed *Black Robe* as an "honest, historically sound film," because it is handled with an appropriately "journalistic rather than moralistic . . . tone."[14] He then pro-ceeded—while simply ignoring facts as obvious as that the Cree verbiage uttered throughout the flick was *not* the language spoken by *any* of the Indians to whom it is attributed—to offer his readers the sweeping assertion that the epic's "[sole] historical departure" is that "the actors playing the French characters . . . speak English."[15] Scott is joined in applauding the "evenhandedness" with which *Black Robe* unfolds by reviewers like Caryn James of the *New York Times*, who concludes that it "pulls off a nearly impos-sible trick, combining high drama with high ideas."[16] James, in turn, is rein-forced by Vincent Canby, also of the *Times*, who observes that, more than anything, Beresford's work is marked by its "historical authenticity."[17] The *New Yorker*, in its "Current Cinema" section, sums up the view of the status quo by proclaiming the film to be "a triumph" of unbiased cinematic pre-sentation of history.[18]

Nor have reviewers writing for such periodicals been especially shy about what has motivated their praise. James, for example, is unequivocal in her contention that *Black Robe* stands as a useful and necessary counterbal-ance against what she describes as a wave of "Columbus bashing"—by which she means the assignment of some degree of tangible responsibility to Europeans and Euroamericans for their conduct during the conquest and colonization of the Americas over the past five centuries—currently sweeping the continent. The primary strength of Beresford's exposition, she argues, is that it presents an interpretation of early European colonialist thinking and behavior that embodies "no evil intentions." While one is free to disagree with or regret it in retrospect, one is compelled to acknowledge that, because they were "sincere," the colonists "must be respected for [their] motives" in perpetrating genocide, both cultural and physical, against American Indians.[19] Left conspicuously unmentioned in such formulations, of course, is the proposition that with only a minor shift in the frame of reference the same "logic" might be applied with equal validity to the nazis and their implementation *lebensraumpolitik* during the 1940s.

Such use of *Black Robe* as a device in an establishmentarian drive to sanitize and rehabilitate the European heritage in America has been coupled directly to a similar effort to keep Indians "in their place" in the popular imagination. This has mainly assumed the form of juxtaposing Beresford's portrait of Native North America to that developed by Kevin Costner in *Dances With Wolves*, a movie which abandoned many of Euroamerica's most cherished falsehoods concerning how people lived their lives before the coming of the white man. *Washington Post* reporter Paul Valentine, to name one prominent example, took Costner to task in the most vituperative possible fashion for having presented what he called a "romantic view of Native Americans,"[20] which lacked, among other things, reference to the following invented "facts":

> It is well documented, for example that [Indians] stampeded herds of bison into death traps by igniting uncontrolled grass fires on the prairies. . . . For many years afterward, animals could not find food in such burned over areas, and starvation would finish the destruction [of buffalo herds]. . . . Nomadic hunters and gatherers moved from spot to spot seeking food, strewing refuse in their wake. . . . Women [were used to haul] the clumsy two-stick travois used to transport a family's belongings on the nomadic seasonal treks . . . [Indians] practiced . . . cannibalism.[21]

"*Black Robe* is no over-decorated, pumped-up boy's adventure yarn like *Dances With Wolves*," as Canby put it.[22] The *New Yorker* comments admiringly on the "straightforward, unromanticized. . .anthropological detachment" with which Indians are portrayed by Beresford.[23] Scott goes even further, contending that the film is not so much a story about the onset of the European invasion as it is a true "exploration of North American aboriginal history" itself.[24] Having thus equipped his audience with the "inside scoop" on traditional Indian realities, Beresford can, as *Variety* put it, "lead us into unknown territory, and keep on pushing us further and further on, until, by the end, we find ourselves deep in the wilderness of the seventeenth-century consciousness."[25] There, we find, not good guys or bad guys, not right or wrong, but rather "well-meaning but ultimately devastating" European invaders doing various things to a native population which, through its own imperfections and "mystical" obstinacy, participates fully in bringing its eventual fate upon itself.[26]

It's just "one of those things," over which nobody had any genuine control, a "tragedy," no more. No one actually *did* anything to anyone, at least not with any discernable sense of malice. No one is culpable, there is no one to blame. Even at the level of cultural presumption, it's six of one, half-a-dozen of the other. The entire process was as natural, inevitable, and as free of human responsibility, as glaciation. Or an earthquake. As James sums up, her own infatuation with *Black Robe* derives precisely from its accomplishment, through the most popular of all media, of the most desirable objective assigned to "responsible" historiography in contemporary North American society: Spin Control. In effect, Beresford successfully rationalizes the past in such a way as to let her, and everyone like her, off the hook; "[He] criticizes cultural imperialism," she says with evident satisfaction, "without creating villains."[27]

No Villains?

James' smug accolade is, to be sure, partly true. But it is at least equally false. What she really means is that *Black Robe* contains no *white* villains, and that this is what counts in her ever-so-"balanced" scheme of things. The handling of the indigenous victims of Europe's "cultural imperialism" is another matter entirely. The first whiff of this comes fairly early in the movie, when Father LaForge recalls a meeting in France with an earless and fingerless priest (based on real missionary, Isaac Jogues), prior to his own departure for the New World. "The savages did this," the mutilated man points out, and the audience is left to let the horror of such atrocities settle into its collective subconscious. James explains the meaning of the scene as being motivational: "LaForge sees this as a compelling reason to bring his faith to a godless people."[28] Neither she nor Beresford allow so much as a hint that both clergymen are representatives of a church which had only just completed two centuries of inquisitions in which the refinement of torture had been carried to extraordinary lengths, and in which the pyres of burning heretics numbered in the tens of thousands.[29]

Even as the two men spoke, the Thirty Years' War was raging in its full fury as Catholics and Protestants battled to the death over which side would dominate the spiritual, political and economic life of the European Continent.[30] But nary a word is murmured on this score either. Nor is the fact that Jesuit missionaries were hardly acting on the basis of some pure religious fervor, no matter how misguided. Instead, as their own writings compiled in *The Jesuit Relations* and elsewhere make patently clear, they were consciously—one is tempted to say, cynically—using their faith as a medium through which to transform Indians, not just into ostensible Catholics, but into surrogate troops deployed as fodder by the French Crown in its struggle with Great Britain for imperial hegemony in North America (the series of for so-called "French and Indian Wars" commencing in 1689).[31]

In any event, the exchange between LaForge and his senior colleague serves as a prelude, a means of setting the psychic stage for the capture of the priest, his interpreter (Daniel), and their party of Algonquin guides by "violent Iroquois" (Mohawks) while making their way along a 1,500 mile journey to the christianized Huron village of Ihonataria.[32] First the captive men a forced to "run the gauntlet" between two lengthy lines of blood-crazed warriors who beat them severely with all manner of stone clubs. Then, a leering "Mohawk chieftain"—a young male—brutally slashes the throat of an Algonquin child, announcing that the adults, men and women alike, will be ritually tortured to death in the morning. To further make his point, he calmly saws off one of LaForge's fingers with a clamshell. The condemned are at this point left to spend their last night under guard in a longhouse stuffed with the Mohawks' larder of recently killed game, most of it steadily oozing blood. Under the circumstances, the firelit interior scenes which follow take on an aura of nothing so much as a sequence from *The Texas Chainsaw Massacre*. Only a sexual deception by Annuka allows the guard to be overpowered, and the survivors to escape their desperate plight.

Actually, Beresford softened portions of his characterization of the Mohawks in the interest of not driving away even moderately squeamish viewers. In Moore's original novel—a book the director and several of *Black Robe*'s producers found to be so "beautiful" that it simply *had* to be made into a movie—the body of the child is hacked up, boiled and eaten while his family is forced to watch.[33] Even in its revised form, however, the matter is very far from the sort of "anthropological" accuracy, distance, and integrity attributed to it by most reviewers. It is, for starters, well-established in even the most arcane anthropological sources that Iroquois village life was controlled, not by young men, but by elder women—who fail to appear anywhere in the film—known as Clan Mothers. The latitude of the women's decision making included the disposition of captives, a circumstance which led invariably to children being adopted and raised as Mohawks rather than gratuitously slaughtered. By and large, the same rule would have applied to a young woman such as Annuka; she would have been mated to a Mohawk man, perhaps an unkind fate in the estimation of some, but certainly a substantially different destiny than being dismembered and burned alive.[34]

In a project as exhaustively researched as Beresford's, it is unlikely to the point of impossibility that "errors" of such magnitude were unintentional. Hence, it is difficult to conclude that the extent to which the Mohawks were misrepresented, and the nature of that misrepresentation, were anything other than a deliberate exercise in vilification. Such a view is amply reinforced by the employment of more subtle means to convey the impression that these are, indeed, the bad guys. For example, all scenes of the Mohawk village are framed against an overcast and threatening sky, the pervasive darkness evoking a strong sense of the sinister. By contrast, when LaForge finally reaches Ihonataria, despite the fact that it is now much later in the winter than when the Mohawk sequence occurs, the setting is bathed in sunlight. To suggest that these subliminal cues were just "accidents" on the part of a veteran director who is known to do the most detailed storyboarding well in advance of his shoots would be insulting.

Ultimately, the Mohawks are used as mere props in a broader theme which is developed throughout the film. Beresford's play of good and evil goes much deeper than a simplistic notion that one particular group of Indians was "bad." Rather, the Mohawks are deployed only as the most dramatic illustration of a more-or-less subterranean message holding that that which is most emphatically resistant to the imposition of European values and belief systems—or, put another way, that which is most decisively *Indian*—is by definition evil. This is manifested most clearly in a confrontation between LaForge and an overtly anti-Christian Montaignais spiritual leader. The latter is personified as "a shaman (a nasty-spirited dwarf),"[35] his face continuously painted a vibrant ochre, standing in shocking contrast to the somber dignity of LaForge's attire and physical stature. The dwarf (indigenous spirituality) is self-serving, malicious and vindictive, an altogether repulsive entity; LaForge (Christianity), on the other hand, is sensitive and selfless to the extent of self-flagellation and acceptance of martyrdom. Within such a consciously contrived scheme, there can be no question as to which tradition is most likely to win the sympathy of viewers.[36]

Nor do the Algonquins who serve as LaForge's guides, collaborating with the white man but unsure as to whether they should embrace his religion, escape such categorization. To the extent that they remain uncommitted to conversion, clinging somewhat pathetically to the vestiges of their own beliefs, they too are cast as being imbued with crude and sometimes bestial impulses. In his novel, Moore made the point by lacing their speech with obscenities for which their are no native counterparts (e.g.: "Now we will all eat our fucking faces full."), contrasting this to LaForge's austere pursuit of purity. Once again, Beresford cleans things up a bit, substituting a tendency of the Indians to fart loudly throughout the night, the noise and the stench keeping the delicate Father LaForge awake until he is forced to witness an even more disturbing phenomenon.

This last has to do with Annuka's proclivity, fair and unmarried maiden though she is, to copulate voraciously with whatever male she happens to find convenient when the urge strikes. More shocking, she obviously prefers to do it in the dirt, on all fours, in what is colloquially referred to as "dog style" (like a dog, get it?). Well, perchance viewers were too startled by such carnality to fully appreciate its significance the first time around, the director includes a second iteration. And, for those who are really slow to catch on, a third. The only deviation from such canine behavior is to be found in yet a fourth sex scene, when Annuka, Pocahontas-like,[37] falls in love with Daniel, LaForge's young French interpreter. In the best civilizing fashion (albeit still in the dirt, as befits a sin of the flesh), he teaches her the meaning of "the missionary position," still morally—and in some places, legally—defined as the only "unperverted" sexual posture in the United States, Canada, and Beresford's Australian homeland.[38]

When all is said and done, the only Indians exempted from what is plainly meant to be seen as the disgusting quality of indigenous existence are the Hurons, at least those who have converted to Christianity. Unfortunately, LaForge arrives at last to tend this promising flock only to find them mostly dead or dying from an unnamed "fever," perhaps smallpox, introduced by his predecessor. What an "irony" that in their "salvation" lay their extinction. Truly, God works in mysterious ways. Nothing to be done about it but carry on. That's progress, all for the best. Even for the victims, who might otherwise have been consigned to an eternity of farting and fornicating and wandering around at the command of yellow dwarfs. It is well that we remember, as *Black Robe* attempts to insure that we will, that however "mistaken, naïve," or even "wrongheaded" the invaders "may have been at times," they "did what they did for love [of humanity], nothing else, and that is nothing less than sheer nobility."[39]

Conclusion

Returning for a moment to the earlier-mentioned Holocaust metaphor, such a conclusion—which derives logically enough from Beresford's presentation—is quite comparable to a film's serving not only to rehabilitate but to ennoble the nazi exterminationist impulse through a systematic defamation of the Jewish *untermenschen* ("subhumans") based in such "historical documentation" as *The Protocols of the Elders of Zion*.[40] This, of course, was precisely the objective of Josef Goebbels' propaganda ministry and its cooperating filmmakers in producing such works as *Die Rothschilds*, *Jud Süss* and *Der ewige Jude* (*The Eternal Jew*) during the halcyon days of the Third Reich.[41] For all its pictoral beauty and technical sophistication (or because of them), *Black Robe* is different mainly in quality, not in kind.[42]

If there is a distinction to be drawn between the nazis' antisemitic cinema and the handling of indigenous subject matters in contemporary North America, it is that the former were designed to psychologically prepare an entire populace to accept a genocide which was even then on the verge of occurring. The latter is pitched more to rationalizing and redeeming a process of conquest and genocide which has already transpired. *Black Robe* is thus the sort of "sensitive" and "mature" cinematic exposition we might have expected of the nazis, had they won their war. Their state, much like the United States and Canada (and Australia, New Zealand and South Africa, for that matter), would have been faced with the consequent necessity of achieving a complete psychic reconciliation of the horrors of victory experienced by the "Germanic settlers" upon whom it depended for consolidation of the *lebensraum* gained through invasion and subsequent liquidation of native populations.[43]

In the context of the recent Columbian Quincentennial, a symbolic period ripe with opportunity for wholesale reassessment of the evolution and current reality of Indian/immigrant relations in the Americas, and with the potential for some constructive redefinition of these relations, the form and function of films like *Black Robe* speak for themselves: "Nothing was really wrong with what has happened," they proclaim. "Therefore, nothing really needs altering in the outcomes of what has happened, nor in the continuing and constantly accelerating conduct of business-as-usual in this hemisphere. There is no guilt, no responsibility, nothing to atone for. Don't worry. Be happy. To the victors belong the spoils." Sieg Heil.

Notes

1. Moore's earlier screenwriting credits include the script for Alfred Hitchcock's *Torn Curtain*.

2. James' credits include *Driving Miss Daisy* and *Mr. Johnson*.

3. Wellburn's credits include *The Fringe Dwellers*.

4. Alliance Communications press release, March 1991, p. 10.

5. Andrew L. Urban, "Black Robe," *Cinema Papers*, Mar. 1991, pp. 6–12, quote at pp. 10–11.

6. Pinter's credits include *Breaker Morant*, *The Fringe Dwellers* and *Mr. Johnson*. The quote is taken from ibid., p. 10.

7. Ibid.

8. Ibid., p. 12.

9. "Black Robe: Anatomy of a Co-Production," *Moving Pictures International* (Special Supplement), Sept. 5, 1991, p. viii.

10. Ibid. The Australian Film Finance Corporation committed 30 percent of the budget, Canada's Alliance Entertainment 20 percent. The balance was provided by Jake Eberts of the U.S.-based Allied Filmmakers.

11. Quoted in Urban, *op. cit.*, p. 10.

12. Alliance press release, *op. cit.*, p. 10.

13. See, for example, Antoinette Bosco, "Remembering Heaven-Bent Men Wearing Black Robes," *The Litchfield County Times*, Feb. 14, 1992. Bosco is a nun who has authored two ostensibly nonfiction books on the Jesuit missionaries depicted in *Black Robe*.

14. Jay Scott,, "A hideous piece of history wrapped in frosty, ebony shroud," *Toronto Globe and Mail*, Sept. 5, 1991.

15. Ibid. In fact, Scott posits an inaccurate belief that Hurons and Montaignais actually spoke Cree: "the natives in *Black Robe* speak their own languages."

16. Caryn James, "Jesuits vs. Indians, With No Villains," *New York Times*, Nov. 17, 1991.

17. Vincent Canby, "Saving the Huron Indians: A Disaster for Both Sides," *New York Times*, Oct. 30, 1991. Canby also joins Scott and others in asserting that the movie's Indians "speak their own languages."

18. "True Believers," *New Yorker*, Nov. 18, 1991, pp. 120–2; quote at p. 122.

19. James, *op. cit.*

20. Paul Valentine, "Dancing With Myths," *Washington Post*, Apr. 7, 1991. Tellingly, a search of the indices reveal that Valentine has never, despite there being literally thousands of examples to choose from, published a review criticizing a filmmaker for engaging in a *negative* misrepresentation of Indians. Nor has he published anything critical of Hollywood's overwhelming romanticization of Euroamerican soldiers and "pioneers" engaged in the "Winning of the West." His agitation about Costner's allegedly "unbalanced portrayal" thus speaks for itself.

21. Ibid. Most of this is simply bizarre. For instance, it is a well-known principle of range management that burning off prairie grass in the fall causes it to grow back in the spring more luxuriously than ever. In fact, new grass tends to be choked out by dead material after a few years. Hence, occasional burn-offs—caused naturally by lightning strikes—are essential to the health of the prairies and, to the extent that Indians practiced this method of hunting at all (which is dubious in itself) they would have been enhancing rather than destroying buffalo graze. So much for their casually starving herds into extinction. Similarly, insofar as no one has suggested that inorganic substances had been created in precontact North America, exactly what sort of "refuse" are Indian "nomads" supposed to have "strewn in their wake"? Again, there is no substantiation at all for the notion that the travois was designed to be hauled by women. To the contrary, all indications are that it was meant to be and was in fact hauled by the dogs kept by every native group for that purpose. Finally, while there is no authentication whatsoever of a single incident of indigenous cannibalism anywhere in the Americas, there are numerous documented cases in which Euroamericans adopted the practice. Witness, as but two illustrations drawn from the nineteenth century, the matter of Colorado's Alfred Packer, and of the notorious Donner Party.

22. Canby, *op. cit.*

23. "True Believers," *op. cit.*, p. 120.

24. Scott, *op. cit.*

25. "True Believers," *op. cit.*, p. 121.

26. "Toronto Fest: *Black Robe,*" *Variety,* Sept. 9, 1991, p. 65.

27. James, *op. cit.*

28. Ibid.

29. The author has had occasion to visit what is formally titled the Torture Museum, in Amsterdam, in which a number of the utensils developed for use in the French Catholic inquisition are displayed. Included are such items as the rack, the wheel, the iron maiden, the iron mask, special tongs for tearing out tongues, instruments used in drawing and quartering, and coarse-toothed saws created for dismembering living bodies. It is estimated that the Church caused such devices to be used on more than a quarter-million Europeans between 1400 and 1500. Suffice it to say that Native North America offered no remote counterpart to such ferocity, either quantitatively or technologically.

30. See Geoffrey Parker, *The Thirty Years' War* (New York: Military Heritage Press, [2nd ed.] 1978). For thorough (and classic) contextualization of this conflict in France, see James Westfall Thompson, *The Wars of Religion in France* (Chicago: Aldine Publishers, 1909).

31. See Rubin G. Twaites, ed., *The Jesuit Relations and Allied Documents* (Cleveland: Burrows Brothers Publishers, 1919; 73 vols.). Also see George M. Wrong, *The Rise and Fall of New France* (New York: Macmillan Publishers, 1928; 2 vols.).

32. The description of the Iroquois as "violent" accrues from "Toronto Fest," *op. cit.* It is the *only* adjective used with reference to the Iroquois in this article, thus the author must have intended it to be definitive of their character.

33. Here we encounter the standard fable of Indian cannibalism once again. It is noteworthy that even a reputedly progressive publication like *In These Times* seems quite attached to this time-honored Eurocentric fantasy. At least it published a review by Pat Aufderheide ("Red and white blues in the *Black Robe,*" Nov. 20–26, 1991) in which Beresford's film, minus cannibalism, is thoroughly trashed in favor of Nelson Periera dos Santos' *How Tasty Was My Little Frenchman.* Stated reason? Because "the European is dinner" for a group of South American Indians.

34. All this has been common academic knowledge since at least as early as the publication of Lewis Henry Morgan's *The League of the Ho-De'-No-Sau-Nee, or Iroquois* (Rochester, NY: Sage & Brother, 1851).

35. "True Believers," *op. cit.,* p. 121.

36. This is a standard method of distorting native spirituality for non-Indian consumption. See L.C. Kleber, "Religion Among American Indians," *History Today,* No. 28, 1978.

37. The Pocahontas legend is, of course, one of the oldest and most hackneyed of the stereotypes foisted off on native women by Euroamerica. See Allison Bernstein, "Outgrowing the Pocahontas Myth: Toward a New History of American Indian Women," *Minority Notes,* Vol. 2, Nos. 1–2, Spring-Summer 1981.

38. The entire handling of indigenous sexuality in *Black Robe* is analogous to Ruth Beebe Hill's fetish with portraying Indians engaging in oral sex—also considered bestial and criminally perverse under Anglo-Saxon law—in her epic travesty, *Hanta Yo* (New York: Doubleday, 1979). For commentary, see Beatrice Medicine, "Hanta Yo: A New Phenomenon," *The Indian Historian,* Vol. 12, No. 2, Spring 1979.

39. Bosco, *op. cit.* Anyone inclined to buy into the good sister's interpretation of things should refer to the recent work of Osage/Cherokee theologian George Tinker. In a fine study entitled *Missionary Conquest: The Gospel and Native American Cultural Genocide* (Minneapolis: Fortress Press, 1993), he details not only the actions of, but the express motivations and underlying assumptions guiding four exemplary Christian proselytizers among "the savages of North America," each of them representing a particular period over a 200 year timespan.

40. The protocols—attributing a vast and carefully thought-out "anti-goyim" conspiracy to "World Jewry"—were fabricated and distributed by the Czarist political police in Russia during the early twentieth century as a means of whipping up anti-Jewish sentiments and consequent "solidarity" among the non-Jewish population. Subsequently, the utterly invented "historical document" was republished and disseminated by such antisemites as the nazis, and American industrialist Henry Ford, as a means of justifying programs directed against Jews in both Germany and the United States It is currently in circulation again in the United States after having been reprinted by various neonazi organizations. For background, see Norman Cohn, *Warrent for Genocide: The Myth of the World Jewish Conspiracy and the Protocols of the Elders of Zion* (New York: Harper & Row, 1967).

41. See David Stewart Hull, *Film in the Third Reich: A Study of German Cinema, 1933–1945* (Berkeley: University of California Press, 1969) pp. 157–77. Also see Irwin Leiser, *Nazi Cinema* (New York: Macmillan Publishers, 1974) pp. 73–94.

42. Even the quasiofficial rhetoric attending release of the nazi films was similar to that which has accompanied *Black Robe*. According to the minutes of a Conference of Ministers at the Reich Propaganda Ministry conducted on April 26, 1940, Goebbels explained that the films should be reviewed in periodicals such as *Völkisher Beobacher* as if they were utterly authentic in their depictions of Jews: The "publicity campaign for *Jud Süss* and *Die Rothschilds* should [make clear that they portray] Jewry as it really is. . .If they seem antisemitic, this is not because they are aiming at any particular bias." The minutes are reproduced in full in Willi A. Boelcke, *Secret Conferences of Dr. Goebbels: The Nazi Propaganda War, 1939–1945* (New York: Dutton Publishers, 1970). As Leiser (*op. cit.*, p. 76) observes, Goebbels' instruction was motivated by a conviction—apparently shared by contemporary publicists in North America—that "propaganda only achieves its desired objective when it is taken not for propaganda but for truth. In a speech to the film industry on 15 February 1941, Goebbels stated that it was necessary to act on the principle that 'the intention [of a picture] should not be revealed to avoid irritating people,'" thus causing them to resist or even reject the desired "message."

43. For more on what the nazis had in mind in this regard, see Ihor Kamenetsky, *Secret Nazi Plans for Eastern Europe: A Study of Lebensraum Policies* (New York: Bookman Associates, 1961). On preliminary implementation, see Alexander Dallin, *German Rule in Russia, 1941–1944* (London: Macmillan Publishers, 1957).

Lawrence of South Dakota

Well, here we go again. The ol' silver screen is alight once more with images of Indians swirling through the murky mists of time, replete with all the paint, ponies and feathers demanded by the box office. True, we are not confronted in this instance with the likes of Chuck Connors playing *Geronimo*, Victor Mature standing in as *Chief Crazy Horse*, or Jeff Chandler cast in the role of *Broken Arrow*'s Cochise. Nor are we beset by the sort of wanton anti-Indianism which runs so rampant in John Ford's *Stagecoach*, *Fort Apache*, *She Wore a Yellow Ribbon* and *Sergeant Rutledge*. Even the sort of "rebel without a cause" trivialization of Indian anger offered by Robert Blake in *Tell Them Willie Boy Was Here*—or Lou Diamond Philips in *Young Guns* and *Young Guns II*—is not at hand. Yet, in some ways the latest "Indian movie," a cinematic extravaganza packaged under the title *Dances With Wolves* is just as bad.

This statement has nothing to do with the entirely predictable complaints raised by reviewers in the *New York Times*, *Washington Post* and similar bastions of the status quo. Self-evidently, the movie's flaws do not—as such reviewers claim—rest in a "negative handling" of whites or "over-sentimentalizing" of Indians. Rather, although he tries harder than most, producer-director-star Kevin Costner holds closely to certain sympathetic stereotypes of Euroamerican behavior on the "frontier," at least insofar as he never quite explains how completely, systematically and persistently the invaders violated every conceivable standard of human decency in the process of conquest. As to those media pundits who have sought to "debunk" the film's positive portrayal of native people, they may be seen quite simply as liars, deliberately and often wildly inaccurate on virtually every point they've raised. Theirs is the task of (re)asserting the reactionary core of racist mythology so important to conventional justifications for America's "winning of the West."

Contrary to the carping of such paleocritics, Costner did attain several

239

noteworthy breakthroughs in his production. For instance, he invariably cast Indians to fill his script's Indian roles, a Hollywood first. And, to an extent surpassing anything else ever emerging from tinsel-town—including the celebrated roles of Chief Dan George in *Little Big Man* and Will Sampson in *One Flew Over the Cuckoo's Nest*—these Indians were allowed to serve as more than mere props. Throughout the movie, they were called upon to demonstrate motive and emotion, thereby assuming the dimensions of real human beings. Further, the film is technically and geographically accurate, factors superbly captured in the cinematography of Photographic Director Dean Semler and his crew.

But let's not overstate the case. Costner's talents as a filmmaker have been remarked upon, *ad nauseum*, not only by the motion picture academy during the orgy of Oscars recently bestowed upon him and his colleagues, but by revenues grossed at the nation's theaters and by the misguided and fawning sort of gratitude expressed by some Indians at their cultures having finally been cinematically accorded a semblance of the respect to which they've been entitled all along. The vaunted achievements of *Dances With Wolves* in this regard should, by rights, be commonplace. That they are not says all that needs saying in this regard.

In any event, the issue is not the manner in which the film's native characters and cultures are presented. The problems lie elsewhere, at the level of the context in which they are embedded. Stripped of its pretty pictures and progressive flourishes in directions like affirmative action hiring, *Dances With Wolves* is by no means a movie about Indians. Instead, it is at base an elaboration of movieland's Great White Hunter theme, albeit one with a decidedly different ("nicer" and, therefore, "better") personality than the usual example of the genre, and much more elegantly done. Above all, it follows the formula established by *Lawrence of Arabia*: Arabs and Arab culture handled in a superficially respectful manner, and framed by some of the most gorgeous landscape photography imaginable. So much the better for sophisticated propagandists to render "realistic" the undeniably heroic stature of Lt. Lawrence, the film's central—and ultimately most Eurocentric—character.

In order to understand the implications of this structural linkage between the two movies, it is important to remember that despite the hoopla attending *Lawrence*'s calculated gestures to the Bedouins, the film proved to be of absolutely no benefit to the peoples of the Middle East (just ask the Palestinians and Lebanese). To the contrary, its major impact was to put a "tragic" but far more humane face upon the nature of Britain's imperial pretensions in the region, making colonization of the Arabs seem more acceptable—or at least more inevitable—than might otherwise have been the case. So too do we encounter this contrived sense of sad inevitability in the closing scenes of *Dances With Wolves*, as Lt. Dunbar and the female "captive" he has "recovered" ride off into the proverbial sunset, leaving their Lakota "friends" to be slaughtered by and subordinated to the United States. Fate closes upon Indian and Arab alike, despite the best efforts of well-intentioned white men like the two good lieutenants ("We're not *all* bad, y'know.").

It's all in the past, so the story goes, regrettable, obviously, but comfortably out of reach. Nothing to be done about it, really, at least at this point. Best that everyone—Euroamericans, at any rate—pay a bit of appropriately maudlin homage to "our heritage," feel better about themselves for possessing such lofty sentiments, and get on with business as usual. Meanwhile, native people are forced to live, right now, today, in abject squalor under the heel of what is arguably history's most seamlessly perfected system of internal colonization, out of sight, out of mind, our rights and resources relentlessly consumed by the dominant society. That is after all, the very business as usual that films like *Dances With Wolves* help to perpetuate by diverting attention to their sensitive reinterpretations of yesteryear. So much for Costner's loudly proclaimed desire to "help."

If Kevin Costner or anyone else in Hollywood held an honest inclination to make a movie which would alter public perceptions of Native America in some meaningful way, it would, first and foremost, be set in the present day, not the mid-nineteenth century. It would feature, front and center, the real struggles of living native people to liberate ourselves from the oppression which has beset us in the contemporary era, not the adventures of some fictional non-Indian out to save the savage. It would engage directly with concrete issues like expropriation of water rights and minerals, involuntary sterilization, and FBI repression of Indian activists. It would not be made as another *Powwow Highway*-style entertainment venture, or one more trite excursion into spiritual philosophy and the martial arts à la the "Silly Jack" movies. Cinema focusing on the sociopolitical and economic realities of Native America in the same fashion as these themes were developed with regard to Latin America in *Salvador*, *El Norte* and *Under Fire*. Such efforts are woefully long overdue.

On second thought, maybe it wouldn't be such a good idea. Hollywood's record on Indian topics is such that, if it were to attempt to produce a script on, say, the events on Pine Ridge during the mid-'70s, it would probably end up being some twisted plot featuring an Indian FBI agent (undoubtedly a cross between Mike Hammer and Tonto) who jumps in to save his backwards reservation brethren from the evil plots of corrupt tribal officials working with sinister corporate executives, and maybe even a few of his own Bureau superiors. They'd probably cast a nice blond guy like Val Kilmer as the agent-hero, have it directed by some one like Michael Apthed, and call it something really Indian-sounding, like *Thunderheart*. It stands to reason, after all: now that we're burdened with the legacy of *Lawrence of South Dakota*, we can all look forward to what will amount to *South Dakota Burning*. Next thing you know, they'll want to do a remake of *Last of the Mohicans* and try to cast Russell Means as Chingachgook. Yup, the more things "change," the more they stay the same.

Index

N

Nabokov, Vladimir: 140
Nachbar, Jack: 200, 201
nagual, concept of: 36, 45, 57n
Naiche (Apache leader): 181
Naish, J. Carol: 174
Naked City, The (TV series): 90n
Nakia (TV series): 182, 213n
Nanook of the North (film): 169
Naropa Institute: 63n
Narrative of the Sufferings and Surprising Deliverances of William and Elizabeth Fleming (book): 5
Nation (weekly news journal): 8
National Indian Youth Council: 127
National Recorder (newspaper): 113, 114
Native North America
    demography of: xii, 125-6; health data on: xi-xii; impoverishment of: xii-xiii; mineral resources of: xi, 85; subordination of: xi
Naturally Native (film): 224n
Naturegraph Publications: 27
Navajos: *see* Diné Indians
Navajo Talking Picture (film): 204
Nazi Doctors, The (book): 122
nazis/nazism: 97n
    "New Order" of: 83
NBC television network: 180, 182
Neihardt Petri, Hilda: 127
Nelson, Ralph: 188, 189
Nevada Smith (film): 196
Never So Few (film): 170, 201
"New Age" movement: 53n, 54n, 57n, 99, 106, 116-7, 214-5n
New Age (magazine): 28, 43
New Englander and Yale Review (magazine): 8
New Hope for the Dead (novel): 93n
New Statesman (magazine): 28
New York Times (newspaper): 28, 29, 53n, 173, 205, 228, 239; *Higher Educational Supplement* of: 29
New Yorker (magazine): 67, 228, 229
Newman, Paul: 214n
Newman, Philip: 31, 32
Newmar, Julie: 175
Nick of the Woods (novel, play): 217n, 219n
"Nino Cochise": 101
Nobody Loves a Drunken Indian (novel): 207n
Noel, Daniel: 42, 60n
North American Circle of Elders: 127
North American Review (magazine): 8
North of 60 (TV series): 202
North West Mounted Police (NWMP; "Mounties"): 179, 212n

North West Mounted Police (film): 179
Northern Exposure (TV series): 202, 224n
Northwest Indian Women's Circle: 127
Northwest Passage (film): 192, 211n
Nott, J.C.: 220n
Novak, Michael: 139, 143
Nuremberg Doctrine/Principles: 131

O

O'Neill, Eugene: 140
Oakley, Kenneth: 48, 63n
Oandasan, William: 164
Oates, Joyce Carol: 56n
Ogallalah (film): 209n
Oklahoma! (play, film): 209n
Oklahoma Territory (film): 194
Oklahoman (newspaper): 68
On Teaching (book): 106
On the Warpath (film): 170
One Eighth Indian (film): 196
One Flew Over the Cuckoo's Nest (film): 170, 184, 206, 214n, 240
One Lonely Night (novel): 75
Oneida Land Claims: 129-31
Oneida Indians: *see* Haudenosaunee
Ontwa, Son of the Forest (novel): 218n
Opler, Morris Edward: 218n
Oregon Trail, The (film): 181
Ornstein, Robert: 29
Ortiz, Simon J.: 144, 161
Other Fields, Other Grasshoppers (book): 38
Outlaw Josey Wales, The (film): 181, 213n
Outlaw Josey Wales, The (novel): 213n
Outlaw, Lucius: 29
Outsider, The (film): 174
Overland Monthly (magazine): 8
Owl, Barbara: 103-4
Oxford University: 46
    press of: 146

P

Packer, Alfred: 236n
Paget, Debra: 174, 194
Paine, Tom: 124
Paiute Indians: 208n
Palance, Jack: 201
Pale-Face Squaw, The (film): 192
Paleface (film): 169
Palfrey, John Gorham: 65n
Paretsky, Sara: 78, 93n
Parker, Cynthia Ann: 218-9n
Parker, Fess: 211n

Author photo by Leah Kelly

Ward Churchill (enrolled Keetoowah Cherokee) is Professor of American Indian Studies and Communications in the Department of Ethnic Studies, University of Colorado at Boulder. A member of the Governing Council of Colorado AIM, he has also served as a delegate to the United Nations Working Group on Indigenous Populations, as rapporteur for the 1993 International People's Tribunal on the Rights of Native Hawaiians, and as an advocate prosecutor for an international tribunal convened at the request of the Chiefs of Ontario to consider the rights of the indigenous peoples of Canada. His many books include *Marxism and Native Americans, Agents of Repression* and *The COINTELPRO Papers* (co-authored with Jim Vander Wall), *Struggle for the Land, Since Predator Came, From a Native Son,* and *A Little Matter of Genocide: Holocaust and Denial in the Americas.*

CITY LIGHTS PUBLICATIONS

David-Neel, Alexandra. SECRET ORAL TEACHINGS IN TIBETAN BUDDHIST SECTS
Deleuze, Gilles. SPINOZA: Practical Philosophy
Dick, Leslie. KICKING
Dick, Leslie. WITHOUT FALLING
di Prima, Diane. PIECES OF A SONG: Selected Poems
Doolittle, Hilda (H.D.). NOTES ON THOUGHT & VISION
Ducornet, Rikki. ENTERING FIRE
Eberhardt, Isabelle. DEPARTURES: Selected Writings
Eberhardt, Isabelle. THE OBLIVION SEEKERS
Eidus, Janice. VITO LOVES GERALDINE
Eidus, Janice. URBAN BLISS
Ferlinghetti, L. ed. CITY LIGHTS POCKET POETS ANTHOLOGY
Ferlinghetti, L., ed. ENDS & BEGINNINGS (City Lights Review #6)
Ferlinghetti, L. PICTURES OF THE GONE WORLD
Finley, Karen. SHOCK TREATMENT
Ford, Charles Henri. OUT OF THE LABYRINTH: Selected Poems
Franzen, Cola, transl. POEMS OF ARAB ANDALUSIA
García Lorca, Federico. BARBAROUS NIGHTS: Legends & Plays
García Lorca, Federico. ODE TO WALT WHITMAN & OTHER POEMS
García Lorca, Federico. POEM OF THE DEEP SONG
Garon, Paul. BLUES & THE POETIC SPIRIT
Gil de Biedma, Jaime. LONGING: SELECTED POEMS
Ginsberg, Allen. THE FALL OF AMERICA
Ginsberg, Allen. HOWL & OTHER POEMS
Ginsberg, Allen. KADDISH & OTHER POEMS
Ginsberg, Allen. MIND BREATHS
Ginsberg, Allen. PLANET NEWS
Ginsberg, Allen. PLUTONIAN ODE
Ginsberg, Allen. REALITY SANDWICHES
Goethe, J. W. von. TALES FOR TRANSFORMATION
Gómez-Peña, Guillermo. THE NEW WORLD BORDER
Goytisolo, Juan. THE MARX FAMILY SAGA
Harryman, Carla. THERE NEVER WAS A ROSE WITHOUT A THORN
Heider, Ulrike. ANARCHISM: Left Right & Green
Herron, Don. THE DASHIELL HAMMETT TOUR: A Guidebook
Higman, Perry, tr. LOVE POEMS FROM SPAIN AND SPANISH AMERICA
Hinojosa, Francisco. HECTIC ETHICS
Jaffe, Harold. EROS: ANTI-EROS
Jenkins, Edith. AGAINST A FIELD SINISTER
Katzenberger, Elaine, ed. FIRST WORLD, HA HA HA!: The Zapatista Challenge
Kerouac, Jack. BOOK OF DREAMS
Kerouac, Jack. POMES ALL SIZES
Kerouac, Jack. SCATTERED POEMS
Kerouac, Jack. SCRIPTURE OF THE GOLDEN ETERNITY
Lacarrière, Jacques. THE GNOSTICS
La Duke, Betty. COMPAÑERAS
La Loca. ADVENTURES ON THE ISLE OF ADOLESCENCE
Lamantia, Philip. BED OF SPHINXES: SELECTED POEMS

Lamantia, Philip. MEADOWLARK WEST
Laughlin, James. SELECTED POEMS: 1935–1985
Laure. THE COLLECTED WRITINGS
Le Brun, Annie. SADE: On the Brink of the Abyss
Mackey, Nathaniel. SCHOOL OF UDHRA
Mackey, Nathaniel. WHATSAID SERIF
Masereel, Frans. PASSIONATE JOURNEY
Mayakovsky, Vladimir. LISTEN! EARLY POEMS
Mehmedinovic, Semezdin. SARAJEVO BLUES
Morgan, William. BEAT GENERATION IN NEW YORK
Mrabet, Mohammed. THE BOY WHO SET THE FIRE
Mrabet, Mohammed. THE LEMON
Mrabet, Mohammed. LOVE WITH A FEW HAIRS
Mrabet, Mohammed. M'HASHISH
Murguía, A. & B. Paschke, eds. VOLCAN: Poems from Central America
Nadir, Shams. THE ASTROLABE OF THE SEA
Parenti, Michael. AGAINST EMPIRE
Parenti, Michael. AMERICA BESIEGED
Parenti, Michael. BLACKSHIRTS & REDS
Parenti, Michael. DIRTY TRUTHS
Pasolini, Pier Paolo. ROMAN POEMS
Pessoa, Fernando. ALWAYS ASTONISHED
Pessoa, Fernando. POEMS
Peters, Nancy J., ed. WAR AFTER WAR (City Lights Review #5)
Poe, Edgar Allan. THE UNKNOWN POE
Porta, Antonio. KISSES FROM ANOTHER DREAM
Prévert, Jacques. PAROLES
Purdy, James. THE CANDLES OF YOUR EYES
Purdy, James. GARMENTS THE LIVING WEAR
Purdy, James. IN A SHALLOW GRAVE
Purdy, James. OUT WITH THE STARS
Rachlin, Nahid. THE HEART'S DESIRE
Rachlin, Nahid. MARRIED TO A STRANGER
Rachlin, Nahid. VEILS: SHORT STORIES
Reed, Jeremy. DELIRIUM: An Interpretation of Arthur Rimbaud
Reed, Jeremy. RED-HAIRED ANDROID
Rey Rosa, Rodrigo. THE BEGGAR'S KNIFE
Rey Rosa, Rodrigo. DUST ON HER TONGUE
Rigaud, Milo. SECRETS OF VOODOO
Ross, Dorien. RETURNING TO A
Ruy Sánchez, Alberto. MOGADOR
Saadawi, Nawal El. MEMOIRS OF A WOMAN DOCTOR
Sawyer-Lauçanno, Christopher. THE CONTINUAL PILGRIMAGE: American Writers in Paris
      1944-1960
Sawyer-Lauçanno, Christopher, transl. THE DESTRUCTION OF THE JAGUAR
Schelling, Andrew, tr. THE CANE GROVES OF NARMADA RIVER
Scholder, Amy, ed. CRITICAL CONDITION: Women on the Edge of Violence
Sclauzero, Mariarosa. MARLENE